Dedication

To all the people who wrote, called, or came up to me, and said,
"When are you going to write another one, Joni?"
Without each of you, this book would never have been started—
And certainly never finished!
So, since you are just as responsible for it
As I am—
This one is for you.

Booktalk! 2

BOOKTALKING FOR ALL AGES AND AUDIENCES

A SECOND EDITION

by Joni Bodart

THE H. W. WILSON COMPANY
NEW YORK
1985

First Printing 1985
Second Printing 1987

Library of Congress Cataloging in Publication Data

Bodart, Joni.
  Booktalk! 2 : booktalking for all ages and audiences.

  Includes bibliographies and index.
  1. Book talks.   2. Public relations—Libraries.
3. Books and reading.   4. Libraries and readers.
I. Title
Z716.3.B63   1985   021.7   85-14223
ISBN 0-8242-0716-5

Front cover: Ms. Jerilyn Henrikson's fifth-hour freshman English class at Emporia High School, Emporia, Kansas, May 1985.

Cover photos © 1985 by James R. Garvey, Emporia State University Photography, Emporia, Kansas.

Cover design by Martin Connell.

Printed in the United States of America

CONTENTS

ACKNOWLEDGMENTS

I still believe that no book is ever written in a vacuum, and the amount of help needed to write a revision of a previous work far surpasses the amount needed for the original one. There are many friends and colleagues who provided the necessary support and encouragement all along the way:

Larry Rakow and Elizabeth Overmyer contributed much more than their expertise in their fields and the pages of written material that they both gave me for the chapters they wrote. I appreciate their patience and encouragement over the last year and a half, as we all struggled to put this book together. Their willingness to put their money where their individual mouths are made life infinitely easier for me. They both helped make this book what I, and you, wanted it to be, and without that help, it would have been far less valuable, and much shorter!

Christy Tyson shared both booktalks and information, and also encouragement and laughter when the going got rough. Anyone who sits down and types pages and pages of all she knows about training booktalkers in the midst of an "antihistamine fog" surely deserves special credit!

Linda Lapides explained in detail the method of booktalking used at the Enoch Pratt Free Library, encouraged Cathi Edgerton to write to me with lots more information on how it's done at Pratt, and was in general encouraging and supportive.

Booktalkers across the country contributed booktalks, sometimes just one, and sometimes by the dozen. They are listed below, with their hometown or library. Two of these, however, worked with me most closely—Judy Druse and Barbara Lynn. They were extremely generous with time and energy, helping me write the final talks to be included. Without their assistance, I would not have been able to include nearly as many recent titles as I did.

Jonette Hill and Amy Van Meter, my graduate assistants, were both incredibly patient and hard-working. They spent hours setting up files, making mailing lists, and inputting the text on my computer. In addition, Jonette provided hot tea, encouragement, and order out of chaos on a regular basis. Amy dealt with a sea of paperwork that I simply refused to have anything to do with, and got us both through without drowning.

Bob Grover, Dean of the School of Library and Information Management, gave me generous amounts of time, encouragement, and anything else I needed to help me finish this and other projects. He is a very paragon of a boss!

Other faculty members of SLIM—Herb Achleitner, Nancy Flott, Barb Herrin—dispensed everything from jokes and approval to a shoulder to cry on and a beer when necessary, and so helped me keep working. Nancy inspired me to get a computer, and then held my hand through the first traumatic months while I got used to it. This book would never have been finished in time without her!

Norris Smith is still a marvelously patient and perceptive editor, and still makes me—and everyone else—sound much better than I ever believed I could sound. Not only that, she deals beautifully with the author's paranoia that strikes us all every so often. Bruce Carrick is still a source of great encouragement, support—and deadlines. They both knew I could do it long before I did, and were always available to tell me so when I needed to hear it. They were also available to listen to my new ideas, both half and fully baked, and didn't laugh even once (except when they were supposed to!).

I am most fortunate to have a wide and supportive circle of friends, all of whom have taken turns holding my hand and encouraging me, and also rejoicing when things went well. Foremost among them are: Patty Campbell, who laughs at all my predicaments and helps me laugh too, and who listens to my tales of woe or not-woe. Even when she doesn't have time, she makes time. Elizabeth Talbot, who also makes time, and who writes supportive and racoon-decorated letters. Harry Madden, who still lets me call him collect in the middle of the night, and who still says "Of course you can do it!" whenever I need to hear it. Mary Kay Chelton, Dorothy Broderick, and Joan Atkinson, who all simultaneously nagged me about finishing my dissertation and encouraged me about this book. I'm happy to be finishing both. (Now I can work on that *VOYA* column on booktalking!) Susie Achleitner, who talks—and listens—as hard as I do, who cares about both good and bad times, and who never fails to compliment me on my cooking and remind me that at least some of my disasters aren't nearly as disastrous as I like to think they are. Mikie Pepper and Gail Reikers, also recipients of late-night phone calls, who have read manuscripts, shared opinions, and believed in me and told me so when I needed it most!

And finally, to each one of you who took the time to write, call, or visit, and who said, "When are you going to do another one?" or "Why don't you include children's talks (or adult talks, or something else) in your next book?"—thank you. Without your input, your encouragement, your demands, this book would never have been written. I hope you enoy it.

JONI BODART
Emporia, Kansas
May 1985

CONTRIBUTORS OF BOOKTALKS

Linda Susan Angy
  Lambuth College
  Memphis, TN

Joan Ariel
  Irvine, CA

Shelia Barnett
  Memphis/Shelby County Public
  Library and Information Center
  Memphis, TN

Becky Blick
  Prairie Hills Middle School
  Buhler, KS

Joni Bodart
  SLIM, Emporia State University
  Emporia, KS

Beckie Brazell
  Alameda County Library System,
  Dublin Library
  Dublin, CA

Roger Carswell
  Wellington High School
  Wellington, KS

Frances Carter
  Northwest Regional Library System
  Panama City, FL

Christine Chilton
  Tulsa City-County Library
  Tulsa, OK

Karen Cole
  Prairie Hills Middle School
  Hutchinson, KS

Sherry Cotter
  Miami-Dade Public Library System,
  North Dade Regional Library
  Miami, FL

Dorothy A. Davidson
  Jackson Elementary School
  Abilene, TX

Debbie Denson
  Colorado City, TX

Margaret G. Driskill
  Clifton, TX

Judy Druse
  Chanute High School
  Chanute, KS

Kathryn Dunn
  Prince Georges County Memorial
  Library, Beltsville Branch
  Beltsville, MD

Nancy Eager
  Hayward Public Library
  Hayward, CA

Cathi Edgerton
  Enoch Pratt Free Library
  Baltimore, MD

Carole Gastrell
  Bear Branch Elementary School
  Kingwood, TX

Linda Gibson
  Memphis/Shelby County Public Library
  and Information Center
  Memphis, TN

Nancy Gierhart
  Colorado City, TX

Eileen Gieswein
  Lincoln Elementary School
  Concordia, KS

Vicki Grannan
  Memphis/Shelby County Public
  Library and Information Center
  Frayser Branch
  Memphis, TN

Patsy Hamric
  Rotan, TX

Billie Harding
Coahoma, TX

Barbara Hardy
Alameda County Library System,
Pleasanton Library
Pleasanton, CA

Marion Hargrove
Prince Georges County Memorial
Library, Bowie Branch
Bowie, MD

Janet Hellerich
Richmond Public Library
Richmond, CA

Linda Henderson
Wellington Junior High School
Wellington, KS

Diana Hirsch
Prince Georges County Memorial
Library, Surratts-Clinton Branch
Hyattsville, MD

Emily Hobson
Pemberton High School
Marshall, TX

Mary K. Hobson
Vermillion Grade School
Maize, KS

Katie Hoffman
Ft. Riley Junior High School
Ft. Riley, KS

Betty A. Holtzen
Abilene Public Library
Abilene, KS

Donna Houser
Iola, KS

Sarah B. Howell
Northwest Regional Library System
Panama City, FL

Sandy Hudson
St. John, KS

Ilene Ingelmo
Alameda County Library System,
Union City Library
Union City, CA

Bonnie Janssen
ACA County Library System,
Fremont Main Library
Fremont, CA

Zoë Kalkanis
ACA County Library System,
Albany Library
Albany, CA

Sherrill Kumler
Monterey Public Library
Monterey, CA

Linda Lapides
Enoch Pratt Free Library
Baltimore, MD

Pat Lichter
Alameda County Library
Hayward, CA

Sally M. Long
Worcester County Library
Snow Hill, MD

Clara Lovely
Moore, Lee and Crockett
Elementary Schools
Marshall, TX

Barbara A. Lynn
Iola Senior High School
Iola, KS

Billie McKeever
Haskell, TX

Diana McRae
Alameda County Library System
Alameda County, CA

Dwight Malone
Memphis, TN

Lucy Marx
Louisville Free Public Library
Louisville, KY

Avis Matthews
Prince Georges County Memorial
Library, Oxon Hill Branch
Hyattsville, MD

Beverly Montgomery
Junction City Junior High School
Junction City, KS

Claranell Murray
Taylor Elementary School
Abilene, TX

Alan Nichter
Tampa-Hillsborough County Public
Library System
Tampa, FL

Elizabeth Overmyer
ACA County Library System
Fremont Main Library
Fremont, CA

Akiba Patton-Shabazz
Memphis/Shelby County Public Library and Information Center
Memphis, TN

Laurie Peck
Palo Alto, CA

Martha Pillow
Memphis, TN

E. Lynn Porter
North Harris County College
Houston, TX

Faye Powell
Prince Georges County Memorial Library, Oxon Hill Branch
Hyattsville, MD

Pat Powell
Ottawa Public Library
Ottawa, KS

Larry Rakow
Shaker Heights High School
Shaker Heights, OH

Cheryl Ress
Wellington Junior High School
Wellington, KS

Anne Reynolds
Baltimore, MD

Paul H. Rockwell
Alameda County Library System,
San Lorenzo Library
Hayward, CA

Peggy Ross
Abilene, TX

Richard Russo
Alameda County Library System
Albany Library
Albany, CA

Judy Sasges
Stanislaus County Free Library
Modesto, CA

Dee Scrogin
Prairie Hills Middle School
Hutchinson, KS

Judie Smith
Alameda County Library System,
Pleasanton Library
Pleasanton, CA

Suzi Smith
Tulsa City-County Library
Tulsa, OK

Alan Stewart
Memphis, TN

Janet Strang
Memphis/Shelby County Public Library and Information Center
Frayser Branch
Memphis, TN

Judy Thomas
Abilene, TX

Diane P. Tuccillo
Mesa Public Library
Mesa, AZ

Peggy Tucker
Tulsa City-County Library
Tulsa, OK

Christy Tyson
Spokane Public Library
Spokane, WA

Lola Viets
Winfield High School
Winfield, KS

Holly Willett
Chapel Hill, NC

JoAnn F. Young
Tulsa City-County Public Library,
Tulsa, OK

INTRODUCTION

Many things have changed since I wrote the introduction to *Booktalk!*—and many things have not. I may be in a different place, with new experiences, and using a computer instead of a felt-tip pen—but somehow deciding what you will read first when you open this book is just as hard as it was the last time. Nevertheless, here goes!

This book is a response to all the people who asked me to write it. When *Booktalk!* came out, none of us were sure what would happen, or whether another edition would ever be demanded. But demand you did—and sometimes loudly. Newer talks, more details on how to write them, more information about children, children's talks, how does a school librarian manage to find the time to give booktalks, how do you talk to adult groups, and what books can you use? Everywhere I've given lectures, workshops, and demonstrations, people have said, "That was great—I want another one just like it, but I want you to add this, and this, and this." Well, here it is; whether it can answer all your questions any more than the first one did, I don't know. But it's bigger, and I hope better, and includes more information, more booktalks, and more people.

Not all the chapters have been completely rewritten, but they have each been examined and updated. Due to the fact that I have not worked as a YA librarian since 1979, the personal examples I've given are almost all ones from before then. I hope you will still find them as relevant as I believe them to be. I have included more recent titles in the examples given in all the chapters, and given more information on how to write booktalks and organize and deliver a presentation. When it was possible, I have tried to make it clear that the techniques presented are suitable for all age groups, with only minor changes needed.

In response to the requests for information on how to write booktalks for children, I asked Elizabeth Overmyer, from the Alameda County Library System, to write a chapter on preparing and delivering talks for that age group. While we do use the same basic technique, Elizabeth has modified it to suit the various ages of children she works with. I think you will find the information she gives quite practical and easy to follow. Her long experience as a children's librarian has given her an excellent background, and I am delighted she is willing to share her knowledge. At the present time, she is working as the head of the first booktalking project that I know of funded by LSCA funds. Volunteers from the Fremont, California, area are being recruited and trained to go into the elementary schools in Fremont to do booktalks. It is an eighteen-month program, and Elizabeth plans to publish a handbook on how the program was run and how well it worked. As busy as she is with the project, I feel very fortunate that she was willing to take time to work with me on this book.

I have talked to many school librarians who have told me that there is a difference between going into a school as a public librarian, and doing booktalks in your own school. They have also said that there is no time for a school librarian to do talks, because of the amount of other work required, and the number of classes that want to visit the library. Larry Rakow, high school librarian from Shaker Heights, Ohio, is one of the people who commented on the qualitative difference between doing booktalks in your own versus someone else's school. So I asked him to write on just what those differences were—to put his money where his mouth was. I am pleased to report that he has done just that—and done it beautifully, as well. Anyone who isn't ready to "go get 'em" after reading Larry's chapter probably won't ever be ready!

I have traveled all over the United States since *Booktalk!* was published, talking about booktalking, YA literature, and YA's in general. Doing these workshops and presentations has been one of the high points of my life, and I am looking forward to continuing it in the future. One of my favorite things is discovering not only new people and places, but also new ways to do talks, innovations that prove what I have always known—the only limits on how and where and to whom you do talks are the ones you set on your own imagination. I have tried to include a few of these new ideas in Chapter 11—but what you find there only scratches the surface. You can try anything—who knows, it might work! And if it does, let the rest of us know about it!

I have also begun to teach booktalking in a variety of formats, including a class here at Emporia State University. I have included a great deal of new information in Chapter 10, on how you can run a class, a workshop, or a demonstration for a variety of different kinds of groups. You have much more to pick and choose from than was available in *Booktalk!* I have given other people's methods and appended their handouts, when I have had access to them.

Writing a second edition of a book written five years ago means going back and really *reading* it again, for the first time in more years than I care to admit. I was startled at some of the things I'd said—and pleased at some of them, too. But the mistakes seemed to be most obvious. Two of the things that I decided to correct this time through were the sexist language and the absolutes. I think I have caught all of the he's and she's and rephrased them into language more acceptable to me at this time. I also took out all the absolutes that I could see. I am amazed now at my temerity in saying that *this* is the way to do things, and that C *always* results from A + B. You may notice a liberal sprinkling of sometimes's, perhaps's and maybe's. If I ever thought I was the final word on anything, I no longer do—unless it's my own life, destiny, whatever. Life at thirty-seven is much less black-and-white than it was at thirty-one.

Finally, I have included many more booktalks than I did in the first edition, also because of the requests some of you made. These new talks are coded for the age group they would be most suitable for, but you may or may not agree with the codes we have listed. Appropriateness varies with the area of the country, and with the philosophy of the person doing the selecting. I advise you to trust your own judgment when you are in doubt.

I was surprised to discover that writing a second edition of a successful book was much more difficult and nerve-wracking than writing the first one was. It's a good thing I didn't know—I'm not sure I would have ever gotten it started, much less finished it! But I didn't know, I did finish it, and here it is. And it's for you, so let me know what you think of it!

Happy Booktalking!

CHAPTER 1

WHY BOOKTALKING?

What's All the Fuss About?

For me, reading is a way to explore new worlds, new ideas, new people, new experiences. If people, especially teenage people, don't read, it's because they don't think it's fun, or interesting, or "in," or "cool," or "bad," or *necessary.* I do booktalks because I have found this to be the quickest, most effective way to change their minds, as effective with the avid readers as it is with the reluctant ones. Booktalking can interest students in things they may never have thought of before and introduce them to books that will broaden their horizons. Reading can be vitally important to troubled kids, as well. Although solutions to problems are not always found in books, teenagers can at least find there the reassurance that they are not the only people who have ever had to face those problems. And even with the increasing influence of television and computers, the ability to read is still essential to an individual's functioning adequately in our society.

Reading is also recreation—it is fun, funny, entertaining, and emotionally satisfying. It can be an individual or a group experience. It is something to enjoy by yourself or to share with friends. It is portable and adaptable, something you can do almost anywhere with almost no preparation. I see it that way, but then I've been reading easily since I was five years old. Many people see reading only as a painful, difficult chore; they are not able to read well enough to truly enjoy it. They never discover the fun of reading, and so they don't get the practice that might help them read more easily. To me, that's where booktalking comes in. In booktalking, you try to emphasize the fun and excitement of reading. Even if the kids don't listen, or don't check out the books, at least you will have shown them that somebody (an adult who is not a teacher) thinks that books are important and is willing to visit their class to say so. That's the least you can accomplish. But perhaps you'll convince a kid to try reading. Let me tell you about a boy at the Stanislaus County Juvenile Hall whose experience demonstrates what a difference booktalking can make.

1

I hadn't noticed Billy until he picked up *The Haven*. I'd been wondering whether anyone would pick it up—the cover was certainly a "grabber," showing a huge dog's head with slavering jaws, teeth bared in a snarl. Unfortunately, the cover had little to do with the story, a clumsy imitation of Tolkien. I asked Billy to tell me what he thought of the book when I came back next week, since I hadn't given it to any kids before and I wanted his opinion. The next week he was one of the first to come running up to me—he not only loved the book, he'd been reading it out loud to the other boys in his room, and they loved it too! He was nearly through, did I have anything else just like it? My favorite book at the time was Gordon Dickson's *The Dragon and the George*, which I did a booktalk on and which he was equally enthusiastic about. *The Hobbit* was next, then *Star Wars, Splinter of the Mind's Eye,* and several books on body-building. I was rejoicing at having found not only a real reader but also one who could inspire his peers. *The Haven* was so popular it didn't surface again for months, and *The Dragon and the George* soon disappeared as well. Imagine my shock when Billy came up to me the week before he was transferred to CYA (California Youth Authority) Camp and said how much he appreciated all my help and suggestions—before he came to Juvenile Hall, he said, he didn't read much and almost never finished a book. Now he really liked to read and was reading faster then he ever could before—and he planned to keep on even after he got out!

That's what booktalking can do, and that's why I do it.

Billy is five years in the past now, and one of the memories and prods I use to keep myself going when I get tired of dealing with kids, as a booktalker, librarian, or therapist. But I run into "Billys" almost every time I booktalk. There are plenty of people out there who are ready to enjoy reading.

What Is a Booktalk?

In the broadest terms, it's what you say to convince someone to read a book. It's what I was doing as far back as grade school and as recently as yesterday when someone said, "Joni, you've read a lot, tell me a good book to read." It's sharing your enjoyment of a book with other people and convincing them that they will enjoy the book too.

A booktalk is not a book review or a book report or a book analysis. It does not judge the book's merits; it assumes the book is good and goes on from there. As a dramatic art, booktalking has something in common with storytelling, although in content it more nearly resembles an unfinished murder mystery—it doesn't say "whodunnit," but it makes you want to find out. A good booktalk reaches out to the listeners and involves them so they become not merely listeners but participants. It makes them care enough about the people in the book to want to read it and see what happens after the end of the talk.

A good booktalk is enticing. It is a come-on. It is entertaining. And it is fun, for both the listener and the booktalker. However, a booktalk should not be better than the book it's about. Overselling a book merely means that your credibility will be reduced for future talks. If the first three chapters are slow and the rest of it is great, say so. Don't let your audience think it's great from page one—they may not make it to Chapter Four!

Booktalks are long or short, memorized or just learned, and written down or not. Each method has its own rationale and usefulness—and its own drawbacks.

Long booktalks average three to five minutes but sometimes may run up to seven minutes. Usually they are written down and then learned or memorized. They are used in somewhat formal presentations. Short booktalks are one to three minutes long and are used both in reader's advisory work and in formal presentations. In reader's advisory work, the short talks are delivered impromptu, as needed, and are not written down, but in a formal presentation brief talks may be written out beforehand and then used between longer talks, to vary the pace of the program. With experience, most booktalkers learn to size up an audience and can often decide on the spot whether to give a long talk on a particular title or use a brief version instead.

There are two ways to learn a booktalk. It can be memorized, word-for-word, or the general content of the talk can be learned, so that while the exact words and phrases vary, the ideas and their sequence stay the same. Booktalkers who memorize use this technique for excerpted sections of a book, which have to be word-perfect and can then be delivered as booktalks. And some people also memorize talks they have written themselves. Memorizing has good and bad points. Reciting a selection from a book is an effective way to get the author's style across, and if the selection is chosen with care, it will capture the audience's attention and appeal to their imagination. In addition, excerpts work with a variety of age groups, from children to adults. However, memorizing is risky, since if you forget the next word, phrase, or sentence, you've lost your cues for the subsequent ones as well. Ad-libbing at this point is difficult, and many (even most?) people panic, freeze, turn red or white, and even fall apart. Of course, that's not to slight the cool heads who cover up, ad-lib flawlessly, and go right on. They simply seem to be a minority—except among very experienced public speakers. (In case you were wondering—I'm in the first group, *not* the second! I can only ad-lib flawlessly when I haven't memorized the talk in the first place.)

The other way to learn a booktalk is to do what I call just that—learn it. That involves *not* memorizing it word-for-word but remembering ideas or the scenes that are included and their sequence. There are various ways to do this, which I will cover later. The advantage is that, should you forget something, you aren't tied down to a sequence of sounds as you are with a memorized talk. It is much easier, therefore, to say in different words what you want to convey. In addition, you are more flexible and able to adjust better to your audience's needs. It's hard to cut down or to lengthen a memorized talk (virtually impossible, I should think, with a memorized excerpt), but very easy to do that with a learned one. Flexibility is essential to a booktalker, since entertainment is a primary goal. You must keep your audience listening and your presentation moving in order to sell books.

However, there is one disadvantage to a learned talk that doesn't apply to a memorized excerpt. The booktalker must create the talk—must use his or her own words and imagination to describe the book in a way that will entice readers to it. This is more difficult for some than for others, and is the sole reason (well, not *sole*—laziness comes in there, too!) I am a proponent of shared talks.

Another problem is getting the author's style across—relatively simple with an excerpt. I will discuss this more later, but it can be frustrating to try to capture the tone of a book in your own words. One way, however, is to use some of the author's key words and phrases in your talk, as I did in my presentation of *The Quartzsite Trip* by William Hogan—one of my all-time absolute favorite books (criticize it at your own risk!).

Booktalks vary in another major way—they can be written down or not. Many people I've talked with lately simply don't have time to write down talks. Several school librarians have said, "I'm so busy, if I stopped to write them down, I'd never *do* any!" Disadvantages are obvious—unwritten talks can't be retrieved easily; they may vary more in quality from program to program, depending on how much preparation time is available; and they can't easily be shared. Written booktalks are, for me and most others, the way to go. I will cover methods and techniques in detail later.

But no matter what method you use, all booktalks have one thing in common. They are a come-on, capture the listener's attention, lead up to a climactic moment, and stop, without giving away the ending.

The audience always knows there's something else going on that they haven't heard about yet—and so must return to the book to discover it.

Singin' the Red Tape Blues

The first step in doing booktalks is to persuade your administration to sponsor them. If you don't know what your library's policy is on outreach activities, or on services that might be considered "untraditional," find out—quickly and quietly. Official attitudes are probably well understood by the senior employees. If going outside the building to bring in new patrons is encouraged, thank your lucky stars—you are fortunate! So are you if booktalking has already been written into your job description. However, you may discover that no one has ever done booktalking in your library, school, or town, and that your administration is a bit skeptical about letting you try something new, especially something that will involve time and money, not to mention a chance for you to get out of the library for a while in the middle of the day. Even if you find that librarians have asked for similiar programs in the past and been refused, do not give up hope. You may be the one who succeeds. Plan your presentation carefully and try to use words and terms your supervisor can relate to. Talk about what booktalking can do for (and to!) the library, and be as realistic and thorough as possible.

You should prepare your presentation as carefully as you would a booktalk. They are both in a sense sales pitches, and you want to be successful. Remember that you will communicate with dress and body language as well as with words. Practice your presentation on a friend if you're nervous, and ask for feedback.

Some of the basic points you may want to discuss are: how a booktalking program can benefit the library, the school, or the community (or all three); what the costs are likely to be, in money and in time; how a booktalking program may affect the workload of the entire library staff; what problems can be anticipated and how they can be dealt with.

Booktalking does have many benefits. You may want to cite any facts and figures you can find about circulation increases as a result of booktalking. These data can be hard to come by, but if you talk to other people who do booktalking, you should be able to get some information from them. For instance, Judy Druse, a high school librarian in Chanute, Kansas, recorded a threefold increase in circulation after four years of intensive booktalking. June Level published the results of an informal study of the effects of booktalking on middle-grade students in *School Library Media Quarterly* (Winter 1982). She found that circulation increased overall (especially for paperbacks), and that reading among lower-ability students rose markedly. Descriptions of my own experiences and others' are scattered throughout this book, as they seem to fit in. I am currently working on a dissertation on the impact of booktalks on the circulation of the titles talked about—the results of this study should be available late in 1985 or early in 1986. If you can't find anyone to talk to locally, write to me or one of the contributors to this book. Or search the journals yourself—there aren't a lot of articles on this subject, but every little bit helps when you're trying to convince a skeptical administrator. And by all means refer to your own experience, if you were ever part of a successful program somewhere else. The fact that you have actually participated in such a program will increase your credibility.

In addition to boosting circulation, booktalking can change attitudes toward reading, libraries, and librarians. It gets librarians out into the community and promotes a positive image of the library and the people who work there. It's not just the confirmed readers who raise the circulation figures, it's people who have never been near a library before, who are drawn in by an intriguing program and a friendly librarian. Booktalks can be presented at schools and at meetings of community groups. They can also be used in a review column in a school or town newspaper, or recorded for broadcast on radio or television. They bring the library to people's attention, making it appear more accessible, more fun, and more relevant to daily life. At a time when library service is increasingly mechanized and computerized, it seems to me important to focus on people-oriented individual services and to continue to promote reading as pleasure and as recreation. Booktalking, individually or to a group, does this. Most children's and YA librarians agree that booktalking is also the most cost-effective way of promoting books and reading.

But starting a booktalking program, even on a small scale, can mean a change in the library's routine, and new hassles, as well as new opportunities, for the staff. You must be ready to discuss potential problems with your administrator—no gains without pains! While there is usually not much outlay for equipment, booktalking may necessitate purchasing extra copies of some popular titles, and it does involve staff time. The number of requests usually increases, sometimes dramatically, and so does the workload of the department that handles them. Titles and authors may be incorrectly given or indecipherable, again increasing workload. And if you (the booktalker) are given release time from desk coverage to prepare talks and present them, other staff members will be expected to make up the difference.

You need to be prepared to discuss how much preparation time will be necessary, both now and after the program is underway; how many extra copies of titles will have to be purchased and when; how much money will be spent, and why it will be well spent; how much time you'll be spending outside the building; how your booktalking will affect your ability to do your required hours of desk coverage and other duties, and why that change (if there is one) is defensible.

Handouts can be helpful in making your point and in reducing the demands on your director's memory. First, you may want to present a written statement of your goals—what you hope to accomplish by initiating or expanding a booktalking program—and then an outline of the steps you plan to take, listing people you intend to work with and the schools and community groups you'd like to contact. (Needless to say, you should *not* make commitments to any group until your proposal is approved.) You may want to include copies of relevant statistics showing the effects of booktalking on circulation, and you should present cost figures and perhaps a chart showing the amount of work time involved (include time spent contacting schools or community groups, filling requests, setting up displays, and selecting new titles for future talks). You may be able to establish a ratio between preparation time and time actually spent booktalking, although you should realize (and point out) that this ratio will change as you gain experience. A sample schedule of visits would be helpful, also a list of some of the titles you plan to talk about. Any handouts you prepare should be neat, easy to understand, and concise, and there should be a specific reason why you want your administrator to have the information each sheet contains.

Your administrator will probably be concerned about the effects of a successful program on the library as a whole, and about the reactions of the rest of the staff. You should be concerned about these matters too. It is essential to educate the entire staff about the goals of a booktalking program and to involve them as much as possible, so that there will be no slow-burning resentment against the program as it develops. (After all, there is not much point in enticing new patrons to the library if they are going to be treated as pests by a cross, overworked staff once they get there.) If any of your colleagues share your enthusiasm for booktalking, include them in your plans. And offer to do whatever you can to ease the impact of a successful booktalking program on the support staff. There are a number of steps you can take: helping fill requests, instead of just passing them along; talking only about titles that are available in paperback, or in multiple copies; giving the public service desk a bibliography of the titles you talk about, and a list of alternative titles to recommend when these are not available; setting up a display of booktalk materials, so that the service desk staff will have only one place to look. Make it clear that you are proposing a cooperative effort, not an ego trip.

Of course, the more classes or groups you talk to, the greater the impact on the library. If your administrator is not willing to commit a large amount of the library's resources to a booktalking program, then take what you can get and keep track of any increases in circulation, library usage, requests, and reference questions that come from the groups you have addressed or pertain to the titles you have promoted. Send memos to your supervisor with carbons to anyone else who matters (you know who they are!) pointing out the wonderful results you are having. Be assertive, but do be careful not to be too aggressive, or to demand too much all at once. It's not unreasonable for an administrator to want to start small. While you keep your nose to the grindstone, cranking out all those talks, also keep your ears flapping in the wind. Be sensitive to the climate around you, and listen to the news on the staff grapevine. Once you have started a program like this, that can be viewed as frivolous by administrators and clerks alike, it is important to keep both happy, so that the program can continue and even expand.

Good luck!

CHAPTER 2

WRITING A BOOKTALK

Nuts & Bolts & Everything Else— Including the Kitchen Sink!

There are two unbreakable rules in booktalking:
1. Don't tell the ending of a book.
2. Don't talk about a book you haven't read.

There are good reasons for these rules. In a booktalk, you are trying to persuade people to read a book by telling them just a little bit about it, and if you tell the whole story, including the climax, there will be no reason for them to read it. The idea is to make them want to read the book by withholding information, so that their curiosity is piqued. The reasons for the second rule are just as obvious. How can you talk about a book that you haven't read? If you're using someone else's booktalk, and you learn it and do a marvelous job presenting it, all your work will be wasted if, afterwards, someone comes up and asks a question you can't answer. Then, on top of that, if you are really lucky, there'll be a bright kid around to listen to you fumble that first question and say (loudly): "You didn't *really* read that book, didja?" I know it happens because it has happened to me—and I can categorically state that there are no holes in floors to sink through in such a situation. In addition, your credibility goes down the drain! It's simply not worth it, so read the book you're talking about, even if you are using someone else's booktalk.

The first step in building a collection of booktalks is to read as much as you can. There is no danger of reading too much. You will not be able to write talks on everything you read, and probably not all of the talks you write will be successful, at least the first time you give them. As you read, jot down notes about the book. These can be written on a three-by-five card for a file box or just on a piece of paper, to be stuffed in a drawer with all the other miscellaneous pieces of paper on booktalking. However you take the notes, try to keep them all together, so that when you have a chance to start writing booktalks or need some new ones you'll only have to look in one place. Your notes should include the author's name, the title, a brief one- or two-sentence plot outline, the names of important characters, incidents you thought were funny, interesting, or intriguing—and don't forget the page numbers, so you can find the scenes again.

All this notetaking may seem somewhat forced at first, and time-consuming as well. However, it saves time in the end, when you don't have to search the new-book shelves for the elusive title you can't remember, that would be perfect for the class you're talking to next week—or for the eager kid who's standing at your elbow! If extensive notetaking is something you simply will not do, try just keeping a list of the titles and authors of books that look like possibilities. Anything that will jog your memory will help. If I can, I set aside a copy of the book so I'll have it when I want to start writing—that way I don't have to take notes either! (I do need to be careful I don't reread each book completely as I skim it for ideas—it's easy to forget why I'm reading it, slow down, and enjoy it all again. But booktalks don't get written that way.)

How can you tell what books will be easy to booktalk? Basically, the ones you liked yourself. (How can you convince someone else that reading a book will be a pleasurable experience when it wasn't for you?) The book you choose doesn't have to be a literary gem that can withstand the ravages of time and reviewers. However, the qualities that make any book "good" are important—a strong, fast-moving, believable plot, lifelike characters who fit into the setting; emotional impact of one kind or another, a chance for the reader to become involved in the story, a way to identify with what's going on in the book. Paula Danziger's *The Divorce Express* is one example of a book that booktalks well. Others are Richard Peck's *Are You in the House Alone?* and *Ghosts I Have Been; One Child* by Torey Hayden; *Long Voyage Back* by Luke Rhinehart; *I Know What You Did Last Summer* and *Killing Mr. Griffin* by Lois Duncan; all of Stephen King's novels, including *Carrie, Firestarter, The Shining,* and *Pet Sematary.* The sample booktalks at the end of this volume may give you some more ideas.

Basically, however, it is the book *you* like that you will be able to sell. This rule holds true almost without exception in regard to long booktalks. In a one-to-one situation, though, especially when you're acquainted with the person you're talking to, you can say, "I didn't like this book, but I know you like books on this subject, so I think you will. It's about. . . . " Do be honest with kids—they are startlingly perceptive most of the time, scorn lies, and respect honesty.

The Long Booktalk

Now that you have an idea of the kind of book to choose, have selected one and read it, and maybe taken notes to jog your memory, you're ready to plan your talk. How do you pick out a scene or series of scenes to build your booktalk around? Since booktalking is essentially just sharing your enthusiasm about and enjoyment of a book with someone else, imagine what you'd say to friends about the book to convince them to read it. Why was it funny, exciting, suspenseful, intriguing, frightening? Why did you keep on reading it? Was there a point at which you realized you couldn't put it down? Maybe that would be a good place to stop your booktalk, if it's not too far along in the story, since kids will want to pick the book up to see what happened next.

Look at the source of excitement or focus of interest in the book. Does the book center around the plot, a character, a particular scene? Build your talk around this focus.

I divide booktalks into four major types, based on where the interest or excitement focuses: scene/anecdote/short story, plot summary, character description, and creation of mood.

Scene/Anecdote/Short story

The scene you choose may or may not be a major one, but it should be one you can enjoy and identify with. It may not be the same one someone else would choose, but if it works, it's the right one for you.

Generally, look for a short scene with lots of action, perhaps something funny or suspenseful, that takes place early in the book so you don't give away too much of the plot. The scene should be complete in itself and should convey the feeling of the book. You want to find a scene that will show your listeners what to expect in the rest of the book. For example, in Harold Krents' *To Race the Wind,* a good scene would be the description of how he learned to drive a car—as a very drunk senior in high school. Another funny anecdote is his response to being classified 1-A for the draft—he was delighted, informed all the news services, and wrote a poem about how he would be glad to go and defend his country, if someone would just tell him which way to shoot.

Other examples of good scenes to use are: learning how to play chicken in *Red Sky at Morning;* Blossom Culp's ghost imitation or how she suddenly got the second sight in *Ghosts I Have Been;* Arthur's first glimpse of himself as a dog in *The Dog Days of Arthur Cane;* Ramona's problems with wearing her new pajamas to school, or with toothpaste, or almost any of her other mishaps and escapades in the Ramona series; the wedding scene in *The Day the Senior Class Got Married*; or the scene in *First the Egg* when the class is divided into couples and receive their eggs. Lead up to the scene you choose by sketching the plot so far, if that's necessary, or telling why these stories were collected into one volume. Then concentrate on the episode or story itself. Try to capture the excitement, humor, or human interest of the scene, and don't forget to mention any interesting or odd details. Then stop at a crucial point or after the punchline, and you have a booktalk.

Episodic books are easy to talk about in this way. James Herriot's books are an excellent example. You can start with a sentence or two about Herriot and how he ended up in the Yorkshire Dales. Then go right into one of the anecdotes about the animals he treated. In *All Creatures Great and Small*, Nugent's troubles with his "little jobs" is a funny scene, or perhaps you could tell about the mistreated dog whose love was able to give an old woman a new lease on life, in *All Things Bright and Beautiful*.

This technique of centering a talk around a particular scene or anecdote can also be used for short story collections. Rather than telling one scene, tell one story. Some examples are: "Priscilla and the Wimps" from *Sixteen*; "The Man in the Middle" from *The Headless Roommate*; the title story from *Summer Girls, Love Boys* or from *Dear Bill, Remember Me*; one of the lives that Hissune experiences during his adventures in *Chronicles of Majipoor*. Choose a story that particularly appeals to you and is representative of the entire collection. Tell the story, all of it, in your own words. Don't try to memorize it—use *your* words to make the story your own, to make it come alive. Then add a final sentence or two to the effect that " . . . this is only one of the exciting/romantic/suspenseful/terrifying [choose one] stories in this book!"

Plot Summary

In this kind of booktalk, you summarize the plot up to a climactic moment, and then stop. If you do this well, the talk can be extremely effective (as well as frustrating for the listener, who wants to know what happens next). It can sell the book immediately. This kind of booktalk is definitely a teaser, a cliffhanger, and so shouldn't reveal too much. Action, suspense, or adventure novels lend themselves to this treatment. Some examples of books you can treat this way and the points at which you can stop your talk are: *Are You in the House Alone?* (Gail wakes up in the hospital, realizes that she's been raped and that no one will believe her story); *Firestarter* (Charlie turns to defend her father from The Shop—with fire); *Lord Valentine's Castle* (Valentine understands who he really is and why he must make a pilgrimage to Castle Mount); *Deathwatch* (Ben starts to walk across the desert without food, water, or clothes); *Bid Time Return* (Richard lies down on his bed in 1975 and begins to convince himself he will wake up in 1896); *Ordinary People* (Con realizes that his brother's death was *not* the cause of his own suicide attempt—but what was?); *The Chocolate War* (Jerry decides to defy both the school administration and the Vigils); *The Queen's Gambit* (Beth wins her first chess tournament and becomes the Kentucky State Champion at thirteen); *The Dragon and the George* (Jim/Gorbash discovers Angie has been imprisoned in the Loathly Tower and knows he must lead a quest to rescue her). Booktalks on some of these novels appear in the booktalk section.

How much of the story to tell is up to you—a few pages may be enough to involve the audience in some books. For others, you may have to sketch in up to half the book, as in *Are You in the House Alone?* The point is to involve and to entice, not to reveal all. You need to tell enough about the book to interest and involve the audience, and then make sure they know something else exciting is going to happen. But do not tell them what. It's better to tell too little than too much. You never want to give your listeners the feeling that they don't need to read the book because you've already told them all about it. When you say, "To find out what happens next, read . . . ," the response should be, "Oh no! Go on! Go on!" If the book has a complicated plot, it's not necessary to give all the details. You should sketch in the main highlights, leaving out more than you include. Include action; leave out most descriptive details. Paint with a broad brush, not a fine one. Remember also that you have a time limit to consider. Let your listeners discover some things about the book themselves. Don't go on and on and on. You'll suddenly discover your audience hasn't come along with you. Plan your talk—it should have a beginning, a middle, and an end. When you get to the end, quit. It's essential for your audience to know that they'll be missing something if they don't read the book. They have to be interested and stay interested so that when you're through, they'll still be intrigued enough to go to the library and get the book.

You may occasionally find that it's unnecessary to get very far into the plot. All you may have to do is set the stage and reveal the crucial conflict. *Save Queen of Sheba* (Moeri) and *Amanda/Miranda* (Peck) are two books that can be handled like this, and booktalks on such titles can be very brief.

Character Description

There are several situations in which you might want to base a book-talk on character description. One is obvious—when a person (or an animal or an entity) is the main focus of the book itself, and events of the story are presented as they affect that character. This is almost always true of biographies and often of novels as well. If you find that what you remember best about a book is a character, then you should consider building your booktalk around character description, because your own involvement will communicate itself to your audience. To see some of the ways this approach can be used, look at the description of the tragic Mara in the talk on *Sunflower Forest* in the booktalk section, or the sketch of the undersized, picked-on hero of *Slake's Limbo,* or the account of the battling stepsisters of *Gardine vs. Hanover.* Judy Thomas' talk on *The Best Christmas Pageant Ever* is almost entirely character description—an extended, getting-funnier-by-the-minute rap sheet on the mean and rotten Herdman kids.

Going a step further, you can not only describe but temporarily embody a character by speaking in the first person, a technique that can add drama and immediacy to your presentation. This approach will come most naturally if the book you've chosen is written in the first person. Chances are, the narrator will describe himself or herself somewhere in the story, and that description can be used—instant booktalk! For example, Chrysta, in *To Take a Dare,* describes her own transformation from sweet Chrissie, who never said boo to anyone or did anything unusual, to the wild and dramatic Chris, whose outrageous behavior forced everyone to notice her. This account makes a very effective talk. Autobiographies like *To Race the Wind* and *Joni* can be introduced quite successfully simply by letting the central characters tell about themselves.

The first-person technique can also be applied to books written in the third person—it just takes a little more imagination (or a touch of ventriloquism!) Judy Druse has written a first-person talk on *Roadside Valentine,* although the book is written in the third person. You can even adopt the point of view of a minor, unimportant character. Just pick one who is well placed to observe what's going on and try to imagine what that character would say—get inside the mind of the nosey neighbor, or the policeman who discovered the crime. In Linda Susan Angy's booktalk on *Here I Stay,* a large black cat named Satan tells the story of the haunted house and its occupants. Satan is not the narrator (or even the hero) of the book itself, but the cat's-eye view in this talk is a fresh and intriguing way of presenting the story.

Fantasy and science fiction are absolutely crawling with fascinating nonhuman characters—dragons, space aliens, androids, and the like. Descriptions of exotic characters are almost irresistible—who wouldn't want to know more about the Named of *Ratha's Creature,* or the shape-changers of *The Riddle-Master of Hed?*

Finally, you can use character descriptions to introduce a murder mystery or a survival story—any book in which a motley crew are brought together by a common emergency. Short thumbnail sketches of the players in *The Westing Game* or of the passengers on the Orient Express can be used to create suspense: Which one of these people is the murderer? Which ones will come out alive? Lists are almost inherently interesting, and a list of suspicious or endangered characters is no exception.

Creation of Mood

Basically, this is a technique that is best used in combination with one of the other methods I've described. If a certain mood or a distinctive writing style is an important focus of attention in the book, it's necessary to capture (if you can) that mood or style in your own talk. This may mean using some of the author's words or phrases, or tailoring your style of writing and delivery to the author's. In a talk on *The Quartzsite Trip,* I used Hogan's own phrasing style to write the talk, pulling many of the sentences directly from the text. Since the style is so important, it is essential to learn this kind of talk very well, so that if you need to present the material in a slightly different order, you will still be able to maintain a consistent tone.

The Headless Roommate, a collection of modern folktales (the scarey stories we all told each other as adolescents—remember "The Hook"? It's included!), depends on atmosphere for its impact. In their natural settings, in dimly-lit rooms or around campfires late at night, these stories are terrifying in the way virtually impossible to duplicate during the day. The booktalker, however, can create a spooky atmosphere with tone of voice, pauses, intensity, and emphasis, drawing in the listeners and making them believe in a tale that might otherwise seem a little silly in daylight.

Overall Hints and Tips

But no matter which method or combination of methods you use, there are a few things to remember. Don't always rely on the same format for your talks—try a new approach occasionally. Feel free to use talks of different lengths. If all you really want to say can be covered in two minutes, don't feel you have to stretch it to three and a half or four. Other talks may demand a full five minutes. Don't worry about it. Talks of different lengths and types vary the pace of the program and help provide interest. And that is essential to keep your audience involved.

Lists of things are interesting and can be worked into almost any type of booktalk. Try listing the bits and pieces the Wortmans rescued when their boat sank (*Almost Too Late*), or the names of some of the Class of '62 on *The Quartzsite Trip*. In *Ace Hits the Big Time,* a list of the items that combined to change his life can be effective, and so can a list of the mixed-up classes from *The Alfred G. Graebner Memorial High School Handbook of Rules and Regulations* or of Isabel's religions and diseases from the same book.

Just a note here about reading an excerpt, and the dangers involved. Reading is not a substitute for learning a booktalk. Although some people disagree with me, I believe that reading can easily become boring and shouldn't be done at all unless you're extremely good. Even then the amount of reading should be strictly limited, within both the individual booktalk and the entire presentation. The hidden disadvantage to reading is that it limits eye contact between you and your audience and puts something—the book—in between. Eye contact is one of the things that brings you and your audience closer together and that makes your presentation more personal. It keeps your audience involved with what you are saying and lets you be constantly aware of their response to the material. Some of this contact will be lost when you read from rather than tell about a book. Reading also makes the situation seem more static and formal, rather than relaxed and free-flowing. Finally, it is very difficult to read aloud well—much more difficult than simply to tell a good story. If, however, you must read a passage for some reason, then be sure that you know that section *very* well, so that you will not have to look at the text all the time. Just a very brief glance every now and then should be sufficient. If you aren't sure how good you are, read to someone who you know will be critical rather than tactful, or try reading one excerpt before an audience and gauge their reaction. If they listened and wanted to read the book, okay—but don't get too enthused. If they were bored and didn't want to read the book, forget it. You also need to be aware that the author's style of writing may not fit in with your style of booktalking. In that case, what you have written and the excerpt you have chosen will clash. If the transition is awkward, the talk would probably be smoother and more flowing if you told the scene entirely in your own words.

Poetry, on the other hand, must be read, unless you can recite it perfectly. But limit yourself to one or two, possibly three, short poems—no more.

I used to read quite a bit, occasionally doing whole scenes several pages long, until I realized that I was enjoying this much more than my audience was. Now, if I read aloud at all I choose a short passage or a few crucial sentences. I use this technique in my talk on *The Minds of Billy Milligan*—I read the list of the different personalities because I want to get the details exactly right, but I describe Billy's situation in my own words. What you're trying to do in booktalking is sell the book; if reading doesn't sell it (and for most people it doesn't), don't do it.

You can add "inside information" to your booktalk if you know something about the author or how the book came to be written. Perhaps you've heard an author speak, or chatted with a writer at an autographing session—that's a source for interesting personal information. Rosemary Wells used her family as models for some of the characters in *None of the Above*—and they found out about it! Richard Peck's inspiration for one scene in *Representing Superdoll* was a real incident that occurred backstage in a TV studio just before he went on the air.

Watch the media for information—according to *People,* June 6, 1977, Hal Krents and his wife divide up the household chores (he takes out the garbage) and he reads Braille picture books to his son, Jamie. These sidelights on the author are now a part of my *To Race the Wind* booktalk. An article on James Herriot in the March 1979 issue of *Good Housekeeping* gives not only his real name but a new view of him as a veterinarian, as distinct from an author. Did you know Stephen King has bats and spiders on the custom-made iron fence and gates that surround his house in Bangor, Maine? (*Fine Homebuilding,* Oct./Nov. 1983.) Or that Billy Milligan is out of the hospital, apparently cured of his multiple personalities? (*20/20,* April 5, 1984.) Check book review magazines and news stories also—you never know where you'll find a fascinating new tidbit! Publishers have biographical pamphlets on many authors, or they may have small newsletters on what authors are doing or have done recently and where they're going to be speaking—*Dell Carousel* is only one of these.

You can also say something personal about yourself to introduce the book: "After I stayed up all night to read *Carrie,* I slept with a light on for weeks"; "I was so interested in finishing this book I snapped at my supervisor when she interrupted my break, and nearly got fired!" This kind of recommendation is an attention-getter, and makes both you and the book seem more "real."

Some booktalkers think being impersonal is best, but I disagree, up to a point. Since booktalking is an individual art, you should always work towards what is right for you and what works for you. If you can handle including personal touches, and the audience responds to them, fine. But if this makes you uncomfortable, don't do it. Both approaches are valid and defensible. If you do decide to include something personal, remember to be matter-of-fact rather than cutesy or coy about it. Your straightforward attitude will make it okay for people to accept and enjoy a reference to your private life. Be aware that your listeners will immediately pick up whatever emotion you project. If you aren't completely at ease with yourself, your audience, and what you're saying, forget it. This is one of the things that's either a huge success or a total flop. Be prepared, and be careful.

As I've said, a booktalk is not an evaluation or a book review. It is not a discussion of the book's literary merit. One of my friends is a former English teacher and constantly has to be reminded that all the reasons he thinks a book is interesting are not necessarily what a teenager wants to hear about. Teenagers appreciate realistic characters, believable settings, good writing, symbolism, and a plot they can identify with too, but they just don't use these terms. All these things don't need to go into a booktalk. The center of a booktalk is *action*—what is happening in the book, who does what, and what happens then. Analyze the symbolism with your colleagues, but don't discuss it in a booktalk.

The title and author of the book should be the first and last things mentioned. Give this information before you start your talk and after you finish—and don't read from the cover of the book. Know the correct title and the author's name.

The two most important sentences in a booktalk are the first and the last. The first sentence should be a "grabber"—something that will catch and hold the interest of your audience. The first sentence determines whether everybody or nobody will keep listening to you. If the word "grabber" is intimidating, let me say it another way. The first sentence should be interesting, catchy, and attention-getting. It should also provide an immediate lead-in to the plot or the dilemma of the central character. If the first sentence isn't too long, it can set the scene, with the second sentence getting into the action. But don't wait longer than the second sentence to get into the meat of the talk, or you'll lose your audience. You can lose them in the first thirty seconds of a talk and never get them back, which makes first sentences very important! Some examples of first sentences that work are: "Horace stared at the ghastly sight in the mirror—his first day at JFK High School, and he had a sty the size of an egg yolk!" (*Ace Hits the Big Time*) "In October, 1977, the Columbus, Ohio police arrested 22-year-old William Stanley Milligan—The Ohio State University 'Campus Rapist.'" (*The Minds of Billy Milligan*) "On my thirteenth birthday, my dog got run over, my father called me a slut once too often, and I lost my virginity—or what was left of it!" (*To Take a Dare*) "In the Methuen Home in Mt. Sterling, Kentucky, Beth Harmon got two tranquilizers a day." (*The Queen's Gambit*)

I also think the first sentence is the hardest one to write. Once I've made a start, the rest of the talk seems to flow more smoothly. If you're stuck on the first sentence, there are several things you can do to help yourself get started. Try writing an annotation. Because it has to accomplish some of the same things, it can give you a place to start. If you've done a short talk or told someone about the book off the top of your head, think about what you said. Or try reading that dust jacket or the back-cover blurb. It's a ready-made come-on, and that's what you're looking for. Maybe you could write a short booktalk—it might be easier than a long one, since you don't have to make so many decisions about what to put in and leave out. You can always start in the middle of the action, and go back to fill in the details in your next few sentences. "They were running—it seemed like they'd been running for years!" is the first sentence of a booktalk on *Firestarter*. Why they're running and who they're running from all come later. The purpose is to grab your audience right away. When you start with description or background, you may lose them. Start in the middle of the action, and then go back to explain how and why when you've got their interest firmly hooked! Details can always wait, but action can't be delayed too long.

The last sentence of a booktalk is also important—it may be all some people remember, so make it a grabber, too. It should imply that something else will be happening but not say what. Leave them hanging in mid-air, or at least aware that they're missing some of the action if they don't read the book. Some good final sentences are: "Patty has her favorite performer, I have told you about mine, but you can pick your own favorite busker from *Passing the Hat*, by Patty Campbell." "Can you sue your parents for malpractice? Read the book and see!" (*Can You Sue Your Parents for Malpractice?*). "That afternoon when Til got home from school, the table was set for dinner—with *butcher knives!*" (*The Girl Who Lived on the Ferris Wheel*). "The wisewoman's prophecy came true, but not till April, 1912, when the two women set sail for New York—on the unsinkable new ship, *The Titanic!*" (*Amanda/Miranda*).

The ending should come at a specific point. Unless you plan an ending, you may ramble on and on, completely losing your audience as you do. A booktalk needs to have a definite structure.

• First sentence(s): a lead-in to the action or an introduction to a character

• Body of talk: action; what happens in the book or in the scene you have chosen; the dilemma of the character

• Last sentence(s): the talk stops without telling everything, letting the audience know that something else will be happening. A booktalk isn't a speech—you can't afford any extra words. It must be concise—at the most, you have only six or seven minutes to make your point. If you don't plan what to say and when to stop, you can easily just go on and on and on, not realizing what you're doing until your audience starts to snore. Avoid such embarrassing moments by knowing when to stop.

When you write your talk down, it should be in a format that is convenient for you to use in a presentation. Opinions on this format vary widely. Booktalkers each have to decide what will work best for them in their own situations. I usually do my rough draft on a yellow legal-size pad but my final copy on a five-by-eight card, which is what I take with me. I write down my rough draft, correct it, and sweat over it; then, when it's as good as it's likely to get, I put it away for several days to see what it sounds like cold. The difference is amazing sometimes, and the strengths and flaws are suddenly very clear. If the draft needs changing, I make the final revisions and then copy the result onto the five-by-eight card. I write down everything I intend to say, word for word. When writing, I try to limit myself to one and a half pages of legal-size lined paper for my rough draft and to both sides of the card for my final copy. That way, I know my talk will be about the right length (three to five minutes), and thus I no longer have to time each talk. Practice reading your talk aloud before you make a final draft. It should be only two to four minutes long in rehearsal, to allow for hesitation and a different pace when you actually give it. Work out how long your written talk should be to equal three to five minutes in the classroom. Once you know that, you shouldn't have to time yourself so carefully. But until you know, *do* time yourself, and every so often go back and check. I wrote a ten-minute talk the other day, and didn't even know it till I started watching the clock! Don't let your talks get too long— shorter is usually better.

Other methods include using three-by-five cards that can be filed in a box or drawer later; using sheets of paper rather than cards; writing down only an outline or key words and phrases to jog your memory;

and writing down the first one or two sentences but using an outline from there on (see the talk on *The Headless Roommate* in the booktalk section). Some people type their notes, some don't. Marianne Pridemore, of the San Jose Public Library, uses a combination of methods. She writes out her whole talk and uses that version to practice with; then she condenses it to an outline written on one or two index cards, which she takes into the class with her.

When I make a presentation, either in a classroom or elsewhere, I always have my notes with me, so I can refer to them right away if I get stuck. That way my lapses of memory aren't quite so obvious. Mary Moore, a YA librarian in Stanislaus County in California, used to write her very brief notes (sometimes only characters' names) on slips of scratch paper or three-by-five cards, which she left in the book she was talking about. Now, however, she also writes her talks down in a more complete format, having discovered it saves time in the long run. Marion Hargrove, from Prince Georges County in Maryland, doesn't take her notes with her at all, just reviews them before she goes out to visit a class. Use the method that works best for you. The purpose of notes is to keep your booktalk flowing as smoothly as possible, even if you suddenly go blank. And that does happen, even to the most experienced booktalker, although if you're good it's usually possible to cover up. Ad-libbing takes a lot of experience, however, and occasionally even experience doesn't help. Several years ago I was visiting a freshman high-interest/low-reading-level class in California with one of the other Alameda County YA people. It was all going along as usual—neither of us was nervous, and we were both experienced with class visits and familiar with the teacher and the school. In spite of this, halfway through one of her favorite booktalks my partner forgot what her next sentence was. She stopped, looked horrified, struggled through one more sentence, then told the class that she had forgotten, and went back and started the whole talk over, using the exact words she had before. She stopped at the same place she had the first time. This time there were more than the few scattered snickers there'd been at first. She gave up and went on to another book, saying, "Well, I just can't tell you about that book, I guess." Needless to say, her impact on that class was somewhat lessened, not only for that booktalk but also for her other ones, which were shaky too.

That's the worst horror story I've ever heard about what happens when your memory evaporates and you don't have any notes. It's always been an inspiration to me to take mine along, even when I'm very familiar with the talk. There are, however, a few ways of coping with a suddenly blank memory. I'll cover some of these in Chapter 6.

Once your talk is down on paper, it needs to be practiced and polished before you present it the first time. (It's not necessary to be able to do it in your sleep, but practicing while in a light doze is a definite advantage!) More polishing will take place after you've done it in front of an audience several times and discovered that it doesn't sound quite right, or that people respond better where you emphasize one thing instead of another. Just because a booktalk is written down doesn't mean it can't be or shouldn't be changed. Most of my older talks have been revised, and what I say now bears little resemblance to what I wrote down initially, several years ago.

There is no substitute for practice, something I rediscover every time I think I can do without it. An audience can be distracted from the talk itself if the speaker is fumbling for words. The audience then get nervous *for* the speaker, hoping he or she won't forget what to say. The audience can relax when they are sure the speaker is in control of what's happening. How you practice really isn't important, although you will need to rehearse aloud, just as if you were actually talking to a group. Some people use a tape recorder or videotape when practicing. Both can be helpful, and a videotape can show you not only how you sound but also how you appear to an audience. The only disadvantage to either of these methods is that you have to be detached enough to learn from them. Hearing and seeing how you actually look and sound can be a rather disturbing experience, which can prevent any real learning. If you are uncomfortable with video equipment or don't have access to it, a full-length mirror can be an adequate substitute, letting you see immediately how you look (including how you stand).

Occasionally I find time to practice booktalks at work. More often I don't, and so have gotten into the habit of practicing at home. It's not the best of all possible arrangements, but it involves me in the fewest hassles. At work I am usually sitting down and don't do much projecting. This doesn't help my newest bad habit, which is to shift my position constantly while delivering a talk. When I teach, I stand up and move around, even pace. Once I realized the habit had carried over from teaching to booktalking, I began to rehearse my entire presentation at home, disciplining myself to stand still. Even with experience, you need to practice to keep your performance up to the mark. It is essential to remain aware of what you are actually doing—not just what you *think* you're doing.

I read my talks aloud over and over again, at least one time in front of someone else, in case there's some glaring error I haven't noticed. For instance, my ability to remember numbers is nil, and if I forget one I tend to plug in another that seems appropriate—only someone else can catch me on that. It's better if it isn't a member of the audience who's already read the book.

While practicing your talk, practice not only the words but also the way you deliver them. Actors rehearse gestures and movements as well as lines. When movements become automatic, it's easier to concentrate on the lines themselves. And booktalkers can definitely borrow from actors. In a booktalk, eye contact is essential, so practice looking around the room as you talk. Making eye contact with chairs, windows, plants, and so on may make you feel a little foolish, but it will help you to remember to look around when you're in front of a class, from habit, if nothing else. (My cats, however, have never learned to respond to the multitude of talks they've heard. They've even refused to learn to read!)

You should also practice speaking in the tone of voice you will use during the actual talk, if you possibly can. This is especially important for people who speak softly and need to remember to practice speaking more loudly and enunciating clearly, making sure to project the voice all the way to the back of the room. Breathing deeply from the diaphragm will help do this. Modulation and tone of voice should be pleasant and easy to listen to—this is also a time to practice that. If you have trouble with any of these things—enunciation, tone, projection, or modulation—practice with a tape recorder is very important, at least until these problems are corrected. Don't change your voice when you do talks, either in practice or performance. Many people tend to talk down to children, teenagers, or the elderly, adopting a "special" voice or one that's higher than normal. This is obviously patronizing, and the audience will be aware of it.

Any time you practice, you should work to make it seem as close to the real thing as possible. Begin to form good habits in your practice sessions, and they will stay with you in front of a group. For instance, I have practiced talks standing up in the center of the room, because at the time my worst fault was the way I stood and what I did with my hands. Working in front of a mirror can also help you eliminate various kinds of awkward postures and poses. If nothing else works, be creative, I make sure that if I'm going to a place where I'll be the least bit ill at ease I wear something with pockets—that way I'll know where to put my hands! I try not to juggle the books around. I hold them up briefly and then set them up on a table, so I won't distract the audience by demonstrating my lack of dexterity. I usually pick up each book and show it to the audience again at the end of the talk as I repeat the author's name and the title. I only pick up a book during a talk if I want to show pictures, which should, of course, always be marked ahead of time to avoid fumbling.

Some librarians practice their talks on tape. They write a talk out, record it, and then file the written version. They listen to the tape over and over again, at any convenient time, until they've learned it. If they decide to change something, they change the written version, but may or may not change the tape. These tapes can be the permanent record of the talks, and can help the librarians first to learn talks, then to review them later, if it's been a while since they were done. These folks may or may not take notes into the class with them, but don't memorize talks and so feel free to change them.

You should practice a talk until you feel comfortable with it and don't really need to check your notes to see what comes next. You may or may not have memorized it. If you haven't, it may not always be the exact same talk every time you give it, but it will seem more spontaneous. And you will have more freedom to tailor your words for the people you're talking to. I also think knowing rather than memorizing a talk makes it harder to forget or go blank. If you've memorized a booktalk and then forget one sentence, you can't go on, since the missing sentence is the key to the next one. If you haven't memorized it, you can simply use different words to express the same idea. In learning a talk, you might try to remember a series of scenes or ideas rather than specific words, visualizing a comic strip or TV show in your mind as you speak. Pictures are harder to forget than words. If you can actually *see* what you're describing as you do it, the picture you create for your audience will be more vivid, and you will help them create their own interior "visual aids."

When you know your booktalk well, set it aside and go on to another one. Which brings me to a point about which I have become adamant and rather cynical. I keep all my booktalks—I still have the very first ones I did, back in 1969. A booktalk represents several hours of hard work and creativity. Replacing or rewriting a talk that I have not given in several months can take just as long or longer than it did to write it the first time. I know because I have had to rewrite several talks I naively loaned to people who never returned them. I am all in favor of sharing booktalks, and often exchange with other people. But now I only share *copies* of my talks. The four hundred or so booktalks I have represent several times that many hours of labor, and while I don't mind if someone else uses my talks word-for-word, I want to retain the ability to give them myself as well, and so the original stays with me.

I also keep my talks in title order*—it makes it much easier to locate a specific one quickly. This sort of filing may not be necessary at first, but as your write more and more talks, you may find that locating something filed in random order can be very time-consuming. Arrange your talks in the way you find easiest to deal with—maybe even by your own system of subject headings.

The Short Booktalk

A short booktalk can be used in several ways: in on-the-floor reader's advisory work with one or more people; for a change of pace from long booktalks during a presentation before a group; in radio or TV spots to promote YA services or the library; or as a basis for a longer booktalk.

The method for writing a short booktalk is basically the same as for a long one; the difference is simply that the short talk doesn't include as much. A short booktalk is close to a long annotation, or a dust-jacket blurb. For example:

> *To Race the Wind,* by Hal Krents, is his autobiography and tells how he refused to let blindness stop him from doing anything—including learning how to drive a car when he was a senior in high school and playing touch football with his friends when he was in college.

> In *Slake's Limbo,* by Felice Holman, Aremis Slake gets tired of being beaten up by all the gangs in New York City and so escapes by going to live in the subway tunnels for 121 days.

> When Gail wakes up in the hospital examination room with her parents and doctors hovering over her, she knows what's happened. She also knows no one will believe her when she tells them she's been raped by the son of one of the town's most influential families. *Are You in the House Alone?* by Richard Peck.

---

*That's still true for my talks on cards, but since most of the booktalking I do now is part of teaching workshops, I no longer have new talks on cards. I have them only on lined yellow-pad sheets, messily scribbled, or on printouts from my word processor, and they are crammed into a folder in haphazard order. Needless to say, this "filing system" is much less efficient and much more time-consuming than the old title-order arrangement. Were I to go back to doing the number of booktalks I used to do, I would have to change—I may have to anyway! That fat file folder is getting fatter and messier by the week!

Although short talks can be written and planned, they are more often brief, spontaneous retellings of what was to you the most important part of the book. This is especially true for books you've already done long talks about. Include a good first sentence and something about what happens—that's all. This isn't always as easy as it sounds, since the tendency is to go on and on, making a short talk into a long one. Pick out the crux of the plot—what scene or character does the story move around? (*Not* the scene that gives away the ending, though!) Tell about that scene in just a few sentences, as in the examples given. Your remarks ought to be short, snappy, and most of all intriguing. You have only those few sentences to hook your audience—they have to really count!

Giving short booktalks isn't difficult for some people, but others may find that they need preparation until they get the hang of it. It becomes easier with practice. A question Mary Moore and I answered over and over again during our visits to the Juvenile Hall was, "What's this about?" Not many kids wanted to listen to more than about 30-45 seconds' worth, so we became, of necessity, adept at the short booktalk. The talent has stood me in good stead ever since. Doing bibliotherapy with emotionally disturbed adolescents, I found they would seldom listen to more than about a minute on a book. By that time, they'd decided either to read it (and didn't want to know more) or not to (and wanted me to go on to something else).

The "Memorized" Booktalk

As I have pointed out before, some librarians present word-for-word excerpts from books as booktalks, using the author's words rather than their own. (I call these talks memorized, but have been cautioned by Linda Lapides that the Enoch Pratt Free Library, which sponsors talks of this sort, does not use this term—hence the quotation marks.)

When I was introduced to booktalking in 1969 during my internship at Dallas Public Library, Judy Kuykendall, the YA coordinator, and her staff regularly did this kind of talk. I trained in the style I now use—the learned booktalk—with Genevieve Dixon in my YA literature class that same year, and later refined the technique with Hazel Furman, who taught YA services when I was working on my MLS. So far as I have been able to determine, the learned talk is the dominant style among booktalkers today, mainly because of the advantage it offers in flexibility. A learned booktalk is not, however, necessarily more effective than a well-done "memorized" talk and you may want to experiment with both styles.

The "memorized" booktalk is used extensively both in the Enoch Pratt Free Library and in Prince Georges County Memorial Library system. Several talks prepared by librarians in these two locations are included in the booktalk section, to give you an idea of what kind of excerpt to choose. Ideally, the selection should do all the things that a talk you'd created yourself would do. It should have lots of action and excitement or humor. It should give an idea of what's going on in the story and be complete in itself.

Prince Georges County Memorial Library's Young Adult Services has drawn up a list of hints about how to fix an excerpt in your mind.

1. Type out the section or chapter.

2. Concentrate—remove all other thoughts from your mind.

3. Set a deadline of fifteen to thirty minutes for memorizing each day.

4. Read the whole talk over several times—at least once out loud—to get the smooth flow of events in your mind.

5. Concentrate on the names of characters and places.

6. Outline events in progression.

7. Concentrate on the key words of paragraphs.

8. Work on sections, several paragraphs at a time, each time adding another section.

9. Try putting the whole talk together from memory, noting "blank" spots—then work on those.

10. Use a tape recorder to play back your delivery and use your aural memory—listen—hear the words in your mind.

11. Don't worry about forgetting a word or words—you should be memorizing the progression primarily. Know the talk well enough so a temporary loss of memory doesn't throw you.

12. *Allow enough time for the talk to sink in*!

These hints may also be helpful if you want to incorporate a short poem or a quotation from the text into a booktalk that you have written yourself. If you're taking a passage directly from the book, you'll want to be word-perfect, which means either reading aloud or speaking from memory.

CHAPTER 3

PLANNING A BOOKTALK PRESENTATION

A Time for Every Talk . . .

Once you have decided to visit a school class or a community group, you need to find out certain things about it, so you can choose books that will be interesting to the audience and avoid starting off on the wrong foot.

1. Subject of the class, or nature of the group. If it's a class, what is it called? (English? History II? General Science?) What is the teacher teaching? (the short story? the Civil War? astronomy?) If it's a community group, what is the basis of the association? Do the members share a common interest in a particular subject (the environment, historic preservation, gardening) or a common life situation (senior citizens)? What books have been read in class or discussed in the group recently?—you will want to avoid these. The subject orientation will affect the scheduling as well as the content of your program, since you may need more preparation time for some subjects.

2. Purpose of visit. What does the teacher or the leader of the group expect of you? Why have you been asked to come—to give recreational reading ideas or book report suggestions, provide background information for an assignment, or explain what is available on a particular topic? You should let the person in charge know what you can and cannot do, and what your standard presentation includes, if this is not clear already. You may also want to tailor your appearance to the teacher's or leader's expectations. If you look too much like a teenager yourself, you may have trouble getting support or cooperation from some teachers. With an adult group, too, it's wise to find out in advance how much informality is appropriate, both in your appearance and in your style of presentation.

3. Composition of audience. What is the age level, the reading level, the ratio of boys to girls, or men to women? Does the audience have a long or short attention span? How large will this audience be? What are some books they have recently read and enjoyed? Do they have any

28

special interests or preferences—sports? mysteries? biographies? These are things you will need to know when selecting books to talk about. If it's a men's group, or a class with more boys than girls, you will need more male-oriented books. If the attention span is short, as it sometimes is with low-reading-level classes, longer booktalks won't work as well as a series of short, snappy ones. With school classes especially, both age and reading levels are important, since you want to select something the students will be interested in *and* able to read.

4. Length of session. How much time will you have to talk? If it's a class, do you want to talk for the whole period or only for part of it? What would the teacher prefer? If it's a community group, how long do their meetings usually run? How much of that time will be allocated to you? Will there be a social hour afterwards, during which you can answer questions?

5. Location. Be sure to get the exact address, including the room number if there is one. It's very embarrassing to be late because you got lost or because you had to go by a main office first to find out where you were supposed to be.

6. Exact time the session starts and ends. Easy, with an adult group, but teachers and school librarians run on a totally different schedule from the rest of the world. They go by periods—first, second, fifth, and so on—not by hours. And knowing you have to talk to a third-period class does not tell you when to be there! Be sure to find out if third period starts at 9:15 or 10:27—there's usually no rhyme or reason to it, and every school is unique. You also need to know exactly when the class is over so you can wind up your presentation before the bell rings, and not get caught in midsentence as your audience rushes past you to the door.

A booktalking visit can have a variety of purposes, which will determine the content of your presentation. Are you advertising the library or just promoting books? If part of your purpose is doing PR for the library, you will want your introduction to include information on what materials are available there (magazines, records, films), the rules and regulations for using them, the library's hours, its location, and so on. Including some actual reference questions that were particularly funny or unusual can make the point that the library is a place for finding all kinds of information. This introduction can be very brief or as long as ten minutes. If you have mentioned various materials, you may also want to include samples of them either as part of your introduction or after your booktalks, in a wrap-up. For me, the latter way works best. After my last booktalk to a school class, I show a variety of magazines students can check out, adding the names of others I don't have with me as I go. The same technique can be used with an adult group—many people can't afford to subscribe to all the magazines they'd like to read. With hi/lo school classes, I also talk about "adult picture books"—big books on a variety of subjects, that contain more pictures than text. Some of these books might appeal to senior citizens as well, along with large-print materials that are easy to see.

If you do not want to include any general library information, your introduction can be very brief. You should include your name, your title, where you work (which branch), and where the books you're going to talk about can be found—the location of any special areas (young adult or browsing collections) in your branch and in any other nearby libraries. Then just go right into your first booktalk. My introduction, whether I am pushing the library or just books, is usually only about five minutes long, since I have noticed that people are less interested in hearing about the library than in the books I've brought.

Choose books for each class or group with its composition in mind. Vary long and short booktalks; otherwise, you may create a static and measured effect, when a more interesting pace is what you want. Keep in mind the amount of time you will have and be sure to plan to include enough books to fill it up. Underestimating can create problems, such as being left with twenty minutes at the end of a class and nothing to say. Depending on the length of the class period and the other things I want to present (a long introduction about the library or samples of various things available there other than books), I can do from six to fourteen talks of varying lengths per class. I usually have one or two books left over if I do fewer talks. Some people deliberately take more books than they could possibly use so that they can choose titles according to the audience's response. To do this, you have to find the right balance—not carrying too many books but still giving yourself maximum flexibility as a performer.

Keep a list of the titles you plan to talk about for each visit. I make a separate Information Card for each group or class I'm invited to. For classes I list the school, teacher, subject, grade level, time, room number, date, and any other miscellaneous information I might want, and the books I plan to talk about (see Figure 1). For other groups I list the name of the group; the location, time, and date of the meeting; leader's name and phone number; length of presentation; book titles; and so on. I keep these cards clipped together in date order in the drawer with all my other booktalk materials, where I can find them at short notice. I try to keep three weeks or so ahead of myself when I fill out the cards, so I don't have too many last-minute decisions to make. After the visit is over, the cards provide a record of what I talked about, in case I want to do the same or different books the next time I visit that class or that group. The cards are also handy if you have a subject that is difficult to locate books on, and you have to do that particular subject every year. The cards give you something to build on, so that you only have to start from scratch once.

SCHOOL   TEACHER   CLASS   ROOM   TIME   DATE
Basic information necessary for choosing books— reading level, make-up of class, etc.
Booktalks presented—use abbreviated titles
CLASS VISIT INFORMATION CARD

Figure 1

I also list the sequence in which I plan to talk about the books, although many booktalkers do not bother to do this. But a pre-established sequence can be very helpful to the beginning booktalker, or to anyone who needs the security of a set program (as I do sometimes). It can also result in a more flowing presentation, with fewer pauses or hesitations between booktalks and smoother transitional sentences connecting them.

Some people find this method too rigid, because it does not allow for last-minute changes or the idiosyncrasies of a particular situation. Beginners, however, may find it easier to start with more structure and move away from it when they have more experience. Structuring is one way to minimize last-minute panic, hassles, and mistakes. Knowing exactly what is coming next can also combat stage fright, allowing you to grit your teeth and carry on without having to make any decisions of the what-now variety. Such structure can be useful as a crutch, to be discarded if it doesn't help or when it's no longer necessary. (I still use it almost all the time!)

Whether or not you decide on an exact order for all the books you use, it is a good idea to plan at least the first one or two and the last one you will talk about. These talks are just as important as the corresponding sentences in an individual booktalk. If you are a beginner or if you tend towards stage fright, as I do, start off with a book you particularly enjoy doing to help you relax. This first talk is the one you will be judged on. During it, your audience will decide whether you are worth listening to. The talk should be exciting; it should also be one you are able to do well in spite of encroaching stage fright, to which even experts are not immune. Perhaps you can find several books you can use as your standard openers, as I have. I have used *The Shining, I Know What You Did Last Summer, Center Line, Quartzsite Trip, Ace Hits the Big Time,* and *To Take a Dare* as some of my openers with young adults. (*Q.T.* is my favorite, though.)

I also make sure that my second book is a "grabber," just like the first one, to make absolutely certain I have everyone listening. However, if the students are mostly girls, my second book will probably be more female-oriented, though still something boys might read. Two of Richard Peck's novels fit in well here—*Through a Brief Darkness* and *Are You in the House Alone?*

The last book you talk about needs to be one that will end the presentation on an upbeat. Whether the book is funny or suspenseful, it should definitely leave your audience wanting more. It's the last thing you're going to say to them. It should leave a definite impression, preferably positive. *The Headless Roommate, The Minds of Billy Milligan, Killing Mr. Griffin,* and *Firestarter* are all good candidates.

If you are talking to a mixed audience, try to alternate male-oriented and female-oriented books in your presentation. Usually teenage boys are the hardest to hook and the easiest to lose. The quickest way to make them lose interest is to talk about several books in a row they wouldn't be caught dead reading—love stories, for example. Put *See You Thursday, To Take a Dare,* and *Annie on My Mind* together and nine times out of ten you'll lose the male part of your audience. All this sounds sexist, I know, but I have also found it to be true. And as we know, teenage boys often *are* sexists. Not that we should cater to their attitudes (in fact, we have a real responsibility to counter them in the books we talk about); but it doesn't matter what you say if your audience isn't listening.

The 1979 BAYA (Bay Area Young Adult Librarians) Hip Pocket Reading Survey (*Top of the News,* Summer 1979) showed that a number of teenagers are interested in classic authors, such as the Brontës, Dickens, and Steinbeck, and in "semi-classics" such as Agatha Christie. The 1982 version of the same survey (*School Library Journal,* December, 1982) included *Of Mice and Men* and *To Kill A Mockingbird,* as well as some perennial mystery favorites. You might try including one or two of these, especially if you are working in an English class with a conservative teacher. While I don't talk about the classics because I dislike reading them so much, I was delighted to see a recent article by Hazel Rochman called "Booktalking the Classics" in *School Library Journal,* February, 1984. I recommend it to you.

You can also use films as a part of your presentation to a class. Many YA librarians do so with great success. The best time to show a film is after your booktalks, since it is very much a "dessert" and the kids may not be interested in listening to you after they've seen the film. This may not be everyone's experience, however, so show the film at the point it works best for you.

Lists of short films for use in school classes are published by NICEM (National Information Center for Educational Media) and by *School Library Journal,* among others. One of the all-time favorite shorts is probably *Bad Bad Leroy Brown.* When we showed it to a freshman English class in an open classroom school, we attracted not only that class but kids from all the classes around. They crowded in six deep and had a marvelous time. Their teachers were somewhat less appreciative, and requested that we please *not* bring that film again. Oh well, I guess you just can't please everyone! The best films to use are short (no more than ten minutes), fast-moving, and fun—pure entertainment. Animated cartoons work well for lower grades, and *Frank Film* has been used very successfully with juniors and seniors. Two spoofs—*Blaze Glory* and *That Rotten Teabag*—and two sports films—*Turned On* and *The Olympia Diving Sequence*—were very popular in Alameda County. But any good film will remind the kids that the library can be fun. A list of short films you might want to use is included in the back of this book.

Before scheduling a film, be sure to get the teacher's approval. Also ask if you can use a school projector, since you already have to lug around a film, a stack of books, and other stuff. Allow enough time before your presentation to set up the equipment and rewind the film, so all you have to do later is turn on the projector. It should be all ready to go when you start your presentation.

Of course, there may be technical problems. The film may break, the projector may not work—be prepared for the worst. If anything does go wrong, try to keep your sense of humor. Don't panic—it happens to everyone. If you can't remedy the situation, forget it. Teachers show enough films these days for kids to know that occasional mishaps are inevitable. But they usually yield to the inevitable somewhat less than quietly—be ready for that, too.

You might also consider using a videotape instead of a film—they're easier to carry, for one thing. And I'd like to think that less goes wrong with them, but I am not at all sure that's accurate!

Some YA librarians do a slide show as part of their presentation, showing the library, the YA area, and various programs and activities. Although I have never tried this, I'm sure a snappy, fast-moving presentation of this sort could be very effective. Here again, you might try a videotape rather than a slide/tape. The latter is easier, but I think the former is more interesting.

Another AV aid you can use with young adults is rock music. Tape selections from the library's popular records and play them before and after your presentation, or as background for a slide show. You could either tape a few complete songs or excerpts from a variety of songs, performed by different groups. This can be a very effective way of letting the kids know something different and *fun* is happening.

You can also take a box of paperbacks into the class with you and let kids check them out right there. These can be either copies of the books you've talked about, or other titles, or both. The major disadvantages to doing this are the poor return rate and the amount of time even the most minimal processing takes. I feel, however, that with a sufficient supply of paperbacks, the advantages far outweigh the disadvantages. It is fun, and the kids love it. It is the ultimate way of striking when the iron's hot, especially with hi/lo classes. If those students don't get the book they want to read *now*, they may lose interest and never read it at all. (This is, of course, a risk with any group, but especially with hi/los.) At Alameda County, we didn't require a library card. We just stamped the books with a date due and kept a record of how many went out, to add to the branch circulation. We also found that it was a good idea, when talking to several classes in a row, to hold back copies of some of the most popular titles so that last class would have just as good a selection as the first one.

If you have to cancel a visit, do so as far ahead of time as you can. If something serious comes up at the last minute, it is especially important to let the teacher or the group leader know you won't be there. So if you wake up with laryngitis on the day you have three class visits scheduled, starting at 8:00 a.m., don't just call the school and hope someone in the office will tell the teacher what's happened. Call the school librarian as well, and ask him or her to go over and tell the teacher personally or have one of the library aides do it. The librarian should always know about canceled visits, anyway, and may be able to provide valuable help in a last-minute emergency. Or one of your colleagues may be able to pinch-hit for you. Booktalking is supposed to create good will for the library. Not showing up for a visit without letting anyone know you won't be there is bad public relations (and bad manners, too). If you tend to oversleep, try using two alarm clocks or get someone to give you a wake-up call.

The library staff needs to be prepared for the results of a successful booktalking program. School visiting will bring in kids, kids, and more kids, all wanting the same books, most of which they can't identify by either title or author, only by bits and pieces of the plot and the fact that "somebody came to my class and talked about it." And a successful presentation to an adult group may result in a run on certain titles or a flurry of requests in one subject area. Children's and reference staff members can get very annoyed, to say the least, if they are caught unprepared for the onslaught.

A list of the books you talk about should be on hand at both the adult and children's reference desks, even if you are addressing only school classes. If you are not doing too many visits, it could be organized by teacher and school, or by name of group. If possible, this list should be annotated, at least briefly, since titles and authors may mean little or nothing to the people who come in. Don't forget to make sure all branches near the places where you talk have lists, as well as the main branch.

Have as many copies of the books you talk about ready in the library as possible. Borrow from other branches ahead of time if you can't buy enough copies, especially of hardback books. If you have space to do it, you can set aside several shelves in your office or work area for multiple copies of the books you talk about. That way the library staff has to look in only one place for extra copies.

You can also make a separate display for "Books Everybody's Talking About" and use it only for booktalked books. Again, it means the staff has only one place to look. At Fremont Main, I had all the books I talked about stamped "Booktalk Display," and the pages automatically shelved them in that area. It saved a lot of wear and tear on everyone concerned, and, once it was set up, was easy to maintain.

Since you will be taking copies of the books with you when you go booktalking, you need to pull them ahead of time and keep them by your desk or in your office. You should start doing this toward the end of the summer, if you plan to begin giving school talks in September or October. The copies you pull should be nice looking, with dust jackets if they are hardbacks. But use as many paperbacks as possible. Many readers (and most kids) prefer them, they're easier to carry, and you're more likely to have multiple copies in the library, so the one you pull won't be missed. You should keep these sample books during the whole time you're doing booktalks, so that you know they'll always be available when you need them. Make sure other staff members understand that these copies are not to be moved for any reason. At 8:15 in the morning, when you're running late for a 9:00 class, suddenly noticing that three of your booktalk books are unaccountably missing can wreak havoc with your carefully planned presentation and with staff relations as well, not to mention what might have been a beautiful day! If you explain to staff members precisely why you must have these books available at all times, and add a "Please Do Not Touch, Ever!" sign to your shelves, hopefully you will have no problem.

If you are handing out booklists to the classes or groups you visit, you should probably have a copy of each book on the list in your desk collection. You will be booktalking some or most of these, and the rest are your potential talks. If you want to or have to change the program at the last minute, these copies will be useful.

CHAPTER 4

GIVING A BOOKTALK PRESENTATION

How to Hold an Uncaged, Untamed
Audience in the Palm of Your Hand

Preparation is the key to a successful presentation, whether you're an expert or a novice. Plan what you're going to do, including the presentation of your talks, how you will display the books, where you will stand, and what you will do with your hands. Work out what you're going to say in your introduction, writing it down if that is easist; if not, just making notes to remind yourself what comes next. Practice until you are completely at ease with what you'll be saying.

Make doubly sure you have copies of all the books you will be talking about, especially if they are books you haven't used before. Kids are going to be more interested in a book that they can actually see. Also, you may discover that it's easier to talk about a book if you have it with you. Sometimes I only half remember what I want to say until I pick up the book itself. If I have to talk about something I don't have on hand, I flounder, forget what to say, and generally do a rotten job. (It's either magic or osmosis!)

I carry all my paraphernalia for visiting in a large, sturdy canvas bag, which provides, I feel, the easiest and least awkward means of transporting all this gear and eliminates juggling several different packages. The book bag is used only for booktalking visits and usually stays at work, so I know where it is. Make sure that any sack you use is sturdy enough to carry the weight of everything you will be putting into it, and large enough so that you *can* put everything into it. It should also be shaped so that it's easy to carry when full.

When I was at Alameda County, some of us on the Fremont YA staff worked up a class visit evaluation form that's been used there ever since. (See Figure 2.) Mary and I also used it in Stanislaus County and Christy Tyson has used it in Spokane. It offers a chance to get feedback, encouragement, and (occasionally) helpful pointers about how to

TEACHER'S CLASS VISIT EVALUATION FORM

Teacher _____ Librarian(s) _____

Class and Grade _____

School _____ Date _____

Please be honest—our feelings won't be hurt—and we really need to know how to improve.

1. How would you rate the visit?

EXCELLENT   SATISFACTORY
UNSATISFACTORY   HORRIBLE

2. In what ways was it satisfactory or unsatisfactory?

	GREAT	OKAY	AWFUL	OTHER
General Presentation	___	___	___	___
Length of Booktalks	___	___	___	___
Interest Level	___	___	___	___
Number of Talks	___	___	___	___
Appropriateness of Titles	___	___	___	___
Reading Level	___	___	___	___
Other (specify)	___	___	___	___

Comments on any of the above:

3. What things did you particularly like about the visit?

4. How could the visit be improved?

5. Would you be interested in further visits?

6. Would you recommend to other teachers that we visit their classes?

7. What opinions/reactions did your class have after we left?

8. Other comments/questions.

Figure 2

improve your performance. It's relatively simple, and I always tell the teachers they can spend as much or as little time on it as they wish. Replies vary widely, from the casual to the meticulously detailed. (And do be prepared for criticism. You asked for honesty, remember! Nine times out of ten, all you get is positive feedback, but do watch out for that tenth reply! Not all teachers are careful to be tactful.)

The day before a visit, I load books, booklists, a film if I'm using one, visit information cards (Figure 1), teachers' evaluation forms (Figure 2), request cards, booktalks, and appointment calendar into the book bag. If I'm going to an early class or meeting, the bag probably goes home with me, so I don't have to stop by the library and pick it up the next morning, when I could have slept fifteen minutes longer. If it's a later appointment, I'll take home the talks I need to practice and leave everything else at work, ready to go.

I have reasons for taking everything with me in spite of the fact that I occasionally have rather a heavy load. Books and booktalks, films, information cards, and evaluation forms are obvious items to take. Booklists are nice to hand out to the audience, to suggest other things they might like to read. These lists should be bright, eye-catching, and annotated. Almost any format will do. Some booktalkers want to squeeze more titles onto these lists and skip the annotations, but most audiences seem to prefer annotations because they give an idea of what the book is about. More information on booklists is included in Chapter 9.

Bringing enough copies of the books you have mentioned to fill requests on the spot is a nice touch that many people will appreciate. Or you can take requests and fill them later. Allow about ten minutes or so for checking out books, or for passing out the request cards and getting them back. Usually all that people really need to put down on a card is the title of the book they want and their name, address, and phone number. Process the request cards when you get back to the library and call as soon as the books are available. My record number of requests was fifty-seven from three classes, but response can vary widely from class to class, or meeting to meeting.

These procedures *are* time-consuming. Finding all the books and calling each person can take hours, and many of the books may never be picked up. You may have to go through the request shelves a week later and retrieve all the orphans to fill other requests. However, when your audience does respond, the request cards can work very well, and the ones who get the books will appreciate the special attention. But every person has to decide individually whether the response is worth the work involved.

Be sure you always take your appointment calendar along in your book bag. Teachers, especially, often want to know when their next visit will be, if they can schedule another one, or if they can change to another day. Other teachers may drop by the classroom, the staff lounge, or the library to schedule new appointments. The one day you forget your calendar is the day when all of the above will happen, I guarantee!

When you are deciding what to wear for a booktalking visit, remember that you're going to have a whole roomful of people—usually kids—staring at you. Wear something comfortable that will stay in place without adjustment and allow you to move naturally—something you can forget about once you've put it on. Your individual style will determine exactly how you dress, but no matter how you look, you should give your audience something nice to look at. Be attractive. That can mean wearing your newest outfit or the old standby that always makes you feel good. I usually dress up a little and make an effort to wear something at least close to the latest style (as interpreted by adults, not teenagers). There's no use in trying to look like something you aren't, but I still try to do my part to change the old, staid Marian-librarian image. However, if the latest thing isn't *your* thing, then wear whatever is right for you. Some people prefer to be as unobtrusive as possible, in order not to distract from the books. Others dress to be noticed. Take your choice—neither is wrong.

"Classic" styles that don't go out of date can be a sensible choice. They save you money and keep you from being labeled "unprofessional" by audiences, teachers, or community leaders. Since that label can be damaging in some situations and can even jeopardize your standing in the community or school system, you should consider your appearance from this angle. There is a fine line between looking approachable—which can be difficult when looking "professional"—and looking too casual or downright sloppy. The location of this line is often dictated by the locale. What is acceptable in California may be completely inappropriate in another place, such as Kansas. Try talking with other people in your area who work with children, teenagers, or community groups to discover what look will allow you to be considered both approachable by your audience and professional by the powers-that-be. When in doubt, however, it is probably wise to err on the side of formality. A warm, friendly and open body language can do much to make a conservative outfit less intimidating; it's harder to compensate for clothes that turn out to be too casual.

There are also more immediate practical considerations: Pockets can be useful if you have trouble deciding what to do with your hands. (For me they are *absolutely* essential! I have discovered that I also require pockets to be able to teach, since I tend to wave my arms around when I'm in front of a group, no matter why I'm there. In fact, I buy almost nothing without pockets—salespersons just don't understand why I'm so picky!) And no matter what else you wear, be sure to choose comfortable shoes. Four-inch heels or the new boots that you like so much may look super, but don't wear them unless you can stand up in them for four hours at a stretch without turning your ankle or getting grumpy! It's difficult to think about anything else when your feet hurt, so make sure they don't.

Your hairstyle should be as attractive and comfortable as your clothes, and not one that has to be fussed with frequently. I generally try for something that I can check on briefly before or after the presentation class and then forget, knowing I look as good as I can for now. You may want to consider a style that doesn't wilt from stress or heat. If you do several presentations in a row, you may have little time for repairs in between. A style that doesn't hide your face is probably also a good idea, since you want your audience to be able to see your face and expression. In summary, dress to feel comfortable and look attractive. Be aware enough of how you look that you can forget about it, and go on to more important things.

Obviously, I have written this from a woman's point of view, but the principles hold true for men, too. A three-piece pinstripe suit may be appropriate for a meeting with the library board but may not be right for a classroom of high school students. They may respond more readily to someone in less formal clothes, say, a sports coat and casual slacks, with or without a tie. Being considered approachable by your audience is the most important thing, whether you're male or female. That often means a fairly casual, up-to-date appearance that also manages to look professional and adult. Decide for yourself what is right in your location and in your life. Years ago my mother told me that the reason she had such a large wardrobe when she was a high school English teacher was that the students in her classes had to look at her all day, and she felt obligated to make sure that they had something nice to look at. As a booktalker and a teacher, I feel the same way.

Get to the school or meeting place ten or fifteen minutes early so you have a chance to find the room. If you're at a school, go by the library and say hello to the librarian. You may also be expected to stop at the office so the school administration will know you're on campus. Don't interrupt a class if you arrive before the bell rings. Wait in the library or in the hall near the room. When the period is over, gather your things and go in. (Here are two more reasons to look professional—you may have to meet or may run into school administrators, and you don't want to be mistaken for a student when waiting in the hall.)

When you enter the room, introduce yourself to the teacher or group leader. Make sure part of a desk or table can be cleared off so you have a place to display your books as you talk about them. In school classes, ask the teacher not to leave the room, and explain that you can't be both a disciplinarian and an entertainer. There is usually no problem about this; most teachers assume they'll stay in the room. However, it's a good idea to mention it when you're visiting a teacher for the first time or if a class looks as though it might be particularly loud and difficult to handle. You might also ask the teacher to introduce you, so that there will be a definite beginning to your presentation. This is more effective than the teacher just taking roll and wandering off to the back of the room, leaving you to get the kids quiet and introduce yourself. An introduction can be very simple: "This is _____ from the library who's going to talk about some books you might like to read." Carol Starr tells a funny story about a teacher who introduced her the first time she went to his class with a five-minute speech on the theme, "I've given up my valuable class time for this speaker, so you better be quiet or else!" The next period she also spoke to one of his classes, and he introduced her as follows: "This is Carol Starr, and she's going to tell you about some really neat books." A one hundred percent improvement!

Set your things up in the order you are going to need them. Give the teacher or group leader an evaluation form, if you intend to use one, before your presentation starts. If you plan to talk about the books in a certain order, stack them up in that order. Stack your notes or booktalks the same way. They should be placed where you can unobtrusively glance down at them if you need to do so. If you can't see well enough to read your talks when they're lying on a table, you have several options. The talks themselves can be written large or typed on a large-print typewriter. If you do this you may have to use larger sheets of paper or bigger cards to get the whole talk on one of them, or else use more than one sheet or card per talk (make sure the order is correct, and that all cards are typed to be turned over the same way). In a classroom or meeting room, there may be a table lectern available; put the talks on it and stand to one side of it so you can see the talks by glancing sideways. Don't stand behind the lectern if there is any way to avoid it—it looks to formal and forbidding, especially to kids.

Decide where you're going to stand—beside or behind the table where your books are is best if you are likely to have to refer to your notes at all. If you don't have notes or aren't using them frequently, you can stand in front of the table or desk and lean or even sit on it. Make sure the way you move or stand will not look awkward—practicing or just taking time to think about it will help here. Women need to be aware of how they sit when they wear skirts. "Keep your knees together" may sound like something your mother used to say, but not doing so can be distracting and embarrassing for you and your audience.

Just as the best clothes to wear when booktalking are those that make you feel comfortable and at ease, the best way to act in front of an audience will depend partly on your own personality. Move and stand in a way that feels natural, comfortable, and right for you. Leaning against a classroom blackboard, a wall, or the side or front of the desk where your books are, or standing away from the desk in the open are all equally good. Sitting on the desk, either on the edge or completely on it, may be more difficult to carry off, but if such a position is one you like, as I do, try it. (However, be aware that the informality such a posture suggests may make some adults and even an occasional student uncomfortable.) Standing away from walls and desks makes it easier to use body language as a deliberate part of your talk, but also makes your unconscious body language more obvious. Standing with your hands on your hips or arms folded can convey the idea of "parent" or "lecture" without your intending it. If you are ill at ease with your hands at your sides, link them loosely in front or in back of you; put one hand at your side, the other in back of you; or put one or both of them in your pockets. You can use gestures during your talks, but be very sparing. A speaker with windmilling arms can be easy to mock, amusing and distracting. Remember to look pleasant as you talk, and smile when you can. Your facial expression, as well as your body language, can turn people on or off.

The last thing to do before you start talking is relax. Remind yourself that you are going to be fine, and that even mistakes can be dealt with and are *not* major crises. Remember you are promoting books for recreation, even if the reason you're there is to help a class find something for a required book report. *You* have to enjoy yourself if you want your audience to have a good time too. Take a minute to be aware of that. The people you're in front of want to enjoy the program, and no matter how monstrous they may look right now, they're just folks. Most of them are probably pretty nice. Wait until everyone is quiet and the attention is on you, take a deep breath, *smile,* and begin.

As you begin to talk about each book, pick it up and show it to the group, giving its author and title as you do so. Then stand it up facing the audience, so they can see the cover. Sometimes a teacher will insist that the class write down all the authors and titles you mention, and you will have to repeat or spell them, but try not to delay your talks any longer then necessary. Point out that the students can get the information off the book jackets when the presentation is over or from the lists you will distribute, if you use booklists. Or just go on holding up the book as you start your talk, so everyone can copy from the cover. (If you choose to do this, be sure to hold the book steady.) As you set down one book after another, make an effort to display them in an attractive arrangement, with as many titles visible as possible. If some books have to be hidden, they should be the ones you talked about first. The cover of the book you are currently talking about should always be visible. Sooner or later, some of the books you have arranged may fall down, sometimes knocking over several more in the process. If you can reposition them unobtrusively, then do so. If there are more than two or three to deal with, then just make sure the book you're talking about is visible and set the others aside in a pile on the desk. You can set them out in the display when the presentation is over and there is time for your audience to come up and look at the books. In general, don't let the accident interrupt the flow of your talks any more than absolutely necessary.

Some booktalkers choose to show only one book at a time, setting up or displaying only the title they are talking about. Other titles are stacked or laid flat on the desk or table, if there is room, so the covers are showing when people come up to look at them when the presentation is over. Both methods seem to work equally well—it simply depends on which you prefer to use. If you don't have much display space, however, you might want to use the latter method, since that can be done more gracefully with a limited amount of desktop space.

If there is a picture you want to show the whole group, walk in front of them, holding the book just above their eye level. Be sure to hold the book straight up and down, not with the top tilted back toward you. Give the group as long and clear a look as possible without losing the sense of your talk. It isn't necessary to talk the whole time you're showing pictures, but don't let the silence build up for more than thirty seconds or so. If someone says, "Hey, wait, I didn't see it!" remind them that they'll have another chance to look at the books and pictures after you finish talking.

When you finish your last booktalk, invite the group to come up and see the books and ask any questions they may have. If you are taking requests, explain as briefly as possible how to fill out the cards and be ready to hand them out. Talk to those who come up about the books, and be ready to suggest other titles to people who have already read the books you talked about. Responses to your invitation to come up and look at the books can vary widely, to say the least. Younger kids will have a more enthusiastic response than older ones. A group of children or junior high school kids may even elbow you to one side in their eagerness to get at the books. Many times, in a junior high class, every single student has come up to examine the books and talk to me. (And examine is the accurate word. There was one small nude photo in *The Rock Almanac*—I didn't have any idea it was there until it was found by a rather gleeful eighth-grader. Someone found it and made a big deal about it in almost every junior high class I went to—I finally gave up and took *The Rock Almanac* only to high schools. That age group is too cool to make a fuss over something like that.) On a junior high level, it doesn't seem to matter much whether the kids are good readers or not, either. They *all* want to see what's going on. High school classes are much more blasé. You hardly ever get a stampede, even out of sophomores. Maybe one or two kids will oh-so-casually drift up to look at the books and pick up a booklist. When you're doing a lot of book-talking, it can be a real shock to switch from one age group to another, if you aren't aware of the different styles of response. The adult groups I have had experience with have not been particularly eager to look at the books, and have also responded less obviously with facial expressions and body language than either adolescents or children. Be prepared—an underwhelming response may *not* mean that you just bombed or insulted someone unawares. If you have booklists, leaving them on the table where the books were displayed for listeners to pick up afterwards seems to work better than passing them out. Fewer will be made into paper airplanes or just thrown out, depending on the age of your audience.

Don't judge your presentation by the number of people who come up to talk to you afterwards. There are many factors besides the presentation itself that may influence them. If a teacher is a strict disciplinarian, students may not be inclined to move without permission. Or they may be waiting for someone else to go first—no one wants to appear too eager. (This seems to be true of adults as well as young people—I once had an audience of high school teachers who behaved exactly like their students in this respect.) If you suspect shyness or a reluctance to go first, a few more comments can break the ice and put people at their ease. Hand a couple of those in the front row some of the books that they seemed most interested in and strike up a conversation with them. Listen to what they are saying and watch what they're doing for a clue about why they're pretending to be bumps on logs. It may or may not have anything to do with you. In any case, don't worry about it until *after* you get out of the room.

If two people can visit groups together, that makes booktalking easier in almost every way. The preparation is divided in half, as is the pressure. With two different personal styles, there is more variety in the program. Each person has a chance to relax and catch a breath while the other one is talking. One person can do the introduction, the other the final wrap-up, and the two can alternate booktalks in between, each person doing one or two at a time. I prefer alternating to having people do all their talks at once, but every team needs to work out its own arangements. After the visit, you can also take the opportunity to get feedback from your partner. It's easy to just let a booktalk get longer and longer, unless someone reminds you to keep it short. Your partner can help you realize how you affect other people, too. It was one of my partners who told me that while putting my hands on my hips might call attention to the ten pounds I'd just lost, it was also making me look like a lecturing parent, and alienating my teenage audience. I was able to tell one woman I worked with that part of one of her favorite talks was really too graphic for some kids, and she toned it down a bit. You can also learn new booktalks and tricks of the trade from your partner, and pick up some new ideas. If you want to experiment with something a little different, it's nice to have someone there to help rescue you if you flop, and also to give you information on how the group reacted, things you may not have been aware of, since you were busy performing.

It can also be interesting to take a non-booktalking library staff member with you on a visit, either as a participant or an observer. If your colleagues are cynical about your exhaustion when you get back from a booktalking presentation, have them go with you and perhaps even do just one talk. Unless they are very unusual, that one talk will exhaust them as much as all of yours do you, since you have had more practice. (This is not always true—the person may already be an experienced public speaker and comfortable with the age group you are addressing.) Even if you do the whole presentation yourself and the visiting staff member just observes, the amount of energy and preparation required should be obvious.

If you are asked to do a presentation on a particular subject (for instance, business, law, history, biology, biography, or psychology) or to talk about a particular section of the reference collection, have a reference librarian who knows about that subject and section work with you to prepare the presentation and, if possible, go with you to help present it to the group. For example, if you are asked to go to a class and explain how to do research for a major term paper, you need to give the students an idea of where to start, how to proceed, and what reference tools to consult. You should request a copy of the assignment sheet, if there is one, and poll the reference staff to see who would like to go. (This often translates as whose arm can be twisted until they agree to go. This is the time to call in all those favors you've been doing for people!) Try to get someone who can speak effectively to a group and who doesn't have a strong negative bias against the age group you will be talking to. If at all possible, make sure the person you take with you has an interest and some expertise in the subject under discussion. Or give the entire reference staff all the information you have about the group and let them choose the books you will talk about. If your volunteer has never spoken to a group (especially a class) before, explain what needs to be done. The easiest approach is probably to take a sample question and follow it through several reference books, using as many kinds of tools as possible. The speaker should include both basic and specialized tools and spend from two to five minutes on each one, explaining the kind of information it covers and how to use it. Take as many of the books with you as possible, and allow about ten to fifteen minutes for the group to examine them after the presentation. Passing them around during the presentation can be very distracting for both listeners and speakers—don't do it.

You may want to supplement the reference talk with general information on the library—where it is located, the reference phone number, what kinds of questions can or can't be answered over the phone, how to ask a reference question and request a book, what interlibrary loans are and how they can be used, and the problems inherent in trying to do a major assignment when it is due the next day, since specialized or even sufficient information is not always immediately available.

If the class is also required to do a book report or can do one for extra credit, you might give one or two of your short booktalks after the reference presentation. The books you choose can be fiction or nonfiction, tied in to the sample question or on an entirely different aspect of the subject.

You can take a wide variety of other staff members to a presentation for just as wide a variety of reasons. Beginning booktalkers will have a better idea of what it's all about if they've actually seen one or more visits. An added advantage is that the beginners' mistakes won't seem so earthshaking to them after they've seen an expert fumble, recover, and go on. And even the most expert booktalker can and does make obvious mistakes that aren't easy to cover up! The novice needs to know that everyone can recover, gracefully or not. (More about that later, in Chapter 6.) If the mistakes are successfully covered up, the expert can always point them out to the novice later, and show how the coverup was done.

If there have been mountains of requests generated by booktalk presentations, perhaps someone from the interlibrary loan department would enjoy seeing just what you have been doing that has increased their workload so suddenly. The same holds true for the circulation and reference staffs, since they're the ones actually facing the people who come in after books and other things you've suggested.

Involve the rest of the staff in your booktalking program as much as you can. Even when the program is focused on school visiting, its impact is not limited to the children's and young adult staffs—it affects everyone who works in the library. If everyone knows what you're doing firsthand, and why the people who hear you are so excited about the books you talk about, they may be more understanding about the fifty-first request for this month's or this semester's leading title, and more sympathetic to the fifteenth kid who walks up and asks for *Killing Mr. Griffin,* when there are only ten copies, and three of them are overdue, and nobody wants to put in a request, everybody just wants the book!

CHAPTER 5

DOING BOOKTALKS IN SCHOOLS

On the Road Again. . . .

School visiting is one of the most effective and popular ways of book-talking. It gives you a chance to reach the maximum number of teenagers and children in the minimum amount of time. In Stanislaus County (California) two of us visited schools between February and May 1978, and talked to more than 3,000 students. At Emporia High School (Kansas), all the English classes can be visited in only two months at the rate of one or two per day—that's about 1,500 students. The results of school visiting are measurable and often immediately apparent—circulation figures go up, reference questions increase, requests for particular titles that have been widely talked about can skyrocket. So the staff can usually tell right away how effective the school visits are (especially if the books requested are already in short supply). The image presented to the students of the library and librarians is a new one—less staid and conservative; more fun, relevant, and interesting. Talking about the various AV materials the library has can bring in kids who would never ask for a book, but might check out the latest rock record or maybe a film or videocassette. The kids who come in also know they'll recognize at least one face when they get inside the library, and that face will be a friendly one. Children and teenagers are tomorrow's taxpayers—the very life of libraries may depend on convincing them the library is good for something other than school assignments. And who knows, someone sitting at one of those desks listening to you booktalk may be inspired to become a librarian because of you! (It sounds corny, but it does happen.)

Research on reading attitudes shows that as children move into junior high school and then into high school, they no longer see reading as a recreational activity, preferring TV or being with their friends. They see reading only as a way to gain information for school assignments, not as a source of pleasure. Fewer parents today read either in front of or to their children. Reading is not valued in the home, and books may not be readily available to children and teenagers in their homes.

Booktalking is one way this trend can be countered. It shows that books are fun, and while it presents the group with information on a limited number of titles (perhaps twelve or so at the most), it also permits the individual to make the final choice. Again, research has shown that the most effective procedure for helping a child or adolescent select a book is to personally recommend several and allow the person to choose among them. This is what booktalking is. No wonder it works so well!

A successful school visiting program takes time, energy, and dedication, but it does bring results. Occasionally, when you have a waiting list of fifteen for a popular title and no more money for duplicate copies, you may even wish the results weren't quite so good! Because of the effect the program can have, school visiting should involve not only the YA or children's librarian who makes the actual visits, but also the whole library staff. Without support from staff members, the program will fail. Include them as much as you can, from making sure they know what books you will be talking about, to inviting them to go with you either as participants or observers.

The first essential for school visiting is a lot of booktalks. You need a collection to work from so you don't do the same ones over and over, or spend hours frantically writing new ones by the dozen for each new class. Between twenty and thirty booktalks covering an assortment of subjects and age levels is a starting point. If you will be visiting several age or grade levels, be sure that you have talks appropriate for all of them. Twenty or thirty booktalks may sound like a lot, but isn't in actuality all that many. Each time you select books for a class, try to add a few new ones to supplement the ones you already have. That way you should have, at any one time, only three or four talks to prepare for a class. As your booktalk file grows, the number of new talks you need will decrease, although you should continue to add to them from time to time to keep up with the new titles being published and also to spread out the requests over a larger number of books. If you have only a few talks and have to do them over and over, you will get so tired of those talks you won't be able to convince anyone to read the books. The essential spontaneity and joy of sharing will be gone, and with them your effectiveness. A variety of talks averts boredom for everyone, booktalker and audience alike.

The second essential for a successful school visiting program is books. Unless you can buy multiple copies of hardback books, you should do most of your talks on titles available in paperback. At times

I have bought popular titles by the case so I'd have enough to fill requests from the five schools in the area. It's not really fair to generate
interest in something you can't provide, and it is bad public relations
besides. If you talk about a book that's in short supply, tell the kids
they'll have to wait for it and give them some substitutes, if possible.
Assume there *will* be requests for the titles you talk about frequently—
and for some you talk about infrequently, as well.

Often kids lose interest when a book isn't readily available, but
sometimes they surprise you. I talked to a psychology class just after
I'd gotten a review copy of *Why Am I So Miserable if These Are the Best
Years of My Life?* by Andrea Boroff Eagan. I couldn't resist mentioning
it. Although my talk was very brief, five girls requested the book. I explained that I'd just ordered several copies but that it would take them
a long time to arrive and be processed. Would anybody be willing to
wait six months or a year? They all said they would. I saved the requests
until the books were ready, a year later, and then called each of the girls.
They were all still interested, they all picked up the copies I had reserved for them, and a couple even came back to say how much they'd
enjoyed the book. It *had* been worth waiting for!

Most kids won't wait that long, however, and some won't wait at all.
You need to be frank when a delay is inevitable, so the kids will know
what to expect. And you need to collect a lot of books that can be
checked out right away—they are essential for a good school visiting
program.

Contacting schools to let them know you are available can be done
in a variety of ways. A letter to the principal or the school librarian—
perhaps both—explaining who you are and what you'd like to do can
be a good beginning, especially if you have a large number of schools
to contact. Include details of what you are able to do for the school—for
instance, visit classes and talk about books and the library, to encourage recreational reading or suggest ideas for class assignments, such as
book reports; provide booklists or bibliographies to support your visits;
work with the school librarian—whatever you are prepared to do. If
you're willing to visit special subject classes, say so—for instance, sociology, ancient history, business, law, remedial reading, poetry, creative
writing, psychology, sex education. The list is bounded by only three
things: your creativity, your willingness to work, and the amount of
time you have available. (Finding twelve or fourteen books on psychology for hi/lo readers is *not* my idea of the easy life!) You may also want
to point out your willingness to work with teachers and the school librarian on finding materials for mass assignments, to make them easier
on all concerned. Suggest a meeting so you can discuss these things with

the faculty as a whole or with the department heads. Such a presentation will probably take about fifteen minutes and could include a demonstration booktalk.

If you have fewer schools to contact, a phone call can be a very effective and more personal method of conveying the same information. If you aren't sure about school policies, I suggest contacting the principal first, either by phone or in person, to explain what you'd like to do. If the response seems favorable, ask if you can speak to the teachers, at a faculty meeting if possible. Ask for no more than fifteen minutes at the beginning of the meeting. If there are no faculty meetings, then see if you can speak to a meeting of department heads, on the same basis. Find out the name of the school librarian, and before you speak at that meeting, call or visit to make sure the librarian knows what you're planning to do and what you'd like to accomplish.

Include the school librarian as much as possible in your school visiting program. Some librarians will be willing to do a lot for you—contact teachers, spread the word about you, help schedule classes, etc. (Cultivate these people: They are, in my experience, rare and need all the positive feedback you can give them.) Other librarians will be less helpful, and you'll have to do more work in their schools. Occasionally, you may find a librarian who has enough time to visit classes and do booktalks with you. These librarians are also fairly unusual and should be appreciated, even if they just introduce you or do only one or two booktalks per class.

When you speak to any faculty group, you should take no more than fifteen minutes of their time. Be as formal or informal as seems appropriate, but remember you are trying to convince your audience that you can make a lively presentation that "will turn the kids on to the library and to books." If you bore the teachers, they'll never believe you won't bore the students. It has been my experience that large faculty meetings allow more freedom to be expressive. I have a fast, lively presentation for the teachers, including an explanation of what I can do for them and what they can do for me. I give some information about what's available in general at the library, outside the YA area, and mention any current programs they might be interested in. I usually include several comments that should make them laugh, and always the challenge: "I dare you to show me a kid that I can't persuade to read one book. Maybe not the first, or even the fifth—but sooner or later, I'll find the book that kid will read!" So far, I'm batting a thousand in classrooms, and not doing badly outside them.

Tailor your presentation to your own personality. Maybe you can't be as flip as I can and get away with it. Maybe you don't want to. If formality is what you are most comfortable with, then be formal. Just be sure you're interesting. Until you're in their classroom, all these teachers see of you is that brief presentation at the faculty meeting. You have to sell yourself. Try several approaches—if one doesn't work, another will. And the same technique may not be equally successful every time. Be flexible. The same approach may not be right for all schools.

Be sure to mention how you can be contacted and leave a minute or so for questions. You might want to pass out an information sheet on YA and reference services at the library, one that includes information on how the library as a whole (not just the YA department) can serve teachers. I've never included a demonstration booktalk in my faculty meeting visits, since I have always had to deal with a very limited time period and frequent pauses for laughter. However, if you have time, a demonstration can be a very effective way to let teachers know what you're going to be doing in their classes. It can also lend credibility to your claims of being able to persuade or inspire kids to read. If you can persuade teachers to read a book, surely you can persuade their students.

Tie in current events and interests whenever possible: the Olympics, the latest movie craze, controversy over nuclear energy, or maybe something local, especially if it's funny. Avoid boredom at all costs! Elizabeth Talbot once decided to convince a faculty group that she was serious about wanting to talk to their classes by wearing a clown mask, to show she *wasn't* just "clowning around"! They got the point.

If the entire faculty isn't meeting at a convenient time or at all, you can give a presentation at a meeting of department heads. For some reason, these gatherings tend to be more formal than teachers' meetings, so be ready to tailor your presentation accordingly. If you arrive a bit early so that you have a chance to watch people come in and listen to the conversations preceding the meeting, you should be able to read the ambiance of the group and make an appropriate presentation. It should include the same information as the one for the faculty.

Make sure you meet the heads of the English and social studies departments. These two departments will probably give you most of your booktalking business. However, you don't have to limit yourself to booktalking. If the library has display space, the art department head should know about it, not only for students' pictures but for any objects that might be produced in that department or other departments: wood carvings, jewelry, models, quilts, clothes—anything that would fit your display space. Working with the journalism department could get you a book review column in the school paper, or at least a list of the books you talked about at that school. Mention these possibilities, or at least note the appropriate people to talk to at a later time. Also ask if you can go to an English or social studies departmental meeting and talk to the teachers directly.

If you have spoken at a meeting of the whole faculty, the main reason for going to a separate department's meeting will be to schedule teachers for individual classroom presentations. Be sure to take your calendar, and check before you go to make sure you've got all of your commitments on it. If you haven't visited a faculty meeting, or have only gone to a department heads' meeting, a single department's meeting gives you a chance to tell teachers directly what you'll be doing, as well as schedule your visits. You should include more detail about exactly what you can and cannot do, and why you should be allowed to speak to their classes. Give both serious and not-so-serious reasons, from encouraging kids to read to giving the teachers a chance to relax, a no-effort class, and some ideas for their own reading. Departmental meetings tend to be fairly relaxed, and you should be able to form some opinions about the various teachers from what they have to say in the meeting. You may want to adapt your class presentations to their personalities and teaching styles. Teachers vary in the amount of freedom/ discipline they allow/impose in their classes, and a booktalker has to be aware of this. Students do what the teacher expects, and their response to outside speakers is definitely included. Be aware of teachers' personalities as much as possible, but don't forget that first impressions can be very deceiving. Some of my most enjoyable visits in Stanislaus County were to four classes taught by a woman whom I had been dreading. I was sure she would be very much into control, so that I would have to work three times as hard to get a response. In fact, she was able to blend freedom and discipline so well that her classes were eager to respond and yet ready to be polite. Needless to say, she was at the top of my list from then on!

If you've done a good job selling yourself, you may find several of the teachers in a department wanting you to go to all five or six of their classes. Working out a schedule during the departmental meeting, when your time is limited and you're under pressure, can be frustrating and confusing. Just make a list of the names of the teachers and the names of the classes, noting when and where they meet and any other pertinent information, and draw up the schedule later. Arrange to leave messages for the teachers saying when you will visit their classes. Ask them to get back to you if the times aren't convenient. Do not depend on the department head to deliver these messages for you after you've given him or her a list of all the visits. The department head should have the complete schedule, but you also need to notify each teacher individually. The school librarian should also have a schedule of all visits. In some schools the librarian or one of the teachers may volunteer to set up your school visit schedule and let you know the results. This is only practical when you have large chunks of free time, so that as few conflicts as possible develop.

If this isn't your first year at a school, you may be able to skip some or all of these meetings simply by letting the teachers whose classes you've visited previously know that you're ready to come back again. A personal note might be easier than a phone call, since teachers are occasionally rather difficult to reach. Do be sure to notify the principal and the school librarian that you'll be in the school in any case.

There is always the question of when to make these contacts and go to these meetings. If you can get yourself included in the agenda for the first week the teachers are back in school in the fall (without the students), that might be a good time to start acquainting them with what you can do. Another logical time would be at the beginning of a semester or grading period—probably two or three weeks into the semester, to give teachers and students a chance to settle down. If that means contacting the school in early October instead of September, you may gain the advantage of cooler weather. Even in hot parts of the country, many schools are not air conditioned, and it's hard to fire up the audience when they (and you) are wilting away.

When you're planning visits and contacting teachers, it's helpful to have a copy of the faculty roster at hand, so that you can deal with people by name rather than by title. "May I speak with _____ " works better than "May I speak with the ninth-grade English teacher." If you can't get a copy of the roster from the school secretary, the librarian should have one you can duplicate. The roster will also give you the correct spelling of the names.

Scheduling school visits can be compared to doing a jigsaw puzzle—sometimes it's very frustrating when all the pieces don't go where you'd like them to! Before any school contacts have been made, you and your supervisor or administrator should establish priorities. Is school visiting your first responsibility, or does it fall somewhere further down the line, to be fitted in around more important things? Will you be able to schedule as many school visits as you like, or will you be limited to a certain number of hours, days, or classes per week or month? Are you responsible for staffing a service desk a certain number of hours per week? Does this have a higher or lower priority than school visiting?

Once you have listed your various job responsibilities in order of priority, give each of them an hour-per-week value. After you complete this analysis, you should be able to tell how much time you can spend preparing for and making school visits. I usually need one to three hours of preparation for each class, depending on how many booktalks I have to write.

The two county libraries for which I have done most of my school visiting are good examples of the different priorities school visiting can be assigned. In Alameda County, where I worked under the direction of Carol Starr, I was responsible for service to young adults in four branches and at five high schools. School visiting came third, after book selection and collection maintenance. I was also assigned to the reference desk about twenty hours per week, occasionally more, and I was not allowed to cut down on this time to increase the number of school visits I made, although my desk time was usually fitted in after my visits had been scheduled. At a maximum, then, I could do school visits only three days a week, three classes a day. I usually did do this maximum during most of the school year. I could switch the days of the week around but not increase the number of days per week or classes per day. Because the person doing the scheduling usually worked several weeks in advance, I had to require at least two weeks' notice from the teachers. I turned in a schedule of planned school visits every two weeks. School visiting was given a fairly high priority in Alameda County, but had to be worked in around other things. I talked to about 150 to 200 classes a school year, reaching approximately 3,000 to 4,000 students. Some classes I did alone, some with one of the two other YA people in the region.

Priorities were set differently in Stanislaus County. Mary Moore and I were the only YA librarians in the county, and we had the freedom to set up our own schedules and priorities. During the school year, we each worked one night (four hours) a week on the reference desk, and we spent one afternoon a week together at the County Juvenile Hall. (We did the latter twelve months a year.) Our other duties were fitted in around school visiting, which took 35-40 percent of our time during the school year, including preparation time. From February through May, 1978, we visited about 250 classes and talked to over 3,000 students. We visited junior high and high schools throughout the entire county (a total of about 30 schools), and were occasionally visiting as much as four days a week, one to four classes a day. Usually we went separately, but occasionally together.

There are advantages to each approach. In Alameda County, I was more often visible when kids came in looking for the books I'd talked about. There was a smaller area to cover, and it could be covered more thoroughly; however, the number of classes that could be visited was set ahead of time. In Stanislaus County, there was no set number of classes to visit; consequently, Mary and I were, some weeks, out of the library more than we were in it. Kids usually didn't see us when they came in, though we tried to encourage them to come on Monday or Tuesday nights, when at least one of us would be working, and to ask for us if we weren't right there at the desk. A heavier burden was placed on the reference staff, who sometimes couldn't tell what book a kid wanted from a vague description without a title or author. We would leave a list of the books we had talked about most frequently at both the children's and reference desks, but this didn't always solve the mystery of an elusive title. With such a large area to cover, we were forced to do fewer visits per school and could not get to every school every year. With no limit on how many classes we could go to, we had to be very aware of overscheduling and burn-out, especially near the end of each semester, when we were tired and teachers wanted to be sure and schedule us before the term was over. "No" was the word we had to learn to use, frustrating as it sometimes was for both us and the teachers.

The number of school visits a person can do depends upon individual stamina. A beginner shouldn't try to do more than one or two a day, two or three days a week. While booktalking is fun, it is also true that a forty-minute presentation to a group of teenagers is very tiring, both mentally and physically. It is very difficult, if not impossible, to psych yourself up enough to do a good job if you're tired. Until you know your limits, try to stay well below them, and progress slowly. Some classes will be more tiring than others, depending on how much work you have to do to get and hold the class's attention. If the kids are right there *with* you, interested in what you're saying, you'll find it takes less effort to booktalk than it does if you're talking to a group that isn't interested and doesn't want to listen, so that you have to work just to get the class's attention, never mind putting the books across. It's difficult to describe the difference between a group that's with you and one that's not, but even an inexperienced speaker can recognize it.

Therefore, it may be fine to schedule three or even four classes in one day if you're talking to kids who love to read and want some new suggestions. It's not such a good idea to schedule three or four classes of reluctant readers on one day, since you'll be expending more effort and energy per class and may not have enough left to do a good job with the third or fourth group. However, responsiveness doesn't always correlate with reading ability. A seventh-grade group of interested non-readers, even though they may be full of wisecracks, is easier to talk to than a group of senior honor students who are too blasé to react or let any emotions show. A teacher who allows a class the freedom to react to your comments (while still maintaining discipline) will have classes that are more fun and easier to talk to than the teacher who demands absolute silence from the students. If possible, schedule the classes you think will be the most difficult first, so that you'll give them your best shot. If you have a good class later, you will usually be able to psych yourself up from the positive feedback during your presentation. In other words, even when your energy is running low, it's easier to put on a good show for an appreciative audience than it is for one that doesn't care.

When you begin scheduling classes, remember you'll have to allow for a lot of preparation time writing and learning new booktalks, maybe for every class. Increase your school visits slowly. It's better to say No and give everyone full measure than it is to accept every invitation and end up so tired that some classes get a less than first-rate presentation. The teachers who sit through a poor presentation won't ask you back, and may also tell their colleagues that you don't do a very good job. You are your own best advertisement, so you need to be sure you do the best possible job with every class. You will be working more effectively and your reputation will be better if you do a modest number of very good visits instead of a lot of mediocre ones.

If your supervisor doesn't set limits, set your own and stick to them. It is difficult to do talks at more than one school a day, especially if travel time is more than five or ten minutes. I can do an absolute maximum of four classes a day, and I have to have a break sometime in between so I can relax. I cannot be onstage for four hours straight and still do as good a job with the fourth class as I did with the first. (Some people can, however. Marion Hargrove, from Prince Georges County Library, does a whole day of classes—six or seven periods, with a break for lunch—and does it with great success. She has had a lot of experience and must schedule herself heavily in order to cover the number of schools she has to visit.) You will need to consider how many days a week you will be visiting as well as how many classes you will talk to a day. You may want to limit yourself to two or three days a week. It is easier to do four classes for two or three days than for four days, especially if you need a lot of time for traveling. Consider your own convenience as well as that of the teachers when you plan your schedule. Make it as pleasant for yourself as possible. If you have several classes you think will be difficult to talk to, schedule them next to or between classes you think will be easy. Try to schedule all the classes for one day in a block, so you don't have to make several trips to the school or kill a great deal of time between appointments. For example, classes at 8:00 a.m., 9:00 a.m., and 11:00 a.m. would be fairly easy to cope with, and three in a row easier still, unless you prefer not do do three at one time. When you have extra time between classes, you might take the opportunity to talk to the school librarian and let him or her know what you're doing, not only in class visits but in your whole YA program. You can get a cup of coffee and sit in the teachers' lounge, maybe drum up some new business or just rest your voice and not talk for awhile.

I usually stay in a class for the whole period—35–55 minutes. Most teachers seem to prefer that to an interrupted class period, and it also gives me time for a more relaxed presentation. Some librarians simply don't have time to spend a whole period with each class and so only take 20 minutes, meeting two groups per class period. This method works, but is more wearing, means more hassles and more pressure, and can cause burn-out. For these reasons, I can't really recommend it. Sue Tait, of the Seattle Public Library, points out that there *are* advantages to doubling up, though. It is not very tiring if there are not many schools to visit, and beginners often find it easier to prepare a 15-minute presentation than a 40-minute one. Also, some teachers may prefer not to lose a whole class period. At the end of the year, you may use short presentations to do a quick blitz of all the schools you can get to—an effective way to remind kids that there will be things going on at the library during the summer or to give them summer reading ideas.

As you get more experience you may find that you have more endurance than I do, and can go virtually all day, every day. I envy you. However, if you don't build up to that gradually, you may end up doing a poor job, not having a good time, and disliking booktalking altogether.

When you know you're going to be at a school all day, be sure to take your lunch, or scout out a convenient fast-food place so you can get away from campus if you want to. A toothbrush, deodorant, and a few basic toiletries are also important. A few minutes of "freshening up" can make you look and feel more presentable.

Burn-out does happen with school visiting. It usually starts for me about a month before school's out, when I have a very full schedule. I start counting down on the number of classes I have left. By the time the last one is over in May or early June, I'm sure I never want to do another booktalk again! That feeling lasts about a month or six weeks; then I start looking forward to school again and writing new booktalks as fast as I can. The best way to combat burn-out is not to do too much, so you don't get too tired. If you feel yourself getting tired of school visiting, slack off for awhile until you can get your enthusiasm back.

How far ahead of time should you require teachers to ask for a class visit? Again, this depends on your experience and on how much preparation time you need and have available. In Alameda County, I required two weeks' notice for "standard classes"—straight English classes, with no special subject to work around, just recreational reading. For "special classes" (ones I would have to read many new books for—history, psychology, religion, poetry, fantasy, mythology, anything not standard), I asked for four to six weeks, since I needed time to read the books (up to a dozen new ones for each class) and write the booktalks. In Stanislaus County, with a substantial file of booktalks, Mary and I still asked for a week or so advance notice, so we could be sure of having some preparation time, even for a standard class. When we were heavily booked, teachers were sometimes forced to schedule us up to three or four weeks ahead, simply because our time prior to that was already taken. Since we were both experienced and had complete freedom to make our own schedules, we did not always require much advance notice. The main thing to remember in setting up a schedule is to allow yourself enough time to plan the visit carefully, and to write and practice any new booktalks you may need.

When you schedule visits, try to set them on the days of the week when the students will be the most receptive. Friday afternoon is probably the worst time, followed by Monday, both morning and afternoon. Try to do most of your visiting on the three middle days of the week, especially to those classes you think may be most difficult. Likewise, the beginning and middle of a semester are probably the best times for heavy visiting. Toward the end of the term, everyone's worried about finals and more interested in vacation than in you.

The school librarian can be very helpful in working out the best times for you to visit and may even be willing to do all or most of the scheduling for you, especially if you've been to the school before and the teachers all know you already. The librarian can also leave reminders with the teachers about your forthcoming visit several days in advance, if you have scheduled it several weeks previously. (You should do this yourself if the school librarian won't do it for you.) Work with your school librarians; include them in the program as much as possible, even to doing one or two booktalks with you, if they are interested and have time. They may be willing to let the class meet in the school library, so that the students can browse and maybe check out some of the books you talked about. Always let the school librarian know when you'll be in the school, and provide a list of the books you intend to talk about so the library can be prepared for requests. The librarian may want to purchase some of the titles for his or her own collection. You might even consult with the school librarian when you plan your presentation, so that you can include as many books as possible that are already in the school library. Then the students will have access to them there as well as in the public library.

Don't ever make the school librarian feel that you are competing. While your basic function is the same, your areas of emphasis are different. You should complement each other and work together. (For a better understanding of the school librarian's situation, see Chapter 8.)

If your schedule gets very full, some teachers may ask you to talk to their combined classes—eighty or ninety kids at one time. Think twice before accepting!! I have nightmares remembering the times I agreed to do this and then bitterly regretted it. A larger group is harder to control, and is likely to include more kids who enjoy making trouble. Even the kids who usually listen or at least keep quiet will find new people to talk with when two classes meet together—people who seem more interesting than their familiar classmates. You will have less chance for eye contact, and you will have to speak louder than usual just to be heard in the back row. Teachers who may be able to keep a class quiet in their own rooms aren't always able to do so when there's another class present. In short—noise, hassle, and a less than effective presentation. Perhaps someone somewhere can communicate as effectively with large groups as with small ones—try it if you think you can. But if you can't don't hesitate to refuse!

The only time I have spoken to a large group and been successful was when I went to the Fort Worth County Day School and talked to the entire student population in one morning! Debby Jennings, the librarian, wanted something exciting for their Book Week celebration. (I thought talking to hundreds of kids all at once would *definitely* be exciting!) So I spoke to two groups of between two and three hundred each. Since they couldn't all see the book jackets, Debby had slides made of them, and they were flashed onto a large screen behind me. That meant the room had to be dark, so I had to have a little light on the lectern to see by. Talking to a roomful of wiggly junior and senior high school students that I can't really see but can hear is *not* my idea of ideal conditions. But Debby had been very persuasive, and I was surprised that it all went off quite well. The kids were great—almost all of them were quiet. Debby sold copies of the titles; by the end of the day she had sold almost everything she and all the local bookstores had.

I have heard other stories about successful booktalks for very large groups in auditoriums, and have decided that while 15–30 is the easiest number of people to work with, perhaps 200–400 is the next; 40–60 is the *worst!* I'm not sure why that seems to be true, and it's only my opinion, but there it is.

CHAPTER **6**

HASSLES AND HOW TO HANDLE THEM

Murphy Was Right!

Murphy's Laws are, for me, a statement of reality. If anything can go wrong, it will, and in the worst possible way. Preparation can avert some problems, but others are unavoidable. Even the most expert and experienced booktalkers occasionally fall on their faces. When it happens to you, all you can do is to get up as inconspicuously as possible, dust off your bruised nose, knees, and pride, and go on as if nothing unusual had happened. The mark of a professional entertainer, whether storyteller, actor, comedian, or booktalker, is the ability to cover up all but the most obvious mistakes and not let them affect the rest of the performance. It has also been my experience that when I am nervous, I am almost waiting to make a mistake. Once I've made it, however, the waiting is over, and I can get on with what I'm doing. The feeling is "if I make one mistake the whole world will fall apart!" But then, once I've made that mistake and gotten it over with, I discover that neither I nor the world have been shattered, that I have been neither booed nor lynched by my audience, who may not even be aware that I have made some monumental error, and that as long as I laugh at myself, they won't laugh *at* me but *with* me.

Once, when I was talking to an eighth-grade class of reluctant and non-readers, I mentioned in the course of my talk on William Sleator's *House of Stairs* that there were three boys and two girls in the story. This sentence had occasionally elicited giggles from the front row, but I'd ignored them. After I'd finished my presentation and the kids were milling around the table where I'd set up the books, one of them picked up *House of Stairs* and said, looking at the cover of the paperback copy, "Where's the other boy?" I looked at the cover, and sure enough, there were three girls and two boys. The reason for the giggles was obvious. I admitted my mistake, thanked the boy who'd pointed it out to me, and laughed about it. In another class of eighth-graders, which I had visited the previous year, I asked if they'd already heard me talk about

Through a Brief Darkness. Only one girl had, and she'd read the book as well, so I began by saying I'd have to be really careful, since she'd catch any mistakes I made. Everyone laughed. I began, and as I progressed, the girl who had read the book kept smiling and nodding. In the middle of my talk, however, she suddenly stopped smiling and shook her head. Since this was a class I had a good rapport with, I felt it would be okay to stop and see what I'd said wrong. (This would *not* be okay in every class, since it breaks the continuity of the presentation and focuses the class's attention on something besides the talk. Also, it can make you look *very* foolish.) I couldn't get her to say what I'd done, so I shrugged, passed it off, and got back into my booktalk. End of incident.*

Obviously, mistakes aren't limited to the inexperienced or the nervous. Everybody makes them, and the probability of the mistake being a stupid one increases with the importance of the people watching you, their uncanny ability to see every error, and the likelihood that they will comment—loudly. All you need to know is how to recover with a maximum of ease and grace. The most important thing to remember when trying to achieve this is, *don't panic!* Panic can make you freeze and forget what to do. It makes any mistake seem worse. If you keep your wits about you and stay calm, you can recover one way or another from *any* mistake, even if it seems impossible at the time.

My most recent horrible experience with forgetting and not controlling the resulting panic was at a state library convention. I had just moved to Kansas, this was the first time I had spoken locally, and I was being sponsored by another member of the SLIM faculty. It all meant a certain amount of pressure, and I was nervous to begin with. I had also been very busy and hadn't had time to practice my booktalks, but figured I could just wing it. Wrong!

The room was packed when I got there—three times as many people as we'd expected or that the room could comfortably hold. They stood around the walls and sat on the floor in the aisles. To top it all off, the lectern and microphone I'd requested were unavailable. I took a deep breath, looking at the mass of tightly-packed bodies (which someone had estimated numbered about 150), and using my very best-projected voice so I could be heard above the speaker on the other side of the accordion-folding wall and above the noise from people using the back of the room as a hall, I began. Halfway through my first talk, I had to stop while they set up and adjusted a *handheld* mike with a *very* short

---

*Until I reread the book, that is. Then I discovered that about half my talk had nothing to do with the novel. Over the years, I'd gradually invented a story of my own—no wonder she'd been shaking her head! I wrote a new talk as fast as I could, and it was accurate.

cord. It took a while to get used to that, and about the time I was starting to think I'd probably survive, I started my talk on *The Westing
Game*. This talk is almost entirely characters' names—sixteen of them,
and horribly easy to forget! I tried to look at my notes, realized they
were too far away on the table—I couldn't read them, floundered along
for what seemed like an eternity, gave up, reached for my notes, and
read the names off, trying to not show that I wanted to die of embarrassment. Finally I stumbled to the end and was able to go on to another
talk I was more familiar with.

As I started my explanation of how to do booktalks, I used this fiasco
as an example of how not to do them, of why practice is important and
how even experts can make mistakes and survive. The most amazing
thing was that I really did survive, and the audience enjoyed what I had
to say in spite of the mistakes. If that's true with adults, think how
much more forgiving kids are likely to be! After all, you're the one
who's getting them out of class!

The worst, or at least the most obvious, mistake is forgetting what
comes next in the book or the booktalk. This is for me the most nerve-
wracking thing that can happen when I'm in front of a class. It takes
all my will power not to run screaming from the room. My first line of
defense is my notes, which I always have unless I've been doing the talk
for a year or so. I keep the notes on the table where my books are, and
if I feel I'm going to need them, I move around to stand in back of the
table so I can see the notes by just glancing down. This position is a little
more "teacherish," but seems to be the best stance for checking notes
inconspicuously. You should know your talk well enough that you
don't actually need to read it, just glance down at it two or three times
to make sure you're on the right track. If you realize you aren't sure
what's coming up, glance down and check *before* you completely run
out of words, if you can. If it's not the next sentence you have forgotten
but the next word, you may not be able to keep talking as you check
your notes. *Don't panic* when silence falls. Find your place and go on.
A break of a few seconds in a talk isn't a tragedy. Usually the kids are
so impressed at all you're remembering that they don't really react
much when you have to check your notes. And sometimes kids will be
too embarrassed about an adult making a mistake to laugh immediately, especially if you maintain your poise. The silence is probably much
louder and longer to you than to anyone else anyway. (Warning: This
is a sweeping generalization, of course. Some kids *always* notice
everything. Don't worry about them—they seem to be in a minority,
and are occasionally not even appreciated by their peers!)

If you don't have notes to fall back on, recovering from a suddenly blank mind is more difficult. Again, don't panic. Slow down and stay calm. If you know that you have a sentence or two to go before you run out of words, take as long as possible to say those sentences, to give yourself a maximum amount of time to remember what you've forgotten. *Think* about what you're saying—after all, you've read the book. You *know* what comes next. This is where knowing rather than memorizing a talk comes in handy, since all you have to remember is a scene, rather than an exact sequence of words. If you have memorized your talk and have lost the exact words of the next sentence, try paraphrasing until you can remember. Sometimes a couple of extra sentences elaborating on the last thing you remember will give you enough time to recover. Struggle on as far as you can before you give up completely.

If you can't remember anything about the book no matter how calm you stay and how carefully you think—admit it! Say something like, "I've suddenly gone blank; I have no idea what comes next! To find out, you'll just have to read [title]." Or, "This is ridiculous! I didn't intend to tell you the ending, but now I can't even remember the middle! But it's still a neat book; read it yourself and find out." Be as casual and unnervous as you can. Laugh about it, make a joke. You want your audience to laugh with you, so *you* must laugh first. If they laugh first, they may be laughing *at* you instead. Do whatever you are most comfortable with, but don't make a big deal about having forgotten something. It *isn't* a big deal, unless you make it so. Be brief in what you say to wrap up the talk you don't remember, and immediately go on to your next one. No matter how colossally bad your mistake was, it should only involve that one booktalk and not the rest of your presentation. Work to wipe out the memory of that mistake with the rest of your performance. The show must go on, no matter what. It should go on superlatively!

If you leave something out, and don't realize it until several sentences later, you can always fix it then. There are several ways to do this—the most obvious way is to be obvious. "Oh, I forgot . . . ," add whatever you left out, and pick up your booktalk again. You can also work in whatever you left out in a more subtle way if you can think quickly. This means not stopping to add what was left out as soon as it occurs to you but waiting until you reach an appropriate place in the talk to insert it. Or you can assess the importance of what you've left out and decide not to include it after all. An experienced booktalker will find it easier to add to or rearrange a booktalk while giving it than will a novice. For a novice, the least awkward tactic may be to either admit something was left out or not mention it at all. There are actually few details in a booktalk that are one hundred percent essential, and if you leave one of *those* out, you will soon realize it. Listen to what you're saying—make sure it makes sense. Then you'll include all the really necessary parts.

There are two schools of thought about what to do if you forget names or numbers. One suggests that you insert any handy name or number and go on. The other holds that you should not make up what you've forgotten but just do without. For a number, use "many," "several," or "a few." Instead of giving a name, describe the character by personality, role, or appearance, or use only "he" or "she." Each method has its pitfalls. Too many nameless characters can be confusing, but it's embarrassing to get caught when you've inserted any handy number in place of the correct one. I hadn't reread *Deathwatch,* by Robb White, for years; I'd just talked about it. After a while, Ben wasn't walking fifty or sixty miles back to town but two hundred! Mary had to bring me back to reality.

Forgetting part of your talk is only one of the problems you will run into. The other big ones are an uninterested class, a series of unexpected interruptions, and an uncooperative teacher.

Teenagers have myriad ways of expressing their lack of interest. Ostentatiously reading a different book, doing homework, writing notes or letters, daydreaming, talking, whispering, looking at magazines, making noise, fiddling, and generally acting as if you were a minor annoyance that might go away are only a few of their tactics.* Any behavior of this sort will make it harder for you to get the books across. You will feel that you are using up mental energy without getting anything back in return.

Just hope that the teacher won't let things go too far, so the class doesn't get completely out of control. If there are more than one or two troublemakers, things *are* getting out of control, and if the teacher doesn't do anything (in spite of the fact that you explained ahead of time that you couldn't double as a disciplinarian), there is one simple technique that usually works quite well. Stop talking, preferably in the middle of a sentence to make it more obvious, and look at the ringleader. Wait till she or he quits talking, then go on as if nothing had happened. If you get any smart remarks like "Whatcha lookin' at me for? I ain't doing nuthin'!" you can say, "I was just waiting till you finished

---

*Of course, some teenagers use the same techniques to disguise a genuine interest. Just as I've seen kids do homework, listen to the radio, and watch TV at the same time, I've also found that they can follow a booktalk closely while combing hair, staring into space, twiddling pencils, etc. It's just unfortunate that it's usually hard to tell whether they are actually listening or not, because you'll be tempted to assume the worst—they're bored!—when in fact they may be hoping to hear more.

talking" (or "making noise," or whatever). Maintain your cool and self-possession, in spite of your ardent desire to wring the kid's neck—hard—or to run out of the room screaming. The troublemakers are trying to hook you into their game—don't let them.

Another way to make a noisy group quieter, if not silent, is to get the rest of the class interested, so the other kids will tell the noisy ones, "Shut up, I can't hear!" Aim your talk at the kids you can reach, especially the ones who look as though they might be class leaders. Or try to get the troublemakers themselves interested. You may be able to do this by talking directly to them or by choosing books they will like. Perhaps rearranging the order of your talks will catch them. Work harder to make you talks interesting—build suspense as high as possible, and make the funny parts even funnier. If only the best will interest them, do your very best. Try using body language; come out from behind the desk or table and use your whole body to show what's going on in your talk. Use a book with pictures, such as *The Minds of Billy Milligan,* since everyone will want to look at them. If conversations continue afterwards, they may be about the book; many times the talking will stop altogether. If one thing doesn't work, try something else. Be aware of what you were doing when the noise stopped, if only for a minute. Try doing that again, if you can. There are some classes that are going to talk and not listen no matter what you do, and these classes always seem to have teachers who let them get away with it. (Remember Murphy's Laws?) Don't let these classes discourage you. Just hide your fright, smile, and struggle through. Every booktalker gets a fair share of classes like this—no one gets left out. It is a good idea to remember the teachers who allow this kind of behavior, so that in the future you can remind them again that your primary function is entertainment, not discipline. If they are still not willing to do their part, schedule their classes in tandem with good ones, psych yourself up, and valiantly ignore the uproar. Do-nothing teachers are, in my experience, few and far between. Most teachers want to make sure their classes act properly, and will take the steps necessary to quell unruly students.

But even the most conscientious teacher can have students who turn into demons as soon as you're alone with them. A junior high (eighth-grade) reading class gave me one of the worst times I've ever had. I was just getting over a cold, it was my third class that day, and my voice was giving out. I asked the teacher to get me a glass of water before the class started. I'd hoped she would send one of the students out for it, but she didn't. She trusted her class and had faith in me (I had done talks for her several times), and so she took roll, introduced me, and walked out to get my water. I had ten seconds of sheer panic as she disappeared in the middle of my introduction, but I kept talking. The trouble started with the first booktalk—the main character's name was the same as a smart-aleck's in the front row. "Oh joy!" I thought, and kept on going. Then pencil-tapping, hair-combing, face-making, and talking erupted all over the room. I struggled along for a minute or so, then stopped. After several eternities, the racket quieted down a bit, and I went on. So did all the students. I stopped again. Several comments were made by the two or three kids who were listening—"Shut up, I can't hear!" I said, "Come on, y'all, I can't talk over you." New comments about my "y'all." I went on, holding on to the shreds of my dignity, but now all was lost. More racket! Then I got out the heavy artillery (not really a good idea, actually a *bad* idea, but I was desperate): "If you don't want to listen, I'm sure Ms. Silva will be glad to assign you some homework when she gets back." (Where *is* she, anyway?) Rude comments, made by the kids who were listening to the noisy ones, but the noise level stayed about the same. I finally stopped one last time, "Come on, guys, mellow out, *please!*" That elicited a lot of imaginary joints and appropriate noises, but they got reasonably quiet. About the time they all settled down, of course, the teacher came back, and they transformed themselves into little angels. The rest of the period was blessedly unremarkable, but if the teacher hadn't come back when she did, I might have been up for manslaughter!

Noisy-rude classes are to be distinguished from noisy-interested ones. Loud comments about your talks or a discussion with another kid can be signs of interest. An interested class can be almost as noisy as a rude one, and yet be right there with you, giving you the support, attention, and feedback you need. The difference is especially noticeable in the timing of the noise. In an interested class, the noise may rise between talks, starting after a talk is over, as kids comment on it, and last sometimes even into the first part of the next talk. But by the end of each talk, the noise will have died down completely, as more and more kids get involved in the story. Then it will rise again in the interval between the talks. You can't expect a responsive class to remain totally quiet and motionless. Noise and movement can mean interest as well as uninterest. The class's attitude makes the difference, and is almost immediately obvious.

You can respond to interested comments and questions. If possible, don't stop your talk, but respond in between talks. If you have to answer a question in the middle of a talk, make the interruption as brief as possible and get right back into your talk. Classes in which a dialogue goes on can be the most fun for both you and the kids. Don't shut the kids off—take part in the fun! But don't go too far. Here again, you need to remember your role: You are the one in charge. Be sure you don't give up that position.

A class can show its lack of interest by a total absence of response. It's as if you were playing to a vacuum. Nothing comes back to you. Perhaps you brought inappropriate books. You're looking at a class of mostly boys, and two-thirds of your books have female leads. You didn't realize these kids all had heard you last year—and you're doing the same talks they heard then. Occasionally you'll find a teacher who doesn't really communicate to you the actual make-up of the class you're going to address. "Good readers" can mean almost anything, and result in your bringing grade-level books for nonreaders. *Disaster!* Suddenly you realize all those blank looks mean that no one has any idea *what* you're talking about—no one in the class could possibly read any of the books you've mentioned. In cases like this, try to pick the few books that are appropriate, talk about them, and either omit the others or do them quickly. You may end up doing a shorter presentation. Since the class has a lower reading level than you expected, concentrate on magazines and "adult picture books," if you have brought any. You can also talk about appropriate books that you don't have with you but that are available from the library. When you do this, though, remember to write the author's name and the title on the board, in case anybody wants to copy down the information. In other words, play it by ear and try to make the best of a difficult situation. But if you feel that the situation is impossible, ask the teacher if you can come back another day with more appropriate books, rather than struggle through with ones that aren't right.

The responses you'll get from junior high and senior high school students will vary from class to class and from grade to grade. Even a lackluster response during and after a presentation doesn't necessarily mean that you've been a flop or that your books were inappropriate. In a high school class, it may just mean that no one wants to be the first person to go up and look at the books, or that they're all practicing being cool and blasé and you're a perfect target. If you want a really enthusiastic response, the kind where you're trampled by kids grabbing for books, go to a junior high class—the need to be "cool" doesn't usually take over until about the tenth grade. Older high school students are probably just as interested as the younger ones in the books you're talking about, but they are much less direct about expressing it.

Another thing you're going to have to deal with is interruptions from the outside. These come in all forms, but never the one you're expecting or are prepared for. Kids straggle in late or have to leave early. Someone comes from the office with a note telling a class member to go somewhere else immediately. There's a fire drill. The public address system comes to life with interminable announcements just as you reach the most exciting part of your talk. Bells ring for unknown reasons in the middle of the class. The easiest way to deal with all of these interruptions is to ignore them, as far as possible (obviously, you can't ignore a fire drill!). The student who comes in late or with a message can be directed to the teacher, who may be in the far corner, with just "Mr. So-and-so is over there," said very quietly, while pointing to the teacher. Teachers usually catch on to this quickly, and may call the student's name and/or stand up to attract attention, so that you can get back to your talk as quickly as possible. There's no way to escape bells or PA announcements. Just shrug and wait. A comment about good timing or not being able to shout over the noise can bring the class's attention back to you when the interruption is over. After a long interruption like an announcement, you should probably repeat your last sentence or idea, to make sure even the kids who quit listening a little early know where you are. This isn't always necessary after a brief interruption.

My "favorite" interruption comes from the kid who is either too dense or too preoccupied to respond to quiet instructions. This student walks in and tries to hand me a late pass, sick excuse, or whatever, and doesn't respond to "She's over there," "Ms. So-and-so is in the back of the room," or even "I'm not the teacher; she's right over there." Finally, I usually give up, take whatever is being handed me, and worry about it after my presentation is over. By that time the whole class is giggling, and the thread of my talk has been lost.

Teachers can be difficult or uncooperative in a variety of ways: for instance, by leaving the room, not keeping the class quiet, interrupting a talk with questions or comments that are not relevant, or whispering to a teacher's aide while you are trying to make your presentation. Explain to the teachers, if you can, what you expect of them and why. I have never been able to bring myself to tell a teacher in class not to whisper, or stop my presentation to eject a student who has been allowed to cause trouble. But I have gotten up the courage to speak to teachers between periods and remind them that I need a quiet, orderly classroom to work in. Fortunately, teachers who whisper during a talk are uncommon, for their rudeness can have a devastating effect. Once you realize that a certain teacher is likely to present problems of one kind or another, you can schedule his or her classes for times when you will be most able to deal with those problems. Try not to do more than two classes in a row for this teacher, and schedule them, if possible, when you'll be fresh and alert. Don't try to handle three classes for a difficult teacher after you've just gotten off a two-hour shift on the desk, without lunch or even a break. You'll be asking for trouble, and you'll probably get it. When it comes to problem teachers or problem classes, make it easy on yourself.

The adult groups I've spoken to have generally been more polite and attentive than school classes. Occasionally, though, I have encountered people who liked to whisper and giggle throughout a talk. Other than making a greater-than-usual effort to involve these people in my talk— by speaking *to* them, for instance—I haven't tried to quiet them down. Their whispering usually isn't a serious distraction to the rest of the audience, and I've often found out later that they were discussing the books. Once in a while I have run into an adult who wanted to ask questions or make comments after almost every talk; in that situation I just explain (nicely) that I'll be ready to answer questions after the whole presentation is over. Adults seem to be more aware and appreciative of the amount of work involved in a presentation than schoolchildren are, and of course adults are not a "captive audience." They are more likely to identify with you, and so less likely to create a disturbance.

CHAPTER **7**

BOOKTALKING FOR CHILDREN

Small Can Be Beautiful

By ELIZABETH ROWLAND OVERMYER

When I delivered my first booktalk twelve years ago, I had no idea what I was doing. No one had mentioned booktalks to me in library school, and I had never heard another librarian do one. It was June, however, and June in the Alameda Country Library System was the time for "summer blitzing." These visits to every kindergarten through sixth-grade classroom included brief announcements of summer programs and—booktalks! After a panicky conference with a slightly more experienced colleague, off I went, *The White Mountains* and *Harriet the Spy* under my arm. Fortunately, what I learned on that first visit would see me through the experience again and again. By the time I walked into the first classroom, I had already done the major part of the presentation—I had chosen favorite books that I could describe with genuine enthusiasm. And by the time I walked out of that classroom, I knew that kids *will* listen when you're telling them about good books, and if you've picked really good books, the author has already done most of the work for you.

Later I attended a booktalk workshop for young adult librarians led by Carol Starr and Joni Bodart. Besides all the practical tips and enthusiasm I came away with, I also became aware for the first time of a commonly-held assumption about booktalking for children as opposed to booktalking for young adults. Many librarians seem to feel that the skills involved are very different, and that those who do booktalks well for one audience may not necessarily do them well for the other. At the time, I was perfectly content to leave this assumption unexamined. Yet as I began to work on this project with Joni, the issue kept cropping up, and I discovered that I had real reservations about the alleged differences. As a children's librarian, I would booktalk *different books,* but would I prepare and present the talks themselves in a very different way? How might booktalks for children be different—shorter? less detailed? more detailed? *Is* there really something very different about booktalking to children?

Having spent the last few months wrestling with these problems and plaguing colleagues for discussions about them, I now feel that the only possible answer is a qualified No, or perhaps a No, but. . . . There are no *essential* differences between booktalking for children and booktalking for young adults or any other audience. The chapters in this book on how to prepare, practice, and deliver a talk may be applied successfully with any age group. But while the guidelines for preparing the talks remain similar, you cannot forget that children are a very distinct and special audience. This will be evident right from the start of a presentation: far more than teenagers, children are willing to accept an adult visitor without imposing an obvious testing period. Reactions are fresher and more openly displayed in elementary school than they will be a few years later; an adult can get direct, valuable cues as to which subjects work and which don't. And the response can be truly exhilarating. Having worked with both age groups, I feel that booktalking to kids is even easier than booktalking to young adults—and more fun!* A good booktalk may be interrupted by a child grabbing for the book or calling out, "Save that one for me!" Most of the books presented may be checked out the same day. Booktalking to kids is indeed so satisfying that kids themselves eagerly participate in it, to an extent unknown in even the most highly motivated high school classes.

Yet despite their fund of ready enthusiasm, children are well equipped to sense a poorly prepared or half-hearted booktalker. The way to provoke the response you want lies not only in the writing, or thinking out, of a good talk but also in the consideration you give to other factors that are particularly important in working with children: the variety of materials available; the range of ages, interests, and reading abilities faced; and the role of other skills, such as storytelling, in the complete program. In the following pages, I will discuss the ways in which basic booktalking techniques can be modified or supplemented in work with children.

Selecting Material for Children

The first step in preparing a booktalk is to select the right books to sell. In most cases, the selection will be entirely up to the booktalker.

---

*Needless to say, this is an issue of long standing between children's and young adult librarians, who each love best the age group they serve.—*JB*

My first concern as a public librarian has always been to select for each age group books appropriate to their age and reading level, and then to present them in a lively combination that will convince listeners of one of the public library's most important attributes: its "something for everyone" quality, its hospitality to individual tastes and needs. Occasionally a teacher may request a program on a particular topic; however, such requests are best left for experienced booktalkers. For the novice, the problems of boning up on one subject and then introducing sufficient variety into the presentation can be daunting.

The first step in preparing any booktalk program is to indulge in an orgy of reading. Read books of all kinds, the ones that are always in demand and the ones that never circulate. To all but the most experienced librarian, this reading is an absolute necessity, and ideally should take place without the pressure of any specific booktalking assignment. *Read,* and give yourself plenty of time for it. Beginning librarians may want to allow themselves as long as six months to become familiar with the children's collection. There will be plenty of other things to do—preschool storytime, displays, reader's advisory and reference work, etc.—but you must make time to read. The better you know the collection, the easier it will be to pick out appropriate books once you are ready to talk to an audience. If you are following in the steps of a well-known booktalker, it can be hard to turn down an eager teacher's request, but do try to be clear on how much time you need to get established, making your point firmly and without apology: "I will be ready to start school visiting in the spring. If you give me your name and phone number, I will contact you as soon as I start scheduling visits." And then, of course, you *do* get back in touch.

Meanwhile, keep reading, and as you go on, look for all the characteristics that were mentioned in Chapter 2—a strong, fast-moving, and believable plot; well-developed characters; and stories with a strong emotional impact. After a time, you'll find yourself creating a mental file of books you like well enough to talk about—the basic selection criterion for any booktalker. Write down the titles of the books you like, along with a few brief notes—you'll appreciate these reminders even more in a couple of years.

As you begin to compile a list of possible books, consider the age level of the materials and the reading experience of the children you'll be seeing. For there is a great deal more variation here than in YA work. It is worthwhile to think carefully about just who your listeners are, and what, in addition to lots of books, you want them to discover through your visit.

Children's librarians are generally responsible for service to children from preschool through either the sixth or the eighth grades, and the great range of interests, reading skills, and enthusiasm you can encounter at those ten or so levels will provide the greatest challenges—and the deepest frustrations—of your job. Before selecting particular titles to booktalk, consider how booktalking supports your library's general goals for each age group.

Kindergarten Through Second Grade

To many kindergarteners and first- and second-graders, the whole idea of a free public library, with stories and books on almost every subject, is in itself brand new and wonderful. In these years, booktalking will usually take a back seat to storytelling and picture-book reading, since you cannot assume that children this young are really sure that they can enjoy books. Yet, as will be discussed later, very short (two-minute) booktalks can be introduced; in fact, easy readers provide some surprisingly good booktalk material. But it is also important not to limit the program to material that children can read themselves. "Here are some good stories to listen to" can elicit some lively discussions on who reads to whom in different families, and can also make it clear that the library is not the preserve of older children and adults, who already know how to read. Remember, too, to bring appropriate nonfiction titles. Even children who have already been read to a great deal may not be aware of books like these, or of the library as a source of information, so it's important to bring in some good, well-illustrated books on science, animals, etc. Collections of jokes and riddles are fun, too.

Third and Fourth Grades

It is in the third grade that the transition from a large measure of storytelling to more booktalking is made, and in the fourth grade booktalking really takes center stage (although there is certainly room for some storytelling in all upper grades). By this time, most children have a fair idea of what a library is, and a good program serves to reinforce—and perhaps expand—the basic concept. The trick here is to focus their attention on titles that will match both their intermediate reading skills and their increasingly sophisticated interests. While some children at this level will be able to tackle almost anything in the library, for most kids this is a tricky period. They are leaving the safety of easy readers and familiar picture books and need a lot of help in finding wonderful titles that won't overwhelm them. Often this is the age at which children begin to come to the library independently and to select books without the help/supervision of their parents. Eight- and nine-year-olds can easily be frustrated if the story you made sound so exciting turns out to be too long or too hard for their first attempt at independent reading. Many kids are ready for longer titles, all will respond to good booktalks, but you must be careful to bring materials for all levels of these in-betweeners.

Upper Elementary and Junior High Classes

In many school districts, some combination of fifth- through eighth-grade classes will be housed in a separate junior high school, which makes it very clear that this age has more sophisticated tastes. These classes demand well-developed booktalk presentations, and extras like storytelling are correspondingly less important. In this age group, you'll be meeting some real readers, so it becomes particularly important to include new titles, a new installment in a popular series, a recent title by an established author, or anything fresh, which you haven't been telling eager readers about for the past three years. This group is more trend- and age-conscious, so in visits to the fifth and sixth grades, I usually bring along a couple of books from the adult and YA sections. For upper junior high classes, perhaps a third of the titles I mention will be drawn from these other collections. Encouraging children of this age to keep reading often means acknowledging frankly to them that they can move on from the children's area to find other books elsewhere. In the seventh and eighth grades, booktalk presentations are basically identical in style and format to YA programs described in earlier chapters, and many of the most popular and suitable titles have been mentioned already.

Consideration of these factors should help you decide how much booktalking is appropriate for each age and how your overall approach should be shaped to fit different grades. There are many specific tools to match age levels to specific titles. In Charlotte Huck's *Children's Literature in the Elementary School,* a five-and-a-half-page chart, "Books for ages and stages," describes characteristics of different age groups, implications for book selection, and examples of just-right titles. Another good source is Donna Norton's *Through the Eyes of a Child,* which matches some of the newest titles with the developmental needs they can meet. ALA's Association for Library Service to Children, many public library systems, and several excellent professional books will supply graded reading lists. But there is an important rule to remember when using any of these lists: only *you* know your kids and your collection. Don't try to fit someone else's ideas into your own plan unless you find yourself saying, "Yes, what a good idea!" or are genuinely curious as to whether something new will indeed work. In fact, your own experience, and that of your colleagues, should be the most reliable tool of all. Are all the fourth-graders reading Judy Blume, or Encyclopedia Brown, or Ursula LeGuin? Have you had lots of requests lately for good mysteries or for books "just like *Charlie and the Chocolate Factory*"? Use these important clues about current outside interests and reading enthusiasms. Dungeons and Dragons buffs may not know the library has specific game-playing titles; they will probably also be interested in new fantasies. *Star Wars* and *Return of the Jedi* enthusiasts will not only enjoy science fiction novels and stories about making the movies, but may also like books about film stunts and trick photography with simple cameras. Thinking about these issues ahead of time will help you plan your visit so that the majority of your books will appeal to a large number of your listeners. And you'll also have the time—and the credibility—to suggest a few special books for listeners of different tastes and/or abilities.

Writing a Booktalk

All right. You've got a good book, one you like and want to talk about, that's appropriate for the age and reading of your audience. So it's time to prepare that booktalk.

I write down my talks, and my box of talks is a talisman against the very real fear of opening my mouth and finding nothing to say. Writing has become a practical habit for me. Yet the majority of people I know never write their booktalks down, no matter how thoroughly they prepare. (A good friend told me what happened the last time she used a thoroughly prepared, written-out booktalk. She delivered it in front of a class she knew well and was reproached for "sounding just like you memorized it all.") Some people do indeed speak easily and spontaneously in front of groups and are constrained by anything more than written notes. Others can only be comfortable and ready to deal with interruptions and last-minute changes when they are completely clear about what they intend to say. The secret lies in knowing just what kind of person you are. If you already know that you are one of those who work best "off the cuff," don't be put off by this talk of writing things down. You can use these guidelines instead to help marshal your thoughts and make preliminary notes.

For me, writing something down is the best way to focus my thoughts, shape them, and breathe life into the descriptions. If my first draft doesn't work, then I've got something concrete to tinker with. I urge new booktalkers to try this method for a while, or, if writing seems too cumbersome and inhibiting, to use a tape recorder to get down what you want to say about the book. In any case, the planning and effort of turning a good book into a good booktalk remain the same.

So far as creating a booktalk goes, the information in Chapter 2 works as well for children as it does for other age groups. But since Joni's examples are drawn mostly from YA and adult literature, I have included some examples from children's literature, to show how I and others apply these techniques.

The first thing to consider is what part of the book you want to talk about. Do you want to recreate an entire incident so that the audience will want to go back and relish it again, along with all the details you've let out? Will you merely set the scene and leave the reader wondering how on earth anyone could survive, or change, that situation, or will you concentrate on introducing the characters themselves? Whether you choose to emphasize the general situation, a specific incident, or a character, it's vital to narrow your focus to a few well-chosen details. As you reread the book you've selected, jot down the things that most surprise, amuse, or just plain stick with you. Then look at them and decide which approach they suggest.

When I booktalk *Julie of the Wolves,* I may approach it from any of several different angles. The most popular one is the survival aspect. Julie has set out across the tundra on her own; winter is coming on; all she has between her and the cold is a backpack containing needles, matches, a sleeping skin, two knives, a pot, and a week's supply of food. But one week after she has left home, she knows she is hopelessly lost. . . . A slight expansion of this outline is all you need to create a good brief booktalk, but occasionally I start out talking about Julie herself (she was married at twelve to a thirteen-year-old boy, lives an intolerable life with him and his mother, has a pen pal in San Francisco, etc.). If I want to reach into the book even further, I describe Julie's fascinating attempts to communicate with the wolves. Sometimes I condense each incident and run them all together; sometimes one of them stands alone.

However you shape your talk, it is details that will keep it from sounding like just another recommendation by a well-meaning adult—details that stick in the listener's mind, niggling and jiggling until he or she just has to know how the story turns out. Pick curious details that the audience will automatically check against their own experience: the list of items in Julie's backpack ("Hmm, is that what I would have taken? Will it be enough?"); Elmer Elevator's list in *My Father's Dragon* ("What on earth is he going to do with twenty pink lollipops?") or the bizarre security precautions in Baker D.'s Slynack-proofed room in *Something's Waiting for You, Baker D.* The details you select must present a vivid mental picture to your audience, one which will last long enough to bring them into the library that very afternoon—or even two months later. Specific details will help *you*, too, for when you start talking, you'll discover that they bring that book alive for you again and rekindle your own memory and enthusiasm.

The most difficult material to work with is character description. The brevity of the standard booktalk drastically limits the depth of treatment possible. It's good to have some booktalking experience before you try this approach. But consider the opening of Richard Russo's booktalk on *Slake's Limbo:*

> Aremis Slake is the kind of person everyone picks on.
> He's small, wears glasses, and can't join any gangs because he always gets sick when he tries to smoke. Not belonging to a gang is bad news in the tough section of New York City where Slake lives; it means you're the one who gets bullied and beaten up. . . .

After this, you're interested in Slake, even before you learn that he will spend 121 days in the subway system—and you're on his side. A book like *Alan and Naomi*, with a plot that hinges on the psychology and interaction of two people, almost has to be introduced through character description; a talk on this title will not work unless you have established who these people are and what unusual circumstances bring them together. In using the character approach, however, be aware that a fictional problem may be a real problem for someone in the audience. Once you've talked about a character who's fat, or maybe smells, and have seen all eyes swivel to one embarrassed face, you'll never make that mistake again.

When you've decided on your general approach and have selected some details to include, you're ready to start developing the booktalk. The beginning and the end are the parts that require the most thorough planning. There is no time for wasting words; you must intrigue the listener with the first sentence. "Janet had a job after school, but it wasn't baby-sitting . . . " (*Baby Needs Shoes* by Dale Carlson, booktalk by Laurie Peck). "Have you ever wished you could find the secret of everlasting life?" (*Tuck Everlasting*, by Natalie Babbitt) or, for the same book, "*Tuck Everlasting* includes a kidnapping, a murder, and a jailbreak—and even those are not as exciting as the secret that Winnie Foster shares only with the Tuck family" (booktalk by Diana McRae). Each of these beginnings is very different: one hints at mystery, one asks a question, one give a thumbnail sketch of the plot. All, however, put the listener right into the middle of things in a very few words.

Some booktalkers begin on a personal note. "Last spring after that small earthquake I began to wonder what I would do if I really had to survive on my own," says Carol Starr as she introduces *Z for Zachariah*. "I always *hated* poetry" may convince those who feel the same way to stay with you a little longer. If you feel comfortable with this approach, it can be a smooth, informal, and effective way to allow the audience to accompany you into a book. But don't force yourself to speak personally if it's not natural to you. If it doesn't work, you run the risk of sounding phony and patronizing. If it does work, it can't be beat, as this classic shows:

> When I was little, my parents were reluctant to take me out to dinner. I wasn't a brat, but I did prefer unusual food—well, actually, the hot dogs I ordered were normal enough; it was the peanut butter I insisted be put on the hot dogs that caused the problem. . . . now, looking back, I can see that my eating habits *were* a bit strange. But compared to Billy Forrester's, my tastes were positively normal. *He* ate worms! It all began with a bet. . . .

Beckie Brazell goes on to conclude her booktalk with a brief description of the plot of *How to Eat Fried Worms* and a few recipes. And adds, "Yes, they always ask if I still eat peanut butter on my hot dogs. The answer is, Yes, but not in public."

Once you're over the hurdle of the introductory sentences, move quickly to the body of the talk and develop the incident, storyline, or character you've selected. Describe it vividly but succinctly. The average booktalk is at most five minutes long, which leaves room for only the essential details. The body of the talk may be as long as one or two paragraphs; as with YA talks, there is no hard-and-fast rule as to how much of the story you tell, as long as you don't tell the ending. In discussing *Harriet the Spy,* I describe the loss and discovery of Harriet's notebook, while I have heard someone else give a terrific booktalk on nothing but Harriet's spy outfit. It's always better to focus on one particularly fascinating aspect of the book than to throw in *everything* and risk confusing your listeners or getting bogged down yourself in the intricacies of the plot. Remember that the ultimate storyteller is the author. With booktalks that run more than five minutes (at the most), you are in danger of presenting your own version of the story rather than the author's, or of turning the booktalk into an entertaining mini-story complete in itself, rather than a "hook" that will entice others to read.

With a beginning and middle established, go back and read what you've written out loud. If you bore or confuse yourself, you'll certainly do the same to your audience. I find this is also the point at which my writing style gets softened a bit, so that it becomes more colloquial and easier to listen to:

> . . . That Hairy Man was sure ugly, hairy all over; his eyes burned like coals, his teeth were big and sharp and white, and he was swinging a sack. Wiley was so scared, he quickly climbed a tree. "What's in your big old sack?" he asked the Hairy Man. "Nothing, yet," said the Hairy Man. . . . [*Wiley and the Hairy Man,* by Molly Bang]

The ending is just important as the beginning and should be worked out carefully beforehand. Don't just flounder to a stop; the audience need to know that you're winding up. They may want to write down the title of that terrific book; you, of course, should make it easy for them by repeating the title and the author's name. Occasionally you can cleverly work the title into the last sentence: "Will he be stuck forever in a dog's body?" (*Dogsbody*). "Listen to them, in *Listen to Us!.*"

But too many clever endings can be distracting, and the audience may begin to anticipate them instead of listening to the meat of the talk. It's perfectly acceptable to end with a simple sentence and a plain repetition of the author's name and the title. A good device—one that throws the initiative back to the listeners—is to end with a question: "Is there something wrong with Emma and Willie—or with their parents?" (*Nobody's Family Is Going to Change,* by Louise Fitzhugh). "Would Irene be the fifth Mrs. Berry to meet with an unfortunate accident?" (*Johnny May,* by Robbie Branscum).

And so you've got a booktalk! Quick, use it! Try out the first few sentences while you're doing reader's advisory work on the floor or recommending books to a colleague. You may be surprised at the enthusiastic response, and that will make it easier to use the talk again, and to start working on the next one.

Like Joni, I recommend saving your booktalk somehow. I file away the written version; other people file their notes or record their talks on cassettes. A collection of booktalks makes it much easier to prepare the next presentation, and gives you extra time for writing new talks. But remember that a booktalk is not frozen forever just because it has been recorded on tape or on paper. It will change: with time, with the audience, and with your own changing state of mind. Sometimes what has always worked before will fall flat; sometimes an ad-lib from you or a child will result in a change that you'll want to keep; sometimes just looking at your work anew will suggest a fresh approach. As you build your repertoire, you will also discard some titles from your book-talk file, just as you do from your shelves, when interests and trends change or when the books themselves become dated.

Planning a Program for Children

When you've prepared one booktalk, you can prepare another—and another. But sooner or later, you have to stand in front of a real group and deliver them. Chapters 3 and 4 describe in detail the most impor-tant factors in preparing and practicing your delivery of a booktalk. I would like to concentrate here on putting together a whole program and adapting it to the needs of various age groups. I will also suggest ways to vary the standard program and discuss the very first step of all—getting yourself invited into a classroom.

A good booktalk program can be as short as fifteen minutes or as long as forty-five. With any short presentation, the key to success is making sure that absolutely every book is one that you yourself love—and then allowing that enthusiasm to show. My own introduction to booktalking came through what the Alameda County Library System calls "school blitzing," in which the children's staff would visit each class in every elementary school at the end of the school year to discuss summer programs. Booktalks were included as an important incentive for using the library in the summer. At any time of year, a blitz-type program is a great way to test the waters and introduce yourself as a booktalker. You can be simple and direct: introduce yourself, the pub-lic library (kids love to give other kids directions to the library), and make sure everybody knows that the card is *free*. Then all you need to add is that you've brought some of your favorite books, or some new books you'd like to tell them about, or some books that will give them ideas of what to look for next time they're in the library, and you're off.

As you expand your allotted time, variety and pacing become important; here's where you add two more very traditional children's librarian's techniques: "flashing" or the mini- (often mini-mini-) booktalk, and storytelling. Both are skills you've probably been developing since the first day you worked at a public library.

Flashing

Flashing, or giving a mini-booktalk, occurs almost spontaneously as you respond to the query, "I want a *good* book." Sometimes it's as easy as literally flashing an appealing title (*Monsters From the Movies* or *The Reggie Jackson Story* or *Karen Heppelwhite Is the World's Best Kisser*) or one that that's already established on the children's own grapevine (*Tales of a Fourth-Grade Nothing, The Cat Ate My Gymsuit, Charlie and the Chocolate Factory*). More often, you need one or two brief sentences: "When her uncle beats her brother and almost kills him, Nell throws a pitchfork at him; now she's on the run" (*To the Tune of a Hickory Stick,* by Robbie Branscum). "If you liked *Freaky Friday,* here's another story about Annabel, her best friend Boris, and her brother ApeFace" (*A Billion for Boris,* by Mary Rodgers). Full-fledged booktalks pack a lot of information and excitement into five minutes or so, and you hope that the listeners will get so caught up that they will *have* to read the book. These mini-talks are less intense; they give both the listener and booktalker a chance to relax a bit and handle a wider variety of materials in a more casual way. They also offer the opportunity to highlight special-interest materials and a lot of nonfiction, that you can't hope to interest everyone in: electronics experiments, motorcycle books, gymnastics, etc. There are many handsome nonfiction titles that need only be held up, while the pages are slowly turned. Using these "teaser" methods in a formal presentation makes it possible to vary both the pace and content of the program, and to include many more titles than you can with the standard booktalk format. Any program longer than ten or fifteen minutes will surely include a lot of this sort of flashing.

Storytelling

Storytelling is one of the most powerful tools a children's librarian has. It should be obvious that the storyteller's experience in recreating incidents and characters in front of an audience provides terrific training for a booktalker, and also heightens one's awareness of the turns of phrase and pacing that will create the most immediate visual picture. But storytelling recreates an entire incident; booktalking never does. Yet storytelling in conjunction with booktalking can be the most effective way to get across the message you're bringing: the pleasure of reading, and the amazing variety of information, good reading, and fun that can be found in the public library. The addition of storytelling gives those children who don't have much reading background the chance to experience first-hand just what is meant by "the pleasure of reading." Here it is, live: the characters, excitement, humor, self-recognition, and rich language that can be yours anytime you open a good book. Storytelling gives a child reasons for becoming a reader. A good story can also break up the repetitive frustration of *never* telling, or hearing, the ending. A story after a string of booktalks acknowledges that the appetite to read has been whetted enough; it's fun for everyone to relax at the end with something they can take away whole.

Combinations for Different Age Levels

Booktalking, flashing, and storytelling each have a place in a program for children; together, they provide variety of materials, welcome changes of pace, the richness of shared reading pleasure, and the impetus to follow up on books independently. How and in what proportions you combine these three techniques depends on the individual audience. Yet there are a few age and grade generalizations that may prove helpful.

— Preschool

We want preschoolers to become readers; we don't expect them to be readers already. In order to read well, they must first develop a listening vocabulary, and so we tell them lots and lots of good stories. Music and stretch activities also have a place here, in working with preschoolers' limited attention span, and in offering a wide range of language and listening experiences.

—Kindergarten and First Grade

Of course you tell stories and read pictures books here, lots of them. But booktalking can start at this age, as long as you keep it all simple, and never more than about a third of the program. Easy readers can make wonderful booktalks, like this one by Diana McRae on *Detective Mole*:

> Detective Mole had just graduated from detective school when Mrs. Chicken asked him for help with their ghosts. Spooky voices were calling out every night, "Don't make your children each spinach; don't send your children to school." I wonder if any of you can guess who those ghosts turned out be be. Read this book, and find out if Detective Mole is as smart as you. . . .

Don't be surprised if at this age kids don't recognize the difference between booktalks and storytelling and come in asking to hear the story of Detective Mole all over again. It's easy to oblige, and then show them that they can read more about Detective Mole on their own or with their parents. While the books you talk about and the stories you tell should introduce new titles, flashing books often involves reminding kids of the familiar—*Harry the Dirty Dog, Where the Wild Things Are,* etc. To the newcomers, familiar titles make the library seem less strange, while the kids who are old hands usually enjoy the chance to show off their knowledge.

Booktalks for this age are very, very short.

> Have you ever called anyone "stupid"? Do you really know what that means? Well, this book will tell you for sure. . . . This family is called the Stupids because under a picture that looks like this [show picture of a fish] they write D O G, and when they want to take a bath they don't run any water into the tub because they're afraid they'll get their clothes wet [show picture] and that's only the beginning of their stupid ideas. Find out about all of them in *The Stupids Step Out,* by Harry Allard.

There should be plenty of talk about books for the children to practice their own reading on, but also talk about finding other people to read to them. No child should ever be made to feel that the library is only for readers.

— Second and Third Grades

This is the real transition stage between the dependence on storytelling in kindergarten and first grade and the heavy reliance on booktalking from the fourth grade up. Second- and third-graders continue to enjoy a great deal of reading out loud and storytelling, but they are definitely aware of the purpose of a booktalk and interested in hearing and following up on one. After introducing myself and the library, I usually start out by flashing a wide variety of books (up to ten), pick two or three for slightly longer talks, and then settle down into reading and telling stories for the last twenty minutes or so.

For this age the booktalks are still very short, all of the basic teaser type. "Phoebe was thirteen when she got her first job—as a spy! Read this true story to discover how Phoebe spotted her first murderer and saved George Washington's life" (*Phoebe and the General*). (Whenever a story is based on a true incident, I am careful to point this out; it seems to add an extra element of interest at any age.)

— Fourth Grade and Up

By the fourth grade, the general pattern of more booktalks than stories is established and remains fairly constant throughout junior high school, changing more to accommodate the teacher's or booktalker's own preference or inside knowledge than for any particular age/grade considerations. Storytelling continues to have a place here, for all the reasons originally suggested, but it is important to understand that this older audience may initially be leery about storytelling. You need to move the listeners beyond their "Three little pigs" notions immediately. Rather than sprinkle stories throughout the program, as I might in the younger grades, I usually pick one and save it for the "dessert" at the end. I hope there's been some good hard listening going on, and this finale is a way to enjoy together one last story and let everyone relax a bit. A basic upper-grade program will usually begin with a brief introduction (who I am, where the library is, it's *free,* etc.) and then open with three to five good basic booktalks (about fifteen minutes' worth). A five- to ten-minute interlude of flashing titles and giving mini-booktalks leads on to two or three longer talks and then a story. Announcements of specific library programs may come with the introduction or be saved until the end.

While you're planning the program, you should also consider how you want to handle the issue of reserves. Although I used to take reserve postcards with me to use in any class from fourth grade on up, I have stopped doing this in the elementary grades. It was not unusual to leave a classroom with over forty reserves, and no matter how well we'd planned for extra copies, we couldn't predict exactly which titles would be the hot ones. We began to feel that the reserve cards just raised everyone's expectations too high. When you simply invite the kids to come to the library after school, you've got a better chance of knowing how long a wait they're really facing and of suggesting a good substitute title. By now most of the children with whom I work have had a great deal of experience with our easy and reliable reserve system, and most live within walking distance of the library. In another situation, I might be more committed to taking reserves during every visit. I continue to do so in junior high classes, where interest in reading appears to drop off slightly and I want to do anything I can to reverse that trend.

Particularly in the older grades, it's a good idea to give some thought to how you will end your entire presentation. It's all too easy to peter out lamely "and that's all. . . . " Just as you restate the author's name and title at the end of every booktalk, remember to remind the class where these books are, and how to get them. If you're going to take reserves, explain this clearly and make sure kids know that even though you took their name, they may not be able to get a copy of the book they want today. Kids understand when this has been explained, but are very disappointed if you've raised their hopes too high—particularly if they don't realize that although they were the first to reserve the book in this class, others in a previous class may have signed up ahead of them. And as Joni has stressed, it's worthwhile to do everything you can to speed the loan of extra copies and to prepare the rest of the staff to suggest substitutes. Always leave a few minutes for questions at the end of the program, and time for kids to come to the front of the classroom and browse through the books on their own.

As you take these guidelines and work with them to choose the exact titles and plan the combination of booktalks you'll use, and as you prepare yourself for an appearance before a live audience, remember the basic principle of flexibility. Perhaps the teacher has misrepresented the average reading level of the class—bring along a couple of harder and easier titles just in case. Perhaps the teacher is reading aloud the very title you were going to start off with. Bring another one equally exciting. Perhaps there is a disproportionate number of boys or girls in the class (as Joni has pointed out, this does make a difference). A few extra books can help you adjust. Use your knowledge of the collection to give yourself some leeway as you plan your program.

Variations on the Standard Booktalk Presentation

Any program of well-thought-out and confidently presented book-talks is bound to be successful. Children have virtually no access to this kind of information, and as Jim Trelease says over and over again in his *Real Aloud Handbook* (which also makes a great selection tool), once children know what awaits them between the covers of a book, you've got them hooked. Yet no booktalk is forever fixed in one form; the art and techniques of booktalking can change too. Among the following suggestions are some that I have tried and some that I haven't (yet). There are times when experienced booktalkers are ready for more than just freshening their repertoire and want to think about experimenting with other styles, reevaluating their strengths, and expanding their range.

—Nonfiction

One of the first changes I ever made came several years into book-talking when I realized that I booktalked fiction, period. I always brought nonfiction titles with me and pointed them out, but I always counted on the subject or the illustrations to sell those books. I realized that nonfiction held more possibilities than this when I worked with Joan Ariel and heard her booktalk not only biographies (an obvious place to start) but also such things as travel guides, a science experiment book, and a book on holidays. Since then, although I continue to flash most nonfiction, I have slowly collected a variety of other formal and informal ways to present it. The most important consideration here is that fully developed nonfiction booktalks should make a subject interesting even to the nonenthusiast. Only a few students will want the name of "a new book on science experiments you can do at home." A lot more will be interested in "the wilderness and adventures you can find if you only go exploring indoors. . . . Did you know that there's a river that runs through your house, or that a murder may be happening every day among your houseplants?" These lines, from a booktalk by Joan Ariel on Linda Allison's *The Wild Inside,* show the same infectious enthusiasm and concern for lively, specific detail that characterize a good fiction booktalk. Nonfiction also lends itself to activities and participation. Magic books may be introduced by enticing lists of tricks—or by the trick itself. ("Do you think I can go through this catalog card?" is a particularly good one for librarians.) Books on UFO sightings, on ghosts or superstitions always yield good stories and can be the springboard for class discussion. Books of optical illusions and drawing guides can supply blackboard artwork; books on wild animals or household pets often yield unexpected and surprisingly entertaining facts, coupled with cunning and/or spectacular photographs.

Longer nonfiction booktalks can be built around titles for all ages. Tomie de Paola's *The Quicksand Book,* Jean Fritz's *And Then What Happened, Paul Revere?,* Seymour Simon's *Animal Facts, Animal Fables,* and Vicki Cobb's *Supersuits* are good titles for early elementary grades. *The Wild Inside; Wild Foods,* by Laurence Pringle; and *Cross Your Fingers, Spit in Your Hat* by Alvin Schwartz, are good for upper elementary listeners. Jim Murphy's *Weird and Wacky Inventions* can be introduced simply by getting kids to list inventors they've learned about in school; then a brief planned talk can suggest the number of unsung inventors, and the multiple choice format of the book can be adapted to a participation finale. Vicki Cobb's science/trick titles offer the opportunity to teach the group a simple trick ("Can you write your name *and* swing your foot in a circle at the same time?") and give kids a chance to stretch and share other tricks too. Often the interest you generate with such an activity gives you a chance to mention a few other titles too. Joke and riddle books suggest obvious breaks, that work well with all ages. Once you've tried describing a joke book ("You wouldn't believe all the funny riddles there are about dinosaurs . . . ") you'll be delighted to move on to the real thing: "What do you get when dinosaurs crash their cars? Tyrannosaurus wrecks; which is the title of this dinosaur riddle book by Noelle Sterne."

Nonfiction can also be effectively paired with fiction. Often a fiction title provides a good way of introducing a nonfiction title that might be tricky to booktalk in isolation. Either Orgel's *Devil in Vienna* or Haugaard's *Chase Me, Catch Nobody* can lead naturally into *The Diary of a Young Girl* or the more difficult *How Democracy Failed,* by Ellen Switzer. A book such as *The Upstairs Room,* by Johanna Reiss, which goes well with the previous titles, might then lead into *Nothing Is Impossible,* Margaret Aldis's intriguing biography of Beatrix Potter, who for very different reasons spent much of her childhood in an upstairs room.

The possibility of embarrassing individual listeners by mentioning intimate personal problems in your fiction booktalks has already been discussed. The potential for similar embarrassment is even greater with nonfiction. Even when no one else in the audience is aware of a particular difficulty, the child who suffers from it may think the whole world knows, and be not only embarrassed but resentful when the subject is brought up. I often bring *Listen to Us!* to junior high classes and introduce it by referring to some of the less serious topics, e.g., "What's the most embarrassing thing your parents ever did?" I say that it's the only book of its kind that's written by kids themselves—over a thousand of them, all between the ages of ten and sixteen. I list some of the other topics very quickly (divorce, dealing with bullies, parents in jail, living in an institution) but I don't focus on any one in particular.

A good way to introduce some of the more specific self-help books (like *Living with a Parent Who Drinks Too Much* or *Learning to Say Goodbye*) is to bring them along and display them prominently with other materials, without discussing them. Usually when I do this, I'll end up with one or two reserves on these titles; the kids (or the teachers) who need them have found them, but they've been allowed to do so on their own.

Broadening your approach to the use of nonfiction titles is more a change of selection habits than of technique, but as you begin to booktalk nonfiction, you may be surprised at its popularity. Imaginative, well-written nonfiction can be as much of a novelty to comfirmed readers as to reluctant readers.

— Reading Aloud and Dramatics

Many people combine the best of storytelling and booktalking into a booktalk that includes whole chunks of the book itself. The booktalk by Sherrill Kumler on *The Indian in the Cupboard* included in the booktalk section combines standard descriptive narrative with brief, well-selected excerpts.

Cindy Barnett, storyteller and literature consultant in Groveland, California, acts out dialogue in her booktalks. She prepares an extended script, which may or may not start off with a brief introduction. As she explains, "I have selectively omitted 'he said,' etc., and some other portions that I felt were unnecessary. . . . I try to become as familiar as I can with the passage I choose and try to get as much out of the words as possible to create a mood. For character changes, I use an interpretive reading technique known as 'off-stage focus.' This means that I look to the right (above the audience) for one character, left for another, etc." Here a storytelling background becomes particularly important; this is a sophisticated technique, not easy for everyone.

Jan Lieberman of the Division of Counseling Psychology and Education at the University of Santa Clara is the editor of *T'N'T,* a wonderful inexpensive newsletter on children's books. She has presented many books through Readers Theatre. She prepares several copies of a typed script ahead of time and selects children to act out the scene in front of their classmates. Good visual scenes with obvious opportunities for hamming it up make the best choice here, scenes that offer good roles for both girls and boys. Dialogue is taken almost verbatim from the book, and a narrator supplies continuity where it is needed.

Esther Woll, Marin County, California, uses a similar technique. She too prepares a script of dialogue betwen two or three minimally-identified characters, e.g., "a man," "a girl." While some children act out the script, the others try to identify the book and the characters. The trick here is to choose books that are already familiar—it's really a follow-up activity to other booktalks.

Peggy Tollefson, Alameda County Library System, is an accomplished puppeteer and slips booktalks into the mouths of her puppets during show intermissions.

—Teamwork

Teaming up with a colleague to visit classes is another effective technique. Preparation may be slightly reduced (but don't count on this); the main advantage comes from the extra energy and variety a second person can bring to the program. Two people have a richer pool of reading and other interests to draw on, and their different personal styles give the audience a built-in change of pace. While these advantages hold true for any age, they are particularly useful with the upper grades, especially junior high. In these classes, the program consists almost entirely of booktalks, and two faces are a good substitute for the variety that storytelling, reading aloud, and booktalking supply in the earlier grades. It is particularly effective to have a children's and YA staff member work as a team in the junior high classroom. The sixth-, seventh-, and eighth-graders have probably been seeing the children's librarian all through school and even before, in preschool storytime. The introduction of a young adult librarian is a concrete way of marking the transition to adulthood, acknowledging the kids' new maturity and their interest in moving beyond the children's collection.

When working with someone else, it's important to map out the program ahead of time, so that each person knows what to do when. I usually let the first person introduce the program and the booktalkers and then give three or four booktalks. The second person does another three booktalks and then flashes some more books informally. The first person comes back with a couple of mini-talks and moves on to one or two longer talks; the second person returns with a couple more and concludes. Team storytelling, which has been popularized recently by storytellers such as the Folktellers, Barbara Freeman and Connie Regan-Blake, is a great conclusion for a team presentation in the upper grades. Because it is so close to drama, it quickly convinces the reluctant listener that stories are not just for little kids.

As with any technique, you need to be comfortable with teamwork yourself, which means comfortable with your partner. Different styles may mean a more varied program, or one that never quite jells, depending on the ease of the partnership.

—Other Activities

Simple activities and visual displays can enhance many booktalks. Maps are a classic visual prop. You can point out the island of San Nicholas (*Island of the Blue Dolphins,*) or Haiti (*The Magic Orange Tree*). You can show or pass around objects from different times or different places, to make the unfamiliar more tangible and intriguing. Pam Kloiber, Western Heights Junior High, Oklahoma, brings a horseshoe to show after her booktalk for *Superstitious? Here's Why.* She also uses food in her programs (in appropriate ways—after talking about *Superstitious? Here's Why* she gives away apples so her audience won't have to see a doctor.) She points out that a toaster oven is portable, clean, safe for student use, and can bake just about anything. While a snack is baking, another booktalk can be going on.

The list of booktalk-related activities could go on and on. A particularly good source is Caroline Bauer, whose three books, *Handbook for Storytellers, This Way to Books,* and *Celebrations* are chock-full of creative dramatics, puppet booktalks, and other ideas—even directions for a working volcano! She also includes examples of entire programs, from beginning to end, giving all the transitions from one book/story/ activity to the next.

Remember, though, if you're thinking of stylistic innovation, to look for something that *you* enjoy and feel comfortable with. You can't go cooking up a storm if you feel self-conscious doing it, any more than you can wholeheartedly talk up a book or tell a story that you don't like.

And even though we're all ruefully aware of the short attention spans we face, I recommend that you resist the inclination to tart things up *too* much. A good booktalk *is* fun to listen to. One sketch on the blackboard, or two or three short jokes or riddles, or one magic trick is enough to provide a quick change of pace without distracting from the other booktalks. Remember, you're introducing books—not yourself as a performer. As a new booktalker, you may be particularly tempted to use some of these ideas to expand a program, but you'll probably be better served by first becoming thoroughly familiar with the basic techniques. Relying too heavily on theatrics may result in trivializing your most significant contribution—your knowledge of a variety of good books, and your well-developed ability to share this knowledge.

Finding an Audience

In my experience, teachers are eager to schedule booktalking sessions, but of course they have to know about them first. Letters to the teachers (with copies to the principal and school librarian) can introduce the program and invite teachers to contact you. A short presentation at a faculty meeting can introduce you, the library's services, and booktalking in the most effective way of all—with a few good booktalks.

Before you do this, however, it's important to consider just what your own capabilities are. How much booktalking can you handle in your schedule? What other responsibilities do you have to maintain? Preschool storytimes, book reviewing, contacts with day care and after-school groups, meetings and other administrative duties all require not only attendance time but planning too. Can you cut back on some of these while you concentrate on building a class visit program, or must you be cautious in the number of class visit appointments you make? My ideal has always been to visit every public school class twice a year—once for a booktalk program and once for the end-of-school "blitzing." This was possible when I made school visiting the top priority, but when other commitments began to claim more time, I had to reorder things. Recently I have been targeting specific grades (k, 2, 4, 6, 8) for booktalk visits, and letting teachers of other grades know that they are welcome to make their own individual requests, which I will accommodate when possible. Other situations may suggest focusing on one or more specific schools (the closest, or the farthest away, or perhaps the one with the lowest rate of library use). If you're just starting out at this kind of programing, it is sensible and reassuring to set modest goals.

When you're clear about just what and how much you're offering, work with your school contacts to make the actual appointments. School librarians and principals are the most obvious contacts, but if you want to try your wings in just one or two classes at first, consider all the other acquaintances a children's librarian makes. The teacher who always asks for ideas or warns you of a major assignment, the avid library user or preschool storytime parent who's also a classroom aide, the enthusiastic parent—any of these can get you an invitation to their own, or their child's, classroom. Most school librarians, when available, are delighted to help arrange a visit; remember to acknowledge this with generous references to the school as well as the public library. Good relations here may lead to later teamwork.

Scheduling

You may decide to take teachers and their classes as they come—a sixth grade here, a kindergarten there. Or you may want to tackle a whole school, with the full range of three to six or more different grades. This is fine as long as scheduling permits adequate preparation. If preparation time is short, however, or if you want to start gradually, consider scheduling a block of same-grade visits. This will allow you to use the same booktalks and stories in several classes and build your repertoire grade by grade. Remember, remember, remember, that no matter how much booktalking you've done, it remains a time-consuming activity. You need to allow yourself adequate time to prepare, not only to write new booktalks but also to read new books (or reread old ones). Although all of us are rushed at times, overscheduling shows up quickly in not-quite-right booktalks and a falling-off in enthusiasm and confidence.

The actual scheduling may be handled one-to-one over the telephone or through a note. When visiting one whole school or set of grades, I usually draw up a sign-up sheet to be placed in the staff room or circulated at staff meetings or from room to room. In this way, time conflicts can be worked out among the teachers themselves. When using this scheduling method, think carefully about the times you are available and say so clearly. Don't just hope teachers will spread themselves out conveniently. You should also be clear about whether you're inviting classes to the library or yourself to the classroom—or whether either is fine. The class trip to the library is easier on the librarian and has the obvious advantage of allowing children to check out books on the spot, but the distance between school and library may be too great for walking and buses unavailable for field trips. Scheduling the same grades one class after another into the library also has the drawback of causing the corresponding part of the collection to disappear. If this is your scheduling plan, you may want to leave a few days between visits so that the collection can build up again and you can pick out a few books to highlight.

Visiting a Classroom

Once you've wangled an invitation to a classroom and have prepared a booktalk program, many of your remaining concerns will be purely practical, and most are covered in Chapters 4, 5, and 6. Know where the school is, and then leave plenty of time for locating the classroom and setting up your books. Like Joni, I advocate drawing up a checklist of items to take along—you probably won't forget your books, but it's easy to think so much about them that you forget other materials. If you're planning to utilize reserve cards, bring extra pencils or pens. (These shouldn't be hard to find in a classroom, but you'd be surprised how much time can be wasted while kids stand in line for two pens.)

Most of the librarians I know use a sturdy cardboard box or heavy canvas bag to carry their books and supplies. Some have used suitcases with luggage wheels. Judie Smith and Barbara Hardy of Pleasanton, California, have gone a step further: they have a portable folding luggage cart with stretchy cords that can tie down boxes or bookbags (holds up to 250 pounds). Their cart has been particularly useful when they've had to walk long distances, such as across a large parking lot. But be careful not to bring more books than you can physically handle; you'll still need to find space to display them all.

As soon as you arrive, it's good to check on exactly how much time you have to talk and adjust your plan accordingly; there may be a special reason why you need to be through five or ten minutes before the period ends. If you're planning to take reserves or to allow some time for browsing, make sure you figure this into your calculations. In most cases, teachers will be delighted to see you and will do everything they can to help out. But there are occasional exceptions—be prepared to introduce yourself and to commandeer your own space for setting up, if you have to. I try to set up the books where I can reach them easily as I begin each talk; as I end, I often place the book I've been talking about on the ledge of the blackboard.

Alternatives

Occasionally you may encounter real stumbling blocks to working in (or with) the schools. If none of the above suggestions works, it may be time to think of all the other places/times for your program. "Good books—find them here!" might work as a short regular Saturday morning or after-school program in the library, or as a quick end or beginning to a regular film or story program. Scouts and other youth groups are usually delighted to find someone willing to bring a program to their meetings, and of course day care and other after-school programs abound in almost every community. Many of these groups do have transportation problems; decide ahead of time whether and when you are willing to go to them instead of having them come to the library.

A number of librarians have experimented with making booktalks available on tape in the library. Rita Wilson, school librarian at Travis Air Force Base, California, uses a tape recorder to give students a chance to record their own booktalks. Pam Kloiber requires that each of her student library aides prepare and videotape a booktalk. These recordings are stored in the library and can be played back whenever another student is looking for "something good to read."

Conclusion

And so you're off. It's easy to assume that once you've started, you'll just keep booktalking as much and as long as you want. Of course, that isn't always so. Changes in the curriculum, overdependence of teachers on the booktalker to make initial arrangements, personnel changes in the teaching or administrative staff in school or library, are just some of the factors that can slow down a well-established program. If you do hit a dry spell, letters to the faculty, along with a new booklist, or just person-to-person contact in the library ("I've missed seeing your class this year, and I know some good new books I'd like to talk about") may start things going again. Try not to waste time berating yourself. My experience is that if you're really terrible, you know it right away, and the time to start improving is the very next class. If you've been booktalking for a while and generally enjoying it, if you've been conscientious about adding new material, you needn't agonize over occasional and inevitable slumps. Remind people of the service, and pep yourself up, too, by making sure you've got some good new material so that you can be as enthusiastic as when you first started.

Which is where we started. Booktalk books you enjoy, and enjoy the booktalking you do. Remember that booktalking is a complicated skill that requires continual polishing, time, and energy to keep fresh. You may find yourself described, as I once was, as "the lady who's read all the books in the library but never has time to finish them"!—but you will also find that all those books are being read and ultimately booktalked again and again by the most effective booktalkers of all—your satisfied listeners!

Selection Tools

Much has been written on the subject of selecting books for children. The sources below are some of the more current and are readily available through public libraries.

Bauer, Caroline F. *Celebrations.* Wilson 1985.

_____. *Handbook for Storytellers.* ALA 1977.

_____. *This Way to Books.* Wilson 1983.

Elleman, Barbara *Popular Reading for Children: A Collection of "Booklist" Columns.* ALA 1981.

Hearne, Betsy. *Choosing Books for Children: A Commonsense Guide.* Delacorte 1981.

Huck, Charlotte. *Children's Literature in the Elementary School,* 3rd ed. rev. Holt 1979.

Kimmel, Mary Margaret and Segal, Elizabeth.*For Reading Out Loud!: A Guide to Sharing Books With Children.* Delacorte. 1983.

Lieberman, Jan, ed. *T'N'T (Tips 'n' Titles).* Newsletter published three times a year; available for one dollar (cash or stamps; no checks) and three self-addressed stamped envelopes from Jan Lieberman, Division of Counseling Psychology and Education, University of Santa Clara, CA 95953.

Norton, Donna. *Through the Eyes of a Child.* Merrill 1983.

Sutherland, Zena. *Children and Books.* Scott, Foresman 1981.

Trelease, Jim. *The Read-Aloud Handbook.* Penguin 1982.

CHAPTER **8**

BOOKTALKING FROM THE SCHOOL LIBRARIAN'S PERSPECTIVE

or, Selling Snake Oil to the Masses

By LARRY RAKOW

—Hey, hey, Mr. Librarian, what'cha got for us today?

—Hey, hey, Mr. Student, I've got books to dazzle your mind, alleviate the grind, and help you unwind! I've got stories as fresh as tomorrow's headlines! I've got tales to curdle your blood and chill your bones! I've got love stories so tender they'd make a quarterback cry! I've got a little bit of this and a little bit of that, but I have one book whose story just won't wait, so I'm going to tell it to you right now!

Long ago, long before marijuana and LSD became household words, powerful mind-altering drugs were given to college students and members of the military as part of psychological experiments carried out by the government to assess these substances as potential weapons of war. That's *true!* Now, *Firestarter* is not a true story, but it's based, at least in part, on real incidents that occurred in this country during the wild and woolly Sixties. When the book opens, two students—Andy McGee and his girlfriend, Vicki—are taking part in just such an experiment. They've been given a drug that's described as being a thousand times more powerful than LSD. . . .

I'm really rolling! Part snake-oil salesman, part shaman, part cheerleader, and part educator, I'm doing what I do best: hawking books in an electronic age, selling airplane tickets to astronauts. I use every device at my command, every gimmick that Madison Avenue drilled into me during countless hours of *Bonanza, The Untouchables,* and *The*

Twilight Zone, to reach kids with the truth about reading. That it's exciting. That it's tough. That it can be your best friend in hard times. That it's worth the effort.

There are several popular canards that have retarded the attempts of many school librarians to become active booktalkers. First, most of us working at the secondary level suffer from the misconception that junior and senior high school students are too old to be told stories. Pity our kids! It's been years since anyone sat them on a knee and spun fantastic yarns, or told them a bedtime tale, or took them to a library story-hour. Television fills the gap for most of them: a nonstop storyteller that makes up in quantity what it lacks in quality. I harbor an irrational faith that any librarian who loves books and loves kids can learn to tell stories better than a TV. Can you meet these criteria?

Second, we should dispel the notion that unrestricted reading occupies a lower rung on the educational ladder than school-directed reading. Ask a school librarian to describe the primary function of the library and you'll probably hear, "To provide materials in support of the school curriculum. Mr. James teaches biology and needs a good book on the digestive system of the earthworm. That's easy; I'll check an AAAS booklist and see what's available. Ms. Fisher teaches American history and has asked for a supplementary text on the causes of the Civil War. No problem; let's see what's recommended in the *High School Catalog.* Math is tough, but I have my ways, and religion is rougher yet. Mo matter; each is important, so I'll have to pinch pennies and make sure I have a balanced, representative collection that responds to teachers' requests and 'supports the curriculum.'

"Richard Peck? Judy Blume? Stephen King? Rosa Guy? I'm certain no teacher of mine ever requested them, and besides, no one said that recreational reading is part of the high school curriculum. Did they?"

Call it self-preservation, but I still believe in the power of the written word. And I believe that a student who is motivated to read S. E. Hinton (or Harry Mazer, or . . .) today will be qualified to choose what he wants to read tomorrow. I try to make reading, *all* reading, a major focus in my library. Students know that, and they respond by reading all kinds of books: classics, contemporary fiction, poetry, and nonfiction, as well as "fun stuff." Leisure reading is not only a part of the school curriculum, it is both its starting and ending point. Kids who can't or don't read outside of school will resent and resist being forced to read inside it. One of the purposes of traditional public education in this country has been to turn out educated readers, to provide a basis for lifelong learning. Reading is an important survival skill, not only during the school years but before and after them as well. Ask anyone who can't.

Most school librarians don't have to be convinced of the efficacy of recreational reading as a remedy for general school blahs, but many still feel chained to their circulation desks, and with good reason. The federal monies that flowed into school libraries during the 1960s have long since dried up, leaving cutbacks in personnel and materials in their wake. Most school libraries are staffed by individual librarians, responsible for everything from filing catalog cards to ordering projector bulbs. The third stumbling block, then, is a practical one: How can I booktalk outside my library when I'm its only staff member?

Close it down. Or invite classes in and close it to others (if that makes you feel better). Look at it this way: you've already identified booktalking as an essential part of the library program; the fact that you're understaffed is a given fact-of-life, and you're not likely to get more help until you've become absolutely essential to your colleagues and the administration. Booktalking is assertive. It reaches out to the classroom teachers, to kids, and to your supervisors in ways that answering a difficult reference question never can. It expands the traditional role of the librarian and centers attention on you and your place in the school community. Talk to your principal, honestly and openly; list the benefits that booktalking will produce for students and faculty. Help the administration see booktalking as a vital component of the educational program. Get them on your side. If they're concerned about community or professional reactions to a closed library (assuming that you are the sole librarian), offer to start small. Close one period per week and publicize the closing as a special on-going event well in advance. After a while, people may begin asking why you have to close the library in order to booktalk to kids. Tell them. You can't possibly be in two places at once. If enough people with enough influence like the job(s) you are doing, they may see their way clear to a solution: a call for more aides, student help, parent volunteers, teacher relief, or even (gasp!) another librarian.

Finally, the "overworked" excuse is almost as popular as the "understaffed" one. I'm talking about students, mind you, not librarians. In our school, for instance, it's in vogue to point out that the kids are given so much homework that they "have no time for outside reading." This excuse makes everybody look good: the teachers are earning their salaries; the administration appears tough and committed to traditional values; and the students seem earnest and hardworking. How ironic that the truth should conceal a lie! For while our teachers, students, and administrators are all that we claim, our kids *are* reading. Yours probably are too. They read what we read when we want to relax, mostly good trash: romances, science fiction, gothics, horror stories,

YA problem novels, and sexy bestsellers. Sometimes they read things that you can't even find in libraries (at least not in the Midwest). Often what teachers and librarians really mean when they gleefully boast that their students have no time to read is that they don't read great literature. It becomes a question of semantics. Fortunately, we educators are not required to divulge our private reading preferences in front of our peers. Otherwise, many of us would profess to be "too busy to read" too.

> . . . Strange and horrifying things happen to most everyone who takes this drug! Some go immediately crazy and have to be institutionalized for the rest of their lives, others commit suicide by jumping out tenth-story windows, and a few become so self-abusive that they tear their eyeballs out and their skin off! Yet others survive—not unscathed, but they survive. That happens to Andy and Vicki. Andy develops a strange new power through which he can influence the way that people behave by "pushing" with his mind. Vicki, on the other hand, becomes psychokinetic; she can move objects by using her brain-power alone! In time, Andy and Vicki get married and they have a child, Charlene, Charlie they call her. When Charlie is still an infant, her parents realize that she has been born with a unique talent: she can start fires by willing them to happen. She is pyrokinetic! . . .

There are a thousand reasons why school librarians don't booktalk. We're like the abused wife on the radio program I heard this morning who patiently explained why she stays with her husband, even though he's beaten her for fifteen years. Irritated, the radio psychologist blurted out, "I don't want to hear all the reasons you can't do things that are good for you!" Booktalking is good for you! More than that, it's good for your students, your teachers, and your school. It's healthy for students to perceive us as something other than file clerks and trivia-mongers, and exciting for fellow teachers to recognize that we're able to hold a class's rapt attention in a room other than our own. A non-threatening booktalk can help build good relationships with students unfamiliar with libraries and the services they provide. Many students' worst enemy is boredom, and your enthusiasm, for books or anything else, can be contagious. Scared? Join the club. Unaccustomed to public speaking? Only one way to get over it.

It is not as though we're among enemies. Booktalking in schools has long been the public YA librarian's turf, the method for introducing students and teachers to local library resources; it makes sense to view the public librarian as a strong potential ally rather than as an intruder. If you're new at classroom visiting, you might plan some joint forays; the YA specialist probably knows the territory. If neither of you has had much experience booktalking, you can provide sympathetic support for each other. There is strength in numbers! Drop by the public library and introduce yourself; you may be glad you did.

As a school librarian, you possess certain keys to success that a public librarian couldn't beg, borrow, or steal. You know the curriculum. You are a member of the faculty (with all the rights and privileges appertaining thereto). You eat lunch with other teachers and may even see them socially. You maintain a close relationship with many of the students; some may work with you in the library. Perhaps you've cultivated the principal's ear. You may sit on faculty committees or help prepare reports for the Board of Education. You're a member of The Team in a way that an outsider, even a well-intentioned one, can never hope to be. Cultivate these relationships and use the power that has been handed to you.

How do you begin? Maybe you find yourself in a situation similar to one I was in several years ago: a good school with good students being taught by good teachers who had not read a book written for adolescents since they themselves were teenagers. The first remedy I attempted was an inservice meeting for the English faculty, an informal lecture entitled, "A Brief History of YA Literature." Ken Donelson and Alleen Pace Nilsen's excellent text, *Literature for Today's Young Adults* (Scott, Foresman, 1980), provided the background for the presentation, but the historical focus was a smokescreen. It permitted me to contrast the past and present (with a heavy emphasis on the present); it allowed me to booktalk some of my favorite YA titles.

The English teachers liked my talk. I felt like an archaeologist, having unearthed a body of literature of which they were only dimly aware. Shortly thereafter, solicitations began to appear in my message box, invitations to present my talk, or something like it, to their students.

The "something like it" was the hard part. Shortly, every student in the school had heard my "Brief History . . . " at least once and were clamoring for more; history teachers had been apprised by their colleagues in the English department and were petitioning for equal time; even the school principal had made rumblings about "booktalks at the annual teachers' luncheon." Success can be mighty gratifying, but so can an orderly reference desk in a quiet corner of the library. How can a person balance the two?

. . . Charlie wreaks havoc in her neighborhood. A visiting child attempts to take her teddy bear and winds up with his hair on fire, and the same almost happens to Andy and Vicki when they try to reprimand her. They attempt to control her through operant conditioning: whenever they see their daughter about to use her power, they shout, "Charlie, don't do that or we won't love you anymore!" It works. But Charlie grows up a very conflicted young girl. On the one hand, she has an overwhelming desire to use her bizarre power; on the other, she desperately wants to retain her parents' love. She's able to keep her desire in check . . . until she becomes a young teenager. As normal physical changes develop, so does the magnitude of her power—five-, ten-, a hundred-fold—until the secret agents of the U.S. govemment, men who have been tracking the survivors of the original experiment for all these years, realize that Charlie could stare at the sun and cause it to go supernova! They know that they have but two choices: they either have to capture Charlie and train her to become the most awesome weapon in the arsenal of the United States . . . or they have to eliminate her. If she falls into the hands of the enemy, the whole ball game's over! . . .

Organizational skills are the hallmark of a good librarian, so use your talents well. Color-code your calendar; mark booktalks in bright red to avoid overscheduling yourself. Roll into the classroom with a full truck of books, *and* with checkout cards, date-due stamp, and ink pad. Claim your captives at the battle site! Check your books out as soon as you finish your talks—immediate gratification for both you and your students. Multiple paperback copies give everyone a fair shot at the prize title, but bring lots of good books and be prepared to give impromptu ten-second booktalks to the losers. Other titles by the booktalked authors can help ease their anguish too.

Plant your seeds early in the year, but don't spread yourself too thin. Address one department meeting each fall, present booktalks specifically for that subject area, and express a willingness to help department members and their students in any way you can. Distribute current subject bibliographies and bookmarks highlighting recent acquisitions in their field. Handouts have a life of their own; they either hit the garbage immediately or are jealously treasured and turned to year after year. Your public will let you know when you're doing a good job. So will your circulation records.

It's a sad fact that some teachers don't read. It's a happy fact that most teachers do. But even the best of teachers is hard-pressed to keep abreast of new materials in his or her field. Librarians accept this task for others; as materials specialists, we help shape curriculum as well as inspire readers. Teachers and librarians, working together, can create curricular units that neither could achieve alone. Establishing realistic limits helps guarantee successful collaborations. Do you need three weeks to prepare a set of nonfiction booktalks on pulsars, quasars, and black holes for your science teacher? Say so, straight out! Are Thursdays your chosen booktalk day? Spread the word! Teachers deserve reciprocal courtesy: their schedules are as tight as yours. Approach colleagues with booktalking ideas well in advance of the presentation date. Most teachers will welcome you with open arms, especially if you've worked well together before, but never lose sight of the fact that you are performing in *their* classrooms. Avoid an us/them approach that tacitly puts the teacher down ("Aren't these books fun compared to the dreck you're reading in this joker's class?"). You're an invited guest, so act like one.

Keep your supervisors updated on what you are doing and why, the measures you've taken to implement your program, and the results, tangible and perceived. If your circulation has doubled during the last year as a direct result of your booktalking, make sure the principal and library supervisor hear about it! Note the number of talks you've presented and the number of students addressed in your annual report. Prepare a program for your PTA or PTO; parents appreciate knowing the new materials available through the school library.

Flushed with victory, you may be tempted to repeat your first successes over and over again. Move ahead! There are innumerable ways to integrate booktalks into the school library program:

• Booktalk reference books. I introduce the *Reader's Guide* to classes as honestly as I can: "Some books in the library are significant and others are trivial. Some are exciting and others are dull. The *Reader's Guide to Periodical Literature* falls within the main category 'Important' and the subcategory 'Boring.' It's one of those books you must know how to use to succeed in high school, but I can't make it sound like fun. . . . "

• Use booktalking to liven up your annual orientation sessions. Sandwich a booktalk in between your explanation of the Dewey Decimal System and the card catalog, right when everyone needs a lift.

• Give a booktalking tour of the library. Select one outstanding book from each major classification as an introduction to the nonfiction collection.

• Develop multimedia booktalks. A local school librarian worked with a teacher in her building who had been awarded an Accelerated Learning Grant. Sets of paperback books were purchased, and students were divided into groups. Each group prepared a booktalk and presented it to other classes in the school. Their talks were audiotaped, and the tapes and sets of books were housed in the library. Other school librarians have used lists such as YASD's "Best Books for Young Adults" as the basis for annual slide-tape presentations. Each book jacket is photographed, a brief synopsis is taped, and the whole is edited into a self-contained unit, complete with projector and sync-recorder, that can travel to classrooms, be set up in the library, or be featured at meetings without the librarian's being present.

• Try your hand at extemporaneous booktalking. Grab the seven or eight kids who never seem to have anything to do in the library, drag them into your office or the library classroom or a quiet corner, pick a few familiar titles off a nearby shelf, and booktalk them into submission. It can't hurt to try.

• Combine library displays, school holidays, bibliographies, handouts, and booktalks for a total assault on blasé reading attitudes. Personalize the library; feature rotating displays of admired teachers' favorite books. Booktalk trashy romances during prom week. Include bookmarks listing new acquisitions with each check-out. Hang up a copy of every promotional bulletin or bibliography you produce in a prominent location, or tape them to the face of your circulation desk. They took time and effort to prepare, and you should get as much mileage out of them as possible.

Above all, have faith in yourself and your mission. The honest fact that reading can be fun is one of the most difficult things to prove to a kid who doesn't believe it. For those who have been denied a personal history of pleasurable reading experiences, it's hard to accept an assertion that a good book's characters are more real than those they meet on TV or that a novel's plot can be more exciting. One of the most immediate and successful ways of spreading the word about reading is booktalking; hearing a suspenseful story skillfully told is a thousand times more effective than being reminded that "reading is good for you." Ten minutes of engrossing yarn-spinning turns more kids on to reading than a year's worth of book reports. Booktalking is one of the school librarian's best weapons against student apathy.

> . . . And that's the way the book starts out. Charlie and her father are on the run, trying to get away from the government's secret hit team that's out to get them. Vicki has al-

ready been eliminated by the same brutal agency. Will little Charlie survive?

You know, I was talking with a librarian friend not too long ago and she pointed out that *Firestarter* was a terrific read and a safe one to put into a high school library. "There's so little sex in it," she said, "just good, clean, all-American violence!" *Firestarter* is not the kind of book that's ever going to win the Nobel Prize for Literature, but it's the kind of page-turner that will capture you on page one and keep you reading until you finish the last word.

I have a copy right here. Anybody want to check it out?

CHAPTER 9

HOW TO TELL WHEN YOU'RE A SUCCESS
AND WHAT TO DO ABOUT IT
Without Getting a Swelled Head

I t's easy to tell if your booktalking program is a success. People will appear at the school and public libraries asking for the books that were talked about, requests will pile up, circulation will increase. Kids and adults will recognize you in a variety of places, from the library to the grocery store to the movie theater lobby, and come up to ask you about a title they've forgotten or to tell you how much they enjoyed reading one of the books you mentioned.

There's also a ripple effect, as those who read a book as a result of your talk recommend it to others, and the news reaches those who never even heard you speak. Teachers have a grapevine, too, and successful visits to one or two teachers' classes can prompt the rest of the faculty to ask for visits. Encourage teachers to spread the word—a colleague's recommendation can be much more effective than your own assertion that you can interest their classes.

Some of these signs of success can be very annoying to other library staff members, who have to deal with multiple requests for the same book, incorrect title or author information, and urgent demands for another book just like the one you talked about in Mr. So-and-so's class, or at such-and-such a meeting. There are a number of ways to make life easier for everyone inundated by hordes of demanding patrons. A separate display area for booktalk books is one way I've already mentioned. Booklists and bibliographies of various kinds can also help.

Annotated booklists to pass out after booktalking can let your audience know that there are other good books in the library besides the ones you talked about. Be sure these lists are also available at the public service desks—reference, children's, young adult, reader's advisory— and any other desks where staff might be asked for the books you've been talking about. Very often booklists can confirm a title or author, or help a librarian locate something else when the specific book wanted isn't on the shelf. In Alameda Country, I used three booklists at the same time, each including some books we talked about regularly and some we didn't talk about that were more likely to be on the shelf. Lists like these should be kept current and revised about every other year, if possible. In theory, the more lists you use, the wider the requests will be spread, because there will be more titles for the students to choose from. In fact, requests still pile up for the books discussed in class, but the lists are a good source of second choices.

Booklists should be just as attractive as possible. Bright colors and catchy covers will help ensure they'll be read and not made into paper airplanes. Ask an art class to design some lists for you as a class project. Maybe you have a graffiti board in your library—use part of it as the cover, or perhaps as a halftone background for the entire list, with the annotations typed on top. It can really be fun when people in the class recognize their own artwork! Play up current popular movie themes—"It's a bird! It's a plane! It's Superbook!" with an S-emblazoned book emerging from a phone booth was on one of the Stanislaus County YA lists. TV shows can be used as well—pick something "everybody" is watching. Humor always attracts attention. One of my favorite booklist titles came from Carol Starr and completed a cover with a large shark and a skindiver on it—"Books you can sink you teeth into!" Maybe Captain Kirk or Mr. Spock could recommend some titles—or one of the Star Wars characters. Collect booklists from other libraries, not only for ideas about titles to include but also for covers. If someone else has a good idea, see if you can adapt it for your list. Annotations are easier, too, if you have someone else's to work from. Be careful not to use anything without asking permission first. Most of the time people are quite willing to share.

If you don't have the time or money needed to produce an annotated booklist to pass out to classes, you should prepare a typed bibliography for the staff at the various public service desks. The bibliography can be annotated or not, depending on the time you have to spend on it and the extent to which the people using it will have to depend on it, rather than on YA staff members. It can be arranged by author, title, or subject, depending on which seems most useful. It should include all the books you plan to talk about frequently, and also others to suggest when those are checked out. If this list is not annotated, notes on similarities between books can save valuable time. A few words are all that's necessary—"for fans of _____" or "A book like _____"—just enough to get the idea across.

Both booklists and bibliographies should be made available to school librarians, who will get requests also. Teachers may appreciate having copies, too. Many will post them in their classrooms so that kids will be able to refer to them.

Another way to let library staff members and school librarians know what you have talked about is to Xerox your class visit information cards or summary sheets—your own records of what you've talked about in each class, with the names of the schools and the teachers. If a kid can't remember the title of the book, all the school librarian or staff member has to do is find the correct sheet or card. Alameda County booktalkers use a Class Visit Summary sheet to record not only what books have been talked about but other information they may want to refer to in the future (see Figure 3). A clipboard or notebook with copies of these sheets, filed by school or by date, would be easy to maintain and handy to refer to at any or all of the information desks.

A subject file of booktalks cross-indexed by author and title is useful, though time-consuming to prepare. It can be made on three-by-five cards for a desk file drawer, and used not only for booktalk information but also for reader's advisory help. I spent one whole summer making such a file at Fremont Main, where it was used frequently. This type of file is as time-consuming to update as it is to create, however, which may mean that the updating doesn't get done.

You may be asked by school librarians or teachers to draw up bibliographies on various subjects for classroom use. Whether or not you do this should depend not only upon the time you have available but also on your relationship with the school in question. If you are having trouble getting into a school and would like to get a department head or school librarian on your side, making future visits easier, then your time and energy will probably be well spent compiling such a list. Otherwise, you might want to consider refusing. The problem is one of time. I have yet to meet a children's or YA librarian who had more than enough, or even sufficient. Consider your priorities when deciding whether or not to take on extra work that could conceivably be done either by the school librarian or by the teacher. In refusing, you can point out the time factor—and offer to help when or if they do come in to work on the bibliography.

Another way to deal with this question is to start collecting a file of bibliographies and booklists, arranged by subject. Then, when someone asks you for a bibliography, say, "I can't do one especially for you, but you can look at my file of materials on that subject," and the blow will be softened. You will have given them something to look at and build upon, without spending too much of your valuable time in the pro-

CLASS VISIT SUMMARY SHEET

DATE OF VISIT: _____ TIME: _____

SCHOOL: _____ ROOM: _____

TEACHER: _____ DEPARTMENT: _____

TYPE OF SERVICE REQUESTED: _____

_____

_____

NUMBER OF STUDENTS IN CLASS: _____

NUMBER OF REQUESTS TAKEN: _____ (List titles below)

BOOKTALKS (List titles below)

COMMENTS:

Figure 3

cess. Be sure you get all your file materials back. It's very annoying to see your files shrink little by little, as other people make use of them.

Being a successful booktalker is fun but it means making everyone involved—library staff, group leaders, and faculty members—think it's just as good a thing as you and your audience do. Ensuring that the information teachers and librarians need is readily available will help make this possible. A booktalk hasn't really *worked* until a person has the book he or she wants to read. You won't always be there to hand the book to this person, so make sure someone else will be able to.

CHAPTER 10

TEACHING BOOKTALKING

A Not-So-Brief Note About Cloning Yourself!

The next step in booktalking is, or course, proliferation—*not* doing it all yourself. Offer to share your skills with other staff members. Everyone who works with children and young adults needs to know how to do booktalks, but they aren't the only ones who can profit by developing these skills. The reference staff will be able to deal more easily with the reader's advisory questions if they know the basics of the short booktalk. The use that school librarians can make of booktalking has already been discussed, but what about those librarians, no matter what department or type of library they work in, who are asked to go out into the community and talk about books? Perhaps booktalks would be just as well-suited to community needs as the more traditional book reviews. The column in the local paper that lists new acquisitions might take on new life if a few brief booktalks were included. Then there are local cable TV shows, radio spots, and even programs in the library for all ages—booktalks fit into these settings as well. And since both English and reading teachers can use booktalking in their classes, not to mention the use elementary school teachers might make of it, perhaps it would be good public relations to invite these people to take advantage of the training program you are proposing to the powers-that-be in your library, system, or region.

But once you have convinced your administration that booktalking is not only essential but the neatest thing since sliced bread, how do you go about training all these people to do booktalks? There are a number of different ways; the one you choose will probably depend on how much time and money you have to put into the project. The simplest method may be to purchase a number of copies of this and similar books and say, "Read these and go do this." Unfortunately, this is also the least effective way to teach booktalking.

The essentials of writing a booktalk can be conveyed to an audience of any size in sixty to ninety minutes through a *lecture/demonstration.*

Little audience participation is involved in this sort of program, however, and its ultimate success will depend not only on the enthusiasm that the speaker can engender but on the ability or willingness of the audience to "take the ball and run with it" once the program is over. A lecture/demonstration is usually what is offered when a speaker is sponsored by a state or regional organization. Follow-up programs on a local level can greatly enhance the effectiveness of this approach.

A one-day or half-day *single-session workshop* for the librarians and teachers in your area is probably the cheapest program you can plan that will actually get people to go out and do talks. I have used this format extensively for the last five years, and know of many other librarians across the country who have as well.

However, if time and money are sufficent to allow staff members to attend a *multi-session workshop* led by an experienced booktalker, with videotaping facilities available, the results will be even better, for the multi-session workshop is undoubtedly the most effective way to teach booktalking. This method is also used across the country, and is the method I prefer in teaching my classes on booktalking.

Each of these three approaches has its advantages and disadvantages. It is necessary to choose the format most suited to the situation and the participants. Try to find out as much as you can about the people who are likely to attend the program. Are they school librarians, public librarians, or teachers? What age levels do they serve? Are they all novices, or are some of them doing talks already? And most important, what do they expect from *you*? What are the specific goals of the program? Once you have this information, you can tailor your presentation accordingly; you will also be able to discuss the options—long or short workshop, or lecture—with the group leader or with your administrator in a realistic, mutually helpful way.

Multi-session Workshop

This is the way I prefer to teach booktalking, and is also the way that many library systems teach it, including ones in California, Arizona, Maryland, Washington, and New York. The program works best with no more than twelve people (and preferably only eight) in the group, and with four sessions, each from two to four hours long. When a class is structured as a multi-session workshop, it is usually offered for one or two hours credit, and the format is adjusted to allow for outside assignments that are not needed in an on-the-job training situation.

The first step is to create a cohesiveness in the group, a feeling of camaraderie—"we're all in this together!" Doing booktalks for an audience of peers who are evaluating you and before a camera that is recording your every move is enough to make even an experienced speaker quail. And these people—the participants in the workshop—are probably *not* experienced. If they know each other already, cohesiveness will come more easily and with less effort on your part. But whether the group members know each other or not, whether they are all librarians or a mixture of teachers and librarians, whether they are enrolled in a class or receiving on-the-job training, some time ought to be allocated during the first session for icebreaking and "getting to know you" games.

My situation is somewhat different from that of the YA, Children's, or Readers' Services Coordinator who regularly does training workshops and who knows and is known by the participants. I teach booktalking to graduate students in library science and to working teachers or librarians who come from all over the state on four Saturday mornings or eight weekday evenings to take this course. Many of the people who attend are strangers to each other and to me. A person working within a library system doing training may not need to spend as much time as I do breaking the ice. However, even a group of co-workers may need some help in forming a cohesive unit—one in which they will feel free to give and receive honest (and perhaps not always tactful) feedback.

I have two games I like to use to bring a group together. As I join in these games, I also watch the other members of the group, so that I learn something about how comfortable they are or aren't in front of an audience, how much about themselves they are willing to reveal, and how they respond to others, whether talking or listening. I always do one of these games, both if I have time. By the end of the session everyone has had a chance to get to know something about everyone else, including me, and we have all laughed together. The first of these games is simple and has been called a variety of things—I call it Paired Introductions. Have everyone in the group (including the leader) pair off with someone they either don't know or don't know very well. They are each to spend five minutes telling their partner something about themselves. The leader decides on the content, but it usually includes their names, where they work, why they came to the workshop, and some kind of personal information about their families, recreational preferences, or maybe reading preferences. As a rule, any information that could be interesting to the group and is not upsetting to reveal is fine. If some of this information is already generally known, the leader can be more creative, asking, for example, "If you could be any bird [fish, animal, literary character, age, color, piece of furniture, town, book, spice, or anything else] or if you could live in any period or place, or as anyone you've ever wanted to be, what would you choose and why?" This should be fun—and usually is! The partners take turns interviewing each other, switching roles after about five minutes (you call time). Then each person introduces his or her partner to the group, using the information obtained in the game.

The second game requires a prop—a roll of toilet paper. It should be obviously but casually displayed during preceding activities, with no hint given as to its purpose. The leader takes the roll of toilet paper and says, "Each of you is to take as much as you need to play this game." When group members protest that they don't know how much to take, the only response should be, "Take just as much as you need." Allow each person to tear off anywhere from one to twenty-odd sheets, the only requirement being that each player take at least one. The more mysterious the leader is, the funnier the game can be. The leader also takes several sheets—more than one or two, so as not to give anything away. When everyone has some toilet paper, then the leader explains that for every sheet taken, a player must reveal something personal that the group doesn't already know. These personal revelations should be innocuous and even silly, and one way to set the tone is for the leader to go first and reveal something quite simple or trivial—some of my "secrets" have been my most or least favorite food, restaurant, or dessert; things I own or collect; how I am feeling at the moment; whether or not I had breakfast; an accomplishment or a sport I've tried; or a career goal I've been dreaming about. The leader may have to help some of the group members find things to tell—and the whole group can help in this as well. You can also use the "If you could be anything you wanted to be . . ." ploy from the first game, with a different kind of choice for each additional sheet. Make sure that no one is uncomfortable and that there are a lot of laughs.

If these two games or exercises seem a little forced—they are. They are an artificial way to help strangers get acquainted. If you are uncomfortable using these exercises, use others or find another way to accomplish the same purpose. If you have never done anything like this before, you might practice the games on your family or friends before trying them out in the workshop.

Introductions and getting acquainted should take thirty to forty-five minutes, and maybe less, depending on the size of the group. Next, it is important to tell the group exactly what the class or workshop will consist of, and what they will be required to do, in class and at home.

Members should understand that after an introduction to booktalking they will be expected to prepare booktalks themselves, present them in the group, and discuss them afterwards. Explain the role of videotaping and discuss the appropriate ways to give and receive feedback. I have handouts on the tricky business of feedback (see Figures 4 and 5). The crucial point to remember is that for ninety-nine percent of the people in this world, negative feedback sounds much louder than positive. Therefore, it is important to offer more positive feedback than negative. If the ratio is reversed, the person may be overwhelmed—unable to take in all the negative information at once and unable to pick out the positive component either. The sandwich technique is a good way to ensure that feedback is made as palatable as possible. Start and end with something positive, and put the negative material in the middle, where its sting will be lessened. Another good rule of thumb is to give someone feedback in the way that you would like to receive it. Make sure that criticism is constructive, i.e., directed toward something that can be changed. "You sound great but your hands are really shaking!" is not particularly constructive because you can't will your hands to stop shaking; "Why don't you try keeping your hands in your pockets, so we can't see them shake" offers help.

When listening to feedback, listen to the content and try to remember that there is a reason for it. Trying some of the suggestions may make you a better booktalker. Deliberately relax your body and remember to breathe deeply and evenly. A calm receptive posture can help you be mentally receptive too, and make it easier to accept what someone else is saying. (The leader of the group needs to be aware of the body language of the person receiving feedback, and in a nonthreatening manner may even remind the person to relax and breathe. The leader can also ask for some positive feedback if the session seems too negative.)

Once all these points have been covered, it's time to start talking about booktalking. The first session (if there are four sessions, the first two if there are eight) should include a demonstration of booktalking, either live or on videotape (both, if possible); detailed information on what booktalks are, why they should be done, how to write and deliver them; information on how to put titles together in a presentation; and advice for those working in public libraries on how to get into a school and start a booktalking program. The demonstration should show several different styles of booktalking; a videotape is good for this, as is a live demonstration by several people who use various approaches. The leader should be one of the demonstrators, and the differences between a live and taped presentation pointed out. If an actual class visit

CRITERIA FOR GIVING FEEDBACK

Feedback: A way of helping another consider changing his or her behavior; communications to a person (or a group) that give information about how he/she/they affect others.

Feedback should be:

1. Descriptive rather than evaluative.
2. Specific rather than general.
3. Sensitive to the needs and goals of both receiver and giver.
4. Directed toward modifiable behavior.
5. Solicited rather than imposed.
6. Well-timed.
7. Checked to insure clear communication.
8. Checked with observers in group to establish how generalized the reaction is.

Figure 4

CRITERIA FOR RECEIVING FEEDBACK

1. Relax. Take a deep breath. Assume a comfortable position. Clear your mind of other things.
2. Listen for the essence of the content of the person's message.
3. Listen for the essence of the feelings experienced by the other person.
4. Pause and try to label your gut reaction in your mind.
5. After the person's statement, repeat what you heard, both the content and the feelings.
6. Ask the person to define some words or provide more clarification if you are unsure about some particular meaning.
7. Assume responsibility for your own behavior. Do not try to be responsible for the way the other person feels about it.
8. Check the accuracy of the feedback statement within yourself and with others.
9. Decide what you want to do with the feedback.

Figure 5

can be shown on videotape, that would be very helpful in getting across the difference between doing talks for a workshop and doing them for a class of real kids. People will take the workshop more seriously and accept criticism more cheerfully after a glimpse of the front lines.

Make sure to allow time in the first session for lots of questions and answers, and for lots of reassurances. Be ready to suggest titles that members may want to use for the booktalks they will present in the next session. Handouts that summarize what's been said about booktalking techniques and school visiting can also be helpful—see Appendix A.

The next sessions are all alike. Group members are taped doing one or two booktalks, depending on the amount of time available and the size of the group. After a break, the tape is played back, and each person has a chance to see his or her own performance, evaluate it, and receive feedback on it. We are our own worst critics sometimes, and frequently other group members will disagree with a person's self-evaluation. If video equipment is not available, then the feedback should be given after each person's talks, rather than at the end of the session. After all the group members have performed, evaluated their own performance, and discussed it with the group, a general wrap-up time of perhaps ten or fifteen minutes can be used to make sure that all the opinions have been aired, that there are no feelings of ill-will, and that all questions have been answered. During the final workshop session, the wrap-up can also include a written evaluation of the workshop itself. The evaluation form in Figure 6 is one that I find helpful; it was used by Carol Starr at Alameda County Library.

The sessions should be scheduled from two weeks to one month apart, to give the participants time to read books and write and practice their talks. New talks can be presented at each of these sessions, or talks done previously can be redone for improvement. Attention should be paid to the content of the talks as well as the style of delivery, and mistakes in that area corrected. The experience of creating an entire program can be simulated by asking the group members to draw up a list of materials for a visit to a specific community group or class, real or imaginary, and then write talks on some of the titles. These lists can be analyzed just as the talks themselves are.

When the workshop is over, copies of all the talks (in their final, corrected versions) should be given to all the participants. That way each person will have access to many talks immediately, even if some of them are not usable without adaptation.

If the group members serve different age levels, each person can present talks that are appropriate for the specific clientele served. Or each person can do talks for more than one age level, perhaps doing

BOOKTALKING WORKSHOP EVALUATION FORM

Did you find the workshop valuable?

What did you like best?

What did you like least?

How could it be improved?

Are the sessions too long? Too short?

Should there be more sessions? Fewer?

What would you have liked to have concentrated more on?

Was there anything you wanted to learn that was not covered?

Any comments?

Figure 6

talks in one session for children, in another for young adults, and in yet another for adults. Within each of these three broad categories there are further divisions that can be made, of course. A person working with children might want to do talks for elementary grades and for middle grades separately. A person serving YAs might want to treat junior and senior high separately, and there are many ways to categorize the adult users.

Single-session Workshop

The single-session workshop is basically a one-day, capsule version of the multi-session workshop and can accomplish many of the same things. The disadvantages of the shorter program are obvious: fewer chances to rewrite talks and polish delivery, and no opportunity to improve performance over a series of practice sessions. However, if a group has limited time or money and needs something more intensive than a lecture/demonstration, the single-session workshop is the answer. This sort of program works well as a preconference activity or as an in-service day for teachers or librarians. The techniques of the single-session workshop can be used with small groups and with large audiences, as long as the large audience can be broken up into smaller units when the real "workshop work" begins.

When making arrangements for the program, try to find out something about the participants, so that you can tailor the workshop to their needs. Every person who signs up should bring along at least one book—tell them to pick something they have read, like, and want to share with their clientele.

As in a multi-session workshop, the program should start with a brief get-acquainted activity (ten or fifteen minutes long) and some information on how to give and receive feedback. Demonstrations and detailed information on how to write and deliver booktalks should follow, and the rationale for booktalking should be explained, in a way that will help members deal with administrative personnel. Again, all this material should be tailored to the needs of the audience. Information on informal booktalks that can be given on the floor of the library or in the classroom may be more important than information on longer, more formal presentations. Or perhaps these people want hints on how to work with a particular age group, or how to get invited to community meetings. They may also want lists of titles that are "just like" some of the popular ones they're already using. (To develop such lists, the small groups could brainstorm and exchange results after all the members have finished their talks.) Both the demonstration and the lecture should include various kinds of talks, but should emphasize the particular kind this group is interested in. Leave plenty of time for questions to make sure all the details are clear, since this will be the only time during the workshop when information will be presented formally.

After a lunch break, the participants can spend one to one-and-a-half hours writing and rehearsing a booktalk on the book they have brought with them. Some people will have brought two or three books, and the leader can help in selecting a title to start with.

During this time, the leader circulates around the room, and is available for consultation as needed. I usually make it a point to ask each of the participants at least twice if they need or want any help. Knowing which scene to talk about, where to stop the talk, and how to write the first sentence seem to be the most frequent problems. If the group is larger than fifteen or so, it is helpful to have two leaders, especially during this time, so that everyone has a chance to get all the help needed. In addition, two leaders may mean two styles of doing and writing booktalks, which can be very beneficial.

When the participants have finished writing their talks, the group, if bigger than ten or twelve, should break up into small groups of six or eight. Everyone in each small group should read a talk aloud and get feedback from the group. Then the group selects a few of the best talks—two or three, depending on the amount of time left—and these are read aloud when the large group reconvenes. If possible, have one of the leaders work with each small group. If this is not possible, however, the leader(s) can continue to circulate around the room. Membership in the small groups can be decided on by the leader, numbering off, or by the audience itself, as members are allowed to form their own small groups.

After the large group has re-formed and the best talks have been read, an evaluation of the workshop should be made, either orally, as a wrap-up activity (what I learned here today), or on paper, as a formal evaluation. The talks written during the session should be collected, reproduced either at the time or later, and distributed to the workshop participants.

Christy Tyson, YA Coordinator at the Spokane Public Library, also uses the single-day workshop format, and shared some of her tips on making it work. After an hour of information on how to do booktalks, and some samples, the group divides up into small groups of about four or five, each with an experienced booktalker as a facilitator. They write their talks in these small groups, taking about forty-five minutes. Then they practice delivery for about forty-five minutes, get feedback, and rewrite their talks. After lunch, they practice their rewritten talks, get feedback, and pick one representative from the group to deliver the talks to the whole group. When the large group reconvenes, the person chosen from each small group shares that group's talks with the whole workshop.

Christy's talks are quite a bit shorter than the ones I do—she does about twenty books in a forty or forty-five minute class. Because the talks are shorter, people have a chance to both write and rewrite their material. She also uses handouts, developed from those created by Carol Starr, to supplement the lecture or instructional information.

While this format works well with very large groups, a minimum of about twenty participants is needed, breaking down into four groups of five each. Two factors are "carved in granite," Christy says. First, all the participants must *participate,* not just sit and observe. Second, the workshop cannot be run in less than five hours, or for fewer than fifteen people.

Lecture/Demonstration

This is the format most suited to large audiences, although its disadvantages include lack of audience participation and difficulty in sustaining the level of enthusiasm generated. It is the least expensive kind of program, even if an outside speaker is required, since it takes the least amount of time.

In giving a lecture/demonstration, it is necessary to tailor your presentation to your audience's needs and vary the pace so your listeners don't go to sleep. One to one-and-a-half hours is about as long as your whole presentation should be. After that you may begin to lose your audience both mentally and physically—and the latter can be quite distracting, to say the least. Divide your presentation into three parts: a demonstration of booktalking, a lecture on how to do it, and a question-and-answer period. The length of each section can vary, but the most successful combination for me seems to be fifteen to thirty minutes of demonstration, thirty to forty-five minutes of lecture, and fifteen to thirty minutes of questions and answers. The pace should be lively, and the program should move rapidly until the question-and-answer session. The first question sometimes takes a long time coming. There are two ways to handle this. You can simply relax and wait until someone decides to go ahead and ask. While waiting, make sure your body language is open and receptive, rather than closed. *Look* as though you want to answer someone's question. And remember, the silence always seems longest to the person standing in front of the group. Of course, you can always "salt the audience"—have someone whose job it is to ask the first question and get the ball rolling. In fact, you can even have several someones. Usually once one or two questions have been asked, then others will follow. Keep an eye on the clock, and don't let the question-and-answer period last longer than thirty minutes, unless there's a lot of enthusiasm.

The most common questions I'm asked have to do with what a particular clientele would like and whether I talk about a particular type of book. Then there's the one that goes "Can you recommend a book just like_____?" Frequently I end up with a nervous smile, suddenly sweaty palms, and a completely blank mind. If I have brought bibliographies along, I can refer to them; if not, then I usually throw the question back to the audience, hoping that they are less nervous and more able to improvise than I am. That gives me some breathing space and a chance to rack my memory. The amazing thing is that most of the time, once I have had a minute or two to think and to listen to what other people have to say, I remember the titles or the method I would use in the situation described.

Other questions have to do with things I have simply left out of my lecture, usually because of time, and those are easier to answer. It's a good idea, though, to check after answering each question to see if the person who asked feels satisfied. You may have misunderstood the question completely or may not have answered it in enough detail. Any questions that I cannot handle on the spot, I offer to answer later by phone or mail. I try to make sure that some attention has been given to every question before the program ends.

The guidelines for dress and appearance discussed previously all apply here, too, with an emphasis on looking professional. After all, you are most probably talking to teachers and librarians, and you want them to accept you on a professional level.

I think comfort comes before fashion, and I make sure that my shoes are low-heeled and that there are pockets in my skirt or dress. (By this time, I have very few "work clothes" that don't have pockets!) A suit with pockets in the skirt as well as the jacket is always my first choice, and my second is a dress with a blazer. Both are easy for me to wear, and I feel I look good in them—two essential points. Wear what looks professional, is easy to wear, and makes you feel confident.

Then relax and enjoy what you're doing. You know how to sell books, now you're selling how to sell books. Your presentation can be casual or formal, whatever your personality and your audience dictate. Dress appropriately so that you can forget what you're wearing. If possible, familiarize yourself with the room where you'll be speaking ahead of time. Make sure that all the props you'll need are there, and that the microphone is adjusted properly, so you can speak into it comfortably and still glance at your notes easily and unobtrusively. If you want to set up a display of books and materials, find out if there is a table you can use. If you are using any kind of audio or video equipment, check it ahead to time, so that all you'll have to do during the program is turn it on. If you don't know how to handle the equipment yourself, arrange for someone to help you and make sure that person will be there when you arrive. Also, you need to plan what you will do if the equipment doesn't work, for whatever reason. Remember, the more hardware you have to depend on, the more chances there are of a failure somewhere along the line. Take care of every possible problem ahead of time, for plenty will come up at the last minute to keep you busy (Murphy's Laws again!).

However, you don't always have to do everything yourself—the group that asked you to speak will probably have designated someone as a host or guide. That contact person can deal with some of these details ahead of time for you. For instance, I always ask for not only video equipment, but also someone to run it and to check it out for me as well. That way, the equipment is set up, loaded, and ready to go. All I have to do is push the right button and hope it works, and have ready something to do if it doesn't.

I have been asked more than once how to combat stage fright when speaking before a large audience. I didn't have the answer in 1980; I don't have it now. And I *still* have to deal with stage fright. I can control my nervousness in front of a group of children or teenagers, but faced with a sea of adult faces, I find it very difficult not to cut and run. Sometimes my nervousness goes away as I get into my presentation, but sometimes it doesn't; sometimes my hands are shaking just as badly when I ask for questions as they were when I stood up to begin. However, there are things I do for myself that help me control my stage fright.

I prepare. I know exactly what I have to do, and the order in which it needs to be done. I have my booktalks down cold. I relax *before* I have to go on, and try to get a minute or two to myself. (This may mean a last-minute trip to the restroom, if no other private place is available.) I relax my muscles and just sag for a minute. I tell myself whatever I want someone to tell me to make me feel better. (*You're beautiful . . . talented . . . you can do it . . . those people may be just as nervous about meeting you as you are about meeting them . . . you know your stuff . . . you know just as much about this as they do, probably more . . .* and so on. Whatever I want to hear.) I breathe deeply and remind myself to continue to do so when I get onstage. I check my hair and makeup one last time, tell myself that I'm a *winner* and picture myself giving the presentation of my life, with all the congratulations that I'll get afterwards. Then I'm ready.

After that prep—and yes, I really do tell myself all those things, and yes, they really do work for me, and yes, I really do need them—there's a period when you have to sit in front of the group and wait while you are introduced, or while some other business is taken care of. I don't look at the audience then; instead I quietly go over my notes for my first talk, or for the first few things that I am going to say. I know that if I can get through the first minutes of the presentation and get the first laugh from the audience, my stage fright may vanish.

Then I'm on. If my hands are still shaking, I either stick them in my pockets or hold them where they can't be seen by the audience. I hide my shaky knees behind the podium, take another deep breath, smile, and jump in. I may or may not tell the group how nervous I am, but if I do, I make it something that we can all laugh about. I make sure that I remember to breathe, and I pause to take a deep breath after announcing the title and author of the first book, before launching into the booktalk itself. For the first talk, I use only an "old friend," usually *The Quartzsite Trip*. As I start out on the initial sentences, I consciously relax my body and let myself become aware of how much I enjoy doing this talk. This was a deliberate tactic at first, but now has become automatic, at least with this title. (I didn't realize just how automatic until recently, when someone ripped off my program copy of *The Quartzsite Trip* and I didn't even have the dust jacket along, to put on another book and fake with. I missed those built-in cues and once again had to make a conscious effort to calm down.) Another title, also an old friend, that works well for me as the first talk of a presentation is *To Take a Dare,* but for entirely different reasons. I get so involved in this story that I forget entirely about being nervous. I usually finish this talk with tears in my eyes, so concerned about Chrysta that I don't have time to worry about me.

I never use a new talk as the first in a presentation if there is the slightest chance of my being nervous about it. It's hard enough to remember to stay calm without having to remember new material as well. I sandwich the new talks in between the old ones, and make sure that I have something really zippy to end up with.

Mostly, I do my best to just take it easy with myself when it comes to being scared. Stage fright happens to everyone, and while it may not be curable, it certainly is controllable and nothing to scold yourself about. In the end, everybody has to find out what works for them, and use it. Maybe some of my tricks will help you, maybe they won't. Either way, you ultimately have to do it yourself. You stand up there alone, even if there's someone right next to you, and you have to depend on yourself. But if I can do it, so can you!

The three methods of teaching I have described are used with groups, large or small. But booktalking can be just as easily taught to one person. If you know or work with someone who wants to learn booktalking—show them how, teach them. You may end up with a partner or someone with whom you can share talks, and then you'll have twice as many!

Finally, booktalking is not a static skill. It isn't something that's learned once and for all, like how to tie your shoe or ride a bike. It is a skill that must be constantly polished and that can always be improved. New techniques for both writing and delivery are constantly being tried out in the field and either adopted or discarded. Many library systems have their booktalkers get together regularly to exchange talks and ideas. (This process can also be good for morale.) Sometimes in the midst of doing something, it's hard to see just how much or how well you are doing. Someone else's experiences may give you a perspective on your own work and perhaps some new ideas or useful practical tips. Sue Madden, YA Coordinator of the King County (Washington) Library System, uses a Booktalking Awareness Sheet (Figure 7) that rates the booktalker's voice, gestures, diction, and eye contact. This can be filled out by teachers during a school visit, or by colleagues, as part of a sharing and practice session. It would also be useful in a booktalking class or multi-session workshop. Sue also uses a mini-survey when she does talks (Figure 8) to get a feeling for the needs and interests of the people she's talking to. This could be an invaluable tool for booktalkers who don't know much about the community they are working in, and it is brief enough not to be intrusive.

A partner or co-worker can be a big help, because you can bounce new ideas off each other. People who present booktalks as a team get together informally to do this, and both have the opportunity to improve continually. A colleague's candid appraisal is one of the most valuable aids I have found: "That was GREAT!" or, "You really screwed that one up, why don't you do it this way next time?" Perceptions of the audience's reaction can vary—someone else can help you see more clearly when you've misjudged a response. This ongoing training is one of the most valuable assets any booktalker can give or receive.

BOOKTALKING AWARENESS SHEET

Booktalker _____

Title of Book _____

Rate 1 to 10 on scale

Voice	Audible		Too loud/soft

1   5   10

Gestures   Appropriate   Too stiff/loose

1   5   10

Diction   Clear   Mumbly

1   5   10

Eye Contact   Talking to me   Distant

1   5   10

Would you want to read the book? _____

Summary of best features

Areas that need attention

Overall   Excellent   Needs Improvement
impression

1   5   10

Figure 7

MINI-SURVEY FOR SCHOOL VISITS

Date: _____

School: _____

Age: _____

Local public library most used: _____

1. Favorite book read in the past two years—could hardly wait to get a friend to read it.
   Title:
   Author:

2. Best movie in the past twelve months that you paid to see:
   _____

3. Cassette or album you want *now* (please circle format).
   Group:
   Title:

4. Do you have a personal home computer? _____ VCR? _____
   Brand _____
   VHS_____ Betamax _____

5. Subject area(s) for a program you'd be willing to attend at your local public library: _____
   _____
   _____

   Best time and day: _____
   How do we tell you? _____

[If you've time/need, add or substitute the following:]

6. How often do you go to the public library?
   _____ Never
   _____ 1 or 2 times a year
   _____ 5 or 6 times a year
   _____ 1 or 2 times a month
   _____ 1 or 2 times a week

7. Do you go for:
   _____ Homework
   _____ Recreational (pleasure) reading
   _____ Films, video, records and cassettes (media)
   _____ Other (please specify) _____

Figure 8

CHAPTER 11

OTHER WAYS OF BOOKTALKING

Doing Your Own Thing

or, Whatever Works Is Right

Booktalking is such an individual art that there is no one way to do it. Larry Rakow, Elizabeth Overmyer, and I have told you something about how we and people we know do it. But that isn't anywhere close to the whole picture. Even the additional ideas I'm going to suggest in this chapter won't do more than give you some additional glimpses of a complex and changing field. However, it isn't necessary (or even possible) to know all the ways booktalking can be done. I may at one time have thought I did know it all, but I have changed my mind—and chuckled at my own naiveté. All you really need to know is how *you* do booktalking; some examples and hints from a few experienced people will give you plenty of ideas to use in developing a style of your own. Remember what was said earlier about writing a booktalk and sketching in the details very sparingly? Using a broad brush to draw the outlines of the story, and allowing the readers to learn the details on their own? It's the same principle. I can't possibly tell you everything about how everyone does booktalking—and I don't want to. We each need to discover something about this fascinating art ourselves. I don't want to rob you of that excitement, that discovery. Even if what you discover is not new to someone else, it is still brand-new and shiny-bright to you. So here you will find ideas from a dozen or so booktalkers whom I have talked with or who took the time to write and let me know how they do it. There are thousands whom I don't know or who didn't write, and each person who starts to booktalk only adds to that list. Try out some of these ideas; see if they work for you. Discover your own unique method, style, technique—your individual place in the picture.

I write down my talks, and I recommend that as the best way to learn. I also use notes in my presentations—even today, and even with some of my most familiar talks. Other people don't use any notes at all.

Elizabeth Talbot, head of a branch of the Alameda County Library, no longer has time for much booktalking. But when she does talks, she prefers simply to jot down the title, the author's name, and a few notes for each book, and do a completely different talk every time. While she realizes that her improvisatory method involves more work and greater risks, she also says, "I would be bored doing the same talk time after time." Sue Tait, of the Seattle Public Library, uses the same method as Elizabeth. They both meet the audience with some idea of what they are going to say and then talk about various scenes from the "comic strip" in their memories. Peggy Tollefson, also from Alameda County, writes very brief notes on three-by-five cards and "freeforms" her talks in front of the class. Her notes include title, author's name, characters' names along with a few descriptive words or phrases about them, and sometimes three or four words that help her remember the basic plot line.

Booklists can also be used in a variety of ways I have not mentioned before. Linda Lapides, YA Coordinator at Enoch Pratt Free Library in Baltimore, told me about one list that is used there to let the kids themselves decide what books will be talked about. It's an unannotated list of about two hundred books, divided into broad subject categories. It's passed out to the class, and the kids are invited to choose any title they want to hear about. Obviously, someone is going to try to trip up the librarians, and according to Linda the class loves it when a librarian has to say, "I'm sorry, I haven't read that book." There's no way to prepare specific talks the night before; the situation calls for people who can think fast on their feet. My hair stands on end at the thought of trying this, but Linda reports that it's been done successfully for several years. Sue Tait uses a modified version of this same technique: her list is shorter (*only* about thirty titles). She finds that the pick-a-title method ensures variety in the program. The same books are not always chosen, and the booktalkers don't get tired of giving the same presentation all the time.

Linda also described some of the other things the YA people do at Enoch Pratt. They have two humorous slide-shows that they use to publicize the library and its services. They revise parts of these every year. Short films have also been used, much as they were at Alameda County when I was there. (Bringing along spare bulbs and an adaptor has eliminated a number of hassles, and using school equipment can make these presentations even easier.)

When the YA people from Enoch Pratt are talking to many classes at one school and a number of teachers are involved, they ask the school librarian and the head of the English department to set up the schedule for them. This arrangement is particularly efficient when an entire grade or two must be scheduled for talks. To use this method, however, you must let the school personnel know when you are available and not available, and how many classes you can do in one day. And you will not be able to suit yourself with regard to the sequence of classes—you may end up with two "hard" ones together or a notoriously rowdy one at the worst time of day. But letting the school do the scheduling does save time, and the method has been used successfully by the Enoch Pratt staff for several years.

Cathi Edgerton, also from Enoch Pratt, specializes in booktalk presentations around themes, and is not the only booktalker to have discovered that teenagers respond to astrology. She uses two different sources for descriptions of the zodiac signs, one funny, one serious. The class picks out a sign (say, Aries) for her to do, and she has all the students born under that sign raise their hands. Then she reads a funny, irreverent description of Aries people that she found on a comic greeting card. After the laughter dies down, she reads a more serious and (theoretically) accurate description. (She uses the ones she wrote for the 1980 edition of the *Enoch Prattler,* the newsletter published by the library; Linda Goodman's *Sunsigns* and *Lovesigns* are another good source.) Then Cathi does the booktalk for Aries, using one of the twelve titles she brought with her, each chosen to go with a different sign of the zodiac. Even if she doesn't talk about all twelve books, the kids want to read the one about their sign and see if it fits. She also hands out copies of the *Enoch Prattler* for additional suggestions.

The summer reading game Bookjack gives her another way of unifying a program. In this presentation, Cathi introduces Bookjack while doing booktalks. The class play cards against the dealer and win the booktalk of their choice. This game is fun, and also results in her leaving the class with lots of Bookjack registrations.

Some librarians talk about the classics, some don't. I happen to be of the latter variety, but Hazel Rochman and Cathi are of the former. Both use the same basic technique—talking about classics and modern titles at the same time. One of Cathi's favorite opening booktalks is *It All Began With Jane Eyre,* and she talks about the original *Jane Eyre* at the same time. She also combines Foley's *It's No Crush, I'm In Love* and *Pride and Prejudice.* Hazel, who works in the Young Adult Books review department at *Booklist,* also does thematic talks. She usually doesn't do more than one classic per presentation, and never points it out as a "classic"—a surefire way to kill a book. In a presentation with an outsider theme, she might include *Oliver Twist* or Richard Wright's *Black Boy. All Quiet on the Western Front* might be part of a program on war, or *White Fang* part of one on survival. For more information on how Hazel persuades teenagers to read the classics, see her excellent article in *School Library Journal,* February, 1984.

Everyone who does talks knows that sometimes it's not only the talk that sells the book. The talk may be the catalyst that moves the books off the shelf, but if demand continues to grow, other factors may be involved—including the grapevine and peer recommendations. Most people, including adults, want to read whatever their best friend stayed up all night to finish—it's more fun to share the laughter or tears of a book with someone else who's also read it.

Cathi Edgerton decided to put the power of peer recommendations to work in a way that resulted in lots more talks for lots more people. She asked her YA Advisory Board to help her out with school visits to publicize Bookjack, and ran a booktalking workshop to show them how. The young people wrote their own talks and came back to practice them; then they went with Cathi in pairs to about ten different schools. This program was an outstanding success. One of the booktalks done by Anne Reynolds (age fourteen) is included in the booktalk section. However, another talk is not included, although I wish it were. Bill Henry (fifteen), a very talented booktalker who worked with Cathi, did a talk on *Callahan's Crosstime Saloon,* but he refused to write it down, and since Cathi didn't have a tape recorder, there was no way to save it. But listen to what Cathi says about Bill and that talk: "It's one of those books that if you like it, you *love* it. . . . He had read it six times . . . and knew it by heart. . . . He held the rowdy class in the palm of his hand as he brought Callahan's characters to life, describing them in Robinson's words but in his own style . . . the class was . . . spellbound . . . [When it was over] they held their silence for a moment and then did a mad rush to the front of the room to claim their copies." What a talk—that's one for the angels! (Maybe that's why it isn't written down anywhere.) If you are interested in more information on training teenagers to booktalk, you can contact Cathi at the Enoch Pratt Free Library.

Diane Tuccillo (Mesa Public Library, Arizona) also trains teenagers to do booktalks. She and her staff go into the classes at school and tell kids how to write booktalks instead of doing book reports. This seems to be a growing trend, by the way, since I have heard of it from any number of people. And why not? Booktalks are infinitely more interesting than the horribly boring book reports we all had to write and then read aloud to the class back in the olden (or maybe not-so-olden) days.

Sally Long, Youth Services Coordinator of the Worcester County Library in Maryland, does a booktalking column for the local newspaper in addition to talking about books in the schools. "Booktalks" presents the talks in printed form. The column has been quite successful, and students have told her that they read it regularly.

Twila Cavey Ness is the Librarian of Special Programing at the Model Secondary School for the Deaf at Gallaudet College in Washington, DC. She uses sign language to do booktalks for the deaf at the school. I have also talked to other booktalkers who don't know how to sign but want to reach this audience. They have gone to deaf classes or groups and had their talks interpreted for the class by the teacher or group leader. The effectiveness depends on the skill of the interpreter as well as the booktalker, but this can be a very exciting way to do talks.

Rhonna Goodman also does booktalks for the handicapped, going to classes for the blind and the mentally retarded in New York City. She includes storytelling in her programs too, telling one or more stories completely. She uses folk tales and science-fiction or fantasy stories, and reports that they are very well received.

Christy Tyson tells stories in a setting where many would hesitate to do so—in the Spokane Juvenile Detention Center. The kids there are more accepting of stories then one might suppose, and even sixteen- and eighteen-year-olds listen with interest.

Judy Druse and Barbara Lynn, high school librarians in Chanute and Iola, Kansas, are unusual not in the audience they address or in the kind of booktalks they write but in the sheer number of talks they produce. Judy writes talks on almost every novel that goes into her collection and on a great many of the nonfiction books besides, and Barbara covers nearly as many books in her library. Judy was trained by Christy Tyson while she was in Arizona several years ago (information on Christy's training procedures is given in Chapter 10), and was already giving talks at Chanute when Barbara was hired at Iola. When Barbara discovered what Judy was doing, she wanted to do it too, so Judy trained her. Now they give talks in their schools and communities and share a file of more than five hundred talks. Whenever either of them writes a talk, she Xeroxes it and sends it to the other. They sometimes both do talks on the same book, and get new ideas from each other. Barbara's copies are in two huge looseleaf ring binders, and both are stuffed full. Just seeing them is somewhat mindboggling! Both these librarians are interested in sharing with a wider group of people and will exchange talks with anyone willing to send them material in return.* Their ad-

---

*And while you're Xeroxing, I would be glad to start collecting talks for "Booktalk 3." Just be sure your name and address are on each page. Maybe if I get enough, I won't wait four years before I start it!

dresses are given in the list of contributors. Their willingness to share is demonstrated in the number of talks that they were willing to donate to this book.

The idea of talking about virtually every novel in a library collection is staggering, and so I asked Judy how she does it. During the school year, she reads one book a night, usually just before she goes to bed. It's her time to relax, and so she looks forward to it. Since she is asked to talk to groups of all ages in her community, her reading includes books for children, YAs, and adults. As she reads she takes rather specific notes on an index card, making them as brief as possible, so as not to interrupt the story. This was awkward at first, Judy admits, but with practice it has become almost second nature. Most of her notes have to do with the first chapters of the book, since it is unlikely that she'll use much, if anything, from the latter parts. Her notes include all the standard things—characters, plot, passages to highlight.

The next day she makes time in her schedule to write the talk down. Sometimes this isn't easy, but Judy feels that booktalking is a major part of her job and is willing to force herself at times to sit down for an hour and write out the talk for the book she read the previous night. It usually takes her about one class period to write up a talk—there are always interruptions. Before she starts writing, she pulls the reviews from her purchase file, and then works from them, the book, and her own notes. She does two drafts, the first to organize the paragraphs or main ideas in the talk, the second to reorganize if necessary and to polish. She uses phrases of the author's to give the talk the right "flavor." Barbara also uses this technique, and both will revise their talks if their first presentations don't seem to be working. Judy says that after four years of doing talks—she visits each English class twice a year—the circulation at Chanute High School Library has tripled.

Obviously, when you write a talk on virtually every book that comes into a library, you'll be writing some talks on books you don't particularly like. Judy and Barbara agree that their talks on books that they didn't enjoy are not as effective as the ones on the titles they did like. Fortunately, they don't have identical tastes, and since they frequently have two talks to choose from, they can pick the one that works best. In addition, they can discuss a talk that isn't working and perhaps figure out how to change it. Judy also notes that she has trained herself, out of necessity, to do two things: to use multiple reviews in selection, so that she acquires titles with broad appeal, and to concentrate, when writing a talk, on the parts of the book she likes best. These strategies don't always solve the problem, but they certainly help.

Chanute is a small town, and when high school students went home and told their parents what the high school librarian was doing, Judy began to get invitations from community groups. In a program for adults, she usually includes one or two longer talks, of ten to fifteen minutes. Most of her other talks to adults (and to YAs) are shorter, a standard two to five minutes.

Both Barbara and Judy echo the sentiments of Larry Rakow in his advice on how to do booktalks in your own school library. They present the talks in their libraries if they can't do them in classrooms. A clerk takes care of the library while the talk is going on, and if there's no clerk, they close the doors, or take their chances on no one coming in with an unexpected class. They also use student help when necessary. Booktalks are important—and you can always find a way and a time to do what you consider to be really important.

Start with a partial class period if you don't have time for a whole hour. Combine booktalking with fall orientation for the incoming freshmen or sophomores. Listen to the positive feedback you get from the kids—and keep track of your circulation figures. Teachers may also come in for recommendations for books—encourage them to bring their classes to the library or to let you go to them. Classrooms have fewer distractions, and there's some advantage to meeting the kids where they are, rather than requiring them to come to you.

Pick the classes you go to carefully when you're starting out, especially if you're nervous. Go to the ones that are most likely to be enthusiastic, and easiest to talk to. Do the problem ones later when you have some experience to draw on.

Among the tips that Linda Lapides gives to novice booktalkers when they first start into the schools is a cue about dress: favor the layered look. What with central heating and central air conditioning, it is sometimes hard to judge which classroom will be comfortable and which either too hot or too cold. If you have more than one layer, you can add or subtract easily. This advice is so basic and so sensible that I am a little embarrassed to remember that I have not always followed it—and feeling chilly or hot is as hard on a booktalker as having on uncomfortable shoes!

There are three new developments in the world of booktalking that may be of interest to you. Elizabeth Overmyer of the Fremont, California, Main Library is now heading Booklegger, which is, I think, the first booktalking project to be funded under the Library Services and Construction Act (LSCA). Her program trains community volunteers in booktalking and storytelling and uses them to supplement the public librarians in school visiting. This means that the children of the Fremont area will receive many more school visits than could be scheduled using only the library staff. Elizabeth's hypothesis is that a difference in quantity of this magnitude will amount to a difference in kind. Sixty-two trained booktalkers and storytellers will make fourteen hundred classroom visits during the school year, each volunteer giving two hours a week to a junior high or grade school. The Alameda County Library System will provide support for these visits by making available extra copies of the approximately three hundred books discussed in the Fremont area. The program began last fall and will continue through the 1985–86 school year, as funds allow. Elizabeth expects to produce a training manual as part of this project, so that others will be able to benefit from the Fremont experience.

Secondly, the Young Adult Services Division of the American Library Association has recently formed a Booktalking Discussion Group, which meets informally at each conference, Midwinter and Annual. Members of the group share their experiences as well as their booktalks, swapping success and horror stories. Mailings are sent out after each meeting, in case any of the members want to follow up on any of the comments. Local booktalkers are encouraged to come whenever the conference is in their area, whether they are ALA/YASD members or not, and regardless of the age group they work with. You can get your name put on the mailing list and contribute by mail, if you are not able to make it to meetings, by getting in contact with the convenor or discussion leader. (At this time, I am the discussion leader, and my address is given in the list of contributors. The ALA office in Chicago will also forward letters.)

And lastly, the magazine *VOYA* (*Voice of Youth Advocates*) has started a column on booktalking, which I am writing. It will run in every other issue for the first year (1984–85) and hopefully more frequently after that. I want to include what you want to read about booktalking, as well as what I want to write about it. (There *should* be some overlap there!) Some of the topics I'd like to cover include techniques; sources for talks and for training; themes for presentations, and books to use for them; unusual gimmicks or ideas; tricks of the trade; dealing with different kinds of audiences; and "straight on till morning!" Do let me know if there's something you'd especially like to see—write to me at my own address or care of *VOYA* (PO Box 6569, University, AL 35486).

Although there have not been many articles written on booktalking, some that show how other people do booktalks are listed at the end of this chapter. These should be enough to get you started.

We all do booktalking in our own unique and inimitable ways, that are right for us. The only real measure of whether we are doing it "right" or not is whether or not the people we are talking to respond by reading what we've suggested. Although the rules I've outlined won't hold true in every case or for every person, I've tried to make them as broad and as general as possible, and they should work for most people.

Seeing someone else do booktalks is still the best way to learn what to do and what not to do. But don't be intimidated by someone who's better than you are, or than you think you'll ever be. You may not know how good you are—your audience is the judge of that. Are the books you talk about checked out? Is circulation going up? Are more people you recognize from your talks in the library? Do you have a longer list of reserves than you did previously? All these things mean that you are a success—a good booktalker.

But don't rest too easily on your laurels. Keep refining your art, for that's what booktalking is—an art. Compare yourself to yourself—look at what you have already accomplished and then look at what you could do if you stretched just a little bit further. Set fresh goals for yourself when you've reached the old ones. Don't let yourself get stale—be creative, try new things. You'll keep your audience that way.

Booktalking ends where it begins—with enjoying books and sharing the various worlds, adventures, and escapes they offer. It's fun, even when your hands are shaking so much you're glad you have pockets. If you keep going and keep enjoying it, one of these days you *will* convince those people who only read the newspaper, or the kids who don't read at all, that there is an experience, an adventure—laughter, tears, inspiration—a whole new world they'll be missing out on if they don't read the book you're talking about. One book may lead to another (it frequently does), and you've made another convert. As far as I'm concerned, that's the most effective kind of proselytizing you can do!

So relax, stick those shaky hands in your pockets, lean up against the table to help steady those shaky knees, and *smile*. Enjoy yourself. Your audience will enjoy themselves too, whether they are third-graders, senior citizens, or somewhere in between. They may not always admit it, but you'll be able to tell when the books start disappearing from the shelves. They'll be right where you want them—children of all ages; uncaged, untamed adolescents; bored, blasé, or superior adults—held by the bounty you alone can offer, there in the palm of your outstretched hand!

Bibliography

Austrom, Liz, ed. *Young Relationships: A Booktalk Guide to Novels for Grades 6 Through 9.* Written and compiled by members of the British Columbia Teacher-Librarians' Association. 1983. Available from William Scott, Box 985, Hope, BC Z0X ILO Canada.

Chelton, Mary K. "Booktalking: You Can Do it." *School Library Journal,* April 1976.

Cole, Doris M. "The Book Talk." in *Juniorplots* by John Gillespie. Bowker, 1967, pp.1–6.

Dwyer, Edward J. "Encouraging Reading Through Book Talks." *Reading Horizons,* Winter 1983.

Eisenberg, Michael B. and Carol Notowitz. "Book Talks: Creating Contagious Enthusiasm." *Media and Methods,* March 1979.

Grosshans, Marilyn. "Booktalks as Bookbait." *School Library Media Quarterly,* Winter 1983.

Leonard, Charlotte. "Let's Talk about Book Talks." *Ohio Association of School Librarians Bulletin,* May 1976.

Munson, Amelia. "Book Talks" in *An Ample Field.* ALA, 1950, pp.97–101.

Nilsen, Alleen Pace and Donelson, Kenneth L. *Literature for Today's Young Adults,* 2nd ed. Scott, Foresman 1985. pp. 376–379.

Rochman, Hazel. "Booktalking the Classics." *School Library Journal,* February 1984; "Booktalking Them off the Shelves." *School Library Journal,* August 1984.

Spencer, Pamela, G. "Booktalking Seventeen Hundred Students at Once—Why Not?" *English Journal,* October 1974.

Witucke, Virginia. "The Book Talk: A Technique for Bringing Together Children and Book." *Language Arts,* April 1979.

BOOKTALKS

One of the exciting parts of working on this book was receiving a blizzard of booktalks from people all over the country. One of the painful parts was deciding which talks to use and which to set aside. Early in the production process, we decided that we wanted a relatively inexpensive book, one most people would be able to afford. That placed a limit on the number of pages we could devote to booktalks. A huge stack of talks—more than five hundred—had been contributed, but only about half could be included. Norris and I went through the stack several times, and each time it was harder to figure out which talks to omit. The quality of work was excellent—there were no obviously expendable talks (that would have been too easy!).

We developed criteria: in order to include the maximum amount of new material, we eliminated all talks on books that had been covered in the previous edition. We also decided to omit talks on books that were out of print, unless we felt that the omission would leave an intolerable gap in the collection. As the number of talks dwindled down closer to the target figure, the choices got harder and harder to make. Often we had multiple talks on the same title; then we'd agonize over which one would be the most effective. Different approaches to booktalking had to be represented, we felt, and we also worked for variety in age level and genre. I had agreed to the principle of a less expensive book, but that was hard to remember when I had to delete talks I *knew* were good!

Finally the ordeal was over, and I was reminded of the way I used to feel as a committee member when the Best Books for Young Adults list was finished. I never got all my favorites on, and sometimes had to make painful decisions about what to keep and what to omit. I was never completely satisfied, but I was usually close to it. That's how I feel about the selection here. All these talks will work, and by studying them and using them you can learn a lot about booktalking; I just wish we had had room for more.

To those of you who sent in talks that do not appear in this volume, I'm sorry. Maybe sometime in the not-too-distant future, there will be a third booktalk book, composed entirely of talks. Then I will be able to include at least some of those I'm still holding. Please don't be discouraged, or shy about contributing in the future—if I do indeed put together a whole book of talks, I'll need all the help I can get from as many of you as are willing to give it. But for now, these talks will have to do. I hope you will like them.—*JB*

ABOUT DAVID   YA
By SUSAN BETH PFEFFER

Bicycling home one evening, Lynn was disturbed to see the blinking red lights of police cars surrounding the house of her best friend David across the street. As she rushed into her own house to ask her parents what had happened, her usually reserved father quickly gathered her into his arms, saying, "Lynn, I have to tell you something horrible."

Lynn's mind flashed to David, her beloved, troubled David. "Tell me, Dad, please," she begged, holding her breath.

"It's David," he said. "And his parents. They're dead, Lynn."

"David's parents are dead?" Lynn echoed in disbelief. It seemed impossible, unreal.

"Yes, and David is dead too," her father said quietly.

Lynn's head spun sickeningly as the unthinkable facts assaulted her, one by one. Her own mother had found them, entering their friendly, familiar home out of concern when no one answered the phone. All three, David and his parents, Lynn's best friend and her parents' best friends, all lying there dead. There was a note pinned to David's shirt. It said, "Forgive me." For he had shot his mother and his father and then himself.

But Lynn was still living. She had to live through police questioning. She had to tell them David's private feelings, his complicated feelings about being adopted, his resentment of his unknown natural parents for leaving him, his hatred of his adoptive parents for demanding perfection of him. It was unbearable talking to a cop who saw her David as a sick, twisted killer.

And what did Lynn think? She was so confused, she didn't know herself. When asked when she had last spoken to David, she remembered that it was during school lunch hour that very day, the day he went home and killed his parents. He must have been planning it even then—efficient, organized David. But for the life of her, Lynn could not recall one single word of their last conversation.

It only she could remember what David last said to her, perhaps it would all make sense. She just *had* to remember, to bring back David's words, a clue to his feelings, to understand . . . about David.

—*Cathi Edgerton*

ACE HITS THE BIG TIME YA
By BARBARA B. MURPHY and JUDIE WOLKOFF

Horace stared at the ghastly sight in the bathroom mirror—his first day at JFK High School in Manhattan and he had a sty the size of an egg yolk! His little sister Nora had warned him about the Purple Falcons, the most powerful gang at JFK. She said, "They're gonna cream you, Horace." But when he came out of the bathroom, she said to Horace, "They aren't gonna cream you—they're gonna *kill* you!" *Just* what Horace needed to hear!

And if that wasn't enough, he went into the kitchen to get his lunch, and his mother handed it to him in a clear plastic vegetable bag! "What's *this*?" "Not another word, Horace, there's not a brown-paper lunch bag in this whole place—just look at this mess!" She was right— the apartment was full of half-unpacked boxes. Horace decided that discretion was the better part of valor and went off to look for his denim jacket. But after going through all the boxes the *only* jacket he could find was the one his uncle had sent him from Japan—red satin, with a dragon embroidered on the back. "At least," Horace thought, "the pockets are big enough to put my lunch in," So the bagel went in one pocket, the banana went in the other. The only problem left was his eye. What was he going to do about his eye? He tried everything he could think of, including combing his hair down over it—nothing worked. Then he saw Nora's Halloween makeup box . . . maybe there was something there . . . a black eyepatch! Perfect! He was ready: now, if he could just make it past the Purple Falcons.

He got to school and was just hanging around across the street, kind of checking things out and looking for the Falcons, when he noticed these two strange-looking people in a weird purple car. They were talking and looking at him. Then one of them pointed at him, and they began to get more and more excited. Finally, they beckoned him to come over. Now, Horace was no dummy—he knew what you do when strangers try to get you into their car—ignore them! He ducked into the school just ahead of the Purple Falcons. Then, in homeroom, he looked out the window and saw that the weirdos in the purple car were still outside, waiting for him. "There's no way I'm going to survive this day," Horace said to himself. "The weirdos in the purple car outside, the Purple Falcons inside, one way or another—I'm gonna die.!"

But appearances can be deceiving, Horace discovers, and a bagel, a banana, a dragon, an eyepatch, and a brand-new Bic ballpoint pen all combine to give Horace a new look, a new name, and a new career. Because, you see, the Purple Falcons had never seen Horace before, and had no idea why he looked the way he did that morning!

—Joni Bodart

THE ADVENTURES   Grades 5–8
OF A TWO-MINUTE WEREWOLF
By GENE DeWEESE

What would you do if your best friend suddenly started to grow hair on his hands, feet, and face; sprouted long, sharp claws; and grew a cold, wet nose? In other words, what would you do if your best friend suddenly turned into a werewolf—then turned back into a human again two minutes later? Well, Cindy simply said, "Hey, can you do that again?" So her friend Walt tried—and succeeded! In fact, he found out that he could turn into a werewolf or a real wolf at will. And he could use his new talent to help Cindy solve a crime wave. But what was making him turn into a werewolf? Read *The Adventures of a Two-Minute Werewolf* and find out!

—*Sherry Cotter*

AFTER THE FIRST DEATH   YA
By ROBERT CORMIER

A busload of six-year-old campers driven by sixteen-year-old Kate Forrester is hijacked by PLO-type terrorists. The children will be held as hostages on Brimmler's Bridge in rural New England until the ransom demands of the terrorists are met. Young Miro Shantas is one of those terrorists. His assignment is to kill the bus driver, Kate, without hesitation, as soon as the bus arrives at the bridge. He is not apprehensive about delivering death even though he has never committed such an act; he is worried only that he will not do a professional job, that he will not follow the example of his hero Artkin. Artkin has killed three people in Miro's presence in the past two years, each of them in cold blood. And now it will be Miro's turn to justify his existence, to make his life meaningful.

The terrorists make three demands: 1) the release of political prisoners; 2) ten million dollars in cash; and 3) the dismantling of a secret US government agency named Inner Delta, involved at the moment in a brainwashing project. Brigadier General Marchand, the head of Inner Delta, is given the responsibility of negotiating with the terrorists. He pretends to negotiate, all the while planning a surprise attack to rescue the children. However, the success of the attack depends upon his son, Ben. Ben has been chosen to carry a message to the terrorists, but when they start to torture him, he also divulges information about the surprise attack, which he heard his father discussing on the phone. Ben does not learn until much later that his father, the General, had meant him to overhear that conversation, knowing that he would crack under pressure and give the information to the terrorists. The General hopes to trick the terrorists—they will be prepared now for a 9:30 attack, but he will strike earlier, and catch them off guard. If the plan works, General Marchand hopes to rescue the children and the bus driver with no loss of life. But if the plan *doesn't* work. . . .

—Judy Druse

ALAN AND NAOMI   Grades 6–8/YA
By MYRON LEVOY

Alan loved playing stickball and he wasn't about to give up his after-school games for anyone—especially not crazy Naomi Kirschenbaum. World War II was not yet over and he knew that she had been through terrifying experiences in Germany, but even though he was sorry for her, he sure didn't want to talk to anyone who spent all her days in a corner tearing up little bits of paper. And besides, even if she wasn't crazy, his friends would call him a sissy.

Alan never really understood how he changed his mind. But soon he was spending most of his days with Naomi, amazed to find that of all the people she met, even including the psychiatrist she was seeing, he was the only one who seemed able to get through to her. His progress was slow; at first Naomi would cower under her bed whenever she heard her own name. She couldn't leave her room. After an air-raid drill she would crouch in a corner for hours, and always she would tear up those bits of paper. It was months before she would say her own name, or leave her room. Slowly, carefully, Alan and Naomi did become friends, until she was able to leave the apartment and start back to school. Alan was feeling pretty proud of himself and Naomi, until that morning on the way to school—when something happened that seemed once again to be more than Naomi's mind could bear.

—Elizabeth Overmyer

ALMOST TOO LATE   YA/Adult
By ELMO WORTMAN

On Valentine's Day, 1979, the 33-foot sailboat carrying Elmo Wortman and his three children, Cindy, Randy, and Jena, was caught in a violent storm off the Alaska coast. The Wortmans were forced to abandon ship and swim to shore through incredibly rough surf that tore off clothes and shoes and threatened to pull them to the ocean floor. They had just stocked the boat with several hundred dollars' worth of provisions to take back to their island home, but only a few scraps reached the shore—a sail, three foam pads, a rope ladder, a first-aid kit, two oars, and a Japanese glass fishing float the size of a basketball. There were also six battered apples, three onions, some Tang, corn oil, an almost empty jar of Cheez-Whiz, and a package of spaghetti sauce mix.

Because of the storm, they weren't even sure where they were. However, they did know that they were away from the main shipping lanes—rescue from the sea was unlikely. If they were to survive, they would have to get to where someone else was, and not wait for rescue to find them. They had told no one where they were going. They had no close neighbors who would expect them home. The Wortmans' survival rested squarely on their own shoulders, and all four of them realized it.

Elmo, 52, was the only adult. Divorced father, ex-carpenter now disabled by arthritis, independent—he preferred living on the edge of civilization and eating off the land to the hassles of poverty and welfare and red tape to be found in the city.

Randy, at 15, had sound judgment and the ability to size up a situation accurately. His excellent physical condition was in his favor throughout the long ordeal, and was one of the reasons they all survived.

Cindy, 16, was the dreamer of the family, with the gift of intuition— she loved everyone, and everyone loved her.

Jena, 12, was an avid reader, a strong personality with lots of determination. It was this determination that would save her later, helping her through an ordeal few could have survived, no matter what their strength and endurance—and Jena weighed only a hundred pounds!

But each one of these people was determined to survive. This is the story of how they did so—for twenty-five days, without food, without shelter, against impossible odds in the winter sleet and snow, trying to get to civilization before it was too late.

—Joni Bodart

AMANDA/MIRANDA YA
By RICHARD PECK

When the wheel broke on the wagon and eighteen-year-old Mary Cooke wandered off for a last bit of freedom before she went to Whitwell Hall as the new maidservant, she never expected what she found. The Wisewoman's cottage was in front of her before she realized it, and then the Wisewoman herself, who invited Mary inside. Over a cup of tea, the old woman told her what her future would be—"Your future lies far beyond the Whitwell Hall and Nettlecombe, far beyond a mountain of ice where you will die and live again, live in a world so strange that the images I see seem to be trickery, even to me." Then the Wisewoman gave Mary a talisman—an old copper coin. When Mary asked, "When shall I meet the men I shall marry?" "Why tonight—both of them." Then her mother called, the wagon was fixed, and once again Mary was on her way to a life of servitude. Arriving in the kitchen in the middle of a battle between the cook and the housekeeper, Mary was given her first chore—to take a supper tray up to Miss Amanda, the daughter of the house. And no sooner had she walked in than Amanda saw the resemblance between them, renamed her Miranda, and demanded that Miranda be her personal maid. And in fact, they did look quite amazingly alike—they could have been twins.

Miranda's second chore was to help serve the dinner Amanda was avoiding by pretending to be sick and staying in her room. She saw the young American that Amanda was to marry—and he saw her as well. And later that night, she was mistaken for Amanda herself by Amanda's lover, who was the real reason why Amanda didn't want to marry the eligible American.

The Wisewoman had been right about Miranda's husbands, but her prophecy of the "mountain of ice" took longer to be fulfilled. It wasn't to become a reality until April 14, 1912, when the two women were on a ship on the way to New York—a ship called *The Titanic*!

—*Joni Bodart*

AMONG THE DOLLS Grades 3–5
By WILLIAM SLEATOR

What Vicky really wanted for her birthday was a ten-speed bike. What she got for her birthday was an antique dollhouse and five dolls. Whenever she made herself play with the hated dolls, she found that she was making them do really unpleasant things. She made them argue—and their arguments grew worse and worse. She made the mother doll beat the children and throw things at them, and the daughter scream back at her. She made the aunt lock the children in their rooms without any supper, and once someone even threw the baby down the toilet.

And then one day Vicky brought home the worst report card she had ever received. In a rage she ran up to the dolls' house and began pushing them around. Suddenly, the sunlight dimmed, she felt dizzy, and she closed her eyes. When she opened them again, she was inside the dollhouse, with the monstrous personalities that she had created.

—Elizabeth Overmyer

ANASTASIA AGAIN!   Grades 4–7
By LOIS LOWRY

Anastasia Krupnik's family were moving out of their apartment in Cambridge, Massachusetts, to the suburbs. Anastasia thought that at age twelve her life was over. There wasn't any point in living if she had to live in the suburbs. Their apartment had a history, and it was her history, and her parents' history, and it was beginning to be Sam's, her little brother's. It was true they were outgrowing the apartment; Sam's bedroom used to be the dining room. But her parents didn't understand how terrible it would be moving to the suburbs. Anastasia was going into the seventh grade next year; all her friends would be going to junior high with her. But by fall, they might be living in the suburbs.

"She could feel the thought of it affecting her physically. Her stomachache was coming back. She could feel her hair beginning to ooze oil, so she would have to wash it again before she went to bed, and she had already washed it that morning. She could feel a pimple beginning to grow on her chin. Her eyes, behind her glasses, began to blur. Terrific. Now she was going blind on top of everything else. Anastasia pictured herself in the suburbs: seven feet tall, with acne and greasy hair, and blind. She would get a Seeing Eye dog, a ferocious one, and name him Fang. If anybody made any nasty remarks to her, she would simply say in a low voice to Fang, 'Kill.'"

"Anastasia went to her room to sulk. She always left the door open when she was sulking. She had perfected the art of sulking, and one of the essential points was that people had to know you were doing it. So it was important to leave the door open." The more she thought about a new, unfamiliar house, the more upset she became. Her parents were making a list of what features they wanted in a new house. Her father wanted a study with lots of bookcases; her mother wanted a room with lots of light where she could paint; they wanted a yard for Sam. When they asked Anastasia what she wanted, she suddenly realized how she could stop the move to the suburbs. She told her parents she wanted a tower, a house where she could have a room in a tower.

Did that stop her parents? No! They *found* a house with a tower, and a witch for a neighbor. Read *Anastasia Again!* to see how Anastasia survives in the suburbs.

—Judy Druse

ANASTASIA KRUPNIK   Grades 3-6
By LOIS LOWRY

Did you ever keep lists of things that are important to you? Anastasia Krupnik does. Mainly two lists: things she loves and things she hates. She loves Mounds Bars, writing poetry, her friends, and Christmas. She hates her name, her parents, her grandmother, liver, and babies.

Life is occasionally complicated for Anastasia, especially when her parents announce she is going to have a baby brother—and she is almost eleven years old, practically an adult! Not only that, they want her to visit with her ninety-two-year-old grandmother, who never remembers who she is. And then there's Mrs. Westnessel, her teacher. Anastasia works for days on a poem for class. It's a beautiful poem—it even sounds like some of the ones in the books her father wrote. But Mrs. Westnessel gives her an F because it doesn't rhyme! No one ever told Anastasia that poems had to rhyme! Anastasia even hates her name—it is too different, and much too long to fit on a tee shirt, and that means she can't join the club all her friends are in at school.

Besides, it seems as though she has to work everything out alone! To see how she manages and what else she puts on all her many lists, read *Anastasia Krupnik.*

—Joni Bodart

AND THEN WHAT HAPPENED,   Grades 1-2
PAUL REVERE?
By JEAN FRITZ

How many of you know the story of Paul Revere? How he rode through the countryside letting everyone know that the British were coming, and so helped people get ready for the Revolutionary War. If you don't know about that yet, you'll hear about it sometime in school, but you probably won't hear about all the things that went wrong along the way—the narrow escapes and the silly mistakes. They're all here, in *And Then What Happened, Paul Revere?*, a very true and funny story that tells you that Paul Revere not only made silver teapots and spoons, he also made false teeth out of hippopotamus tusks! And once he built a barn for himself, but accidentally built it on his neighbor's land instead of on his own. And when he started off on his famous ride, his wife was mad at him because he forgot to close the door and his dog ran off. But he forgot two other important things too—he forgot the cloth to wrap around his oars so his boat wouldn't make any noise as he rowed it across the river next to an armed ship, and he also forgot the spurs he'd need to help make the horse go as fast as possible. But then what happened? Well, one of Paul's friends knew a lady who lived nearby and he called up to her window and asked for some cloth. She was in such a hurry to help that she just took off her red flannel petticoat and dropped it out the window! And remember that dog that got loose? Luckily it followed Paul, and Paul wrote a note to his wife, attached it to the dog's collar, and told the dog to go home, and by the time Paul had wrapped that petticoat around the oars, the dog was back with Paul's spurs hung around its neck. What happened after that? Some things went well and some things went poorly, and you can find out how, in *And Then What Happened, Paul Revere?*

—*Elizabeth Overmyer*

AND THIS IS LAURA   Grades 5–7/YA
By ELLEN CONFORD

For a long time Laura was convinced she was adopted. That would explain why she was the only ordinary member of a family of overachievers. Her mother wrote novels. Her father was a brilliant scientist. Jill, her sister, was an actress, and her brother Doug was a musician.

If only she could see into the future! But of course that wasn't possible.

The first time it happened, she was sitting at the dining-room table. Her friend Beth had been there. During all the noise and confusion, everything faded away, and she could see her father jumping up and down in the middle of his lab with a huge smile on his face. Laura blurted out, "You'll figure out your problem tomorrow after the man in the white shirt leaves." Well, you can imagine everyone's surprise.

The next time she looked into the beyond was at Beth's house. Laura just closed her eyes and right in front of her was Beth, standing on the stage receiving flowers. It clearly meant that Beth was going to be the star of their junior high play.

Of course, Laura didn't know what it was she was doing or if she was actually foretelling the future. But as soon as she arrived home her father told her that what she had foretold had actually come true, just as she had predicted!

She was putting away some frozen foods when she saw a vision again. A grotesque scene appeared before her very eyes. Her mother was dressed in a child's pinafore, playing with dolls. Then one of the dolls was missing. . . . Her mother was throwing a temper tantrum. What did it all mean? Laura was terrified because the missing doll was her youngest brother Dennis! Could she actually foretell the future? Was she truly psychic? Would she be able to use her psychic powers to find her own brother?

—Lucy Marx

THE ANIMAL, THE VEGETABLE,   Grades 6–8
AND JOHN D. JONES
By BETSY C. BYARS

Twelve-year-old Clara Malcolm and her older sister, Deanie, had been competing for their father's attention since the divorce. They were really excited about their upcoming vacation at the Pipe Island beach house. They would have their father's undivided attention. But their father announced that Delores Jones and her son, John D. Jr., would be sharing the beach house with them. John D. was no more excited about the prospect of spending his vacation with strangers than Clara and Deanie were. After meeting the two girls, John D. felt he had fallen into the hands of creatures no longer governed by human values. Deanie was a vegetable; Clara was an animal; and John D. thought of himself as a tablet, like Alka-Seltzer, dropped between the two to start things fizzing.

—Judy Druse

ANNA TO THE INFINITE POWER Grades 6–8/YA
By MILDRED AMES

Rowan Hart doesn't like his sister Anna. Of course a lot of people don't like their sisters, but Rowan really has good reason. Anna is twelve and a complete brat. She lies, she cheats, she steals—and she's brilliant, straight A's all the time. But Anna is cold. Her mind is like a computer. She never seems to feel anything.

Like a lot of older brothers, Rowan has to take care of his sister at times, since his parents both work. One cold Saturday his mother tells him to take Anna to the museum. But Rowan hates museums (Anna loves them, naturally) so he drops her off and arranges to meet her later in a nearby department store. Anna is late meeting him that afternoon, but he finally sees her over in the clothes department. He goes over and calls her name. She turns—and he realizes this isn't Anna. Physically she looks exactly, exactly like his sister. But she's different—softer, prettier, better-dressed. And she looks at Rowan and says, "Who are you? And how did you know my name?"

Rowan finds out that his sister is a clone—an exact duplicate of another, famous Anna who died thirty years ago. But she isn't the only one. There are dozens of Anna clones, and they're all part of a secret experiment—an experiment that will lead to their deaths and a vastly altered humankind. And Rowan is the only one who knows—the only one who can save his sister—the only one who can save the world.

—Christy Tyson

ANNIE ON MY MIND   YA
By NANCY GARDEN

Annie on My Mind is a love story. It is a story of two people who meet and immediately like each other. As they get to know each other better, they find they have much in common. They never run out of things to talk about, and they can't seem to see enough of each other. They fall in love. Like many couples who are in love, they face obstacles and problems. But their love for each other finally sees them through to better times.

Annie on My Mind is the bittersweet love story of Eliza Winthrop and Annie Kenyon.

The story is told by Liza, a freshman at MIT. She begins their story with the day she met Annie Kenyon just a year before, in November of their senior year. They meet one rainy Saturday at the New York Metropolitan Museum of Art, and Liza immediately knows that something is different. She has never felt so strongly about anyone before.

All through that winter Annie and Liza struggle with their feelings for each other. They try not to touch or say too much. But the intensity of their relationship builds. Eventually, both Liza and Annie come to terms with their feelings and begin shyly to explore their love. As long as no one knows about their love, no one is hurt. But a thoughtless, careless mistake on their part brings their relationship and the relationship of two people they greatly admire into the open. The result is the scorn, anger, and disappointment of friends, family, and teachers. The ramifications of their careless action are great.

Now at MIT, with Annie thousands of miles away in college at Berkeley, Liza struggles with her guilt and her love for Annie. Liza hangs on to the parting words of Ms. Stevenson, who had been her art teacher at Foster Academy.

"Don't let ignorance win," said Ms. Stevenson. "Let love."

—*Barbara Lynn*

ARK ON THE MOVE
By GERALD DURRELL
YA/Adult

Gerald Durrell is a collector of exotic animals, a zookeeper, a rescuer of endangered species, and the only author who can make me snicker, snort, giggle, laugh, and guffaw while reading his books about his worldwide adventures.

His love of animals is obvious from the way he talks about them—almost as if they were human. He began collecting animals as a boy on the Greek island of Corfu, much to the chagrin and disdain of his older brother Larry. (Or perhaps you know him better by the name he publishes under—Lawrence Durrell!) When he grew up, Gerry traveled far and wide collecting animals for zoos, but gradually became both dissatisfied with the way zoos treated animals and concerned about the increasing number of endangered and extinct species. He built a zoo and set up a trust fund on the Isle of Jersey in the English Channel, and began to breed endangered species in captivity.

The *Ark on the Move* is about his trip to Madagascar and the Mauritius Islands to obtain animals for the Jersey Zoo.

However, rather than tell you what Gerry's like, I'll let him speak for himself.

One of his favorite creatures (and mine) is the lemur, several species of which are found on the island of Madagascar. This, of course, is not to slight the skinks, the tenrecs, the pink pigeons, the baby shearwaters, the geckos, and the "endearing and charming" fruit bats, but those are other stories—for now, we'll stick with the lemurs. [Read or describe from page 78; page 90; page 114 "We were particularly . . . sacred to the islanders"; page 116 "These black lemurs . . . " on; page 117; page 120 to "without rancour and animosity."]

But the lemurs, as I said, are only one kind of animal—and Gerry describes dozens of others in *Ark on the Move*.

—*Joni Bodart*

BANANA TWIST   Grades 4–6
By FLORENCE PARRY HEIDE

Jonah D. Krock lived on the thirteenth floor of a high-rise apartment building. He was in the process of filling out an application to Fairlee, a private school. He was desperate to be accepted by Fairlee because he had heard from a very reliable source that they let their students eat junk food, watch TV, and laze around without exercising—all the things he craved and wasn't allowed to do at home.

Under the pretense of going downstairs to the mailbox, Jonah went to the drugstore to get a candy bar. He was on his way back to his apartment when he stepped into the elevator to find a kid carrying a huge bag full of groceries. This guy never realized Jonah was in the elevator with him as he mumbled over the grocery list. When the elevator door opened, both boys started through the door at the same time. They bumped into each other and groceries went all over the hall floor, except the bananas, which were left in the elevator. "Yipes!" said the new guy, "they've gone up in the elevator!" Jonah couldn't understand what was so important about those bananas, but he pushed the button for the elevator to come down and tried to calm this weird kid. Jonah told him that the bananas would be all right. The character was hysterical by then, screaming, "It may be too late! They'll die! They'll die!" Again Jonah tried to calm him, all the while thinking about the good television program he was missing. Jonah decided that soothing talk about the bananas and how they could last for days and not need to be kept in the refrigerator would help calm the little guy (whose name turned out to be Goober), but soothing talk didn't seem to help. Finally Goober went running up the stairs, saying, "I'm going up!" Jonah thought he said that he was *throwing* up. As Jonah stood there wondering what to do next, the elevator started down. The door opened, and out flew Goober, carrying the banana bag and screeching, "They're alive! But I think Emily is dying! Hurry! There's no time to lose!" They rushed into Goober's apartment, and following his frantic instructions, Jonah filled a mixing bowl with lukewarm water. Jonah popped the bananas into the water and began telling Goober that Emily was perking up. Goober stood there looking at Jonah and said, "Are you some kind of nut?" Then he opened the deli carton and dumped his tropical fish into the water.

This is just one of the many mixups that occur in *Banana Twist,* as Jonah tries to avoid his strange newfound friend Goober.

—Debbie Denson

THE BATTLE HORSE   Grades 6–8/YA
By HARRY KULLMAN

The first time Roland saw the Black Knight from the Deepest Darkness with his own eyes was a hot, summery September afternoon. It was the first time he had attended one of the jousting tournaments devised by Buffalo Bill, the great organizer and showman of the neighborhood. Buffalo Bill had gotten the idea for the jousts from the book *Ivanhoe.* The tournament was open only to knights of noble lineage, the rich private school kids on the block, who rode battle horses, the poor public school kids. At the first blast of the bugle Buffalo Bill's backyard was transformed as if by magic into a medieval arena with stamping horses ridden by knights wearing helmets and carrying lances from which flew their colors. Something grand and colorful and heroic that had happened a long time ago was being kept alive. It was the most fantastic thing Roland had ever seen. And the Black Knight from the Deepest Darkness was the most terrifying thing he had ever seen. No one had ever defeated the Black Knight; no one even knew who he was beneath his black mask. Roland is thrilled when he is asked to become a part of an ingenious plan to conquer the Black Knight. But the consequences are more tragic than he could have imagined.

—Judy Druse

BEAUTY   Grades 6–8/YA
By ROBIN McKINLEY

Returning from a trip to the city, Beauty's father was caught in a terrible blizzard, and he came home with a strange and horrible story to tell. He had been traveling through a thickly wooded section of the forest and was lost in the storm. He had almost given up hope when he came across a walled garden surrounding a great castle. Finding the doors unlocked and no one about, he had taken refuge in this castle. Although he had seen no one during the night, he had been wonderfully cared for, by invisible servants. Invisible hands opened doors, poured tea, fed him a magnificent meal, and led him to his bedroom. When he left in the morning, he found his horse had been equally well cared for. But as he left, he stopped to pick a rose from the garden—a gift for one of his daughters—and suddenly a roaring filled his ears and an immense beast appeared. The beast released him, on the condition that he would return within one month and bring one of his daughters.

It was Beauty, the youngest, who returned a month later. She was just eighteen and not beautiful at all, despite her nickname. When she entered the castle she fully expected to be killed immediately. But the truth was far stranger than anything she could have imagined. For she was treated like a princess. Yet she was never allowed to leave, and her only companion was the great beast, who every evening asked her to marry him.

—*Elizabeth Overmyer*

THE BEGINNING PLACE   YA/ADULT
URSULA K. LEGUIN

Hugh's mind was clicking like the cash register at the store as he trudged home from work through the barren suburban development. Ever since his dad had left, Hugh's mom had had a phobia about coming home to an empty house, so she insisted that Hugh stay home and wait for her in the evenings. That night it seemed that the air in the house was trying to suffocate him, to engulf him. Panic seized him, and he ran from the house, his bulky weight hitting the ground in heavy shocks. The air burned his throat and lungs. The darkness thickened like blood. Hugh ran and ran, until he finally fell gasping by a stream in the woods. As breath returned, he found that the air was no longer hostile. There seemd to be a sense of peace emanating from this place. The smells of the stream bank welcomed him. The waters of the stream seemed alive, holy. When he drank it, the water was cold and tasted of the sky. Here it was twilight, and time seemed to stop. After what seemed like hours, Hugh sprang to his feet realizing that his mother was expecting him to be at home. Yet when he got home, she still had not returned and it was still early.

Hugh sat down to sort things out. All his life he had been running— run-and-hide-Rogers—but all his running had never gotten him any- where before. There was no place to hide, no place to be. This time he had stumbled into a wild place where there was silence, loneliness, wa- ter running in twilight, the taste of mint. His thoughts wandered to the college he had hoped to attend, all the smothered ambitions. Perhaps there would yet be a way to get into that quiet world of learning.

Hugh's mom burst in screaming at him for having the lights out, for letting his supper burn, for this, for that, and on and on. Here he was, nearly twenty-one, and she still treated him like a child. As soon as he could escape, Hugh ran and hid in bed. He still felt her bitter hatred in the morning when he found the cups she had broken in her rage. It made him sick. How could he escape to his secret place again? He tried going before work, but had to turn back when he realized that he'd be late. It still puzzled him that he had gotten to the creek, stayed there for a long time and run home all in two short hours. A lady at work noticed he had been running and asked if he had been jogging to lose weight. Hugh pretended that he had and quickly found something to do to hide from her questions.

But from time to time during the day's work he thought of the water in the creek. He craved a drink of that water again. Maybe he could convince his neurotic mother that he was going to take up jogging and make his absence acceptable. His mother's reply was sharp, her hysteria thinly veiled. Ordinarily Hugh would have heeded the warning signals and simply have given in to her demands, but he was driven by his thirst for that living water. He must drink once more from that creek, that mysterious creek in that twilight land where time seemed to stop.

Would he find his way back to the beginning place? What adventures awaited him there?

—E. Lynn Porter

BELOVED BENJAMIN IS WAITING   Grades 6-8
By JEAN E. KARL

What was Lucinda Gratz going to do after her brother, Joel, went off to school? She had two major problems facing her. One: the bad fights between her parents. Two: the threats from the neighborhood gang.

Before Joel left, they decided if the situation at home got really bad Lucinda could hide in the cemetery across the street. Anyone would have to be desperate to hide in the cemetery, especially at night! But Lucinda *was* desperate at times.

Lucinda's parents continued having fights after Joel was gone. The first night she slipped through the almost hidden gate without any trouble. She crouched in the bushes for awhile, really quiet, so no one guarding the cemetery would discover her. Then she saw the caretaker's house. Investigating, she found it had a bed, and she decided it was safer to stay there for the night than to go home to all the fighting.

One day, Lucinda's mother told her that her father would not be coming back. Not long after that, her mother told her she would be leaving for a while and would be gone about a week or ten days. Lucinda's mother left, and the neighborhood gang discovered she was alone and began harassing and trying to frighten her.

Lucinda found refuge in the caretaker's house in the cemetery for the week her mother was gone. She had never felt so alone in her entire life, until one night she heard a low humming noise. A statue of a boy named Benjamin who had died almost a hundred years ago began to come to life. It glowed, hummed, and made noises like words.

Through the statue, Lucinda began to realize that she was not alone.

—*Margaret G. Driskill*

THE BEST CHRISTMAS PAGEANT EVER Grades 4–6
By BARBARA ROBINSON

Remember the meanest kids you ever knew? Bullies, show-offs, liars, fighters—remember them? The Herdmans in Barbara Robinson's *The Best Christmas Pageant Ever* are undoubtedly the meanest kids who ever barely escaped juvenile hall.

They are so mean, even their cat is mean. Claude Herdman emptied the whole first grade in three minutes flat when he took his cat to Show-and-tell.

Claude hadn't fed the cat in two days, so it was already mad. And when he opened the box, the cat shot out, right straight up in the air. It came down on the blackboard and clawed four big long scratches all the way down.

Miss Brandel, the teacher, knocked over the Happy Family doll-house, broke the globe, and smashed the aquarium full of twenty gallons of water and sixty-five goldfish trying to catch the cat.

After that, there was a rule that you couldn't bring anything live to Show-and-tell.

You can imagine how my mother, the director, felt when the Herdmans showed up to try out for the parts in the Christmas pageant. It seems that they'd heard about the refreshments served at the church. Naturally the Herdmans got the main parts in the pageant. No competition—all the other kids knew that if *they* tried out, they would get clonked on the head and have worms put in their pockets.

Having read nothing but Amazing Comics, the Herdmans didn't know anything about the Christmas story—but they got involved quickly. They left the first rehearsal arguing about whether Joseph should have set fire to the inn or just chased the innkeeper into the next county.

My mother had trouble finding a baby Jesus because all the mothers withdrew their babies from consideration when they heard about the Herdmans.

Imogene Herdman wanted to know why they didn't let Mary name her own baby. "What did the angel do, just walk up and say 'Name him Jesus'?" Alice Wendelkin said, "I know what the angel said—she said, 'His name shall be called Wonderful, Counselor, Mighty God, Everlasting Father, the Prince of Peace.'"

"My God," Imogene said, "He'd never get out of the first grade if he had to learn to write all that!"

Well, everybody came to the pageant to see what the Herdmans would do. You are invited to the pageant too—read Barbara Robinson's *The Best Christmas Pageant Ever.*

—Judy Thomas

THE BEST LITTLE GIRL IN THE WORLD   YA
By STEVEN LEVENKRON

Francesca looked at herself in the mirror behind the ballet barre. She was fat . . . horrible . . . ugly! Her thighs were grotesque bulges under the leg-warmers. Above them her buttocks protruded offensively. Her torso seemed to be all flab. She was fat . . . more than fat, she was a monster . . . a five-foot-four, *ninety-eight-pound* monster! And when Madame came by, she said Francesca needed to lose a pound here and there and firm up. Slim and straight, that was how a ballet dancer had to be. Slim and straight. Francesca passed up a hamburger with her friends after class and walked all the way home. She even made up a new name for herself—Kessa. No one could make *Kessa* eat, no one could make *her* fat.

And so Francesca's, Kessa's, diet began—five-four, 98 pounds; 96, 94, 86, 84, 81—and still she was fat! She had ugly bulges of *fat* where only ridges of bone should show through in stark, pure beauty. Finally, her parents noticed, and treatment began. Or rather, a series of games began, with Francesca tricking her parents into thinking she was eating while she continued to starve herself. Then a psychologist, and hospitalization.

Francesca—or Kessa now—is deliberately starving herself to death. And no one can stop her. Obsessed with food, surrounded by people who want her to eat—who even force her to—Kessa is commiting suicide by starving herself to death.

But everyone said what a perfect daughter, perfect friend she was—everything anyone could ever hope for. What happened to make such a perfect girl do this to herself?

—Joni Bodart

THE BIG WAY OUT YA
By PETER SILSBEE

Fourteen-year-old Paul MacNamara awoke to yet another fight between his parents. He couldn't exactly understand the words but he knew the sound, and it was dangerous. Then he distinctly heard his father say, "Don't tell me the past is past! That's what the shrinks tell me. The past is dead! As dead as Jake!" Paul's father was insisting that his mother and he go to Kansas City with him for the funeral of his brother Jake. But Jake had been dead and buried two years; he had shot himself with a deer rifle. Dr. MacNamara, Paul's father, was home again after six months in a mental institution. He obviously needed to go back. He was charming one minute, violent and lordly the next. Paul's brother Tim denied the danger, said the old man was okay now; yet he spent all his spare time at his girlfriend's. Paul's mother tried to protect her husband, but they couldn't go on lying and covering up for him all the time. Finally they fled their California home for upstate New York, where her family was. They had to flee; who knows what would have happened next? However, Tim, the older brother, refused to leave his father and went with him to Kansas City. After Kansas City, Tim and his father headed for New York, to reunite the family. But Paul had anticipated this; he was waiting and watching for them from the top of the town's water tower with a rifle in his hands, seeing the death of his father as the only way out, the big way out.

—Judy Druse

THE BIGGER BOOK OF LYDIA YA
By MARGARET WILLEY

Would Daddy be alive if only he'd been bigger? That was the only thing ten-year-old Lydia Bitte could think about after her father's funeral. So many friends at the funeral mentioned her father's smallness that Lydia began to wonder if her father's size had something to do with his death.

Everything in Lydia's life had seemed normal before her father's death. The fact that she had such a tiny father and mother always made the family seem special. The family had been so comfortable in their smallness, so secure together.

Now everything had changed. Her father was gone, crushed beneath the wheels of a huge produce truck with brake failure. Lydia thought about all the things she had seen crushed because they were too small— insects, eggs, tiny toys left on the floor. She began a notebook entitled "The Bigger Book" in which she collected these thoughts and any other information she could find that had to do with size and growth or danger and death. She had to discover how to get bigger. Her family were no help. After the funeral, her mother fell into a trancelike slumber, getting out of bed to wander around like a sleepwalker. Her sister, Rita, went into her own bedroom, opened her toy box, and built a room-sized miniature city. She played fanatically, peopling the plastic families with at least two fathers. So Lydia took on the responsibility of running the household. And she kept her grades up, too. Gradually, she stopped thinking about the notebook. It was lost and forgotten.

Now, at fifteen Lydia has put all that behind her, but she is still withdrawn and self-conscious about her small size. She is uncomfortable around boys, hates the nickname "Littlebit" her friends at school call her, and considers dropping out. She wonders why people can't see her as she really is—strong, and in her own way independent.

Then Lydia meets Michelle, who is also withdrawn, but for very different reasons—she has anorexia nervosa and wants only to be smaller. Lydia is disturbed by anorexia because it is a process of shrinking and fading, a reversal of her own obsession to grow bigger.

—Judy Druse

BILL KURTIS ON ASSIGNMENT   YA/Adult
By BILL KURTIS

Bill Kurtis, now the co-anchor on the CBS morning news, got his start in broadcasting when he was sixteen years old and received a work permit from the State of Kansas. It was 1958, and Bill Kurtis went to work for KIND radio in Independence, Kansas, his birthplace and boyhood hometown. From that unpretentious beginning he would go on to cover some of the most important stories of the sixties, seventies, and eighties.

From Independence, Bill went to college in Topeka and worked for KTOP-AM and WIBW-TV. He spent a couple of years in the Marines and came back to the University of Kansas in Lawrence to attend law school. During the summer of 1966, Bill was studying for the bar exam, preparing to take a job with a law firm in Wichita. On the night of June 8, 1966, he was substituting at WIBW-TV for his friend Tom Parmley, who was on vacation. Shortly after 7:00 p.m., Bill was handed a bulletin that meant death and destruction for the city of Topeka—a tornado was approaching! Bill broadcast the warning, just before the storm cut right through the city. For Bill, it was a first-hand example of how television could save lives. It was also a life-altering experience. Within a few months, he joined WBBM-TV in Chicago. Over the next two decades, Bill Kurtis would be an eyewitness to many of the most important news stories of those times.

Bill Kurtis was in Iran, as one of the few Western press allowed in after the hostage crisis reached its peak. He was in Poland several times in the late seventies as Solidarity made its bid for power and the Pope visited his homeland. Bill and his news team at WBBM-TV in Chicago were responsible for a documentary that brought the plight of the Vietnam veterans who had been exposed to Agent Orange to national attention. While investigating that story, he was part of the first American press team to visit South Vietnam since the Communist takeover. That visit led to a story on the plight of the children of American servicemen who are still in Vietnam. For each of these stories, Bill Kurtis won an Emmy and several other national press awards.

Bill Kurtis shows you the individuals who lived the stories that make the headlines. He is a reporter, observer, and photographer of some of the most important events of our times—the Islamic revolution in Iran and the holding of the American hostages, the Polish Solidarity movement, the wanton bloodshed of El Salvador's civil war, the waste and plunder of the natural resources of this continent, and more.

—*Barbara Lynn*

A BILLION FOR BORIS   Grades 3–5
By MARY RODGERS

Boris needs a billion *fast,* because he has a crazy mother who spends a lot of money. Annabel doesn't have any money, but she does have a crazy little brother, ApeFace, who has just repaired an old TV set. It correctly predicted a snowstorm that took everyone in New York and Connecticut by surprise. After a few more predictions come true, Annabel realizes that they have a TV set that will predict tomorrow's news today—and they have a dynamite way to earn a lot of money. Boris figures he'll use the money for his mother, but Annabel wants to use it for doing good deeds. But neither of them figures on ending up $12,000 dollars in debt, or with a thirty-year-old boyfriend for Annabel!

—*Elizabeth Overmyer*

BLIND FLIGHT YA
By HILARY MILTON

Debbie is going "upstairs," flying in a small plane with her uncle Walt. Uncle Walt wants to take her mind off her surgery on Monday.

Debbie is sitting in Aunt Eva's sunlit breakfast room drinking her cocoa. "Is it too hot?" Aunt Eva asks. Debbie puts both hands on the table and slides them forward over its polished surface until her fingers touch the mug. She cautiously lifts it to her lips.

Debbie is on her family's monthly visit to Uncle Walt and Aunt Eva's farm. She and Rick love to come to the farm each month. Even though her brother is two years younger, they plan and do things together. Rick is in the barn feeding his favorite horse. It is too bad that Rick is afraid to fly in a plane.

Uncle Walt is ready to go. Flying in a small plane can be chilly business. Debbie feels for her warm stocking cap and pulls it over her ears. She wears her jacket and gloves, too.

As he opens the door for her Uncle Walt asks her where they should go.

"Paris? Rome? London?"

"Moscow!" says Debbie.

Standing next to the plane with her face to the sun she vows she won't worry about her surgery. She sniffs the fresh aroma in the air but she can't put a name to it. Maybe it's the hay (they aren't far from the barn) or maybe the freshly-turned earth by the side of the road. Maybe even a late blooming wildfire flower.

"Let's climb aboard," says Uncle Walt.

He catches her hand and together they cross to the door of the plane. He helps her in, bends over and fastens her seat belt, and then climbs around into the pilot's seat.

Now what Debbie smells is new seat covers, light oil, and fumes from the engine. She reaches forward and lets her hands fall loosely on the dual control wheel. Her feet stretch out and touch the pedals.

With a sudden surge the plane begins moving forward. In seconds the bumpiness of the runway disappears and they are airborne. They seem hardly off the ground when Uncle Walt noses the plane upward. He climbs in a circular pattern and Debbie feels the sun brightly through the window.

"Want to fly?"

"Oh, I wish I could."

"Today, you just keep your hands on the wheel, let your feet rest on the pedals. If you concentrate, I'll bet by the time we land you'll know how to fly. Hey—over there—geese!"

Debbie turns her head but she can't hear them. Except for the sound of the engine and the whisper of the wind, Debbie feels as if she's in another world. No sense of being up or down, no sense of motion, no sense of there being anything else in the world. She thinks about her surgery and wishes she could stay up here forever.

Debbie feels the plane bank sharply and she finds herself leaning to the right. After what seems a few seconds, she feels the left side lower, the right wing come up, and once more she feels sure she is sitting level.

Uncle Walt says, "Now we'll just follow our noses and—*Oh, no, no!*"

Debbie hears a splintering crash, and the plane wobbles. Then it falls off to its side sharply, shakes all over, and noses down briefly before it vibrates once more and rights itself!

Debbie feels the cold wind blowing into the tiny cockpit.

"Uncle Walt! Uncle Walt!"

No answer.

Suddenly Debbie knows what has happened. One of the geese flying south has come through the windshield.

"Uncle Walt—you know I can't fly. I can't even see—I'm blind!"

—Janet Strang

BLISSFUL JOY AND THE SATs   YA
A MULTIPLE-CHOICE ROMANCE
By SHEILA GREENWALD

At sixteen and a half, Blissful Joy Bowman has a chip on her shoulder large enough to qualify as a small boulder. Aside from her name, the list of wrongs done to her by life include the fact that she has been born to a pair of childlike, unreliable, disorganized actors, who have never been able to get their act together to do more than sue for divorce. The divorce was the first project her parents ever completed successfully. It even changed their luck, from perfectly dreadful to merely bad. Bliss had learned at an early age that since she could not depend upon her parents she had best find a careful, mature, unimpulsive person to rely on. Herself. She has planned her life and left nothing to chance or luck. She knows exactly where she's going: to a wonderful college, Vassar; a fine graduate school; a professional career as a psychologist; and a *normal* life. The only thing standing in her way is her low score on the PSAT, the Preliminary Scholastic Aptitude Test. But she is studying hard to improve her score for the SAT. The SAT tells colleges how well a person will perform in college. Bliss's mother calls the tests the PSTUPIDs.

Involvements that might disrupt her plans are to be avoided at all costs. Life is hard enough without getting swamped with affections that could distort one's judgment and cause nothing but pain. Bliss veers from her course ever so slightly when she takes home a stray dog she finds on the subway. It leads to one complication after another, including her first MPRWOS (meaningful peer relationship with the opposite sex). Bliss becomes dreamy and romantic but doesn't want to be. None of her old systems for handling her planned life are working, and worst of all she has nothing to put in their place. After years of reckless, irresponsible behavior, her dad finds a good woman and marries her; her mother gives up acting and gets a job. They pull the rug out from under her. Her life turns inside out—and she begins to see that there is more than one way to conquer the SATs, and that there is more than one way to define "success."

—*Judy Druse*

BLUE HIGHWAYS: A JOURNEY INTO AMERICA   Adult
By WILLIAM LEAST HEAT MOON

"Life doesn't happen along interstates; it's against the law." So when at the age of thirty-eight, having lost his teaching job and close to losing his wife, half-Sioux Least Heat Moon set out on his own personal odyssey of more than twelve thousand miles, he took to the back roads of America, roads that, because they are usually colored blue on maps, he called "blue highways." He was going to stay on the three million miles of bent and narrow, rural American two-lanes, the roads to Podunk and Toonerville, into the sticks, the boondocks, the backwaters, the wide-spots-in-the-road, the don't-blink-or-you'll-miss-it towns, into the places where you say, "My god! What if I lived here!" Into the Middle of Nowhere. With minimal equipment, he set off from Columbia, Missouri, in his old Ford Econoline van, named Ghost Dancing, and headed east, then south, west, north, east, and southwest again until he had circled the country. Following a circle would give a purpose—to come around again—where taking a straight line would not. He talked to the people he met along these rural roads and in the small towns. People like Miss Ginny Watts of Nameless, Tennessee, who once ate some bad ham and got so sick she was "hangin' on the drop edge of yonder"; born-again Arthur whom he picked up near Potlatch, Idaho; and the old man called Stitch in Harbor Beach, Michigan, who had been "healed of an affliction to bear" at age sixteen, the affliction being "feet flat as waffles." These and dozens of other wonderful characters speak to Least Heat Moon in the pages of this book, and bring to mind how little we really know of this country and its people. He ate in restaurants that were recommended not by stars but by calendars: you can get a decent meal in a place with one calendar on the wall, but a three- or four- or (rare!) five-calendar place will satisfy your soul. He slept in the van and traveled by whim, left or right, it made no difference as long as the road went somewhere. He took to the open road in search of places where change did not mean ruin and where time and people and deeds connected. He followed the blue highways to a discovery of the country and, more importantly, of himself.

—Judy Druse

BLUES FOR SILK GARCIA   YA
By ERIKA TAMAR

At fifteen, Linda Ann Garcia is a promising rock musician. It is no accident. Her father, Antonio "Silk" Garcia, was a famous jazz guitarist who has recently been reported dead at the age of thirty-eight. Linda Ann feels his loss even though he was never in her life. He and Linda Ann's mother were divorced when she was two. Afterwards, Linda Ann's mother bitterly refused to speak of him. Whenever Linda Ann mentioned him, her mother got a closed, tight look on her face. Linda Ann wasn't even allowed to ask questions about him. When Linda was a child, she received a guitar from her father and a song dedicated to her, "Blues for Linda Ann." But that was all; he himself never visited. Her father's not coming to see her was partly her mother's fault, but dozens of marriages didn't work out and kids still got to see their fathers. Linda Ann could never understand, condone, or forgive her father for not even making an effort to see her. However, she still feels compelled to learn more about him, especially since she too is a talented musician, also a guitarist. Her search takes her into the world of nightclub musicians, where she pieces together an image of her father from the memories and anecdotes of his old associates. She comes to identify with her father; she is told her features closely resemble his; she also has his drive to excel, which her wealthy, popular boyfriend and fellow guitarist learns when she uses a joint audition he has spoiled as a springboard to her own career. In her search, she also discovers she has more in common with her father than just looks and talent. She has inherited his flaws as well.

—Judy Druse

THE BOLL WEEVIL EXPRESS   YA
By P. J. PETERSEN

"Just tell me where we are."

"Just shut up."

"You dummies want to go to San Francisco, so you hop a train to Oregon."

"Get ready to jump. We're gonna starve to death if we don't get off of here."

Hop off.

"I don't care what kind of town this is. . . . They've got to have something to eat here."

The three runaways, Lars, Doug, and Cindy, find it isn't easy to run away. They are hungry, lost, and seem to be going in the wrong direction. After they decide the Boll Weevil Express train isn't the way to travel, the threesome find a man they can hitch a ride with. Tired and exhausted, they fall sound asleep. Waking up several hours later, Lars, Doug, and Cindy find themselves in Healdsburg, Lars's home town. Lars, afraid he'll be discovered, refuses to go eat with the others.

Feeling too exposed on the car seat, Lars scoots down on the floor. He lies there on his stomach with his knees bent and feet sticking up in the air. He wishes desperately for some kind of cover—a blanket or even a coat. Without thinking, Lars grabs some brochures, tears them up, and puts them over his head. He asks himself, What would people think if they saw me here, jammed in between the seats, with pieces of paper sliding off my head? Answer: They'd figure somebody has a screw loose—and they'd be right. Lars lies there until he hears a tap on the window. He doesn't move. The tap becomes louder. "Hey, Larsy." More tapping. "Larsy, you all right?"

It is Claude. There is no mistaking that wheezy, whiny voice—it couldn't belong to anyone but "The Pest." "Larsy," Claude is calling. "You all right in there?" There is nothing to do but rise up.

Finally, Lars eludes Claude. Doug, Cindy, and the man come back, but this is just the first of their many adventures—fun, scary, and dangerous. What happens to this threesome? The answers are between the covers of *The Boll Weevil Express*, by P. J. Petersen.

—*Donna Houser*

THE BUMBLEBEE FLIES ANYWAY   YA/Adult
By ROBERT CORMIER

Sixteen-year-old Barney Snow is inside an automobile racing out of control down a hill. His hands strangle the steering wheel; his foot pumps the brake pedal. Nothing happens. The car gathers speed. Then he spots a girl down the hill standing at the curb, ready to step into the street, into the path of the speeding car. And then . . . the nightmare always ends there. The nightmare is a side effect of the merchandise given Barney by the Handyman. The Handyman is Dr. Edward Lakendorp, and the merchandise is medicine. Barney has relabeled them, as he always does things he fears or worries about. Doctors scare Barney to death; a handyman, a man as skilled and clever at repairs as a doctor is skilled with needles and drugs, he can deal with. Barney feels secure with the Handyman, but he doesn't really trust him or his experiments. There is always an element of risk. Barney is afraid the experimental drugs he is given will wipe out his memory; he won't even be able to remember his own name. So he writes his name on a piece of paper and hides it under a Band-Aid between his toes. But what if he forgets where he hid his name? The loss of memory is not the only side effect of the drugs. Sometimes Barney finds it hard to concentrate. He tries to concentrate on his mother's face but no picture comes to mind, only the jangling of her costume jewelry as she walks.

Barney doesn't tell the doctor or the other patients about his nightmare or his fears. That might encourage them to discuss problems or symptoms with him and that he doesn't want. He doesn't want to get too close. The others, Alberto Mazzofono, Allie Roon, and Billy the Kidney are terminally ill. They have come to the facility for experimental medicine looking not for a cure, but for some relief or maybe a little improvement if they're lucky. Barney is different: he is not ill; he is only a guinea pig.

But Barney's plan to isolate himself from the other patients is destroyed when Cassie Mazzofono, Alberto's twin sister with the pure blue eyes and the irresistible smile, asks for his help. It means befriending her brother Alberto, reaching through his bitterness, and giving Cassie daily reports on his condition. When Barney gets close to Alberto, he discovers that Alberto has accepted his death but he also dreams of going out in a blaze of glory. When Barney discovers the Bumblebee, he begins to plan one last moment of glory for them all.

—Judy Druse

BUNNICULA: Grades 4–8
A RABBIT-TALE OF MYSTERY
By DEBORAH and JAMES HOWE

This book is written by Harold. Harold comes to writing purely by chance—his full-time occupation is dog. He lives with Mr. and Mrs. Monroe and their two sons: Toby, aged eight, and Pete, aged ten. Also sharing the home are a cat named Chester and a rabbit named Bunnicula. It was because of Bunnicula that Harold turned to writing. Someone had to tell the full story of what happened in the Monroe household after the rabbit arrived.

It all began when the Monroes went to see the movie *Dracula*. They arrived at the theater late, and rather than trip over the feet of the audience already seated, they decided to sit in the last row, which was empty. They tiptoed in and sat down very quietly, so they wouldn't disturb anyone. Suddenly, Toby, who's the little one, sprang up from his chair and squealed that he had sat on something. Mr. Monroe told him to stop making a fuss and move to another seat, but in an unusual display of independence, Toby said he wanted to see just what it was he'd sat on. An usher came over to their row to shush them, and Mr. Monroe borrowed his flashlight. What they found on Toby's chair was a little bundle of fur, a baby rabbit shivering from fear and cold. They took him home and named him Bunnicula, a combination of Bunny . . . and Dracula. It proved to be an apt name, at least as far as Chester the cat was concerned. A well-read and observant cat, he soon decided that there was something odd about the newcomer. For one thing he seemed to have fangs. And the odd markings on his back looked a little like a cape. Furthermore, Bunnicula slept from sunup to sundown; he was awake only at night. When the family started finding white vegetables, drained colorless, with two fang marks in them, it was too much for Chester. He had to save his family from the vampire Bunnicula. Does he succeed? Is Bunnicula really a vampire? Find out by reading *Bunnicula*.

—*Judy Druse*

CAGES OF GLASS, FLOWERS OF TIME   YA
By CHARLOTTE CULIN

Claire Burden, fourteen years old, is a shy, timid girl, afraid of people and especially of her alcoholic mother, who stubs out cigarettes on Claire's bare arms and threatens to kill her if she finds Claire drawing.

Abandoned by her father, a painter, Claire is forced by the court to live with her mother, who buys beer but very little food. It's nothing for Claire to go two days without food.

Neglected and abused by her mother, Claire retreats to her drawing. Drawing is the only joy in her life. Sketching wildlife and leaves, Claire forgets the ugliness of her miserable life.

Will Claire's three new friends, Daniel, a black man who makes beautiful music on his guitar, Clyde and his Irish wolfhound, Jake, be able to help her?

—Frances Carter

CAN YOU SUE YOUR PARENTS FOR MALPRACTICE?   YA
By PAULA DANZIGER

Laren Allen is a fourteen-year-old ninth-grader who thinks she has *no rights!*

Her older sister, Melissa, gets a room all to herself. Her mother is always trying to get on quiz shows to win some extra money for the family. Her father, an insurance salesman, is forever talking about how hard it is to support a family in this day and age. Laren has to share a bedroom with her messy ten-year-old sister, Linda, who thinks she is a stand-up comic and tries out her stupid material on everyone! And then to top it *all* off, her boyfriend, Bobby, has just jilted her for a cheerleader.

Between her parents, her two sisters, and school, Laren feels she has no rights at all. But then she takes a course in Law for Children and Young People, and meets Zack, who is a real hunk. But Zack is only an eighth-grader—even if he *is* nice, cute, smart, and funny.

Gradually, however, Laren realizes that there just *may* be solutions to some of her problems.

Can you sue your parents for malpractice? Read the book and find out.

—Peggy Ross

THE CARNIVAL IN MY MIND   YA
By BARBARA WERSBA

Living in a huge, fancy New York apartment complete with butler and doorman doesn't do much for Harvey. At fourteen, he is obsessed with his height, or lack of it, since he is only five feet tall.

Harvey is so short that his mother never notices him. She is far too busy training her prize-winning Irish setters. The dogs were too much for Harvey's father, who gave up competing with them and moved to Connecticut, where he watches birds. But Harvey is still watching the dogs, trying to figure out why they're so special and he isn't. Meanwhile, the proper butler Holmes, who looks like an aging Cary Grant, is the only person who ever bothers with Harvey.

Everything changes when Harvey meets the woman of his dreams, beautiful, six-foot-tall, twenty-year-old aspiring actress Chandler Brown. It escapes his mother's notice entirely when Harvey leaves to move in with Chandler. Only Holmes is worried, as he should be, for Chandler may be lovely and talented, and she may even love Harvey back a little bit, but she certainly is not what she seems.

And when Harvey learns the truth about Chandler, he faces the most painful shock of his life.

—Cathi Edgerton

THE CASE OF THE ELEVATOR DUCK   Grades 1-2
By POLLY BERRIEN BERENDS

Since Gilbert is a detective who takes his work seriously, he has a regular detective routine worked out. Every morning he checks all the elevators in his apartment house—once up, once down—and memorizes the face of everyone he sees. On this particular morning, he watches everyone leave the elevator, and although he knows he is the only person left, he has a strange feeling that someone is watching him. This is the story of Gilbert's first case—if you think Perry Mason has trouble, wait till you see what happens when Gilbert's first client is Easter the duck!

—Elizabeth Overmyer

THE CELERY STALKS AT MIDNIGHT   Grades 3-5
By JAMES HOWE

By now most of you are probably familiar with Harold the dog, Chester the cat, and, of course, Bunnicula. They are back in this book, *The Celery Stalks at Midnight.* And now there is a new addition to the family. Howie, a wirehaired dachshund puppy recently adopted by the Monroe family. Chester has just finished telling Howie that Bunnicula is a vampire bunny when he discovers the rabbit has escaped his cage. Chester is worried—he stays up all night worrying. Surely Bunnicula is on the prowl, sucking the vital juices from helpless vegetables all over the neighborhood. But what will become of the vegetables Bunnicula attacks? Will the morning come to find the town overrun with legions of zombie-like white lettuce, carrots, celery, and tomatoes—obedient slaves to their vampire lord Bunnicula? Chester can think of only one solution—in the morning he sets out with Harold and Howie, armed with a box of toothpicks to drive like stakes through the hearts of those bloodless vegetables.

—Zoë Kalkanis

CENTER LINE   YA
By JOYCE SWEENEY

Shawn Cunnigan can't stand by any more and watch his brothers get slaughtered. Shawn, 18, Steve, 17, Chris, 16, Rick, 15, and Mark, 14, have had nothing to look forward to since their mother died ten years earlier in a automobile accident except the suspense in wondering whose turn it is to get beaten next by their drunk, abusive father. Shawn has always tried to protect his brothers by taking the blame when he can. But his father is getting worse and worse; someday one of them is going to get killed. Shawn has to do something; and, short of killing his father, all he can think of to do is run away. But he will need Chris's support. If Chris will back him up, he knows the others will follow. It's a big decision because, although it is not illegal for him to run away, it is for his under-age brothers. Nevertheless, he intends to take them with him; he would never consider leaving them behind. Besides, his dad's been getting away with assault and battery for eighteen years, so they ought to be able to get away with disappearing for four years until they are all adults. So Shawn and his four younger brothers take to the open road, searching for a new way to live. They have each other, the car stolen from their father, and Shawn's $4,000 college fund. They do not know what may lie on the road ahead; they do know what lies behind: their abusive father and the law.

At first, being on their own is full of adventure, but as time goes on, Chris begins to doubt the wisdom of what they have done; Rick becomes sullen and plans to take his share of the money and head out on his own; Steve turns cowardly; and Mark begins losing touch with reality. The daily struggle to survive is destroying their unity. Every dollar they spend is one dollar closer to the day Shawn will have to think of something else to keep them going. Meanwhile, their only hope is to keep driving along that highway center line, until they find a haven somewhere—or until they are found by the law.

—Judy Druse

THE CHAMPION
OF MERRIMACK COUNTY
By ROGER DRURY

Grades 3–5

Many of you have read about the mouse and the motorcycle, but the champion of Merrimack County is a mouse on a bicycle. O'Crispin is his name, and he had discovered that the best racetrack he could ask for was the big old bathtub in Janet's house. He pedaled around the bottom, he pedaled around the edge at the top; he did figure eights to get extra speed, and when he had enough speed he could go straight up the sides, right onto the rim. But his best trick of all was the one he called "Rolling down to Rio"—when he plunged straight down from the edge, pedaling all the way into the bottom until he braked at the last moment just before hitting the drain. Only, you can imagine what happens when he skids on a piece of soap just as he is braking. In the terrible crash that follows, Janet and her mother are faced with two tricky problems: how to fix a bicycle wheel the size of a dime, and how to bandage a mouse's dislocated tail, so that he can keep his balance in the great championship race two days from now.

—Elizabeth Overmyer

CHARLIE COMPANY: WHAT VIETNAM DID TO US   Adult
By PETER GOLDMAN and TONY FULLER

During the fall of 1981 and the spring of 1982, a team of *Newsweek* correspondents sought out and asked sixty-five veterans of Charlie Company who had fought in Vietnam in 1968–1969 how they felt about their experiences. Charlie Company was with the Big Red One of the First Infantry Division. They wore the Black Lion of the Second Battalion, Twenty-eighth Regiment. *Newsweek* published their stories in December, 1982, as a feature article. Many of these men had been very quiet after they returned to "the world." Many of them had never been asked about their war experiences.

From these interviews, it was soon obvious that the *Newsweek* team had only begun to tap the riches of the raw material. Thus the expansion of the story into a book was natural.

The *Newsweek* team delved into the experiences endured by soldiers of Charlie Company not only while in 'Nam but also after coming home. The members of Charlie Company were eager to talk. They eagerly unloaded the physical and psychological abuse they had had to shoulder for over a decade.

As one veteran wrote to *Newsweek,* "You [finally] gave us our parade."

The book is full of the veterans' pain—both in 'Nam and back home in "the world." This is an account of the personal hell that soldiers endured in Vietnam. One also gains an insight into the hell we visited upon the peoples of Vietnam, and the wastefulness of it all.

This is not a military history, about strategies of staffs and generals. It is a searing account of the everyday hell of the infantryman.

—Barbara Lynn

THE CHEESE STANDS ALONE   Grades 6–8
By MARJORIE M. PRINCE

Thirteen-year-old Daisy was not expecting any changes. She thought she'd always have her friends on the island to spend the summer with. She thought she'd always want to return to be with them. They'd grown so close, the five of them—two girls and three boys—they went everywhere and did everything together all summer long on that special place called Ellis Island. There was Uno (Charles Hollis)—he was the one Daisy liked the best. She'd always had a special feeling for him, she'd been the one to suggest his pack name (Numero Uno) because he was the best at almost everything, he was the tallest, the strongest, the oldest. She though he had a special feeling for her too, because he suggested her pack name (Numero Dos—which later became Dosy). Then there was Pan or Peter Panzini—he had a wonderful imagination and created stories for the pack to act out—and there was Wiggle, who was very good at appearing and disappearing without a sound. His real name was Bradford Putnam Wigglesworth III, and he'd had lots of practice keeping away from his mother. The other girl was Stinky (Ellen Warner). She started every day with an onion sandwich and was probably the easiest pack member to find. She was also the most agreeable member and seemed the most concerned that the pack stay together and never split up. But over the winter she had changed, and the first time they all went to the island it became quite clear just how she had changed. She had also stopped eating onion sandwiches, so her pack name was changed from Stinky to Boobs. Daisy found this hard to take. The rest of the pack, all the boys, were fascinated with the new Stinky—even Uno; that's what hurt Daisy the most. She could remember when they'd been young and played Farmer in the Dell— whenever Uno was the farmer he would always choose Daisy to be the wife. She remembered feeling sorry for whoever was chosen to be the cheese, especially when they were left in the circle standing all alone. To be left standing alone seemed terrible to her, and now she knew exactly how it felt. Her friends had changed and she no longer fit in. If it hadn't been for Mr. Potter, a newcomer to the island, the summer would have been totally disastrous. Find out how Daisy coped with the changes in her friends and what Mr. Potter had to do with it by reading *The Cheese Stands Alone,* by Marjorie Prince.

—Bonnie Janssen

CHRISTINE   YA/Adult
By STEPHEN KING

It was a lovers' triangle: Arnie Cunningham, Leigh Cabot, and, of course, Christine. It could have been funny if it hadn't been so sad, and if it hadn't gotten scary as quick as it did. It could have been funny if it hadn't been so bad, and it was bad from the start, but it got worse in a hurry.

Arnie Cunningham is a bookish and bullied high school senior. He is a loser, a natural "out." He is out with the jocks because he is scrawny; he is out with the druggies because he doesn't do dope; he is out with the macho group because if you hit him he cries; he is out with the girls because he has a face full of pimples. He takes a lot of abuse, but luckily, he has never gotten killed, yet. When it comes to cars, though, he is some kind of goofy natural-born mechanic.

Leigh Cabot is the beautiful new girl in school who (unbelievably!) is attracted to Arnie. Well, when Arnie falls in love, he falls hard, but with Christine, not Leigh. Christine is a 1958 red-and-white Plymouth Fury. The left side of her windshield is a snarled spiderweb of cracks. The right rear deck is bashed in, and there's an ugly nest of rust in the paint-scraped valley. The back bumper's askew, the trunk-lid's ajar, and upholstery's bleeding out through several long tears in the seat covers, both front and back. It looks as if someone has been working on the upholstery with a knife. One tire's flat. The others are bald enough to show the canvas cording. Worst of all, there's a dark puddle of oil under the engine block. But Arnie falls in love with her anyway.

Dennis Guilder is Arnie's only friend and sometime protector. He really likes Leigh Cabot, maybe even for himself. But Dennis doesn't like Christine at all. When Arnie was considering buying her, there was a moment when Dennis felt like slugging him and dragging him away. He thinks Trouble is a better name for the car and he's right—Christine is no ordinary car. When Dennis got in and put his hands on the wheel, something happened. A vision maybe. It was just for a moment: The torn upholstery seemed to be gone. The worn places were gone from the steering wheel. The cracks in the windshield were gone. The car seemed to say, "Let's go for a ride, big guy. Let's cruise." And then Dennis got out of that car just about as fast as he could. That car bothered him. It was a lot of little things, all adding up to a big itch that needed to be scratched. Dennis didn't like Christine, and it was as if Christine didn't like him either.

Dennis didn't like the guy who sold Arnie the car either. Roland D. LeBay, U.S. Army retired. He was an angry man, out to get those who had done him wrong. The first time Dennis saw his grin, he felt cold and blue inside; it wasn't the grin but the gleam behind the old man's eyes that chilled him. Dennis feels no regret when he hears that Roland LeBay died suddenly a few weeks after Arnie bought the car from him. When Arnie and Dennis meet LeBay's brother at the funeral, he tells Arnie to forget the car. Sell her. Whole or in parts. If no one will buy her for parts, junk her. Do it quickly and completely. He tells them that Roland's daughter choked to death in the car and his wife committed suicide in it.

But Arnie will not give up Christine. He feverishly begins to restore her, an antenna here and a hubcap there. He begins to spend more and more time with Christine, obsessed with the seemingly hopeless task of restoring her. It's crazy and not like Arnie at all. He treats Christine as if she were alive.

Then people begin to die on the streets and roads of town. Seven deaths . . . and they form a deadly ring around Arnie Cunningham and Christine.

—Judy Druse

CITY KID   YA/Adult
By MARY MacCRACKEN

Before Mary MacCracken met Luke Bauer, she'd pictured him to be a muscular kid, big for his age, the typical bully.

At least one person who knew Luke described him as "a stealing, cheating, bratty dumbbell." In fact, that's probably what a lot of people thought of him.

Luke had stolen from the drugstore, the five-and-ten, and from a woman in the local department store. He had set a fire in the hills that had taken the entire fire department two days to put out.

In two and a half years, he had skipped school over a hundred times. He had been arrested twenty-four times . . . all this, and Luke Bauer was only seven years old.

When she finally met Luke, Mary was not prepared for such an inno-cent-looking second-grader, but how could she even *start* to help him? How would *she* reach him when the police couldn't, his mother didn't have the time, his teachers had given up, and his father was nowhere around?

Sure, Mary had helped other kids with problems, but Luke was a hard-core city kid, and helping him seemed impossible.

—Avis Matthews

CLAN OF THE CAVE BEAR YA/Adult
By JEAN M. AUEL

"Kill my baby? Kill him because he's deformed?"

"It's the way, Ayla. You have no mate, you have no man to speak for you. A mother must dispose of a deformed child as soon as possible after his birth. You must do as Brun commands."

The time is the dawn of humanity. The clan, a wandering band of Neanderthals, is a race nearing its twilight. Ayla is Cro-Magnon. Her race will survive to people the earth.

It was a time when man's word was law. Woman obeyed. Men hunt-ed, women gathered food and raised children. Their survival depended on the advantage of the fit.

The people of the Clan of the Cave Bear were a superstitious lot. Ani-mal totems ruled their lives. The great cave lion was the strongest of all the totems, even greater than the cave bear.

Ayla was orphaned during an earthquake, was stalked and gravely wounded by a cave lion. The great scars meant that the lion became her totem after she was found and adopted by a childless woman of the clan.

Ayla was different from the people of the clan, and as she grew tall and fair, she was often an object of ridicule by the squat dark people, especially Broud, the son of the leader Brun.

A man took a mate to tend his fires and cook, but children were re-garded as gifts of the totems. Each month, if the bleeding came, then the woman's totem had defeated the man's totem, and no child would come forth.

Ayla's adoptive mother told her she would never be taken for a mate because she was so ugly, and she would never have a child. Her totem was too strong for anyone in the tribe.

Ayla and the clan were stunned when she became pregnant. They had not connected the need of men to relieve themselves with women, to the fathering of children. The only man who had ever relieved himself with Ayla was Broud, the clan leader's son—her old enemy. And he did it only to humiliate her and because he knew she hated him. By Law, she could not refuse him.

And now she must make a decision. "Brun is leader. His word is Law. If I disobey him, he will lose face and the men will cast him out. This gains me nothing. I won't kill my son, and we will die if we stay. But I don't want to go away." Ayla prayed to the great cave lion, but even he couldn't help her now.

—Linda Henderson

CLEVER KATE   Grades 1–2
Adapted by ELIZABETH SHUB

Kate was kind and loving and hardworking, but no one ever called her clever. When she let the dog snatch the sausage, she chased the dog and forgot that the beer was still running out of the barrel, and when she remembered that and found the floor all covered with beer, she emptied the flour all over the floor to dry it up—now, is that clever? When she dropped a cheese and it rolled down a hill, she rolled a second cheese down the hill after it to bring the first one back, and when her husband sent her home to make sure the door was locked and safe, Kate decided that the safest thing of all was to take the door off its hinges and bring it along with her. No, you wouldn't usually call Kate clever. But the night the robbers stole their golden coins, it was Kate who got them back!

—Elizabeth Overmyer

CLOSE ENOUGH TO TOUCH   YA
By RICHARD PECK

Last June there was Dory and "I love you's" and Fourth of July sparklers and laughter and, it seemed to Matt, everything. But today it's March, and it's cold and bleak—a day full of memories, but not joyful ones. Today is the day of Dory's funeral. Matt feels almost as if the world has ended. He needs to stop and wait for a while to recover, but crying's out, getting permanently drunk is a waste, and there are always people—saying, "It wouldn't've worked out anyway," "You'll find someone else," "There'll be someone else—there's always someone else. . . . "

But for Matt there can be no one else, there's only Dory and his memories of her. Until one day, months later, when Matt's running up by the lake, he sees a blue shape in the grass by the fence—a blue shape that develops into a girl lying in the ditch. A girl in an old-fashioned riding habit—a tight-fitted short jacket, long full skirt, narrow black riding boots, and leather gloves. A girl from another century, lying as still as if she were dead. And not far away is a horse with a saddle. But it's a saddle like no other Matt has ever seen—it has no stirrups, and has horns curving out at odd angles. Where did she come from?

Not far away, as it turns out. She's left her car in the riding academy parking lot. Her shoulder was dislocated when she fell, and Matt takes her to the emergency room, where the nurse at the desk discovers how little he knows about her:

"Relative?" "No."

"Friend?" "No."

"Name of patient?" "I don't know. I just found her in a ditch."

"Hospitalization?" "Beats me."

"ID?" "Didn't see any."

"Next of kin?" "Nope."

"Siddown, you don't know anything."

But later he discovers her name is Margaret—they go to the same high school—and he also discovers he hasn't thought of Dory for several hours. And so gradually Matt decides to recover from his lost, first love, decides to take another chance, admits that life *isn't* over, and so begins again.

—*Joni Bodart*

CONSCIENCE PLACE   YA
By JOYCE THOMPSON

The Place is a secret. No one outside knows it exists. No one inside knows that there is anyplace else. It is home to the victims of nuclear accidents—deformed babies born to the workers in nuclear plants. They were brought to The Place soon after birth—not even their parents know that they exist. Healthy, perfect babies were substituted for the mutated ones within a few hours of birth. In the outside world, life goes on as usual, without any panic about the possible effects of radiation. After all, with so many healthy babies, who needs to worry?

Life inside The Place goes on as usual also—although the outside world, if it knew about the residents of The Place, would not call them normal, but monsters. No one who lives there has a symmetrical body—everyone's body is different. Some have one arm and one leg, some two legs and no arms, some two arms and no legs. Some have fur, or skin, or scales, or flippers; some have increased mental powers, some do not. But each is valued, and all contribute something to The Place as far as they are able. Some sing, some dance, some make music, some write, some paint pictures, some sculpt, and one records the events of The Place on television, so even those who are unable to leave their rooms can also share in the celebrations and the daily life of The Place.

The people of The Place are different in another way, too. They have no concept of gender or sex. Not that they are not of two sexes—they are. But there are no words for gender differences in the vocabulary of The Place. Everyone is referred to as "it," rather than as "he" or "she." And since everyone's body is different anyway, the sexual differences are less important than they might otherwise be.

There is only one person at The Place who does not belong there, who has no mutations at all, who watches, and waits, and guards, and reports back to the outside world what is happening in The Place. Those who built The Place have watched it through the years, have watched it grow, have watched the people there live out their brief life-spans and die, only to be replaced with new infants. But now the mutations are increasing. There is less and less room in The Place, and it has begun to get more and more overcrowded. Something must be done—extermination, perhaps. After all, they aren't really People . . . not quite *animals,* of course, just . . . well . . . not people, but something else. The only one willing to fight for them is the only one who doesn't belong with them, and it is only one person—and what can one person do? Should it reveal the true situation to those who live in The Place? And what could they do if it did? Is there no solution?

The frightening thing about this book is that while it could be classified as science fiction, there is nothing in it that is not possible today. It could just as easily be nonfiction. And how do we really know that it isn't?

—*Joni Bodart*

THE COURSE OF TRUE LOVE NEVER DID RUN SMOOTH
By MARILYN SINGER

Grades 6–8

Becky and Nemi (short for Nehemiah) became friends in the third grade because Nemi did not want to play Baby Bear in the class play. Sensitive about his small size, Nemi hated being typecast, and when

Becky found him crying secretly she switched her part with his, earning his eternal friendship.

Now they are both juniors in a Brooklyn high school. Nemi is still short, Becky is still kind and understanding, they are still best friends and once again in the class play. But now Becky is playing Helena and Nemi is Puck (size-cast again) in *A Midsummer Night's Dream.* Though they love the challenge of performing their first Shakespeare, their attention is not entirely on learning their parts. For during the auditions, Nemi has fallen hopelessly in love with Leila, the beautiful new girl who won the part of Titania the Faerie Queen. And Becky has been sighing over Leila's equally gorgeous brother Blake. Leila and Blake Harris would make the All-American Perfect Couple if they weren't brother and sister. Even their names are perfect.

Now even though both Becky and Nemi are secretly irritated and annoyed over each other's silly infatuation, they behave like true best friends and make a pact to help each other attain the love objects of their dreams. After much calculation, they come up with the Harris Plan. They will write a filmscript starring themselves with Blake and Leila, flatter the Harrises into acting in the film, and shoot it with Nemi's new movie camera. During the long intimate shooting sessions they will each win the heart of a Harris. As a serious film buff, Nemi decides to write a very artsy script with no dialogue, but all Becky cares about is getting a lot of kissing scenes with Blake.

It is no trouble at all to convince Blake and Leila to star in their film. But will the Harris Plan work?

—Cathi Edgerton

A CRY IN THE NIGHT ADULT
By MARY HIGGINS CLARK

Twenty-seven-year-old Jenny MacPartland is divorced, working in a New York art gallery, struggling to support her two little girls, Beth, 3, and Tina, 2. Then she meets Erich Krueger, a handsome artist whose exquisitely peaceful landscapes are making him famous overnight. However, the painting that had originally attracted attention to him was not a landscape but a portrait of his mother called *Memory of Caroline.* Jenny could have posed for that portrait; the resemblance was amazing. And it is that painting that brings Jenny and Erich Krueger together. Jenny is in charge of a showing of his paintings at the gallery where she works. She is standing on the sidewalk one morning admiring *Memory of Caroline* in the gallery window. She takes a step backward to get a better perspective and stumbles into Erich Krueger himself. Within a month, Jenny is married to Erich, and she and her two children are transplanted from New York to Erich's Minnesota Farm. She has found her prince, the man she can truly love for the rest of her life, a man who will not share her with anyone.

But Jenny's past threatens her happy future. Her first husband, Kevin, shows up asking for money as he always did. Erich is exceptionally jealous so Jenny tries to keep Kevin's presence from him. But then Kevin threatens to not let Erich legally adopt Jenny's two daughters.

But it is not only Jenny's past that threatens her marriage. Erich's obsession with his mother Caroline also creates tension. Erich has never been able to overcome his grief at the loss of his mother, even though she died twenty-five years ago, because she died on his tenth birthday. Jenny can feel Caroline's presence and see her influence still on Erich and the farm. The house is still arranged and decorated exactly the way Caroline left it. Even Erich's old bedroom off the master bedroom is still decorated as that of a ten-year-old child. Erich tells Jenny it will please him if she will wear his mother's nightgown on their wedding night. Even though she feels uncomfortable in it, she obliges him.

Jenny begins to feel more uncomfortable after hearing disquieting stories from the farm help. Rooney Toomis, the former housekeeper, tells Jenny that Erich's mother was not happy. She was happy for a while but then things changed. She and Erich's father were going to get a divorce, and she had not asked for the custody of their son. Erich has never been able to accept that fact. Rooney tells Jenny also that the Krueger men are not known for being warm and loving. They are not forgiving, and once angry, they stay angry. Caroline had a feeling something terrible was going to happen, but she felt helpless to stop it. Soon afterwards, she had the terrible accident on the farm that took her life. Jenny doesn't know whether she can trust what Rooney says because other people say Rooney is crazy. Nevertheless, when Rooney offers to teach Jenny to quilt and make something nice before something happens to her, it sends a chill down Jenny's spine.

Jenny doesn't know whom to believe. Happy at first, she begins to feel like a prisoner in her isolated Minnesota home. The long, boring days and eerie nights begin to strain her nerves. She is accused of being places and doing things that she can't remember. Her confusion grows, she is near the breaking point. She begins to doubt her own sanity. If she could just leave it all behind for awhile, get away, she might be able to clear her mind of the confusion. Is this the way Caroline came to feel? Is this why she decided to leave? But Caroline never left. Is the same fate in store for Jenny?

—Judy Druse

CRYSTAL SINGER   YA
By ANNE McCAFFREY

Killashandra Ree had the gift of perfect pitch; she wanted to be a top-rank concert singer. But Maestro Valdi said she didn't have the voice for that; there was a flaw in her voice that could not be trained out. After ten grueling years of musical training, she was still without prospect for a fulfilling future. Valdi hoped that in time she would accept choral leadership. He didn't believe she would just discard ten years of her life in a second. But if she couldn't be at the top of her chosen profession, then goodbye theatre arts. She would be top in something else or die in the attempt. At least she was free, utterly and completely free. No schedules, no lessons, no studies. She would go to the spaceport and leave on a ship as a casual entertainer, searching for something to do for the rest of her life.

At the spaceport, she met Carrik of the Heptite Guild from the planet Ballybran. He was a crystal singer, a miner of crystal. Crystals are used as a power source in many operations, from interplanetary travel to power plants. Carrik told her that singing crystal was a terrible, lonely life. Mach storms on Ballybran would scramble the brain, remove memories, and reduce the mind eventually to a vegetative state. Crystal singers could not leave Ballybran's environment for too long, or they would be seized by violent convulsions. But for those qualified, the Guild was said to provide careers, security, and the chance for wealth beyond imagining. And beautiful music would fill her life, as the mountains returned her symphony of sound during the mining. Not only was perfect pitch required but immunity to a spore—that determined who sang crystal and who did not. There were risks involved, but to Killashandra, they were acceptable.

—Judy Druse

CUJO   YA/Adult
By STEPHEN KING

Cujo was a two-hundred-pound Saint Bernard and the best friend Brett Camber had ever had. Then came the day when all that changed. There were some people in town who knew there was something wrong that summer—something sinister, evil, something waiting. . . .

It was the sixteenth of June, quite early—a lovely warm early morning. Cujo *knew* he shouldn't chase rabbits, but this morning he didn't even try to resist. And with the wind blowing his scent away from the rabbit, he got within fifteen yards of it before the rabbit saw him and took off, with Cujo barking happily just behind—oh boy! Rabbit for breakfast! But just then the rabbit dropped out of sight and into a hole, and Cujo promptly followed him and got stuck half in and half out, right at the shoulders. He couldn't see very well, and he realized he was stuck almost right away—and he could still smell that rabbit. He barked furiously, and the sound echoed around him. For this was no ordinary rabbit hole but a limestone cave, with a roof inhabited by several small brown bats. Unfortunately, this year they were crawling with a particularly virulent strain of rabies. Cujo's barking woke them up, and they flew right at him, only to find they couldn't get out—he had completely blocked the entrance. They swirled around him, and he snapped and barked all the more. Suddenly his teeth crunched on a bat-wing, and the bat retaliated with a swift slashing bite across Cujo's muzzle. He let go, and it fell, already dying. But the damage was done.

Rabies is a disease of the central nervous system, and so bites around the head are most dangerous. Dogs are much more susceptible to rabies than humans—not even rabies vaccinations can guarantee they won't become infected. And Cujo, five years old, two hundred pounds, in his prime, had never had a rabies shot in his life. On the morning of June 16, 1980, he was prerabid, and by the end of the month, Cujo was beginning to feel very bad, very bad indeed, while around him the residents of Castle Rock, Maine, lived their lives unaware of the huge Saint Bernard in their midst, steadily feeling worse and worse—a tragedy just waiting to happen.

—Joni Bodart

DANCE ON MY GRAVE   YA
By AIDAN CHAMBERS

Sixteen-year-old Hal Robinson tells the story of his love affair with Barry Gorman.

> A love affair that lasted seven weeks, from beginning to end.
> Forty-nine days from Hal being soaked in seaweed to Barry being dead.
> One thousand, one hundred and seventy-six hours.
> Seventy thousand, five hundred and sixty minutes.
> Four million, two hundred and thirty-three thousand, six hundred seconds.

In their seven weeks together, Barry and Hal:
> Sailed the *Calypso* twelve times.
> Read eight books.
> Saw four films.
> Ate one hundred and nineteen meals together: twenty-three breakfasts, forty-four lunches, thirty-one suppers, nine picnics, and two middle-of-the-night snacks in bed.
> Motorbiked eight hundred miles, approximately.
> Went to London to see a show.
> Listened to hundreds of hours of music.
> Wrote each other five letters.
> Stayed up all night four times because they were talking so hard and didn't want to stop.
> Bought each other six presents—one each week. The last week was death.

This is the journal that Hal is writing to provide information for his court-appointed social worker prior to a hearing on why he was found dancing on Barry Gorman's grave. Hal is also writing the journal to purge himself of his feelings about Barry, and Barry's accidental death after a fight between them over Barry's fling with a Norwegian girl.

After Barry's death, Hal attempts to visit his body. Hal dresses as a girl because Barry's mother has refused to let him see Barry. He is discovered in the act but escapes. Hal then tries to fulfill a promise made to Barry, a promise he has every intention of keeping. As Barry requested, with fatalistic insight into the future, "Dance on my grave!"

—Barbara Lynn

DANCING CARL   YA/Adult
By GARY PAULSEN

Growing up in McKinley, Minnesota, in 1958 means fishing in the summer and skating in the winter. But the best time of the year is winter, when the whole social life of the town, for children and adults alike, revolves around the skating and hockey rinks that are set up in a flooded parking lot. One winter, there is an addition at the rinks. There is Carl Wenstrom.

Carl is a gray-haired man in a beat-up flight jacket. He is silent, moody, alcoholic, an emotional casualty of World War II. Although the grown-ups see Carl initially as the town drunk, they give him a job as custodian of the rinks and the warming shed (where he sleeps). He is a competent supervisor, but he is also a dancer. He does strange, free-style, mesmerizing dances on the ice to express his mood, what is going on inside him. His dances have movement and color; he has the power to make things normally ugly have a kind of beauty. Through his dancing, Carl teaches about living and loving and being what we are, all mixed into the cold and ice-blue flat of the skating rinks. Carl is a man of mystery. Some say he is crazy, everyone can tell he drinks, but there is an almost hypnotic power about him that fascinates Willy and Marsh. They try to find the reason Carl dances.

As the winter progresses, they learn more about him, but then when they show him a B-17 model, his dance becomes a frenzy of horror, and the boys learn that his own plane crashed during World War II; he was the only survivor. Had Carl begun to heal only to be broken again by memories from the past? Can he ever be whole while those memories still haunt him?

—Judy Druse

DARKANGEL   YA
By MEREDITH PIERCE

The vampyre is the most magnificent, and the most menacing, creature Aeriel has ever seen. He has huge black wings and a startlingly beautiful face. Around his neck he wears a necklace hung with fourteen little vials of lead. Aeriel learns that each of these vials, except for the last, contains the soul of one of his wives—thirteen so far. He chooses the most beautiful women in the kingdom and captures their souls so that they can't die. These women become piteous, bloodless wraiths, almost shadows. Unrecognizable as human, they're always begging for help. When the Darkangel takes a fourteenth wife, he will have control of the world. As he descends upon Aeriel, she believes that she has been chosen to be the fourteenth wife—doomed to live in eternal misery. But the Darkangel haughtily informs Aeriel that she is not beautiful enough to be a wife. He is abducting her so that she can be the servant of the wraiths. Told that she will be strangled and thrown to the gargoyles should she try escaping, Aeriel has no choice but to become the castle's servant.

Life at the castle is not as bad as Aeriel feared. She meets a friendly troll whom she can talk to secretly. The wraiths are endearing. The hideous gargoyles, with bat wings and lizardlike skin, are half-starved, so Aeriel starts feeding them. And she gets to know her master, the Darkangel. Beautiful as he is, the vampyre is evil. Aeriel comes across him breaking the wings of bats and throwing them off the ledge. She begs him to stop, but he says that he's bored and is looking for lizards—they're very easy to torture because it's not hard to poke out their eyes and tear out their tongues. Aeriel tries to amuse the Darkangel by telling him stories, and she begins to look forward to their meetings.

It's almost time for him to choose a fourteenth wife, and, in so doing, gain control of the world. The wraiths beg Aeriel to stop the Darkangel and free their souls so that they can die. The troll offers to help Aeriel destroy the Darkangel. Aeriel knows that the vampyre must be killed, but she's fallen under his spell. How can she destroy someone that she loves? But worse yet, what if she doesn't destroy the most evil force her world has ever known?

—Judy Sasges

DAUGHTERS OF EVE   YA
By LOIS DUNCAN

The Daughters of Eve is Modesta High School's most exclusive club; it has only ten members. Yet the members are not necessarily the prettiest, or the most popular, or the smartest girls in school. For example, the three girls just initiated are Ruth Grange, Laura Snow, and Jane Rheardon.

Ruth Grange is an only girl trapped in a family of conceited, overindulged boys. Her older brothers, Peter and Niles, 18 and 17, are filled with self-importance. Peter goes with Bambi Ellis, the most popular girl in the junior class and also a member of Daughters of Eve. Mrs. Grange works, so Ruth has to go directly home from school to take care of nine-year-old Eric, to clean up the house and the kitchen mess left by her brothers, and to start supper. Even though her older brothers are often at home, they can't be expected to do women's work.

Laura Snow is a junior, not unattractive, but twenty pounds overweight and terribly in love with Peter Grange. Laura was chosen for membership mostly because of the strong support of the club sponsor, Ms. Irene Stark.

Jane Rheardon was a shoo-in because her mother had been a member of the chapter when it had first been established. Jane's mother is always reminiscing about her youth and how popular she was. She expects Jane to follow in her footsteps. Jane's father is an alcoholic who often comes home from work "wound up" and proceeds to badger or beat up his wife.

A really strange thing happened at the initiation ceremony of the three new members. Tammy Carncross fled from the ceremony because she had a feeling; she said that she could see blood dripping from one of the candles lit for the ceremony. Tammy often has feelings; she has been know to accurately predict events before they happen, and she feels that something is going to go awfully wrong this semester.

But Irene Stark doesn't agree. The Daughters of Eve are her children who need her because they are so naive. Irene is determined that no one is going to hurt her girls; no one is going to hold them back or keep them down.

But bad things do happen to her girls. The Daughters of Eve have a raffle and donate the proceeds to the school, earmarked for the girls' soccer team. The money is used to buy new warm-ups for the boys' basketball team. Fran Schneider, the club president, enters a project in the science fair which proves the tendency toward alcoholism is genetically inherited; however, a less spectacular project by Gordon Pellet is selected to represent Modesta High in the competition. And Laura Snow tries to commit suicide after being used by her mysterious new boy friend.

Irene begins to influence the Daughters of Eve not to stand still for such injustices. They devise plans to right the wrongs against them, or at least to get revenge. Their revenge is not only sweet; it is deadly.

—Judy Druse

THE DAY THE SENIOR CLASS GOT MARRIED   YA
By GLORIA D. MIKLOWITZ

Lori Banks is seventeen, a senior in high school, and madly in love with Garrick Hamilton. As she begins her last semester in high school, Lori is faced with alternatives that may be in direct conflict. Lori has always wanted to go away to college and now she has been accepted by Berkeley, her first choice. But Lori has also accepted Garrick's proposal of marriage. Garrick wants to marry Lori in June, as soon as school is out. At first both families oppose the marriage, especially Lori's mother and father, who were married very young and are now divorced. But Garrick's parents soon come around, and as the semester progresses, Lori's mother and father also accept the marriage plans.

In this last semester of high school, Lori and Garrick are both enrolled in Dr. Womer's economics class. During this semester, the students in the class are paired in make-believe marriages. Dr. Womer lets Lori and Garrick pair up together, since they actually do plan to marry in June. Each couple must work through all kinds of situations and problems that young married couples face—rent, food, car payments, insurance, cost of children, etc. Each week they also draw a fate card, which adds another dimension to their make-believe situation. But Lori and Garrick's situation is not make-believe, and they struggle to plan their lives, based on their actual earning power and career possibilities.

Not only does the experiment point toward a bumpy financial future, but it also reveals to Lori much about Garrick that she had not previously understood. And tells her enough about herself and what she wants for her own future to make her question the rightness of her decision to marry Garrick.

As the wedding day approaches, Lori tries to push her doubts aside. Isn't Love all that really matters . . . all that is really needed to carry them through? And about their love Lori has no doubts at all.

—Barbara Lynn

A DEADLY GAME OF MAGIC   YA
By JOAN LOWERY NIXON

Teena grabbed her finger tightly and screamed at me, "How did you know that guillotine was real?"

Only seconds before, her finger had lain on the wooden platform where the tiny guillotine blade had fallen, cutting the rose stem neatly in half.

"I'm a magician, remember?"

My answer to Teena's question caused even Bo and Julian to give me their attention. The four of us are stranded here in this enormous house, alone. The thunderstorm rages outside while our imaginations take over inside. Within the sixty short minutes that we have spent here, we have been confronted by a nameless couple who have left us alone in their home, a mysterious hitchhiker, phone lines suddenly out of service, and deadly magician's props.

What's more, I know we are not alone in this house. Someone is here, for everything is too strangely quiet. I cannot prove my theory because it's just a feeling I have—the feeling everyone has had, when they open the door of their home and know they are not alone.

We are not alone in this house, either. Someone is here, and that someone is not alive!

—Cheryl Ress

DETECTIVE POUFY'S FIRST CASE   Grades 1–2
By CHARLOTTE POMERANTZ

Detective Poufy's first case was a dilly. When she and her family returned from a long weekend, their house had been broken into. Her father loved gadgets, and the first thing they noticed was the noise— every single machine and gadget in the whole place was turned on. When they finally got everything cleaned up, and the police had come and gone, they realized that they had just five clues: an enormous feather, giant fish scales, four chairs, four ice-cream puddles, and three bears.

—*Elizabeth Overmyer*

THE DEVIL'S DONKEY   Grades 2–6
By BILL BRITTAIN

"There are those who say a belief of witches and in the Devil is just superstitious nonsense. Dan'l Pitt was such a boy. The only things that were real to him were what he could touch and measure and weigh on a scale. Much as . . . [Stewart Meade] tried to tell him about Old Magda the witch—how she was pure evil and that she was the old oak tree by the crossroads at the edge of town were not to be mocked—he just scoffed. . . . And because Dan'l didn't believe, Old Magda worked her evil magic on him, and he became a thing that was less than human"—the devil's donkey.

The first time that Dan'l found himself pawing the ground—a flea-bitten donkey, unable to say anything but "Hee haw"—it took him only about a day to break the spell. But Old Magda was stubborn. As soon as she could, she witched him again, and this time he was caught in a barn for over two weeks. You'd think Dan'l would be a little more careful after this, wouldn't you? But that very evening Magda found him again, and this time she took him directly to her own master—the devil himself!

—*Elizabeth Overmyer*

THE DIAMOND IN THE WINDOW   Grades 3–5
By JANE LANGTON

On the day the banker and his secretary threaten to take away their house if Aunt Lily doesn't pay the back taxes, Eleanor and Eddy make a number of discoveries about the home they thought they knew. Looking at its shabby exterior, they see a small window of colored glass and realize they have never looked out through that window. When they find the window, it is in a room they have never seen before, a little round room with two small beds and some toys. Reluctantly, their Aunt Lily tells them about her younger brother and sister, Ned and Nora. One night Lily put them to bed in that room, and in the morning the children were gone.

Aunt Lily's fiancé, Prince Krishna, tried to look for them and he disappeared too. All of this happened before Eleanor and Eddy were born. When the two children go back into the room they notice that in the center of the window is a lump of glass that looks like a many-sided diamond. Of course, it isn't really a diamond, they know. And on one of the windowpanes a strange poem is scratched. To Eleanor it looks like Prince Krishna's handwriting, and she realizes that it is a treasure hunt he had set up for Ned and Nora. If ever the family needed a treasure, it is now, so Eleanor and Eddy decide to follow the clues. They start by spending the night in the little room. And after that first night they realize that the treasure hunt is somehow important for more than money. In some way the diamond in the window is the key to Ned and Nora's disappearance. Each adventure is more fantastic than the last and also more dangerous. Will Eleanor and Eddy be able to come back to their beds, or will they too disappear into the unknown?

—Holly Willett

DIFFERENT SEASONS YA/Adult
By STEPHEN KING

Perhaps you thought Stephen King only wrote horror stories. Perhaps you thought you'd never read anything by him you'd enjoy. Perhaps you were wrong!

These are four short novels by King that aren't horror—but are guaranteed to keep you on the very edge of your seat!

For instance, meet Red, from Shawshank Prison. . . . "There's a guy like me in every prison in America. I'm the one who can get it for you. You name it, I'll get it inside the walls—for a price, of course. Gotta think of myself, you know. I came to Shawshank when I was twenty—big, rawboned kid with a head of bright red hair. But I'm no kid any longer, not after forty years of this place. The red hair's gone gray and started to recede. Sometimes I'm startled when I look in the mirror—time passes, and no one wants to grow old in the stir. Anyway, it isn't me I want to tell you about—it's a friend of mine, Andy Dufresne. When he came to Shawshank in 1948, he was thirty years old.

A small, neat man with sandy hair and gold-rimmed glasses. He'd been convicted of murder—and though over the years I became convinced of his innocence, I might have voted against him if I'd looked only at the evidence presented at his trial. It looked bad for him—real bad. And to make it worse, he was the coolest, most self-possessed man I ever met, and when he told the jury his story, that's all he did—he told it. If he'd cried or even let his voice shake, maybe he wouldn't've gotten life. But he didn't. He just told them his version of the facts, sometimes with a little cynical smile on his face. They could take it or leave it—and they left it. Andy had the book thrown at him and ended up in Shawshank.

"I met him not long after he got there, but it took us seven years to go from nodding acquaintances to close friends. And during that time the legend that surrounded Andy began to grow. It started in 1950, when we were retarring the roof of the plate shop. Andy faced down one of the hardest, toughest guards in the prison—and though there were only nine or ten of us that day, drinking the beer Andy'd gotten for us, by 1955 there must've been two hundred, if you believed what you heard.

"But beer and getting along with the guards were not Andy's main goal—it was getting out, and getting the small seaside hotel and marina in Mexico that he had his heart set on. And he had more determination than anyone ever gave him credit for, even me. He'd said to the warden once, 'What would happen to a block of concrete if a drop of water fell on it once a year for a million years?' The warden just laughed—Andy didn't have a million years. However, he did have more effect on that concrete block than an annual drop of water. . . . Did he get out? Well, see for yourself. But remember—this ain't a fairy story. I may be a con, but I don't lie."

And Red isn't the only one with a story to tell. There's Todd, an All-American kid with blond hair and blue eyes, with his friend Denker—or was it Dussander? An ex-Nazi, or just a crazy old man with too much imagination?

What about Geordie and Chris and Teddy and Vern, who found a dead body—a real one?

And the story Dr. Emlyn McCarron told at a club that wasn't quite a club, in an old brownstone at 249B E. 35th—a story about a pregnant woman who was determined to give birth, no matter what!

They're all here—and even if these tales don't send cold chills up your spine, they're close enough to reality to make your gut clench in recognition—which is infinitely worse!

—Joni Bodart

THE DISAPPEARANCE   YA
By ROSA GUY

Imamu Jones has two defenses against the world: his intelligence and the toothpick between his lips. And he needs them in his Harlem surroundings. He lives in a dirty, dingy apartment with his wino mother. His mother had taken away his rights when she had not come to jail to see him. It was over a month since he had been picked up with Iggy and Muhammed at the grocery store, where Iggy had shot and killed old man Fein. She had to have heard about it. Someone must have told her. But she hadn't shown her face. Not at the youth center, not in the court. One month! That sure had taken away his rights. Imamu knew his mother loved him; she was just too drunk most of the time to know it.

Even though his mother never visited him, someone else did, Mrs. Ann Aimsley. Imamu had seen her the first day of his trial. He had liked her looks. She had class. That impressed folks. He was glad she had been there to impress the lawyers, the judge. When they saw folks like her sitting in on a trial and dug she was in your corner, they didn't use just any old kind of language to bring you down. Everybody showed respect. They went by the rules then. And Mrs. Aimsley had come every day. She had even volunteered to be his foster mother. It was a noble cause, a great gesture that suited her. It went with her plain, intelligent face, the dignity of her gray hair. She knew Imamu would more than likely be sent to one of the state institutions to wait becoming of age if someone didn't volunteer to take custody of him.

The Aimsleys' immaculate brownstone house on a tree-shaded street in Brooklyn is a long way from the dirty Harlem apartment Imamu has been sharing with his mother. Things seem to be looking up.

But Imamu decides the Aimsley house is as bad as the streets. It is just that everything is all fixed up to hide what lies underneath. Gail, the Aimsleys' older daughter, is a phony. Perk, their younger daughter, is spoiled and has a big mouth. Mr. Aimsley tries to be a big man. Imamu will not take any of that big-man stuff. If Mr. Aimsley doesn't want him in his house, all he has to do is say so. Only Dora Belle, Mrs. Aimsley's best friend and her daughter's godmother, seems to be pleased with Imamu's presence, besides Mrs. Aimsley, that is. Dora Belle is voluptuous and eccentric and she begins to flirt with Imamu. Imamu has come to be part of a family, to share family life. Already he has had it.

Then, on his second night at the Aimsleys', Perk, the younger daughter, doesn't show up for dinner; when she is still missing by midnight, Imamu's new life crashes. Both the police and his new foster mother suspect him of having something to do with her disappearance.

—Judy Druse

THE DIVORCE EXPRESS   YA
By PAULA DANZIGER

Phoebe Anna Brooks was feeling trapped—trapped with no place to go. It wasn't fair. A kid should have parents who act more like grown-ups. They were supposed to know what they wanted out of life, and not be confused and constantly making a lot of changes. Not her parents, though. They were still getting their act together. They started getting their act together by breaking up. By the time the divorce came through, the only thing they agreed on was that they should live in the same neighborhood so she wouldn't have any trouble getting to school. Her mother got to stay in their New York City apartment and keep the furnishings. Her father sublet another apartment nearby and got to keep the summer house in Woodstock. They both got her, joint custody. Since they lived near each other, she lived half a week with one parent, half with the other. Weekends were alternated. It was horribly confusing. She had to keep track of everything with a calendar. And her parents seemed to be going in two different directions. Her father really loved the country. He wanted to paint and not work in an office for someone else. Her mother enjoyed living in the city, loved being an interior decorator, and got poison ivy from just looking at pictures of nature.

Something happened to Phoebe after the separation and divorce. Her parents thought they had everything figured out just right. Only they didn't. They forgot that she might have feelings too. So she did lots of things at school. She talked in class all the time, never turned in any homework, wouldn't give the right answers when teachers called on her. One day she got to school real early and snuck in and Krazy-Glued everything she could. The principal said she was shocked to see a girl create such havoc. Phoebe told her that with Women's Liberation anything was possible. Her parents started to see each other again to talk about the problem—*her*. For a while, she thought that maybe they'd even get back together. They didn't. They once again decided what was "best" for her. She and her father would move to Woodstock and live in the summer house. And every weekend she would go to New York City to be with her mother, riding the Divorce Express. The Divorce Express was the bus that left Woodstock on Friday afternoons and returned on Sunday filled with kids who lived with one parent in the country and visited the other parent in the city. It was really public transportation, but because of all the kids, it was nicknamed the Divorce Express. Now, not only does Phoebe have to adjust to the hectic routine but she must learn to deal with her parents dating, sleeping with other people, and maybe even getting married again, at a time when she is just getting interest in dating herself!

—Judy Druse

DOGSBODY   Grades 6–8
By DIANA WYNNE JONES

Dogsbody is about a dog named Sirius who knows in his heart that he's really a star—and he's right, for Sirius used to be a star, shining in the heavens. In fact, he was even a rather important star in his own corner of the universe. But he had an unfortunate knack for getting in trouble, and when he loses a powerful magic device called a zoi, the other stars have had it, and Sirius must stand trial for his life. He's sure that he's innocent, but he can't explain what happened to the zoi, and so he is found guilty. The punishment is death.

There's only one way he can save himself. The zoi is a powerful device for channeling energy among the stars, and if Sirius can find it, he will be forgiven. To do so, he must come to earth, where they believe the zoi was lost. But Sirius obviously can't come as a star, and so he agrees to be placed in a dog's body.

His troubles start almost immediately. No sooner is he born as a puppy than someone puts him in a canvas bag and tries to drown him. That's just his first encounter with the evil force that seems to be racing him for the zoi. To make matters worse, life is very difficult for Sirius in his new body; it seems very small and clumsy, and his tail seems to have a life of its own, and he has trouble remembering that he's really a star. It seems as though he'll never be able to find the zoi—and for Sirius, it's a matter of life and death, for if he fails, he will have to live out the rest of his life here on earth and die in a dogsbody.

—Richard Russo

DON'T EXPLAIN   YA/Adult
(A SONG OF BILLIE HOLIDAY)
By ALEXIS DeVEAUX

[Read nine lines from page 1: "This is a long song . . . Sing it."]

Billie Holiday was born in Baltimore on April 7, 1915, as Eleanora Fagan. She had her mother's last name because her parents didn't marry until she was three years old. Her thirteen-year-old mother Sadie was a maid, and her fifteen-year-old father Clarence was a trumpet player.

Her dad called her Bill because she was a tomboy. She hated her name Eleanora, she changed it to Billie to be like her favorite movie actress, Billie Dove.

Before Billie left school in fifth grade, her dad went off touring with a band and never came back to Durham Street to live with Billie and her mother. For the next few years, while her mother was working in New York, Billie lived with different relatives, until she joined her mother in New York to help earn the rent money. No one would hire her as a waitress, and though she liked to sing, she never did it for pay until, as a teenager, hungry and desperate, she stopped at Pod's and Jerry's on West 133rd Street. The piano player urged her to sing, and she did so well that when the evening was over she took home all the rent money. She continued to sing there for two years, and here Alexis De-Veaux's poetry tells you how she sounded. [Read from page 27: "The audience loved the way she sang . . . sauté, sizzle, or steam."]

Billie grew up to become one of the greatest jazz singers in the world. But her life was never easy. She became addicted to heroin. After reading this book, you might understand why, though Billie herself always said, "Don't explain."   *—Cathi Edgerton*

DORP DEAD   Grades 3–5
By JULIA CUNNINGHAM

Gilly writes this story himself. He's lived in a orphanage since his grandmother died a year ago. Then a strange man named Mr. Kobalt takes him in. Mr. Kobalt makes ladders, and wants Gilly to help him around the house and shop. He gives Gilly a room for himself and nice clothes and good food. But he wants absolute quiet—he only speaks when absolutely necessary. Everything in his house is placed just so. There are five clocks in each room, and everything is done on a strict schedule.

At first Gilly doesn't mind the strict rules. After the crowded, noisy orphanage, he quite likes the quiet and order of Mr. Kobalt's house. And it's great to have a room to himself and decent clothes.

Then Gilly becomes curious about what is in the locked room, right next to his own room on the second floor. One day he climbs out the window, inches along a ledge until he can see into the window of the next-door room. What he sees there tells him that he must run for his life. And run he does, with a madman on his trail.

—Nancy Eager

DRAGONDRUMS   YA
By ANNE McCAFFREY

Piemur was standing in the meadow with Menolly and Sebell, waiting to climb up the huge frame of the dragon for his first dragon flight. He still could not believe that he, a lowly apprentice at Harperhall, was actually to be permitted to ride one of these magnificent beasts. Menolly caught hold of the strap and with her feet braced, climbed up and threw her leg over the neck and settled into one of the neck ridges. Next came Piemur. He hesitated to put his boot on the beautiful skin of the dragon, but the dragon-rider assured him it wouldn't hurt the beast. Piemur followed Menolly's example and wedged himself into the ridge in front of her. Then Sebell and the dragon-rider climbed aboard.

Piemur glanced toward the drumheights. He just hoped Clell and the other apprentices there were watching. They'd be so envious they'd die. Ever since he had been assigned to the drumheights, they had been making his life miserable. He had learned the drum message measures easily, and the other apprentices were jealous. They would have been even more jealous if they had known he was, in truth, the apprentice of the Masterharper himself, but that had to be kept secret from everyone except Menolly and Sebell. Masterharper Robinton was very much interested in the politics of Pern and especially in the connection between some of the Hold Lords and the Oldtimers who had been banished to the Southern Continent. One Hold Lord in particular seemed to have an over-supply of goods—exotic cloth, grains, food substances, and especially fire lizards, the small cousins of the great dragons that were coveted by everyone on Pern.

It was Piemur's job to attend the gathers of the other Holds and listen, to pick up information concerning the Oldtimers. That was where he was going now, to an Igen Hold Gather with Menolly and Sebell.

Menolly explained to him that shortly after the dragon rose in the air, they would enter what was called "between," a sensation of intense cold so that one could not feel anything, not even the dragon under him, a most frightening experience.

The great dragon gave a heave and they were aloft. Piemur made the mistake of looking down and wished he hadn't. Then they were "between" and he was paralyzed with fear. It was all he could do to keep from screaming. He held even more tightly to Sebell in front of him. And just as quickly as it had begun, it was over, and they were circling Igen Hold, hundreds of miles from Harperhall. Thus went Piemur's first dragon flight.

At Igen he picked up very little information of value, but a few weeks later he and Sebell went to another Gather at Nabol. This time they were disguised as beast-herders.

Piemur slipped into the Lord's Hold and pretended to be a kitchen drudge. Surely here he could find out if Lord Meron was indeed trading with the Oldtimers. One thing, for sure, there were far too many fire lizards flying around. Even beast herders had several apiece.

His first job in the kitchen was to unload incoming carts. The work was backbreaking, but he got a good look at the storerooms which bulged with goods. Next he had to go with a couple of the other workers to freshen up Lord Meron's apartment, and while he was there, he saw several pots with fire lizard eggs in them. These he examined carefully and took the queen egg and stuffed it up his shirt. He felt certain he could walk out of the Hold with the other kitchen drudges before the theft was discovered. But not so. Very shortly after the feast, Lord Meron discovered that the prize egg was missing and gave the alarm. Everyone seemed to know immediately that the new kitchen boy, Piemur, was the one who took it. There was no way to escape, only one place to hide for a few hours.

—Billie Harding

DRAGON'S BLOOD   YA
By JANE YOLEN

On the planet Austar IV, the main source of money and entertainment is the spectator sport of pit-dragon fighting. The class of people called Masters are successful at raising and training dragons that win fighting matches and earn a fortune from the bettors. They live in fine houses and have lots of gold. The other class of people are bonders, who must wear a leather sack—a bond bag—around their neck until they can somehow earn enough gold to fill it, buying their freedom and becoming Masters themselves.

Fifteen-year-old Jakkin Stewart is a bonder. He works as a stallboy in the large dragon nursery of Master Sarkkan, and his talent is in working with growing dragons. Even though Jakkin enjoys working with them at the nursery, he has a plan to win his freedom. He plans to take a dragon hatchling, raise it up, train it to be a champion in the pits, and fill his bag with gold.

One night, when things are just right, Jakkin tiptoes out of the bondhouse while the other bonders are sleeping. He creeps into the incubarn and heads toward the nestrooms where the mother dragons and their young are kept. One compartment holds a mother named Heart O'Mine, and Jakkin sneaks in, despite the warning thump of her tail on the floor. The stall card tells Jakkin the father of the baby dragons is a fabled fighter named Blood Type. A dragon from his bloodline would have to be a winner! Jakkin realizes there are nine dragonlings—the count is listed on the stall card. Looking at Heart O'Mine, he thinks what a strange, dark dragon she is, with a yellowish lump above her right ear. He is wondering why Sarkkan would breed a deformed dragon, when suddenly the lump moves! Jakkin is startled, then soon realizes it is not a lump at all, but a new-born, wrinkled, yellow dragonling! This little dragon brings the count up to ten—but the official stall card says there are only nine dragons! This one must have been missed in the count! Bonder's luck—Jakkin can't believe it! With the little dragonling in the crook of his elbow and cradled against his chest, Jakkin picks up his lamp to leave. But first, he says, "You have your nine, great mother. This *one* is mine. I shall make this one a great fighter. I swear it."

But there are obstacles he never expected—and he wonders if he can keep that promise.

—*Diane Tuccillo*

THE DUNGEON MASTER: YA/Adult
THE DISAPPEARANCE OF JAMES DALLAS EGBERT III
By WILLIAM DEAR

It began with a phone call on August 22, 1979, to William Dear, one of the most flamboyant and effective private investigators in the business. Several of his cases have been made into episodes in various TV cop dramas. This phone call would be the start of perhaps his most unusual case, one that he would become more involved in than any other. Only recently was he allowed to tell the story he reveals here.

Dallas Egbert was sixteen, a sophomore at Michigan State University, and a fanatic Dungeons and Dragons player with an IQ of over 180. He disappeared from the campus on August 15, 1979, about 1:30 p.m., leaving behind only one clue—a strange map on a bulletin board in his room.

Dear almost immediately discovered that Dallas had played a live version of D&D in the maze of tunnels that ran underneath the university, connecting the buildings underground, sometimes even running through the walls, and housing the pipes for heating and cooling. But there were also rooms down there, places where a rather small but almost frighteningly intelligent sixteen-year-old could hide practically indefinitely. That is, if the rumors that Dear uncovered about drugs, homosexuality, and witchcraft weren't true. Dallas might be playing a real-life version of his favorite game, or he might have been kidnapped by any of a number of groups on campus that he seemed to have had something to do with. Frequently, that connection seemed to be the drugs he made for them—and he could make almost anything. He didn't have many friends—he was too young and too intelligent. Calculus was child's play for him. but he didn't have any idea about how to make friends with someone. Love and trust were almost outside his vocabulary. He was alone, with only himself for company—that wasn't much company at all. Finally, it wasn't enough.

There have been books and movies about college students that played games in the dark, twisting, and sometimes very narrow tunnels that honeycomb the ground under campus buildings. But they have been just stories. This is the real thing—Dallas and his pursuer are not fictional characters. Their story is true, even if it seems almost unbelievable at times. But no matter how strange the story is, no matter how hard to believe, the people in it *are* believable. Dallas Egbert and William Dear are two people I won't ever forget—and I don't think that once you've met them, you will either.

—Joni Bodart

EARTHSEED   YA
By PAMELA SARGENT

Ship has been their parent, their teacher, their friend and provider. Ship has been hurtling through space for over a century, programmed to find a planetary system with a habitable world. The occupants, all about fifteen years old, were brought to life from the genetic banks stored aboard and have been raised by the motherly electronic person called Ship. They have been reared and educated with Ship's loving and watchful care. Earth people, despairing of their future, designed this project to carry the seeds of humankind to other worlds where the human race could begin again unhobbled by the past. All their brightest hopes are in the genetic material stored aboard Ship. Now, over a century later, Ship has created Zoheret and her shipmates from its genetic banks. Soon they will arive at the Earthlike, uninhabited planet they are to colonize, and Ship, like any parent of teenagers, has great worries about their ability to survive in the outer world—alone and unaided by the living machine that has nurtured them all their lives.

To prepare them, Ship devises a "survival test." They are turned loose in the wilderness-like interior, the Hollow, of the ship to test their survival skills. Ship soon realizes it has made a bad mistake. Although the heroine, Zoheret, and her companions have been educated in the most idealistic manner to eliminate the behavior patterns responsible for the problems on Earth, latent instincts, both good and bad, soon arise as competition leads to viciousness, intimidation, and brutality. Can Zoheret and her companions overcome the biggest obstacle to the survival of the human race—themselves?

—*Judy Druse*

THE EDUCATION OF KOKO   YA/Adult
By FRANCINE PATTERSON and EUGENE LINDEN

What do you think of when I say the word "gorilla?" King Kong, maybe? Certainly a large fierce ape, very dangerous to other animals—and to humans. That's how I always thought of gorillas, until I met Koko and Penny Patterson, in the book by Penny called *The Education of Koko.*

Koko is a 10-year-old-female gorilla who has learned to talk—she has a vocabulary of over six hundred words in sign language. Penny is a 34-year-old psychologist who has been Koko's surrogate mother and her teacher since Koko was about a year old. Koko caught onto sign language quickly, even learning to adapt some signs as obscenities—some of her favorites include, "rotten bad toilet," "stupid devil," "that bad stinker." She is also a great tease and loves a good joke. She's afraid of alligators, except for small toy ones, and one of her favorite games is the surprise alligator attack. She sneaks up on some unsuspecting human with the toy alligator behind her back. When she's close enough, she springs up, waving the alligator fiercely. The human is supposed to look terrified, scream, and run, while Koko howls with laughter. It's amazing that a gorilla might think even for a moment that it *needs* a prop like a toy alligator to scare humans.

Then there was the time when Koko developed her first case of puppy love. He was a workman on the Stanford campus where Koko lived. She called him "foot," and during his working hours, watched for him constantly, blowing him kisses and flirting whenever he came into view.

Over and over again, I found it difficult to believe that Koko was a gorilla—she sounds like a very bright preschool child with a wide stubborn streak. She's one of the most memorable animals I've ever met, this (to use her own words) "fine animal gorilla."

— *Joni Bodart*

THE EIGHTEENTH EMERGENCY Grades 4–6
By BETSY C. BYARS

"Hammerman's after me," said Mouse Frawley to his best friend, Ezzie. Ezzie's pink mouth formed a perfect O. Finally Ezzie said, "You mean Marv Hammerman?" even though he knew there was only one Hammerman in the world, just as there had been only one Hitler.

Ezzie had emergency plans for every situation. For instance, Emergency 4—Crocodile Attack. When attacked by a crocodile, prop a stick in his mouth, and the crocodile is helpless. Or Emergency 5—Being Choked by a Boa Constrictor. While you are being strangled by the boa constrictor, taunt him and get him to bite you instead of strangle you. The bite, Ezzie admitted, might be a little painful, but strangulation was worse. But Ezzie had no solution for Emergency 18—which was Mouse's confrontation with Hammerman.

Marv Hammerman was the eighth-grade bully, and he was bigger than anyone else (he should be—he flunked several years). There was something animal-like about him, with his long limbs and skin-tight clothes. His hair was shaggy and looked as if it had never seen a comb. He loomed in Mouse's mind the way monsters do in horror movies— huge and dangerous, with cold, distant eyes.

Ezzie asked Mouse, "Why is Hammerman after you?"

"Well, when I was passing this chart on my way out of history, Ez, I took my pencil and wrote Marv Hammerman's name on the bottom of the chart and then I drew an arrow to the picture of the Neanderthal Man."

No one in school makes fun of Hammerman, especially a lowly sixth-grader like Mouse.

Several days passed. Mouse was becoming an expert in avoiding Hammerman—until Friday morning, when he met him on the stairs face-to-face and Hammerman told him to prepare for a showdown after school.

Mouse was so overcome with fear he was almost physically ill—ill enough, at least, to be sent to the office by his math teacher and then home for the rest of the day.

When Mouse got up on Saturday morning he knew what he had to do. He could run no more from Hammerman. He would have to face the music.

The Eighteenth Emergency, by Betsy Byars.

—Betty Holtzen

EVERYONE KNOWS Grades k–3
WHAT A DRAGON LOOKS LIKE
By JAY WILLIAMS

Everyone knows what a dragon looks like . . . or do they? Appearances can be deceiving (especially in the case of a dragon).

It all takes place in the city of Wu, perched on a hill just this side of China. A lad named Han is the gate-sweeper. He is very poor, and lives in a tiny hut next to the gate. But he is cheerful, kind-hearted, and friendly, and has a happy smile for everyone who goes in or out of the city.

One day a messenger comes racing along the road into the city with some frightening news: "The Wild Horsemen of the North are coming to destroy the city of Wu and bring war into the land of China!"

Alarmed, the ruler of the city, a splendid Mandarin named Jade Tiger, calls together his counselors to decide what to do. After some heated (and hilarious) discussion, the Mandarin, the Leader of the Merchants, the Captain of the Army, the Wisest of the Wise Men, and the Chief of the Workmen all agree that the only way to save their city is to pray to the Great Cloud Dragon for help.

The next morning, as Han is sweeping under the gate, a small, fat man with a white beard and shiny bald head comes walking up the hill leaning on a long staff. "I am a dragon," he announces.

But when the small, fat man tells the Mandarin he is a dragon, come to save the city, the great ruler laughs. So do the Leader of the Merchants, the Captain of the Army, the Wisest of the Wise Men, and the Chief of the Workmen. They all have their own idea of what a dragon looks like . . . and it certainly isn't a fat, bearded, bald old man.

To find out what happens when the Wild Horsemen arrive to destroy the city, and to see what a dragon really looks like, read *Everyone Knows*. . . .

—*JoAnn Young*

THE EXECUTIONER YA
By JAY BENNETT

Talk 1

"Forget the past," everyone tells Bruce Kendall. "Nothing can bring Raymond back to life." But Bruce can never forget. It's more than the scars on his face, or his limp. It's the terror of remembering the awful night of the accident.

Bruce, Ed, and Elaine were riding home from a party in Ray's car. It has snowed earlier that day, so the roads were not very safe. Ed and Elaine sat together in the back, Bruce sat in the passenger seat. Everyone in the car was drunk except Ray, who was driving. Bruce remembers the laughter, the smell of beer—and the way he reached over and grabbed Ray's arm in his drunkenness, trying to take Ray's hat from him. Bruce remembers grabbing Ray the last thing before the car went out of control on the icy roadway and hit a large oak tree. Ed, Elaine, and Bruce survived; Raymond did not.

Bruce is paying for that fatal night with every breath he takes. The guilt just won't go away. He *knows* it was his fault that Raymond died. But someone decides that Bruce—and Ed, and Elaine—haven't paid enough in suffering. One by one they are destined to be taken . . . by fire, by water, by earth.

First, Ed is killed in a mysterious accident—by fire. Elaine drowns in a lake—by water. And Bruce knows he's next. No one will believe him. The executioner has come—and he, or she, wants revenge for Raymond's death. But who *is* the executioner? And can Bruce escape the fate planned for him? To find out, read the book by Jay Bennett.

—*Diane Tuccillo*

Talk 2

The Executioner. He knows what happened the night Raymond was killed. He will not forget. He knows there were three other people in the death car with Raymond. He waits. Patiently. Hoping that the other people who had been in that car will be punished. But they aren't. So now the Executioner must do the job. He must avenge Raymond's death. Ed, Elaine, and Bruce are his targets. One will die by fire. One will die by water. And one will die by earth. And only the Executioner knows when.

—*Kathryn Dunn*

FAIR ANNIE OF OLD MULE HOLLOW   YA
By BEVERLY C. CROOK

Annie was fifteen and was the first member of the family to go beyond the sixth grade. Pa was proud of her for this, but rarely spoke of it. He didn't want it to go to her head, or for her to start thinking about leaving the hollow and going to the city. Mule Hollow was where all of his family should be and stay, just like they had for generations, and there was no reason to leave, that's what Pa thought. Besides, Otis was coming around pretty regular to visit Annie, so it wasn't likely Pa'd have an old maid on his hands.

Annie's cousin from the city was visiting and had just about talked Annie into leaving for the city with her. Annie was not too fond of Patty Ruth Ann, but her talk of all the city had to offer—the pretty clothes, the boys, the schools—made Annie realize that she was going to have to stand up to Pa and tell him that she was off with her cousin to live in Baltimore. But while she was planning that conversation with Pa, she came face to face with something much scarier.

Annie was off in the hills looking for one of the puppies when she saw a sight she'd hoped never to see—a McFarr up close. He was standing on a ledge, looking down at her, with a rifle on his shoulder. His clothes were even more ragged than her own, his shaggy dark hair looked as though it had been hacked off with a knife. She stood and stared for several minutes, considering whether it would be better to be shot running away or stay and be shot on the spot. She had ventured off their own land and was on McFarr land—and the McFarrs and the Collins had a feud that went back generations and accounted for a lot of blood. The feelings were so bad that the families shot each other just for trespassing—no questions asked.

All of this flashed through Annie's mind as she stared into the eyes of Jamie McFarr. But things didn't go as she expected, and their love story turned out to be one that even their feuding families couldn't ignore.

—*Sarah Howell*

FAMOUS ALL OVER TOWN   YA/Adult
By DANNY SANTIAGO

Before the Southern Pacific Railroad rolled Shamrock Street in the Chicano barrio under asphalt, it was the best street in all Los Angeles, with cozy little homes on both sides solid. Maybe they weren't too new or too fresh-painted, but they were warm and lively, and when the trains passed by, how those little houses used to shake, rattle, and roll. Strangers would ask, How can you stand it? But to tell the truth, fourteen-year-old Rudy "Chato" Medina barely noticed. It was like rocking a baby, and very good for the circulation of the blood, anyway.

Fat Manuel, Gorilla, Hungryman, Pelon, and Chato all live on Shamrock Street; they are Los Jesters de Shamrock, the Kings of the Eastside, and nobody messes with them. Nobody except their archrivals from Sierra Street. Every now and then war will break out, and from time to time corpses are the vivid evidence of those wars. That's one reason half the veterans of Shamrock Street end up in the wrong kind of college, like old San Quentin U. Nevertheless, even though the odds are against him, Chato dreams of a future when he will be "famous all over town," a future he may not live long enough to enjoy.

—Judy Druse

FANTASTIC MR. FOX   Grades 2–4
By ROALD DAHL

Boggis and Bunce and Bean—
One fat, one short, one lean.
These horrible crooks
So different in looks
Were nonetheless equally mean.

Watch Mr. Fox, our hero; his fine family, Mrs. Fox and four small children; Badger, the most respected and well-behaved animal in the district; and a crude creature, Rat, outwit the farmers Boggis, Bunce, and Bean. Or do they?

Find out when you read about the fantastic Mr. Fox.

—Sandy Hudson

THE FAR SIDE OF VICTORY   YA/Adult
By JOANNE GREENBERG

He was surprised there was so little pain—he can barely remember the accident. But it had happened—Eric had run head-on into a car containing a man, a woman, and their three children. Only the woman, Helen Gerson, had survived. Eric had been on vacation, partying, and a hitchhiker he'd picked up had had some laughing gas. The time for laughter is long past now.

Free on parole, Eric goes back to Aureole, the scene of the accident, drawn by something he can't quite identify—guilt, perhaps, or the need for penance. He enjoys being a part of the small town, and small town life. Then one day, someone mentions a woman named Helen—and she turns out to be the same Helen whose family he'd killed. She's also moved to Aureole to begin a new life. He rescues her from a ski slope when she can't figure out how to get down, and he offers to teach her to ski. Months later, he realizes that he's in love. No one in town knows their whole story, but *they* do—what now?

This unusual and beautiful love story has something very special to say about who and why and how we choose to love.

—Joni Bodart

FAT MEN FROM SPACE   Grades 3-5
By DANIEL MANUS PINKWATER

The night after William returned from the dentist, he noticed something interesting: he could hear the radio without actually turning the radio on. He didn't know what was happening until he rubbed his tongue against his new filling—and the volume dropped. When he pressed his tongue against the tooth, the radio stopped. It was his tooth! The one with the new filling was receiving radio programs! William got to be pretty good at playing his tooth. When he touched it with a spoon, he could change the station to rock and roll; with a fork, he'd get news and country and western music at the same time; and with a butter knife in his mouth, he'd get classical music—and he could change stations at school by chewing in different places on the wire binding of his notebook. But then one day he wrapped one end of a piece of wire around his tooth and the other end around a metal chain link, hoping the fence would act as one gigantic antenna, and that he could pick up radio stations he'd never heard before—maybe even from the other side of the country. Well, first William got a shock that knocked him to the ground. But when he came to, he was listening to voices from out of this country—in fact, out of this world. By the time he realized he was hearing space men plan an invasion of the earth, the sky was full of glowing lights descending on William and his tooth—and soon William became the first human to be held in a space burger, and the prime witness of the world's first junk food invasion by the fat men from space.

—Elizabeth Overmyer

FELICIA THE CRITIC   Grades 3-5
By ELLEN CONFORD

Every morning Felicia woke up and heard the temperature being announced on the radio, and every morning Felicia would look at her own thermometer and announce that the radio was wrong. Felicia was the kind of girl you could always count on to tell you that your hair looked awful, and so did your new dress, and to remind that you could get cancer from eating a candy bar. When Felicia began to wonder why she didn't have many friends, her mother pointed out that most people don't like to be told everything that's wrong with them, and so Felicia decided that from now on she would be a *constructive* critic, and help people not only see their mistakes but see how to change them. And how does that work out? Well, it allows Felicia to cause the biggest traffic jam in school history, and to wreck the best wedding she's ever attended! Felicia is afraid that no one will ever like her again, but she's too good a critic to keep quiet!

—*Elizabeth Overmyer*

THE FIFTH SALLY   YA/Adult
By DANIEL KEYES

Nola saw three young guys passing a pint in a brown bag as she walked the Coney Island Beach, dropping her clothes as she entered the beckoning water. Stupid time to have a headache, she thought. She fought the neck pain and the head-splitting thoughts that kept saying no-no-no. Someone was fighting her. Then suddenly, the boys dragged her from the water, under the boardwalk, and dropped their trousers. She fought them. Then Nola split. It didn't take Jinx long to figure out what was happening.

When Sally awoke, she remembered nothing about the night before, but she told the psychiatric social worker she felt other forces inside her. When she started to sign the no-suicide contract, Derry slipped out and signed it, too! Sally was quickly referred to Dr. Roger Ash, a psychiatrist.

Knowing she needed more than her alimony check to pay Dr. Ash, she applied for a waitress job at the Yellow Brick Road. As Sally became flustered and confused, Derry—the happy-go-lucky tomboy—slipped out, crossed her legs, flashed some thigh and smiled, and got the job.

In Dr. Ash's office Bella—the sexpot with a talent for singing and dancing—appeared to tell him that Sally just didn't know how to handle men.

Bella, Derry, Jinx, Nola, and Sally—who are they? Why are they?

—*Patsy Hamric*

FIRESTARTER   YA/Adult
By STEPHEN KING

They were running, it seemed like they'd always been running—for years. The big, shabby man and the pigtailed eight-year-old girl hurried down the New York street. "I can't run any more, Daddy!" Andy McGee picked up his daughter, Charlie, and kept on going, glancing over his shoulder at the deliberately unsuspicious-looking car with the three innocuous men in it that crawled along the crowded street half a block behind them. The men from The Shop—following, waiting for him to slow down, for him to make a mistake.

It had all begun twelve years ago, in 1969, when he'd participated in a psych experiment in college—he'd needed the $200. That was when he'd met Vicky, his wife—Charlie's mother. The experiment was testing some kind of new hallucinogenic drug—one of Andy's friends had told him about it. The psych department was working with a U.S. intelligence service. Not the FBI or CIA; more secret than that—they were called The Shop. The experiment had been awful—he'd seen things and people he was sure weren't hallucinations, though doctors said they had been. But it had been worth it—he'd met Vicky, who'd also been in the experiment. They were married a year later, and two years after that had Charlie (Charlene) McGee, who when she didn't get what she wanted, set things on fire—by looking at them! Andy and Vicky knew they both had some psychic abilities. Andy'd seen Vicky shut the refrigerator door from across the room, and he knew he was telepathic—he could "push" his thoughts at people and make them see what he wanted them to see. But Vicky's abilities didn't really hurt her; Andy paid for his "pushing" with blinding headaches. But they didn't really think much about passing their abilities on to their daughter, until one day her bottle was late—and Charlie set her crib on fire.

Andy and Vicky worked to convince her to never do that again, it was *bad*, but eventually a fire extinguisher and a smoke alarm appeared in every room. Not long afterwards, Andy talked to an old friend, the one who'd persuaded him to participate in that experiment, and found out that the horror that began that day had followed them—their house was probably being watched and their phone tapped. The men from The Shop had found out about Charlie, and they wanted her. With her ability to set fires and make anything burn at unbelievable temperatures, she was the "Ultimate Weapon"—a little pigtailed seven-year-old.

When Charlie spent the weekend with one of her friends, Andy came home at noon from the university sure something was wrong, and found Vicky dead. She'd been tortured and mutilated. Charlie wasn't at her friend's house. She'd been picked up by two men in a gray van who'd said they were Andy's friends, but he knew they were from The Shop—and they had her. He followed, frantic, and managed to get her back—but neither of the men who had taken her ever got over what Andy did to them that hot summer afternoon in the almost empty roadside park.

And now, a year later, they're still running. But an eight-year-old girl can't run very fast, and Andy has pushed too much and too hard. The next time he may not survive. The men from The Shop get closer and closer. Finally, there's a confrontation. Andy's nearly killed, and Charlie turns to fight, with the only weapon she has—fire!

—Joni Bodart

FIRST THE EGG YA
By LOUISE MOERI

Sarah and David are both seniors in a Marriage and Family class, both hoping to get an A so they can make it into UC Berkeley, and neither expecting such a challenge as the senior project—parenting an egg as though it was a baby. Ms. Crandall presents the project and all the guidelines. "If it is absolutely essential for you and your partner to be absent from the egg, you will arrange to have a babysitter."

Silence, followed by the incredulous question, "A *baby*-sitter? for an *egg*?" Crandall continues, "I told you. It's not an egg. For the next five days the egg is a newborn infant." Sarah listens to the words as she wonders who will be her partner. Finally Crandall announces that Sarah and David are the parents and must work together—there's no way out. Sarah worries about her A because David appears to be silent and hostile, uncooperative. Actually what puzzles Sarah more is the reaction of her father when she asks for a babysitter. He is angry, furious, and calls the project "a crazy piece of stupidity and it's not staying in my house." The family situation remains tense throughout the week as her brother decides to move out on his own and her mother shocks Sarah with news that she's unprepared to handle. And David seems to be emotionally detached from nearly all aspects of the egg as he plans to leave town with his friends. Through all of this turmoil, Sarah has feelings, vague memories that she can't piece together, that concern her parents, her brother, and most of all, her younger sister.

This is Sarah's diary of a week of loving an egg and understanding David and coming to grips with her family just as it falls apart

—Katie Hoffman

FLAT STANLEY Grades 1–2
By JEFF BROWN

Stanley Lambchop was a pretty ordinary little boy. That is, until the day a bulletin board fell on him and flattened him flat as a pancake.

After that, Stanley was four feet tall, one foot wide, and about a half an inch thick. Once Stanley got used to being flat, he found he quite enjoyed it. He could go in and out of rooms without opening the door, simply by sliding through the crack at the bottom. And being flat was convenient in other ways. When Stanley's father took Stanley and his brother out to the park, he never had to worry about losing Stanley in a crowd—he just rolled him up like a poster, tied a string around him, and carried him under his arm. And when Stanley was invited to spend a vacation with his friend Thomas in California, Mr. and Mrs. Lambchop didn't have to worry about paying the airfare. They just put Stanley in a large envelope, along with an egg salad sandwich and a flat cigarette case full of milk, and mailed him. In fact, Stanley's unique size and shape came in handy many ways—especially when he helped to solve the mystery at the art museum.

—Zoë Kalkanis

FOOTSTEPS ON THE STAIRS   Grades 6–8
By C. S. ADLER

Dodie's life was P E R F E C T, except for a mother she couldn't talk to, a stepsister who hated her, a stepbrother who was afraid of her, and a stepfather she—well, she wasn't sure about Larry. And if this wasn't trouble enough, all five of them were spending the summer in a beautiful beach house that was haunted! Oh yes, Dodie's life was *perfect*!

When she first learned about spending the summer on the seashore, Dodie was excited. She lived to swim and sail, and so did Larry. Imagine, getting your new stepfather to yourself all summer. Then she learned that Larry's children, Anne and Chip, would be joining them at the beach house. Dodie didn't know if she was angry or excited or jealous or all of the above. She wanted Anne and Chip to like her, but would they? Trying to be funny, Dodie dressed up like a ghost and scared five-year-old Chip so badly he wouldn't get out of the car. Anne thought Dodie was immature and childish, and although both of them were thirteen, Anne looked and acted much older, Dodie much younger.

Even Larry seemed different after Anne and Chip arrived. He wanted to be with them all the time and seemed to forget she even existed. Her mother was constantly nagging at her to dress neater, stand taller, not talk so loudly, and most of all, not to imagine so many things that weren't true.

That was the hardest part of all, for Dodie wasn't imagining. At night, when everyone was in bed and the house was quiet, someone was running up and down the stairs! Someone or something not human was making that noise, and no one would believe Dodie. They all thought she was making up another silly trick to get their attention.

One night as she lay in bed after everyone had fallen asleep, Dodie decided she would find out what was really making the noise on the stairs. Suddenly, there they were again, those mysterious footsteps. Just as she was about to get up, Anne called to Dodie, "Listen. There really are footsteps. I hear them, too!" Who was making those noises?

Read *Footsteps on the Stairs*, by C. S. Adler, and find out!

—*Cheryl Ress*

A FORMAL FEELING   YA
By ZIBBY ONEAL

Anne Cameron's mother was clearly an unusual and talented person—artistic, musical, and literary. She's been dead for a year, but she still haunts Anne, and through her haunts Anne's father, his new wife Dory, and Anne's brother Spencer. Anne has never come to grips with her grief. Spencer tries to tell her that life goes on, but Anne says, "Someone has to remember Mother." Spencer says nobody is forgetting her; getting on with life doesn't mean forgetting Mother. All of the family except Anne want to throw off the oppression of that memory, but when Anne returns home for Christmas, she brings her mother's memory back into the house. It really doesn't matter to Anne if she is at home or at boarding school for Christmas, because she is frozen, numb. She doesn't seem to have loved her mother so much as been in awe of her and her many talents. Still, her frozen state makes her isolate herself from the rest of her family, from her friends, and from Eric. They had started dating last summer, and he would like to take up again where they left off.

Not until Anne faces her true feelings about herself and her mother can she overcome her "formal feeling." Not until her inner isolation threatens to drive her over the brink toward insanity can she finally release her anger over her mother's death and her father's remarriage and begin to get on with her life.

—*Judy Druse*

FRAGMENTS OF ISABELLA: YA
A MEMOIR OF AUSCHWITZ
By ISABELLA LEITNER

Yesterday, May 29, 1944, we were deported. My mother, sisters, brother, and thousands of other Jews from the Kisvarda ghetto in Hungary were deported to Auschwitz. My father was in America trying to obtain immigration papers for his family at the time; he had left his wife and six children behind; he had left so that he might save his family. He was in America when we were deported, packed into cattle cars . . . cars with barred windows, with planks of wood on the bars, so that no air could enter or escape . . . seventy-five to a car . . . no toilets . . . no doctors . . . no medication . . . no room to sit . . . no room to stand . . . no air to breathe. This was no way to die. Yet people were dying all around.

At Auschwitz, our heads were shaved; our possessions were taken away. We stood before the infamous Dr. Mengele, who, with a whistle and a flick of his thumb, would indicate who was to live, who was to die. The business of Auschwitz was death. The four crematoriums could not handle the hordes, so the Germans built open fires and threw the children into them.

Not all of us survived, but those who did heard our mother's final mandate: "Live! Stay alive, my darlings—all six of you. Out there, when it's all over, a world is waiting for you to give it all I gave you. Despite what you see—and you are all young and impressionable— believe me, there is humanity out there, there is dignity. And when this is over, you must add to it, because sometimes it is a little short, a little skimpy. With your lives, you can create other lives and nourish them. You can nourish your children's souls and minds, and teach them that man is capable of infinite glory. You must believe me. I cannot leave you with what you see here. I must leave you with what I see. My body is nearly dead, but my vision is throbbing with life—even here. I want you to live for the very life that is yours."

Giving each other strength, courage and love, we obeyed.

—*Judy Druse*

FRANKENSTEIN MOVED IN   Grades 3-5
ON THE FOURTH FLOOR
By ELIZABETH LEVY

When Mr. Frank moves into the fourth floor of their apartment building, Sam and Robert suspect that there is something peculiar about him. He's not like the rest of the neighbors—he's rude, demanding, uses so much electricity that he causes the whole building to black out, and has lots of boxes of colored wires. Box after box of colored wires. But that's not all: When Sam and Robert meet Mr. Frank, they see that he wears earphones that have wires sticking out, and antennas, and from out of the earphones comes the sound of strange music—music unlike any they have heard before, just moans and groans.

The longer Sam and Robert study Mr. Frank, the more they realize that there is something very peculiar about him: He is thin and pale, uses all that electricity, and nobody in the apartment building likes him. Sam is reading one day when he realizes who Mr. Frank reminds him of: Frankenstein! Now, what would you do if Frankenstein moved in on the fourth floor?

—Ilene Ingelmo

FREAKY FRIDAY   Grades 3–5
By MARY RODGERS

Annabel wakes up one morning in her mother's body. She brushes her mother's teeth and puts on her mother's bathrobe. It's going to be a fantastic day; now Annabel can do anything she wants, just like an adult. When Annabel realizes that, as her mother, she has to kiss her little brother goodbye in the morning and can't call him "ApeFace" as she usually does, she gets a hint that she's in for trouble. When Annabel goes to a parent-teacher conference to discuss the problems the school is having with *her* and then lets ApeFace get kidnapped—she *knows* she's in trouble.

—Zoë Kalkanis

FRIENDS TILL THE END   YA
By TODD STRASSER

David Gilbert didn't have time for Howie Jamison. It wasn't that he didn't like Howie, he did; he just didn't have time for a new friend. David already had a close group of friends, most of them on the soccer team. He was the goalie. He had a girlfriend, Rena, who took up much of his time. And finally, he was studying hard to bring up his grade-point average so he could get into medical school in the fall. He'd talk to Howie at the bus stop, but he declined an invitation to dinner because he didn't feel he had the time to cultivate a new friendship. He didn't think anything about it when Howie didn't show up at the bus stop for several days. He assumed Howie had probably made friends with someone else and was getting a ride to school every morning. He didn't see Howie at school either, but that wasn't unusual; they had different classes, different lunch periods, and David stayed late every afternoon for soccer practice. He felt relieved that Howie had found some new friends.

When David found out several weeks later that Howie was in the hospital, he felt guilty. Howie's mother called to ask David to visit Howie; he was the only new friend Howie had made. David was sorry Howie was so ill, but he didn't see why the responsibility for comforting Howie should fall on him, a virtual stranger. He wanted Howie to know he was concerned, but he didn't know anything about leukemia and felt incapable of helping. All his life, when things had gone wrong, he'd always looked for a way to make them right again. If he said the wrong thing, he apologized, or if he broke something, he tried to fix it, or if someone else had a problem, he tried to help them. But what could he do for Howie? There was only one thing that could make Howie right again, and that was curing him. But maybe, just maybe, having a friend, a friend till the end, would help.

—Judy Druse

THE GANG AND MRS. HIGGINS   Grades 1–2
By GEORGE SHANNON

This is the story of Mrs. Higgins, who was home alone the day the Anderson gang came to visit. The Anderson brothers were the meanest gang in all of Kansas. They only took one bath a year, and if they wanted any decent food they had to steal it. Mr and Mrs. Higgins were among the nicest settlers in Kansas. When the Anderson gang found Mrs. Higgins alone on the farm, they quickly stole all her food, but when they started after her gold—guess who won!

—Elizabeth Overmyer

GARDINE VS. HANOVER   Grades 5–7/YA
By JOAN OPPENHEIMER

It was tense even before they met. And once they did, that was it. The battle lines were drawn, and World War III was on!

There were the Gardines—Jill, 15; Abby, 10; and their mother Frances. And there were the Hanovers—Caroline, 16; Drew, 11; and their father Berk. And when Berk and Frances got married, Jill and Caroline saw to it that they were *not* going to live happily ever after. They began to fight practically from the first moment they saw each other. And the fact that all they had in common was hating each other did *not* help! Jill was short, dark, and pretty. She had lots of friends and didn't particularly care about grades. She didn't like to clean house, and she usually forgot to pick up after herself. Plus, she had a hair-trigger temper. Caroline was tall, redheaded, quiet; always made good grades and had never had many friends. Whenever she was nervous or tense, she cleaned house. When she got angry, she had an endless supply of rude, cutting remarks—the kind most people can't think of till it's too late.

Any time they were in the house together, there was a fight going on. Nothing seemed to keep them from it. Jill would walk in the door, Caroline would let fly one of her zingers, and Jill would explode. Or vice versa—they both worked to keep the feud going.

But they forgot one thing—that there were four other people who very much wanted them to be a family of six. Those four people were the casualties of this war. And maybe there were two more casualties—a marriage that never really got off the ground and a family that never really had a chance to start to become a family.

Frances said, "Once we're a family, we can handle anything." That might be true—but *were* they a family?

—*Joni Bodart*

GHOSTS OF DEPARTURE POINT   YA
By EVE BUNTING

Vicki stands on the cliff called Departure Point. Beneath her, the ocean swirls against jutting rocks. Twelve people have died in car accidents at Departure Point. Looking down, Vicki can see parts of cars from the crashes. There is the truck in which the two men died, over there is the VW bus, and a little further down the cliff, the green Volvo sedan in which the four girls were killed. They'd all been cheerleaders coming home from a basketball game. Their team had won, and everyone was in a great mood, especially Vicki. She was looking forward to the Victory Dance that night and could hardly sit still. She bounced in her seat, hung her head out the window and led cheers. When Carla, the driver, turned around to tell Vicki to quiet down, Vicki shook her pompoms in her face. Suddenly the wheels skidded,

Mary screamed, and the car was going off the cliff. Vicki's last thought was that everyone was going to die and it was all her fault.

But Vicki was thrown clear and wasn't even hurt. She stumbled up the cliff to get help for her friends, but no one would pay any attention to her. She saw her body brought up on a stretcher and heard the doctor pronounce all four girls dead on arrival—including Vicki West. Vicki knew then that she was a ghost, doomed to haunt Departure Point. She can wander around town, observe her parents' suffering, and watch her friends, but no one will ever know she's there. Loneliness and guilt are the prices Vicki has to pay for causing the accident. Then one night she meets a young man in a blue tuxedo. Ted was on his way back from a wedding and was giving the maid of honor a ride home. He'd had too much champagne and he knew it, but he still was behind the wheel. He was at fault when the car went off Departure Point, killing its two occupants. So now Ted is haunting Departure Point as well. He and Vicki get together and try to figure out a way to end their torment. How can they go through eternity knowing that they're murderers?

—Judy Sasges

A GIRL CALLED BOY   Grades 3-6
By BELINDA HURMENCE

Have you ever wondered what life would have been like if you had been born a slave? Would you have run away? Would you have ever learned to read and write? How long would you have lived? Would you have been able to stay with your family? Blanch Overtha Yancey, whom everyone calls Boy, is sick and tired of hearing her father talk about their ancestors, who were slaves in North Carolina. "They deserved to be slaves," she says, "the way they let themselves be pushed around and never tried to fight back or anything. I wouldn't stand for it. They couldn't make me a slave!" When her father shows her the old piece of African soapstone he carries in his pocket and tells her that her great-great-grandfather called it the conjure piece that had set him free, Boy laughs and snatches it from him and runs off along a forest trail. She has been in this part of the state park so many times that at every landmark she can remember the boring speech her father always makes about it. But gradually she realizes that the same old landmarks are somehow different—the trees are no longer summer-green, but bare, as in winter. And the paved trail has disappeared, and where she remembered picnic tables there's an old log cabin, with a wisp of smoke rising from it. Suddenly the door to the cabin springs inward and a huge hand reaches out and grabs her by the arm and pulls her inside. The old man and boy are hard to understand, and they certainly don't understand her talk about the interstate highway that will take her back home. She doesn't think much of their dinner, either—squirrel roasted on a stick over the fireplace. But they won't let her go, and by the next morning she realizes that they think they are helping her—for somehow the time is the 1850s, she is in a slave cabin, and she is a runaway slave. The only things of her own that she has are her clothes, a cheap plastic ballpoint pen, and the conjure stone. She is barefoot, the ground is frozen, notices are posted in every newspaper announcing a $25 reward for her capture, and there are bloodhounds on her trail. Now she will find out whether she can live up to her boast, escape from slavery—and return to the twentieth century.

—*Elizabeth Overmyer*

THE GIRL WHO LIVED ON THE FERRIS WHEEL   YA
By LOUISE MOERI

"It was bad enough to have a name like Clotilde (Til for short), she thought, squinting through the curtains at the empty, windswept street, but why did she also have to live part of her life in a bleak old tomb on Quesada Avenue in South San Francisco and the rest of it on a Ferris wheel at Playland?

"It was Saturday morning again and she could almost feel the creaking, swaying seat of the Ferris wheel under her, the cold wind splashing against her legs, the up-back feeling of being sucked in by some great monster, the out-over lurch as she was again thrust out into space. But if she didn't go—didn't ride the Ferris wheel—it would mean staying home all day. And even the Ferris wheel was better than that."

You see, staying at home was awful. Til's parents were divorced and she lived with her mother. Every Saturday Til's father would come and get her and take her to Playland and to the Ferris wheel. But the rest of the week was spent with her mother. Her mother was different, Til felt, but she couldn't say exactly how. She knew that none of her friends' mothers beat them when they left their coat on the floor or ate toast in the living room or had a picture taken of themselves. But Til's mother did. According to Til's mother, she had to discipline Til because Til was cluttering up her house. Til's mother had wanted a house of her own for as long as she could remember. And now that she had one, she had to watch over it and clean it and scrub it. The house had become like her skin—it protected her from the cruel, killing world. And Til— Til was an intruder and nothing but trouble.

Finally Til's mother decided she had to do something to protect her house—her skin—from the intruder. And that afternoon when Til got home from school, the table was set for dinner—with *butcher knives.*

—Nancy Gierhart

THE GIRL WHO LOVED WILD HORSES   Grades K-3
By PAUL GOBLE

Once there was a Native American girl who loved and understood horses. She would lead them to water and show them the grass they liked best.

One day she was staying with her people's horses and fell asleep on her blanket. "Suddenly, there was a flash of lightning, a crash, and a rumbling that shook the earth. The girl leaped to her feet in fright. The horses were rearing up on their hind legs and snorting in terror. She grabbed a horse's mane and jumped on his back." The herd galloped far away, and soon she knew they were lost.

Next morning, she was awakened by the loud neighing of a beautiful spotted stallion, the leader of the wild horses who lived in the hills. Could she and her horses join the wild band? Read *The Girl Who Loved Wild Horses,* by Paul Goble.

—Patsy Hamric

THE GLORY GIRL   YA
By BETSY C. BYARS

Curled up in the back of the wobbling Glory Gospel Singers bus, Anna Glory stared out the window and thought about her terrible luck. Why does she have to be the only person in Glory family history who can't carry a tune? Her twin brothers, the constantly fighting Joshua and Matthew, her distracted but beautiful sister Angel, all join with their parents in exuberant singing while Anna is left to sell Glory albums in the back of the auditorium.

The bus wavered on the edge of the road, swerving back and forth. The headlights shone first on the trees to the left, then on the stone bank to the right. At that moment the windshield wipers stopped. Mr. Glory peered blindly over the steering wheel; the world was lost in a sheet of water. He hit the brake. For what seemed like an eternity the bus wavered. Anna knew the exact moment her father lost control of the bus. She buried her head in her arms, the windshield wipers swept across the windshield for the last time, and she saw the trees ahead. She held on for dear life.

To find out what happened to Anna and the Glory Family, read *The Glory Girl,* by Betsy Byars.

—*Peggy Tucker*

GOD'S RADAR   YA
By FRAN ARRICK

In Syracuse, New York, Roxie Cable had been just another typical teenager. But the summer before her sophomore year, the family moved to Howerton, North Carolina, because her father was transferred by his company. Roxie's older sister didn't move with them. Glenna, at twenty-two, decided to go to New York City and start her career. Not having Glenna with them made the move doubly hard for Roxie.

The Stafford Hill Baptist Church in Howerton changed Roxie's whole life. Roxie couldn't believe the size of the church. She was amazed at how she could look from Dr. Caraman's real face to his televised face on the screen above the pulpit.

Her parents' decision to join the Stafford Hill Baptist Church didn't just mean meeting new people and attending a new church. It was a way of life! She was taken out of the public high school after only five weeks and enrolled in the private school, the Stafford Hill Christian Academy. Stafford Hill also dictated what you did for your social life and who your friends would be. You could not attend dances, go to movies, ride in cars unchaperoned, or listen to rock music. There were many books that you were not allowed to read.

When Glenna came home for Thanksgiving she exploded. She pointed out in a heated argument with her parents that the church and the people in it had taken over the family's life. Roxie was not allowed any freedom, and her parents were showing no trust in her judgment.

Glenna was angry and scared for her family, but it was Roxie who had to live with the situation and she was totally confused. Who could she trust? Who should she listen to? Her new classmates at the church school were likeable, eager for her friendship, but they didn't allow her to maintain friendships she had begun to make in the public high school. And there was Jarrell, a member of the church . . . but rumored to be wild by her new church friends. Glenna was too far away to be much help. Could her father help her? Maybe not anymore. Her mother? Not since she'd become a true believer. Roxie had to make a choice, or risk being torn apart.

—*Barbara Lynn*

GOOD NIGHT, MR. TOM   YA/Adult
By MICHELLE MAGORIAN

Old Tom picked up a poker and walked to the fire. Little Will thought, "Now I'm really going to get it!" He clutched the seat of the stool tightly. Tom looked down at him. "About Sammy," Will heard him say. He knew he should listen to what Tom was saying, but he couldn't keep his eyes off the poker. He saw Tom's brown wrinkled hand lift it out of the fire—the tip was red, almost white in places, and Will was certain he was to be branded with it. The room seemed to spin, he watched the tip of the poker come closer, and it went dark!

Will was an abused child of a single parent, and he had been evacuated from London to the safety of the English countryside just prior to the outbreak of World War II. He had never known kindness or love and was at first terrified of every strange country sound and sight.

Mr. Tom had lived alone for a long time, but his heart went out to Will. He and his dog, Sammy, taught Will about a world he had never imagined existed before—a world of friendship and affection.

Just when he was becoming comfortable with Mr. Tom, Sammy, and a new friend Zack, who helped him to laugh again, a telegram arrived from his mother. She claimed illness, and asked for him to return to London. Mr. Tom tried to get the mother to come to the country, but to no avail. He spoke to the billeting officer, but got nowhere. Mothers had the legal right to their children, and Will was sent back on the train to the life he had tried so hard to forget.

It was a sad moment when the two said goodbye and Will boarded the train. The whistle blew, and Mr. Tom watched the train puff away out of sight. When Mr. Tom didn't hear from Will, he began to worry. He couldn't ignore that sick feeling he got every time he thought of the frightened and bruised little boy who had arrived at his door so many months before. Finally he made up his mind. He and Sammy would go to London to find Will!

—Beverly Montgomery

GRANDPA—AND ME   Grades 5-7
By STEPHANIE S. TOLAN

Grandpa had lived with Kerry Warren and her family since Kerry was three years old. He had been babysitter, swimming teacher, kite maker, and baseball coach for Kerry and her brother Matt.

But suddenly Grandpa had been doing strange things; he went to the bathroom in the back yard, and he walked to the park wearing his pants wrong side out!

A family conference was held to consider what should be done about Grandpa. All the choices were discussed: sitters, rest homes, etc. "Does *Grandpa* have a choice?" asked Kerry. Later she thought to herself, "There isn't a single choice for Grandpa that isn't rotten!"

But before anything was decided, Grandpa himself made the decision. To see what his decision was, read *Grandpa—and Me,* by Stephanie Tolan.

—*Dorothy A. Davidson*

GREAT CUSTARD PIE PANIC   Grades 1–2
By SCOTT CORBETT

The last time Nick had walked down this street in the fog he had met the terrible Dr. Merlin and had escaped just in time from his magic shop. This time when the fog cleared all he saw was a bakery, with wonderful smells coming out, and a rather odd-looking lady called Aunt Nellie Rim. The cakes and cookies and brownies and pies looked terrific—but before Nick could try them, Aunt Nellie Rim turned into his old enemy, Dr. Merlin, who was about to try a wonderful experiment—substituting the brain of a mouse for the brain of Nick's dog Bert.

—*Elizabeth Overmyer*

THE GREAT GILLY HOPKINS   Grades 6–8
By KATHERINE PATERSON

Gilly Hopkins was on her way to her third foster home in less than three years. She definitely had made a mistake at the first one. She had grown to love her foster family. But they suddenly moved to Florida. They had left her, rejected her, abandoned her. Well, she would not make that mistake again! The second home hadn't lasted lasted very long; she had given her foster mother a nervous breakdown. Now she was on her way to number three.

As she sat in the back seat of the social worker's car, she carefully blew a giant bubble with her bubble gum, that burst and went all over her face and into her hair, which hadn't been combed for three days. So much the better.

Gilly and the social worker stood at the door of her new home. The woman gave Gilly a comb and said, "Run that through your hair." "Can't," said Gilly, "I'm going for a Guinness record." About that time the door opened and there stood her new foster mother, Maime Trotter, a hippopotamus of a woman with a broad gentle smile, and sticking his head around one of her legs was a frail little boy named William Earnest who Gilly immediately decided was retarded. So she made a Godzilla face at him and nearly scared him to death. The house was old and ugly and stuffed with junk. But Gilly knew she could stand anything as long as she was in charge, and she was well on her way.

Later that day Mrs. Trotter sent Gilly to bring their neighbor in for dinner. Their neighbor turned out to be an ancient black man who was blind. This latest addition to the family was too much for Gilly.

That night she wrote a letter to her beautiful, glamorous mother begging her to rescue her from this freak house. Gilly knew her mother would not want her precious daughter to have to live like this.

To find out about Gilly's mother and how (or if!) Gilly survived the freak house, read *The Great Gilly Hopkins.*

—*Billie Harding*

GROUNDING OF GROUP 6   YA
By JULIAN F. THOMPSON

Group 6 knew they were special, but they didn't know why. There were five people in the group, three girls and two boys; they were all sixteen, and none of them was fat. Nat was their leader—he was twenty-two, and was supposed to be their teacher.

When Group 6 arrived at Coldbrook Country School, they knew it was the perfect boarding school—very expensive, discreet, and innovative. They were told to hike into the woods to a distant cove as part of their orientation, and at first didn't think much about it. Then they noticed Nat covering their tracks, and began to wonder just exactly what was going on. It wasn't until later that Marigold, Ludi, Sara, Coke, and Sully learned the horrible, impossible truth—Nat had been hired by the school to take them into the woods and kill them. That's why they were special—and their parents were footing the bill!

There's only one reason why parents don't kill their kids—they're afraid they'll get caught. Coldbrook Country School makes sure they don't!

—*Joni Bodart*

THE HAJ   YA/Adult
By LEON URIS

When Ishmael was eight years old his whole world crashed around him. Until that day, like most Arab male children, he had spent his time with the women of the household and he had been allowed to do anything he chose.

His father was the Haj, the leader of the village, and he sent Ishmael's mother away for a few months. When Ishmael went to the village well for water, the women there taunted him by telling him that his father was going to take a second wife. Some of the children even threw stones at him.

As his father strolled by on the way to the coffeehouse, Ishmael ran up to him; as always, the Haj brushed his son aside. But this time Ishmael was persistent and pulled at his father's coat, demanding attention. As his father turned Ishmael put up his fists and shouted that he hated him.

Without a word his father shook him violently and tossed him into the open sewer that ran down from the top of the village. Ishmael shrieked in desperation, but he realized there was no way to protest or rebel.

His mother urged him to learn to count and to read and write. She told him to count the houses, the fields, and the orchards and to learn who farmed each. His mother suspected that his uncle and his brother Kamal were cheating his father. She was right!

By proving to his father that he could do the recordkeeping, Ishmael was permitted to go to school. But Kamal hated him.

It happened so fast that he had no time to run. Kamal seized Ishmael in the barn, flung him down, choked him, and slammed his head against the ground. "You dog," he screamed, "I'll kill you!

By the age of nine Ishmael had learned the laws he was to live by:

> Brother against brother.
> Brothers against father.
> Family against cousins and the clan.
> The clan against the tribe.
> The tribe aganst the world.
> All against the infidel.

—*Lola Viets*

THE HALF-A-MOON INN   Grades 3–5
By PAUL FLEISCHMAN

Aaron had never wandered so far way from home before. Because
he was born mute, he had always depended on his mother—until the
blizzard came. When his mother failed to return from the town market,
Aaron went out in search of her. Nearly frozen, he stumbled upon the
Half-a-Moon Inn and its terrifying owner, the scheming Miss Grackle.
She kidnapped Aaron and set him to work lighting the fires and peeling
potatoes, while she went about her own business—stealing from her
guests in such a clever way that they blamed everybody but her. She
was delighted to have found someone whom she could count on to keep
quiet. And soon she began to train Aaron in the even more dreadful
business of peeling back the eyelids of the sleeping guests and reading
their dreams—for Miss Grackle's own evil purposes.

—Elizabeth Overmyer

HALFWAY DOWN   Grades 6–8/YA
PADDY LANE
By JEAN MARZOLLO

Each moment of a day must be spent, for when it has passed it is
gone forever. Or is it? Is it possible that the past, present, and future
exist at the same time, twirling like three vanes of a pinwheel rotating
in the wind?

At fifteen Kate Calambra wasn't interested in summer camp and she
was too young to get a job. It seemed that her only choice of activity
for the summer was moving with her parents into an old, rundown
house in North Lancaster, Connecticut.

Kate's parents were thrilled with the move. They enjoyed nothing
better than fixing up old houses. Kate, however, could think of better
things to do than work around the old house.

It was morning, Kate's first morning in the new house. She lay in bed
not turning or opening her eyes. "It was as if only her mind had awakened. Something's changed, she thought. Something's wrong."

Slowly, Kate opened her eyes expecting to focus on the ugly purple
wallpaper. Her heart froze. The walls were gray, grimy gray plaster.

Kate, still in bed, sat bolt upright. The pink nylon nightgown she had
worn to bed was gone. In its place she wore a thin cotton slip.

Panic rose within her as she looked around the room. There were
two beds where there had been only one. The bureau that had held her
clothes was missing, and so was her stereo. A wooden trunk sitting at
the foot of her bed was full of clothes. They were long, worn dresses
with cotton petticoats.

In the beginning Kate thought it was a dream. Soon, though, the dream felt all too real. It slowly dawned on her that, though she was in the same house in North Lancaster, Connecticut, she was no longer in the same time frame.

It was 1850, and now she was Kate O'Hara, daughter of an Irish immigrant, and she worked for pennies a day in the town's textile mill.

—Sally Long

THE HARD WAY HOME   YA
By RICHARD SHAW

Life with parents is never easy, but Gary has just about had it with his dad. They can't seem to get along at all. His father is always on his back, criticizing him and nagging him to do chores and telling him how hard *he* had to work when he was a kid. He also hates rock music, so much that he cuts the cord to Gary's stereo. Gary decides that's the last straw—he'll run away to teach his parents, especially his father, a lesson. After all, he's sixteen, he knows how to take care of himself, and besides, he's an only child. After a few days his parents will be desperate to have him home.

Gary hitches a ride to the nearest town. He gets a room and even a job, and every day he searches the paper for news of his disappearance, but he finds nothing. (That's very strange—in a little town a missing kid is always Big News.) Gary meets a girl who likes rock music as much as he does. Then he remembers he left his rock concert tickets at home.

Gary goes home, watches the house until his parents leave, and then goes to his room. He finds the tickets in his bureau drawer with a note. "Dear Gary, enjoy the concert. Be sure to brush your teeth and eat the right things. Love, Mom." It's almost as though his parents know exactly what he's doing and don't care!

In *The Hard Way Home* Gary finds it's easy to run away but next to impossible to come back.

—Diana Hirsch

HARVEY'S HORRIBLE SNAKE DISASTER Grades 3-6
By ETH CLIFFORD

There were three things that Harvey feared more than anything else on earth: his rotten Cousin Nora, his Aunt Mildred, who was the kind of person who screams and jumps if you just happen to come up quietly behind her, and slithery, slimy snakes.

"Not only was Nora obnoxious and always telling whoppers and never-ever getting into trouble, but now I had to let her have my room for the whole two months that she was visiting. Nora took down all my pennants and told me I could enter—my own room. That was enough, I was mad. There she was with my crystal ball telling me that she had the power to foresee the future. 'Danger,' she yelled, 'danger, beware the snakes—you have been warned.' Now I knew it was just an act—but she still made me nervous, so I grabbed the crystal ball and I yelled, 'I see something, I see you disappearing'—how was I to know that that was just what would happen the next day?"

Harvey dreaded the Big Event—SNAKE DAY—but he dreaded taking Nora to class with him even more.

To find out how an eighteen-foot python got a speeding ticket and how Nora and Harvey finally rescued Slidler, a hog-nose snake that just happened to disappear from the upstairs bathtub, you'll just have to read *Harvey's Horrible Snake Disaster.*

—*Suzi Smith*

THE HAUNTING OF HILL HOUSE YA/Adult
By SHIRLEY JACKSON

"Sitting up in the two beds beside each other, Eleanor and Theodora reach out between and hold hands tight; the room is brutally cold and thickly dark." From the room next door, the room that had been Theodora's until that morning, comes the steady sound of babbling, but too low for the words to be understood. Holding hands so hard that each can feel the other's bones, Eleanor and Theodora listen as the sound goes on and on. Then, without warning, a little laugh starts. The laugh breaks up the babbling and rises up and up the scale until it breaks in a little gasp.

Theodora's grasp loosens, then tightens, and Eleanor wonders why it is so horribly dark. She ought to be able to see their hands, at least! Eleanor rolls and clutches Theodora's hand tigher. "I left the light on," she thinks. And then, screamingly, "Why is it so dark?" She tries to whisper to Theodora but finds she can't move her mouth, and the voice goes on and on.

Now Eleanor is lying sideways in the darkness holding Theodora's hand in both of hers so tight that she can feel the fine bones of Theodora's fingers. "I will not stand this. They think to scare me—well . . .

I'm scared, but I'm not going to take any more of this from this lunatic house—I won't—I'll yell!" Eleanor yells, *"Stop it!"* and the lights are on the way they had left them. Theodora sits up, startled.

"What?" Theodora says. "What, Nell? What's wrong?"

"Good God," Eleanor screams. "Good God—whose hand was I holding?"

The Haunting of Hill House, by Shirley Jackson

—*Becky Blick*

THE HEADLESS ROOMMATE   Grades 6–8/YA
AND OTHER TALES OF TERROR
By DANIEL COHEN

Have you ever heard the story of the man in the back seat, or of the babysitter and the telephone, or of the Death Car? They're all horror stories, passed down from one generation to another, told over campfires or in dimly-lit rooms, and they're wonderfully horrible and deliciously gruesome! Daniel Cohen has collected these stories and written them down so convincingly that they sound like they could have happened to your best friend—or even to you!

When I was a teenager, our two favorites were The Hook and The White-Haired Man—called "The Frat Man" in this book. But the ending *we* gave it was even more awful than this one. But the story I'm going to tell you now is one of the scariest ones I've ever heard. It's called "The Man in the Middle." It takes place in New York City. . . .

Describe subways—rush hour/late at night

Barbara—Queens/Manhattan—show and dinner

"Twilight Zone" subway station—almost empty car—elderly couple

Three men across the aisle

High—drunk—man in the middle staring at her

Scared—afraid to move—no source of help

All three staring at her—middle one never stops—she stares back at him—can't help it

Only two more stops—tries to stay calm

Old man leaves—orders her to get off too—doors slide shut—great relief

"Sorry to order you—doctor—trio of men across from you?"

"Yes—especially the middle one, high or drunk. Terrified!"

"Yes—I noticed him. Maybe high or drunk earlier tonight—not when the other two carried him on. When they got on, he was dead. You were being stared at by a corpse."

—Joni Bodart

HERE I STAY   YA/Adult
By BARBARA MICHAELS

Those who now live in my house call me Satan, probably because I'm the biggest, blackest cat they've ever seen. I know their secrets, but they'll never know mine. I know all the mystery corners of the house, all the hidden mazes, and all the answers. I'll tell you none of them: I'll only ask the questions.

Whose voice called Jimmy from the top of the stairs when the upper floor was deserted? How did the voice know his name? Why is Andrea having nightmares of wings beating against iron bars, struggling to break free?

How can a rose bloom in a Maryland winter when not even leaves are left?

The headstone under the rose reads "Mary Fairfax, Here I Stay." What does that mean? And is the rose on Mary's grave, or on the smaller, neglected one next to hers? Whose grave is this?

They thought the house was empty except for me. When they moved in, I had to discover who they were. Andrea—longtime mother to a much younger brother—had just converted my house into a country inn.

Jimmy, her brother, had just had his life converted. He'd had plans to be a professional football player, but a car wreck had destroyed his leg. It was up to all of us to find something else he could be.

I allow Martin, their constant boarder, to share my room and sleep on my bed. He doesn't bother me. As a writer, he has a different perspective on the questions. But even he cannot understand what is happening.

But I—I watch, I see. I know. I understand.

I know Jimmy writes poems about death. I know he can't leave the rose for long before he has to return. I know what it is he's waiting for, searching for.

I watch. I see. I sit beside Andrea as she listens at Jimmy's keyhole. She can see the empty room—empty except for Jimmy, but I—I see the other. Andrea recognizes only Jimmy's voice, but I know the other. I know who it is weeping softly, desolately, like a child lost in the dark.

—Linda Susan Angy

HERE LIES THE BODY   Grades 3-5
By SCOTT CORBETT

Mitch and Howie might have expected strange things to happen when they started their summer job mowing the grass between the tombstones at Hemlock Hill Burial Ground. But things were pretty normal most of the summer until they came upon the caretaker Ezekiel scrubbing a strange mark off a tombstone in the middle of a thunderstorm while his eerie brother Nathaniel screamed curses at him. The boys soon discover that the mark on the tombstone is the mark of the devil. Then Nathaniel disappears, Ezekiel begins digging a secret grave, a body is missing, and the boys begin to wonder who will end up in the newly dug grave on a wild stormy night.

—Elizabeth Overmyer

HIDE CRAWFORD QUICK   Grades 6-8
By MARGARET W. FROEHLICH

Nothing's right at our house. Worst of it is, I don't know what is the matter. Mama's fine, she had the baby. But Daddy's so crabby, Huie cries all the time, and Roberta and Lizzie are awful! And on top of that, Daddy got this mean woman to come and stay with us.

But finally, that long week was over, and Daddy brought Mama and the new baby home.

"They're here," Lizzie shrieked. "Let's have a look at the new baby."

Watching sleeping babies wasn't too interesting, but in a little while, Crawford awoke with a loud demanding cry. All four girls crowded around to see him.

Suddenly, Lizzie's voice rang out above Crawford's crying, "How come this baby is broke? You should take him back and get a new one."

In the next few days, Gracie's thoughts turned to her little sister's words. And why not? Gracie thought. They wanted a perfect little brother. One that Father would call Robert Charles Prather, Jr., not Crawford. Where did that name come from anyway?

Gracie remembered unwrapping the new yellow dishes and finding the broken cream pitcher. Mother had said, "Oh dear. That's too bad. We'll just get a new one the next time the Jewell Tea man comes."

We wanted a perfect baby, one to cuddle and powder and show off. This was a family problem, Mama had said, so Gracie couldn't even tell Nanny Olive, her best friend. And Nanny Olive was making a present for the baby!

Crawford had a lot of colic, mostly in the evenings around dinner-time. One evening, the potatoes were scorched and the scorch spread over the whole house. Dinner was spoiled and Crawford was wailing. Roberta said she couldn't eat. The baby made her sick. *"I can't stand him, him and his one foot."*

Daddy stood and said, *"Do you think anyone can stand it?"* Daddy left, slamming the door. He left without his coat, even though it was December.

Gracie was terrified. What if Daddy decides to go away for good? What will Mama do? What will become of us?

Find out what Gracie does in *Hide Crawford Quick,* by Margaret Froehlich.

—Linda Henderson

HIGH AND OUTSIDE   YA/Adult
By LINNEA A. DUE

Niki wakes up, her mouth tasting of stale beer. She has a headache and feels dizzy. Staggering over to her typewriter, she tries to proofread the article that she wrote last night for her high school newspaper. But instead of a well-written sports article, Niki sees a page of weird, depressing ramblings that have nothing to do with softball. She decides to go downstairs for some juice before rewriting the article. Her parents never say anything to Niki when she's drunk because they feel it's in bad taste to discuss one's occasional overindulgences. After all, getting drunk is something other people—not social drinkers—do. Both of Niki's parents are social drinkers, and they've raised their daughter to be the same. At fourteen, Niki was drinking wine with her dinner. When she turned sixteen, her father taught her how to make all the usual cocktails and stressed the importance of the cocktail hour as a time for family togetherness. Niki began having cocktails before her dinner wine. Now she's seventeen, and the understanding is that she is mature enough to handle her social drinking. Except that Niki is a social drinker who gets drunk almost every night. She has a fifth of gin stashed in her closet and beer hidden all over the house. She has a fake ID and knows which liquor stores sell to minors. And she also has a hangover almost every day. But Niki still has life a little easier than most people. She gets good grades and scores higher on her SATs than anyone else in her class. She's the editorial page editor for her high school paper and the star pitcher of the softball team. She has her own car and lots of friends, and goes to a lot of parties.

One day Niki wakes up still drunk. She can't tell if it's day or night. The clock says 6:52, so it must be morning. Niki vaguely remembers a party the night before where she drank even more than usual. She can't actually remember what happened there or even how she got home. Going out to the driveway, Niki sees her car parked halfway into the street. That means she probably drove it home herself.

She slowly walks around it looking for dents and scratches. It really scares her to think that she could have run over someone and not even remember it. Finally she tells herself that everyone was drunk and it was just a bad night. But Niki's drinking problem is becoming more obvious to those around her. People are starting to avoid her because she's an obnoxious, aggressive drunk. The drinking and hangovers are reflected in her schoolwork and softball pitching. But it's not until she's kicked off the team and her best friend refuses to see her that Niki forces herself to admit that a social drinker can become an alcoholic

—Judy Sasges

HIROSHIMA NO PIKA   Grades 4–8
By TOSHI MARUKI

Seven-year-old Mii was eating sweet potatoes with her mother and father when the atomic flash devastated Hiroshima. Although some of the pictures here are sad, we see the heroism of people facing disaster, even their concern for future generations.

Every year on August 6th the people of Hiroshima print the names of loved ones who died from the bomb on lanterns. Then they light the lanterns and set them adrift on the seven rivers that flow through Hiroshima. As Mii's mother put it: "It can't happen again if no one drops the bomb."

—Paul H. Rockwell

NOTE: This book should be used with discretion and is best read in the company of a teacher or parent. I never booktalk *Hiroshima No Pika* without permission from the teacher.—*PHR*

THE HITCHHIKER'S GUIDE TO THE GALAXY   YA/Adult
By DOUGLAS ADAMS

Talk 1

It all started the day the bulldozer came to knock down Arthur Dent's house to make way for a highway bypass. Since Arthur Dent seriously objected to the bulldozer, he was lying in the mud, in his bathrobe, in front of the bulldozer to prevent its passage, when his friend Ford Prefect came along to take Arthur to the pub for a drink.

Though it was still morning, Ford was planning to tell Arthur some news that would cause him to need a stiff drink. The news was that the world was going to end in twelve minutes.

What Arthur did not know about Ford was that Ford was an alien from a small planet near Betelgeuse, who had been stranded on Earth for fifteen years waiting for a flying saucer to hitch a ride home on. In fact, Ford was a researcher for that wholly remarkable book, *The Hitchhiker's Guide to the Galaxy.* Ford was very bored with his lengthy stay on this dull planet, and he would not mourn its passing.

Twelve minutes later, when a fleet of Vogon starships vaporized Earth to make way for a hyperspacial bypass, it was thanks to Ford's hitchhiking skills that Arthur and Ford found themselves not evaporated, but safely aboard a Vogon starship, Arthur still in his bathrobe.

There Ford introduced Arthur to the marvels of *The Hitchhiker's Guide to the Galaxy,* an electronic book that told everything you wanted to know about the universe, but were afraid to ask, and other tips for galactic hitchhikers. Inside the cover (which bore the words DON'T PANIC in large, friendly letters), the guide explained such great universal truths as why a towel is the most useful item a hitchhiker can carry, how to stick a babelfish in your ear to instantly translate any language, and why one should under no circumstances listen to Vogon poetry.

The commander of the Vogon ship on which Arthur and Ford were hitching was fairly typical for a Vogon: he was thoroughly vile and he hated hitchhikers. Which is why, when he found them on his ship, he strapped them into poetry appreciation chairs, attached electrodes to their temples, and tortured them with the third-worst poetry in the universe. After which he said with fiendish glee, "Now Earthlings . . . I present you with a simple choice! Either die in the vacuum of space, or . . . " he paused for melodramatic effect, "tell me how good you thought my poem was!"

For further hitchhiking adventures of Ford and Arthur—still in his bathrobe—see the sequels: *The Restaurant at the End of the Universe; Life, the Universe, and Everything; The Meaning of LIF;* and *So Long and Thanks for All the Fish.*

—*Cathi Edgerton*

Talk 2

When Arthur Dent came to, he was lying on the floor of a Vogon spaceship.

"The Earth.

"Visions of it swam sickeningly through his nauseated mind. There was no way his imagination could feel the impact of the whole Earth having gone, it was too big. . . .

"England no longer existed. He'd got that—somehow he'd got it. He tried again. America, he thought, has gone. He couldn't grasp it. He decided to start smaller again. New York has gone. No reaction. He'd never seriously believe it existed anyway. The dollar, he thought, has sunk forever. Slight tremor there. Every Bogart movie has been wiped, he said to himself, and that gave him a nasty knock. McDonald's, he thought. There is no longer any such thing as a McDonald's hamburger.

"He passed out. When he came round a second later he found he was sobbing for his mother."

His friend Ford Prefect, who was really an alien from a small planet near Betelgeuse, was sitting off in a corner of the room, humming, as if nothing unusual had happened. Of course, for Ford Prefect, nothing unusual had happened. Ford was a researcher for that wholly remarkable book, *The Hitchhiker's Guide to the Galaxy.* The destruction of the Earth merely meant one less world to research. Besides, Ford had been stranded on Earth for fifteen years. He was glad to be rid of the place.

So here was Arthur Dent. Stuck on a Vogon spaceship with an alien from Betelgeuse and a book whose only words of advice were DON'T PANIC.

Fortunately for Arthur, everything was just about to get worse.

He and Ford were immediately grabbed by a squad of Vogon guards and taken before the captain of the ship. Now the captain was not your average ugly, nasty Vogon. He was an above-average ugly, nasty Vogon. Matter of fact, he was downright vicious, and he always made hitchhikers such as Ford and Arthur listen to his poetry before he killed them. Vogon poetry is of course the third-worst in the Universe. *Only* the third-worst.

But these distinctions could not comfort Arthur and Ford. They knew they were in for an awful lot of pain and torture regardless of whether or not it was the worst or third-worst pain and torture in the universe. To make the situation even more depressing, after all this pain and torture they were to be shoved out into space without space suits. They would surely die within thirty seconds.

Do Ford and Arthur die, or is this whole episode an inconsequential sideline that has nothing to do with the real story? You never can tell with *The Hitchhiker's Guide to the Galaxy,* by Douglas Adams.

—Anne Reynolds

HOME BEFORE MORNING Adult
By LYNDA VAN DEVANTER and CHRISTOPHER MORGAN

Lynda Van Devanter was a typical All-American girl during the 1960s. She attended private Catholic schools, was a class leader, and a responsible and happy member of her family. Lynda enjoyed sports and school activities, and got along well with her sisters and her parents. She staunchly believed in God and her country. After high school she went on to fulfill her dream of becoming a nurse. Lynda graduated from nursing school in 1969, with her whole life ahead of her. She felt she needed to contribute something to her country, so in 1969 she made a decision that would shatter her secure world for the rest of her life. Lynda Van Devanter joined the army and was shipped to Vietnam.

The army recruiter had assured Lynda that army nurses were never sent to areas where there was actual danger of combat. From her naive perspective she saw the United States pursuing a course that President Kennedy had talked about in his inaugural address: "We were saving a country from communism." She thought she would be nursing brave boys fighting for democracy.

When Lynda Van Devanter arrived in Vietnam her idealistic view of the war vanished quickly. The plane that brought her into Saigon was fired on as they tried to land, and she was immediately assigned to a MASH unit on the front lines . . . so much for what the recruiter had said about nurses and combat zones. The first week that she was there her base suffered from continuous rocket attacks. She worked long and arduous hours in cramped, ill-equipped, understaffed operating rooms. She saw friends die. Witnessing a war close-up, nursing soldiers and civilians whose injuries were catastrophic, she felt the very foundations of her thinking shaken daily. She observed the corruption of the South Vietnamese government and army. There was no way to tell the enemy from the friendly Vietnamese people. One lived in constant fear and danger. She was hourly called on to make life-and-death decisions.

After one traumatic year, Lynda Van Devanter came home a Vietnam veteran.

Coming home was nearly as devastating as the time that she had spent in Vietnam. The day she arrived in Los Angeles, Lynda was spat upon and jeered at by people as she tried to obtain transportation back to Washington, D.C., and home. She came home to a country torn apart by the war . . . to a people that blamed those who were doing the fighting in Vietnam for what was happening. She was viewed by many as a murderer instead of a healer. She felt isolated and angry. Even her family did not want to deal with what Lynda had been through in Vietnam. Their advice was to just put it all behind her. She learned to hide the fact that she had been in Vietnam. In doing so she buried it all. Anger and depression surfaced. Like many other Vietnam veterans, Lynda Van Devanter suffered from delayed stress syndrome. Her depression affected her personal and her professional life. Where would her personal war lead?

Home Before Morning is the story of a generation of Americans who went to war and came back wounded . . . the kind of wound that doesn't always show on the surface.

—*Barbara Lynn*

HOMECOMING   Grades 6–8/YA
By CYNTHIA VOIGT

How would you feel if your mother left you alone with three younger brothers and sisters and never returned? Thirteen-year-old Dicey Tillerman felt right along that there was something odd, something wrong about the trip with her mother, her sister Maybeth, and her two brothers, Sammy and James. They were going to see (and perhaps move in with) the great-aunt Cilla they'd never met. Then Dicey's misgivings were abruptly realized when Momma abandoned them all in a parked car in a strange shopping center.

As head of the Tillerman family now, Dicey knew she had to keep them together. She couldn't go to the police since they might split up the family. The only relative she knew of was Great-Aunt Cilla, who lived miles and miles further south. With almost no money, Dicey's only choice as she saw it was to walk south, hoping maybe for a welcome from her aunt.

Unfortunately, Dicey found it wasn't easy to get far, trying to stay out of sight of adults, with three hungry, stubborn, tired, and whining children.

One way to make money finally came to mind as the Tillermans walked past farms with signs saying "Pickers wanted." Maybe they could earn enough in a day or two to get by for a while. The farm they chose seemed in the middle of nowhere, and the four children approached the house slowly.

"A dog growled and barked, snarled and leaped angrily up against the fencing on the right side of the house. This must be a kennel. This dog needed a kennel. It was a large gray-and-brown ceature, bigger than a setter, with a huge slavering mouth. Its teeth were long and sharp. It charged against the fence, setting up a clamor that would rouse anyone in the house, Dicey thought. She couldn't make herself step any further toward the screen door of the house, not with that dog there, not even to make money.

"The screen door opened and a man holding a napkin in his hand stepped out. As soon as he appeared, the dog stopped barking and crouched, fawning and whimpering. The man started toward the children, looking at them carefully with cold eyes."

Dicey explained about wanting a job, but she felt uneasy—then and later in the day, as she and the other children worked alone in a long field of tomatoes. Mr. Rudyard seemed creepy to her, and she was determined to leave at the end of the day.

In the late afternoon, when the sun was beginning to lower and the mosquitoes were beginning to rise, Mr. Rudyard returned in his pickup truck—with the dog on the front seat.

"What's he going to do?" eight-year-old Maybeth whispered.

"I dunno," Dicey said. Fear climbed from her stomach to her throat. Mr. Rudyard tied the dog to a tree, and when he came back, Dicey had decided what to do.

"We can't pick any more," she said. "We have to go now," she said.

He looked at her out of cold eyes. Then he said, "If the dog runs against that sapling, it'll snap." He got back into the truck and leaned out the window. "I keep him hungry," he remarked. He backed the truck around and drove off.

In the silence, Dicey could hear insects humming. "What does he want?" she demanded.

Nobody could answer her.

It's a lot of responsibility taking care of a family when you're only thirteen and on your own in a hostile world.

—Linda Gibson

HOOPS   YA
By WALTER DEAN MYERS

Seventeen-year-old Lonnie Jackson *could* be a great basketball player. But in Harlem there are lots of other good players, and it is hard for even the best to find a way out. Lonnie decides the city-wide Tournament of Champions will be his way. Sixty-four teams from all over New York will be participating, and there will be dozens of college and pro scouts in the audience. The tournament will be his big break— his ticket into the big time.

Lonnie and his friends have played basketball together for years. They know they are good, but to meet competition requirements, they need a coach. The guy who runs the gym where they practice introduces them to the man he's selected as their coach. Lonnie can't believe it! Their "coach" is Cal Jones, a local wino who hangs around the playground where they sometimes shoot baskets. Lonnie refuses to let him coach. But Cal makes Lonnie a proposition: he'll play Lonnie one-on-one, six baskets. If Lonnie wins, he'll leave. If Cal wins, he becomes coach. Lonnie is sure he'll win easily, but to his amazement, Cal beats him.

This is Lonnie's first clue to Cal's secret past. As the time for the tournament approaches, Lonnie discovers that Cal used to play pro ball, but sold out to gamblers and lost his career and his family. Now Cal has a chance to regain his honor through coaching this young team. But the gamblers haven't forgotten him. They want him to throw the tournament near the end of the final game. The tough choices Lonnie and Cal must make—the choices on which their very lives depend—are the story of *Hoops*.

—*Diane Tuccillo*

HOUR OF THE WOLF   Grades 6–8/YA
By PATRICIA CALVERT

At first glance, Danny Yumiat and Jake Mathiessen didn't seem to have much in common. Danny was a native Alaskan from a village of only twenty-three people. He dreamed of becoming a lawyer. He was a popular student and an excellent dog racer. Jake, on the other hand, came from a wealthy Minnesota family. His father wanted Jake to join his law firm, but Jake wasn't interested. Jake felt like an outsider in Alaska, and he had never been around dogs—much less raced in cart pulled by a team of huskies. When Danny asked Jake to be his handler in the Last Great Race—The Iditarod [eye-dit-a-rod] Trail Race—Jake and Danny discovered just how much they shared. Then when Danny couldn't run the race, Jake substituted for him, joining the others in trying to cover over a thousand miles from Anchorage to Nome by dog sled.

Just imagine you are all alone on a small sled pulled by a bunch of dogs. You stop frequently and check your dogs' feet to be sure they are free from ice balls . . . that means cleaning out forty-eight paws and putting booties on the dogs with sore feet. You may not see anyone for hours, and when you do see another racer you have to be careful not to get your dogs too close or the harnesses will get tangled. If your sled is damaged, you have to repair it yourself or hope for another racer to send for help. Often your rest stops will be in snow shelters you build on the spot. Traveling through the wilds of Alaska is as frightening as it is lonely.

During the long race Jake had plenty of time to think about the Alaskans' fear of the "Hour of the Wolf," the time of day when the wolves come out. And he discovered that everyone has fears no matter what they are called. Since most of us will never be in Jake's place, we'll have to rely on Patricia Calvert's *Hour of the Wolf* to discover what survival really involves.

—Judie Smith

HOUSE WITH A CLOCK IN ITS WALLS   Grades 3-5
By JOHN BELLAIRS

When Lewis' parents die, he is sent to live with his Uncle Jonathan in his old house. Lewis has always wanted to live in a mansion and Uncle Jonathan's house is certainly a mansion—a house of many rooms and many mysteries, complete with turrets and gables and even a secret passageway. Then there are Uncle Jonathan and his friend and next-door neighbor Mrs. Zimmerman, both of whom claim to be wizards. But while Uncle Jonathan practices harmless, entertaining, white magic, the original owner of the house, Isaac Izard, was a powerful and evil warlock. Just before his death, Isaac completed a device that would bring about the end of the world—a doomsday clock. Somewhere, hidden deep within the walls of the house, the clock is waiting. As much as Lewis and Uncle Jonathan try, they cannot find it. Still, it can be heard ticking away morning, noon, and night; sometimes loud, sometimes soft, but always there.

Although Isaac Izard built the clock, even he didn't have enough power to wind the device the whole way. Only someone with even more power than Isaac can make the final adjustment—and that person is Isaac's wife Selena. Since she has been dead many years, the doomsday machine poses little danger . . . that is, until Lewis accidently brings Selena Izard back from the grave.

—Zoë Kalkanis

HOW LAZY CAN YOU GET?   Grades 3–5
By PHYLLIS NAYLOR

The Megglethorpe children—Timothy, Amy, and Douglas Jon—are
perfectly normal children. Timothy is a layabout—he likes to lie about
all summer. Amy likes to be left alone; she does not like to be told when
to go to bed or when to get up, what to eat or what to wear, especially
after nine months of school orders. Douglas Jon, the youngest, has
decided that he does not want to grow up. He has made a vow to blow
soap bubbles and hang by his knees all his life. (He's worried because
he doesn't like blowing soap bubbles as much as he did last year.) Their
parents love their blond, skinny children and accept them as they are,
letting them enjoy a carefree, lazy summer.

This easygoing life changes drastically when Mr. and Mrs. Megglethorpe must go to Boston for a week and Miss Brasscoat arrives to
babysit. She believes that children should be seen and not heard, that
layabout children are no good, and that fat children are the best children. Timothy, Amy, and Douglas Jon have been brought up on hamburger and roast beef and salad, but Miss Brasscoat cooks rutabaga
jumble with okra and eggplant. The children assume that eggplant has
some kind of egg growing on it, okra sounds like something from the
bottom of the ocean, and rutabaga must be a disease of the joints. They
try to talk Miss Brasscoat out of serving rutabaga jumble. [Read section
starting on p. 30, as she serves each child, ending when all are served.]
Miss Brasscoat wakens them with a whistle, makes them dust everything (even Timothy's pyramid of 278 beer cans), and never, ever
smiles. To remedy this, Douglas Jon tapes Miss Brasscoat's mouth into
a smile while she is asleep. Do you think that works? Read *How Lazy
Can You Get?* by Phyllis Naylor, and see if anything can make Miss
Brasscoat laugh.

—*Barbara Hardy*

HOW TO EAT FRIED WORMS   Grades 3–5
By THOMAS ROCKWELL

Talk 1

When I was little my parents were reluctant to take me out to dinner.
I wasn't a brat, but I did prefer unusual food—well, actually, the hot
dogs I ordered were normal enough, it was the *peanut butter* I insisted
be put on the hot dogs that caused the problem. Most restaurants didn't
even keep peanut butter on hand for their customers. So we kept our
own jar of Skippy in the glove compartment of the car, just in case.

I must admit that now, looking back, I can see that my eating habits *were* a bit strange. But compared to Billy Forrester, my tastes were positively normal. He ate worms!

It all began with a bet. His friend Tom had been grounded for refusing to eat salmon casserole at dinner one night. Billy had bragged that *he* could eat anything—*including* worms. Well, one thing led to another (from a brag to a dare to a bet) and before he knew it Billy was trying to figure out fifteen ways to make his wiggly entrées palatable. In the meantime, his former buddies Tom and Alan were cooking up just as many schemes to convince Billy that worms could be hazardous to his health. After all, losing a fifty-dollar bet is no small deal!

If you'd like to find out who wins the bet and how, or if you're just looking for new and different recipes—you'll want to read *How to Eat Fried Worms*, by Thomas Rockwell.

—*Beckie Brazell*

Talk 2

Have you ever thought about eating a worm or a bee or a bug? What would it take for you to eat a worm? Would you do it for fifty dollars, if you would be able to get something you really wanted and had been saving for for a long time?

This is the predicament that Billy finds himself in when he makes a bet with his two friends. And it isn't just one worm, it is fifteen worms, one a day for fifteen days, and on top of that they are night crawlers, the bigger and juicer the better.

Of course, he can eat them any way he wants: fried, stewed, with mustard or ketchup, in a sandwich or raw, *but*—he has to eat them.

Can he? Read *How To Eat Fried Worms* and find out.

—*Janet Hellerich*

HOWLIDAY INN   Grades 3–5
By DEBORAH and JAMES HOWE

Those of you who have read *Bunnicula* will remember Harold the dog and Chester the cat, and how they discovered that the Monroe family's pet rabbit was really a vampire bunny, sleeping during the day only to roam the kitchen at night and suck the juice out of vegetables until they turned white. Harold and Chester are back in this new book, *Howliday Inn*. They've been sent to the Chateau Bow Wow to board for a week while the Monroes are on vacation. And Chester is particularly unhappy about spending a week locked up in a kennel, especially one called Chateau Bow Wow—after all, what self-respecting cat would stay in a place with a name like that?

Their first night there, Chester and Harold are kept awake all night by strange howlings, and the next morning Chester nicknames the place Howliday Inn. But what is howling neither of them knows. Chester has his suspicions, though—only a werewolf would make that kind of noise. And it isn't only the howling that disturbs Chester and Harold— soon Louise, the French poodle, disappears. And when Chester disappears, Harold begins to suspect murder.,

Are there really werewolves at Howliday Inn? Where have Chester and Louise disappeared to? Have they been murdered? Then who is the murderer? It's up to Harold to solve the strange mystery of Howliday Inn.

—Zoë Kalkanis

HUMBUG MOUNTAIN
By SID FLEISCHMAN

Grades 4–6

It was a few days after we'd moved onto Grandpa's riverboat that Mr. Johnson discovered the dead man's hand.

Glorietta and I found a couple of old potato sacks on board and set out to collect buffalo bones. Bleached-out ribs and skulls were lying all along the dry riverbed where hunters had shot the buffalo and skinned them for robes. Mr. Johnson, our goose, always tagged along after us, and we were forever trying to chase him away. He'd just honk and beat his wings, so after a while we gave up and let him follow.

We walked all the way to the end of the old dry riverbed, and pretty soon our sacks were bulging with buffalo skulls and ribs sticking out like pieces of bleached driftwood.

Glorietta and I dumped our sacks near the river. Glorietta looked over our tangle of bones. "How much you figure we got?"

"It's a mighty puny pick," I answered. "A nickel's worth at most."

"That's it?"

"We just got started. What in tarnation do you expect?"

Mr. Johnson was eating grass grown up through a hole in the buffalo ribs. We ambled over. I tried to shoo him out of the curved rack of the ribs. "We gotta collect a lot more'n this to make any kind of money."

"What's Mr. Johnson got?" Glorietta asked. Then her voice jumped sky-high. "Wiley, there's a man buried here!"

Humbug Mountain, by Sid Fleischman

—Becky Blick

HUNTER IN THE DARK   YA
By MONICA HUGHES

He'd done it! He'd got clean away. He'd outwitted the lot of them. But he couldn't have done it without his best friend Doug. It was Doug who had helped with the months of planning that had gone into this final adventure, Doug who had suggested the isolated area in the Freeman River Valley as a campsite. Only Doug knew where he was and why. Only Doug understood how important this secret hunting trip was. He hoped his parents would understand. He had left them a note saying he needed to be alone to think things out. This was his own private war. He had three days' worth of supplies. Three days in which to track and shoot a trophy white-tailed buck. This was the dream that had kept him going through months of pain and uncontrollable, exhausting nausea.

Sixteen-year-old Mike Rankin had leukemia. Because his parents were unable to face the possibility of his dying, they had not told him the exact nature of his illness. Neither his parents nor his doctor would explain the necessity for the devastating treatments he underwent. But he had tracked down the truth about his disease on his own in the library. His parents loved him and wanted to protect him, but he couldn't let them do that anymore. How could he ask them to help him fight the dark when they wouldn't admit that the dark was there? Now, in the woods alone, he had nothing he could use to turn away the dark, to turn away his thoughts about the dark. It was his darkness, and there was no one he could really share it with. The nights were the worst. At night the thoughts that he could usually keep at bay during the day began to slink past his weakened defenses, like hungry wolves sneaking past a dying fire. He must face the possibility of his death. If not by leukemia, then maybe by a stray bullet from a careless hunter or in a snowstorm. There was so much that could go wrong. He had to keep his head, not let his feelings and fears get in the way of his judgment. If he could get his trophy, his parents would have to accept that he was no longer a child and stop hiding things from him. They could no longer keep him in the dark.

—Judy Druse

I AM THE CHEESE   YA
By ROBERT CORMIER

"I am riding the bicycle and I am on Route 31 in Monument, Massachusetts, on my way to Ruttersburg, Vermont, and I'm pedaling furiously because this is an old-fashioned bike. . . . "

Adam Farmer and his family live quietly in a small New England town. His dad is an insurance agent. But Adam slowly discovers that things are not what they seem. Who is the mysterious Mr. Grey who always talks to his father in the paneled room downstairs? Why does Adam's mother make a secret phone call once a week? Why all the secrecy? Eventually, they must tell Adam that his father has been relocated by the government under threat of death by assassins. He was a reporter who had uncovered corruption, and his testimony in Washington led to indictments and arrests. One day the family is told to go away for the weekend, there is grave danger.

Adam is being interrogated by someone trying to get information from him. Is he withholding information? Where is his father? Is he on a drug trip? Is he being held in prison? Who is questioning him? Does he really ride his bike to Vermont? What has happened to his family?

—*Alan Nichter*

I WILL CALL IT GEORGIE'S BLUES   YA
By SUZANNE NEWTON

Dinnertime at the Sloan house is like dodgeball: you spend all your energy staying alert to keep from getting hit. Fifteen-year-old Neal is pretty good at not drawing attention to himself, not making waves. His eighteen-year-old sister, Aileen, intentionally defies their bullying father and draws most of the fire. Meanwhile, frail seven-year-old Georgie trembles like a baby rabbit and cringes when he inevitably attracts his father's attention. They are all hostages to their father's anger and to his demand that they present a good public image as a small-town Baptist minister's children. Their father doesn't care about his children as long as they don't act in any way that will disgrace him. The proper facade hides the fact that family relationships are strained to the breaking point.

Each member of the Sloan family has his or her own method of survival. Aileen is rebellious, striking out against her father's rules. She wants to be a real person, not just somebody's idea of what a preacher's daughter is supposed to be. She doesn't want to die of shame if she fails, which, by the way, she is doing. She is in danger of not graduating from high school, which won't look too good for a preacher's kid. Her father calls Aileen lazy, selfish, a no-good. Neal can maintain his equilibrium because he has found an outlet: he is secretly taking jazz piano lessons from a neighbor, Mrs. Talbot. Mrs. T is his escape hatch, so he can endure what goes on at home. Their mother, helplessly loyal to her husband, refuses to side with her children. Finally, seven-year-old Georgie survives by living in a fantasy world of real and false people. Only Neal, who protects him from his father, is real. Georgie is afraid that he himself will be replaced by a false person; then Georgie will no longer be real. Not even Neal realizes the extent of Georgie's fears. But when the respectable family facade begins to crumble, it is Georgie who is caught in the middle.

—Judy Druse

IF I ASKED YOU, WOULD YOU STAY? YA
By EVE BUNTING

"The Crow who flies alone"—that is the nickname given to seventeen-year-old Charles Robert O'Neill. Crow, the victim of orphanages and foster homes, lives alone in his secret room. The secret room is really three rooms: an apartment. Beautiful, remote Sasha's apartment. But "secret room" is what he'd thought when he'd first discovered this place behind its wooden panel. He'd tripped over a loose lace on his Adidas as he was going up the stairs of the old carousel building, and he'd gone crashing to the side. At the time he hadn't known what was happening when the wall slid away under his hand. Later he'd found the hidden catch. It was so well hidden that he knew it was a million-to-one chance that had let him find it. Inside, the apartment lay shrouded in dust, muffled by time. He could tell it had lain this way for years and years. Now, the secret room, the secret place, is his. It is the first place of his own he has ever had. Crow's Nest. His.

About one a.m. one morning, Crow is standing at the window of the apartment (something he'd never do during the day, because someone below on the beach or on the pier might suddenly look up and see him at the window). Crow sees someone swimming way out in the ocean beyond the breakers. It suddenly occurs to him that the guy is swimming *away* from the shore. It looks like he plans to go on and on till he can swim no more. Then he will stop. And he will sink. And he will be gone forever. Crow runs down to the pier, unties the dinghy, and goes to rescue the swimmer. When he pulls the guy aboard, he realizes it isn't a guy at all. It is a girl.

With trepidation, Crow takes the half-conscious girl back to his room above the old carousel. He wonders what she will do now that he has fished her out of the ocean. He is uneasy, because now she will know about his secret room; one phone call from her and he will lose everything. She is a threat to his safe hideaway. Except the secret room proves to be a safe haven for her also. The girl, Valentine, is hiding from someone or something. And she thinks she has found just the right place to hide. Crow is uneasy about Valentine's presence, but most disturbing are the feelings he begins to have for her. They endanger the defenses he's built up to keep himself safe.

Does he dare care about Valentine? Will she betray him, just as all the others did?

—Judy Druse

IF I WERE IN CHARGE OF THE WORLD   Grades 4–8
AND OTHER WORRIES
By JUDITH VIORST

Here are "poems for everyone who has ever had trouble apologizing or writing a thank-you letter, or talked too much, or burped, or had visions of the very worst happening at the very worst time—here is a little help in turning worries into laughter."

[Read "If I Were in Charge of the World" from page 2 of the paperback edition and "Thoughts on Getting Out of a Nice Warm Bed in an Ice-Cold House to Go to Bathroom at Three O'Clock in the Morning" from page 18.]

—Linda Henderson

THE INDIAN IN THE CUPBOARD   Grades 3–5
By LYNNE REID BANKS

Omri received for his birthday the skateboard he'd wanted forever and also an intriguing gift from his brother, who'd found it in the alley—a white metal cupboard with a mirror, like the kind you find in a bathroom. He liked cupboards and only wished this one locked. His mother gave him a boxful of keys to try. The one with the curly top on the red satin ribbon worked. But what should he put *in* his cupboard, he wondered. He didn't have any medicines. His mother suggested he put the plastic Indian she'd found in his pocket while doing the wash in his cupboard. His friend, Patrick, had given the Indian to him for his birthday, only because Patrick didn't have any use for it. So Omri put the Indian into the cupboard, locked it, and went to bed.

A noise woke him the next morning—a pattering or tapping high-pitched noise. It came from the cupboard. There was something alive inside. Omri was petrified. Cautiously, he tried the door, but it was shut tight; the noise stopped instantly. Then he turned the key and opened the door. The Indian was gone! He peered into the corners and there, crouched in the darkest one, was the Indian, and he was alive! [Read paragraphs 1 and 2, page 7.]

Omri had to touch him. He reached his hand slowly into the cupboard. [Read paragraphs 1 and 2, page 9.]

Omri knew this must be kept secret, but soon Patrick, his best friend, became resentful when Omri rushed home from school every day and didn't want to spend time with him. To save their friendship, Omri decided to let Patrick in on the secret. That's when the trouble began. . . .

—Sherrill Kumler

INTO THE DREAM   Grades 6–8/YA
By WILLIAM SLEATOR

Most dreams are dreamt and then forgotten. Most, even nightmares, fade in the morning light. Paul's dream was different. Each night it grew more frightening and intense, filling Paul with a panic that lasted throughout the day. He tried to tell his best friend Larry about it, without sounding weird. Larry and Paul were the best students in the class and had always understood each other, but this dream was coming between them now. Larry suggested that Paul might be going schizo. Paul withdrew from Larry, his teacher Miss Keck, and his mother. None of them would understand.

Francine was dreaming also. Someone was beside her in the dream, someone who mirrored her fear. They moved in horror toward a glowing sphere, toward a small child who swayed and danced before the eerie light.

When Francine realized that it was Paul who was beside her in the dream, she confronted him at school with her discovery. Although Francine was also in Miss Keck's class, she and Paul were not friends— Paul considered her silly; she thought of him as teacher's pet. He admitted having the same dream, every night sharper and more real. The feeling of danger grew, weighed down upon him until he felt like screaming.

Paul and Francine decided to describe to each other in complete detail the dream as each of them experienced it. They both agreed that the most important part was the sense of danger, of imminent catastrophe, that only they could avert.

In the dream there was a funny low building with letters over it that said STARDUST; they could hear murmuring voices repeating "Jaleela" over and over again; close behind them was a great hulking creature. There is also a little kid, almost in a trance, and he didn't know what he was doing and in a minute something terrible was going to happen to him. Francine knew that it was not just going to affect the little kid—they were in danger too.

The night following their initial discussion, the dream became clearer and more intense—their contact with one another had taken them further into the dream. Paul and Francine realized now that they could read each other's thoughts, finish each other's sentences.

Paul became intent on finding the little kid in the dream; he had to be saved!

How could they go about finding a child in a dream? They decided to start with themselves—perhaps some past experience they shared would solve the mystery. Up until now neither Paul nor Francine had cared for each other. They looked at what they had in common: they were both in Miss Keck's class at school, both of their parents were divorced and they lived with their mothers, and they both had mental telepathy. Further investigation proved that they had both been near Reno, Nevada, at the same time about four years ago—and they had both been staying at the same motel. Imagine their surprise when they found that the name of the motel was Stardust.

Did something happen that July at the Stardust Motel that brought Francine and Paul into the dream? Who or what is that horrible lurking creature? Can they find the child in time to save him and themselves?

—*Carole Gastrell*

ISLAND OF THE BLUE DOLPHINS   Grades 6–8
By SCOTT O'DELL

I have been paddling my canoe from sun to sun and I fear I must turn back, for my canoe is still leaking. I keep stuffing the crack with fiber torn from my skirt, but the crack is getting wider. The thought of returning to the Island of the Blue Dolphins is almost more than I can bear, but I know I must.

It has been many moons since I was left on the island. My tribe was small but we were so happy there, until the Aleuts came, killing my father and many of our men. That was when the hard times came on our village, times of hunger and fear. When the white men came in their big ship to take my tribe to the land across the sea, we were all ready to go with them. But when the ship was almost through the harbor, I looked to shore and saw my little brother Ramo. He had been left behind by mistake! What could I do? I jumped the ship and swam to shore. Ramo and I watched the ship sail away. Soon Ramo was killed by the wild dogs, and I have been alone since that time. I burned the houses in the village; I made weapons. It is against the custom of my people for a woman to make weapons, but I had to fight the wild dogs.

Many moons I have waited for the white men to come for me; but they have not come. So I took a canoe my people left behind, to try to reach the land where my people are. Only two or three suns and I would be there, but I cannot go on in a leaking canoe. I am not sure I can make it back to the island, but still I will try. It is my land. It is my home. And I am Karana. I am the daughter of an Indian chief.

—Emily Hobson

IT AIN'T ALL FOR NOTHIN'   YA
By WALTER D. MYERS

Ever since his mother died, Tippy has lived with his Grandma Carrie in Harlem. He hardly ever sees his father, Lonnie, even though Lonnie lives in the same city. Lonnie is more interested in partying than he is in his son. Tippy doesn't much care, he learned long ago that Lonnie wasn't into being a real father. Tippy is happy living with Grandma Carrie. She gets Social Security and does housework a few days a week, so they get along pretty well. All that changes when Grandma Carrie breaks her hip. She seems to get old really fast and can't work anymore. Money gets tight, and finally Grandma Carrie goes to a rest home. The only place that Tippy has to go to is his father's.

It's hard for Tippy to live with Lonnie. Lonnie never does anything at a set time—just whenever he feels like it. He's gone a lot and never tells Tippy where he's going. There's never any food in the refrigerator, and Lonnie doesn't seem to realize that Tippy gets hungry. Lonnie hardly ever talks to Tippy—he just sits around playing cards with his friends. And Lonnie refuses to let Tippy call him Dad.

One morning, Tippy wakes up early and sees lots of rings and watches spread out on the table. There's no way that Lonnie could afford to buy all those things and he certainly doesn't need them all. Tippy knows that his father has done jail time for stealing, but he thought his father had learned his lesson. Grandma Carrie taught him that stealing is wrong, and Tippy is upset to discover that his father is a thief. Tippy starts hanging out in the streets to avoid being around Lonnie. And he has a drink every so often to help him forget his problems at home. But even though Tippy is working hard at forgetting Lonnie, Lonnie is just starting to think about Tippy. He thinks that Tippy should help him rob a local store. And Lonnie makes it hard for Tippy to refuse.

—Judy Sasges

IVANHOE   Adult
By SIR WALTER SCOTT

His father would not speak his name—Ivanhoe—nor would he allow anyone else in the household to speak it.

Cedric the Saxon had disinherited his son for two reasons. Ivanhoe had betrayed him by becoming a knight and serving the Norman king. To Cedric, all Normans were enemies, their conquest of Saxon England generations before still unaccepted and unforgiven. Worse, Ivanhoe had dared to fall in love with Rowena, Cedric's ward, and a princess in the line of the last Saxon king, Alfred.

But Ivanhoe was certain the days of a Saxon England would never come again, and he believed the Norman king he had chosen to serve would treat all his people fairly. That king was Richard the Lionhearted, and Ivanhoe had willingly followed him to the Holy Land to fight in the Crusades.

Now Ivanhoe has returned to England alone. Disguised, penniless, he learns that his father's bitterness has not faded, his hope of winning Rowena is still remote. Then comes the worst news of all—Richard has been captured in Austria and is held for ransom. A ransom his greedy brother Prince John has no intention of paying.

Has Ivanhoe given up father and love for nothing? Join him for a tournament of sword-play, kidnappings, love, escapes, trial by fire, outlaws, sieges, and adventure. Sir Walter Scott's *Ivanhoe.*

—Christy Chilton

JAKE   Grades 3-5
By ALFRED SLOTE

Jake is the toughest eleven-year-old on the Arborville Little League Team. Their arch-enemies are the McLeod Builders, and this year Pat McLeod has a curve ball—which Jake's team doesn't have yet. And to, top it off, Jake's team doesn't have a real coach, so one of the boys' mothers volunteers. But she knows nothing about baseball; she leaves the coaching up to Jake, who has to beat the team into shape—literally.

—Laurie Peck

JANE'S HOUSE   Adult
By ROBERT KIMMEL SMITH

Jane Klein died in her sleep. Her husband Paul, sixteen-year-old daughter Hilary, and ten-year-old son Bobby never got a chance to say goodbye. Now it was just the three of them, living in Jane's house. And they were coming apart, each in his own way, as they tried to find some method of coping with the hurt that wouldn't go away. With Jane gone, they had lost their very center; it was as if the sun had not come up one morning. Bobby had become silent, brooding, and withdrawn because he felt it was his fault his mother had died. Hilary sought solace in a deep involvement with her boy friend, Peter Block. It was simpler for Paul; he had his answer right in front of him—the children. He had to be strong now for the children. He had to be mother and father rolled in one to keep them all together and functioning. That was his job, his responsibility, and by God, he wouldn't permit them to fall apart. But how do you mend a broken family?

As Paul gradually emerges from his paralyzing grief, he tries to recapture the past by finding a woman to take Jane's place. He falls in love with and marries a young advertising executive, Ruth Gordon. But Ruth feels uncomfortable living in Jane's house—a house that reflects Jane in every corner. She gets off on the wrong foot with the kids. So no matter how much sweet, handsome, totally lovable Paul says not to worry, Ruth *is* worried. She cannot measure up to Jane's standards; she cannot fill Jane's shoes; she cannot live in Jane's house.

—Judy Druse

JENNIFER, HECATE, MACBETH,   Grades 3–5
WILLIAM MCKINLEY AND ME, ELIZABETH
By ELAINE L. KONIGSBURG

Elizabeth had just moved to a new apartment and had no friends at all, until she met Jennifer. And Jennifer was a witch, so of course she couldn't really be a friend either. But she could teach Elizabeth to be her apprentice in witchcraft, and this is the story of how she did. Elizabeth was initiated in a special blood ceremony, and from then on she had to obey Jennifer's orders—such as, eat one raw egg per day—

and she had to observe certain witchy taboos, until at last she was judged ready for the ultimate spell—making flying ointment. Now Jennifer looked pretty ordinary—not like a witch at all—and she did some ordinary things like going to school, but she was definitely a witch. What else could you call someone who could pull a whole wagonload of books down a flight of stairs without spilling a single one, or wear a paper bag over her head with no holes in it, and not trip or bump into anything at all?

—*Elizabeth Overmyer*

JEREMY VISICK   Grades 6–8/YA
By DAVID WISEMAN

When Matthew Clemens tells his history teacher that history is a lot of rubbish, his teacher asks him to go to the graveyard and copy down what he finds on a tombstone there. The tombstone is for one John Martin and his wife and their six sons, who were all killed in mining accidents. But Matthew's attention is caught by another marker—to Reuben Visick and his two sons, who were also killed in a mining accident, and to a third son, Jeremy, whose body was never recovered from the Wheal Maid mine. Somehow, Matthew can't stop thinking about Jeremy Visick. Then he discovers that his own house is on land once belonging to the Visicks—and his nighttime excursions start. Night after night he is woken up and compelled by some strange force to go out to the graveyard, or the old shed nearby. His mother finds him one morning fast asleep in the graveyard, his father rescues him from the shed another night, and soon Matthew meets the real Jeremy and finds himself in the very Wheal Maid mining disaster that took Jeremy's life, and may well claim his own.

—*Elizabeth Overmyer*

JULIE   YA/Adult
By CATHERINE MARSHALL

The surging water was gushing around me. My boots were so full of water that I could scarcely lift them. I stood there, frozen in my tracks, for not twelve inches from me scurrying along the top of a wooden fence were six of the largest, ugliest rats I had ever seen in my life. I wanted to scream, to turn around and go back to the safety and warmth of home, but I couldn't. I had to go on. Dad and the others needed the coffee and sandwiches I carried.

My family had moved to Alderton, Pennsylvania, in September, 1934. Father had purchased the local paper, *The Sentinel,* after the former owner had declared bankruptcy.

"This will be a family business," Father told us as we stood on Lookout Point catching our first glimpse of what was to be our new hometown. "We cannot afford to run it any other way."

My younger brother and sister, Tim and Anne-Marie, were elated, for to them owning a newspaper was a game. Then again, when you're ten and eleven years old, life itself is a game. Mother had the house to operate and the finances to manage, so the "family business" meant Dad and me. I was eighteen, or would be in a few weeks, and all my life I had dreamed about being a writer. Maybe my dreams were to come true sooner than I had expected.

But as I stood in the middle of the rising water, I wanted to cry. The inky blackness was closing in on me, and I had not yet gone halfway to *The Sentinel*'s office. The rain was falling harder now, and my courage ebbed lower as the waters around me rose. I swallowed my fears as best I could and moved on. As I trudged along, I kept telling myself that the dam would hold.

I moved past Exeley's Drug Store and set my sights on the A&P in the next block. "Not long now," I told myself. "You can make it."

Then I heard the thunderous roar as the streetlights went black!

—*Cheryl Ress*

JULIE OF THE WOLVES   Grades 3–5
By JEAN C. GEORGE

Julie is an Eskimo girl who is forced to marry when she is thirteen. She finds living with her husband and his mother so intolerable that at last she decides to run away to San Francisco to visit her pen pal, Amy. And so she sets off across the Alaskan tundra, taking with her a backpack, a week's supply of food, needles, matches, a sleeping skin, two knives, and a pot. One week later she is hopelessly lost. All around her the tundra looks the same—there are no landmarks. Without a compass and with no food now except the grain and insects she can gather along the way, she will never survive the approaching winter. Finally, after two days of watching her only neighbors, a family of wolves, she remembers that her father once told her that helpless people have sometimes asked the wolves for help. Of course he never told her how to ask. But now Julie realizes that her only chance of survival depends on learning how to communicate with the wolf pack.

She must be accepted by them or else she will die.

—Elizabeth Overmyer

JUST ANOTHER LOVE STORY   YA
By R. R. KNUDSON

Dusty loved Mariana more than anything else in the world. There was no one like her, and no one else could possibly take her place. When she said they were through, it seemed easier to just give up and die than to go on living. So he got in his Plymouth Duster and took off for the beach. He was so out of it that all he could really do was drive and hurt. Anyone who said that nobody could die of a broken heart had obviously never suffered from one. He ached all over. He wore a pair of faded striped pajamas, and with his hair sticking up every which way, he looked an escapee from the mental ward. But Dusty didn't care—with Mariana gone, what was there to care about? What was there to live for? Nothing was worth the effort. "Can't live if living is without you . . . ," he sang along with the radio, looking for a place to crash. . . . No place seemed to be quite right—until he thought of the ocean. He'd go back to Long Island, and he'd die on Jones Beach—just drive that old Duster right into the ocean, and the two of them die together, missing Mariana. But he couldn't wait all the way to Jones Beach, and when he saw the sign for Southshore Beach, he decided this was it. Dusty floored the accelerator. He blasted across the Southshore boardwalk. He headed for the pier. Sunbathers stood watching with their mouths open. He was airborne, spinning, and just had time to think that Mariana would think twice before saying "Never" to him again. "Take that sucker," he said to himself as he ran out of pier and plowed into the Atlantic.

But Dusty only thought his life was over, because he was pulled out by Rush, Mr. Long Island, the champion bodybuilder of Muscle Beach. When Dusty first saw him, he thought, "This guy's only in college, and already he looks like Conan the Barbarian." He thought muscles like that were repulsive. Then Rush made him an offer he couldn't refuse— if he would train with him all summer, Rush would help Dusty get Mariana back. The last thing Dusty wanted to do was spend the summer with a bunch of airhead "bubblebuilders," but if he could just get Mariana back, he'd put up with anything—even lifting weights. And if he didn't get her back, there was always suicide, and *this* time, it would be somewhere far, far away from Muscle Beach and Rush to the rescue!

—Joni Bodart

KAVIK, THE WOLF DOG Grades 3–5
By WALT MOREY

Kavik was part dog, part wolf, bred in the icy Alaskan wilderness. From the time he was a pup, Old Charley One-Eye, his owner, trained him meanly and roughly to be the lead dog for his racing sled team. Charley One-Eye's dream was to win the North American sled dog race in Fairbanks, and Kavik did it for him.

But this attracted the attention of a wealthy Seattle businessman, who paid Charley One-Eye $2000 for Kavik and shipped him off by private plane for Seattle. They ran into a storm; the plane crashed. Fifteen-year-old Andy Evans found the cage several days later. Surprisingly, Kavik was still breathing. Andy knew he should shoot the dog, to put him out of his misery. But just then Kavik opened his eyes. And Andy begain to figure out a way to get Kavik home.

—Nancy Eager

THE KEEPER OF THE ISIS LIGHT YA
By MONICA HUGHES

It is Olwen Pendennis' tenth birthday on Isis. By Earth years she is sixteen. Olwen has never been to Earth. She was born on Isis. Her parents had the job of Keepers of the Isis Light, which meant that they were charged with making sure the beam of light from the galactic lighthouse kept sending its signal back to Earth and to space travelers. Olwen's parents were killed by a storm when she was two years old, and she was raised by Guardian, a robot. Guardian and Olwen have kept the light of Isis beaming.

Since her parents' death, Olwen has not seen another human being. To her Guardian has always been human. Then on her tenth Isis birthday, Olwen not only receives a beautiful musical dress from Guardian, but she also learns that settlers from Earth are coming at last to the valley below. Olwen is very upset by this. She wants things to stay as they are. Guardian reminds her that there is nothing she can do about it, as their whole purpose through the years has been to guide settlers and travelers to Isis. Besides, Olwen has the freedom of the whole planet. She has adapted to the strong ultraviolet light and the thin air of its upper plains. The settlers will not be able to move out of the valley, not until they have made atmospheric adaptations, which will not happen for generations. She will still have most of the planet to herself.

When the settlers finally arrive Olwen is ready to welcome them, become friends, and finally to love at least one of them. But the settlers are not ready for the strangeness of Isis, or even for Olwen's strangeness. Suddenly Olwen is faced with the fact that she is indeed different, and that this difference will affect the whole settlement.

—*Barbara Lynn*

NOTE: There are two sequels, *The Guardian of Isis* and *The Isis Pedlar.*

THE LANGUAGE OF GOLDFISH   YA
By ZIBBY ONEAL

Sometimes growing up isn't easy. Thirteen-year-old Carrie Stokes finds it a mind-shattering experience. She is uneasy about the changes in her body, frightened about not fulfilling her teachers' and parents' expectations, fearful of relations with other people, especially boys. Her older sister, Moira, readily accepts adolescence; she delights in new clothes, dances, and her new sexuality. Consequently, a gulf develops between them, which Carrie cannot cross. She is told, "You can't go on being a kid forever," but that is exactly what she would like to do. She is unwilling to let go of her belief in a magic world where nothing can change. She longs to return to the goldfish pond where she and Moira summoned the fish with crumbs and soft whistling noises they called the language of goldfish. Carrie sees the goldfish pond as a sanctuary in a changing world. The tension between reality and the chaos in Carrie's mind makes her have dizzy spells—everything suddenly slips sideways. Inside her head, colors begin to tumble like the colored glass in a kaleidoscope. Trance-like moods overwhelm her, in which she loses all sense of time. Her fear of growing up results in a gradual nervous breakdown, but her parents fail to recognize the trouble Carrie is having. They ignore her calls for help until she attempts suicide; even then her mother talks about "an unfortunate incident." Under the guidance of a psychiatrist, Carrie starts out on the long road to recuperation. Like Lisa Shilling in *Lisa, Bright and Dark,* Carrie gradually learns that there are no easy answers to life's complexities, and that strength to survive must come from within.

—*Judy Druse*

THE LAST MISSION
By HARRY MAZER

YA/Adult

In 1945, during World War II, the crew of a U.S. Air Force bomber flew their last mission over Europe. After this mission, the men were to be returned home. But on this mission the plane was shot down, and everyone was killed except for the middle gunner, Sgt. Jack Raab. He was the only one who had seen the last two men of his crew shot down as they were trying to parachute to safety. He was alone as he struggled behind enemy lines, and was taken prisoner and sent to a German POW camp. He tried to act like a man, while witnessing and experiencing things he'd never imagined. However, he kept his military secrets and his personal one. . . . Sgt. Jack Raab was only sixteen years old. A very young patriot who only wanted a real chance to "play war." He found out too late and too fast that war is not a game, when he flew his *Last Mission*!

—*Faye Powell*

THE LAST TEXAS HERO
By DOUGLAS TERRY

YA/Adult

Homer Jones, Shad "Sparkie" Sparks, and Harold Sims are the heroes of Rutherford Park, Texas—on their way to becoming All-American heroes. All three have been offered football scholarships to Dallas University. They have been courted by Oklahoma and Arkansas schools, but only Coach Burt Carnegie at Dallas U. will take all three. And the three musketeers decided long ago not to let any college split them up.

Homer Jones, a noseguard, has lots of determination that carries him through when his ability stops. He won't stop trying; he keeps going after the others quit. He wants to do great things on and off the football field. With him, it's a matter of discipline and believing in dreams. He is the leader of the group.

Sparkie Sparks, a full-blooded Choctaw Indian and running back, is the best athlete Homer has ever known. He has all the moves and the size of a heavyweight boxer. He has all the moves off the field, too; he is quite a ladies' man.

Harold Sims is a born-again, virgin linebacker who has kamikaze courage and the strength of a bull. He's got speed, agility, and head-hunter abandon. He is the most dedicated guy Homer has ever met.

And so, one August morning, the three start off to the city of Dallas and big-time college ball playing for the Wildcats. They are going to make their mark, to stand tall for the truth, justice, and the American way. But the rules of heroism have changed since the days of the Cheerios Kid and the Lone Ranger, and neither the coaches nor the senior Wildcats are the God-fearing gladiators they appear to be from the stands. There is the defensive coach, Crazy Ray Cutler, who finds "a few good men" by having the players participate in rubber hose fights; there are the cheerleaders willing to do anything for real Wildcats; there is the media machine that insists on ignoring cruelties or pretending All-Americans have to be cruel; there are the psychological and physical pressures that turn friends into rivals; but there are also one professor and a young woman who see through to the heart. They encourage Homer, increasingly disturbed by the methods the coaches use to produce a winning team, to attempt to change the system by restoring dignity and pride. When he takes on the bad guys, he either ensures his future in college football or ensures that he will be a has-been at twenty. . . . no longer the hero of Rutherford Park, Texas.

— Judy Druse

LEROY AND THE OLD MAN   YA
By W. E. BUTTERWORTH

Where can you hide if a gang is threatening to kill you? That is the question facing seventeen-year-old Leroy Chambers. Leroy had seen Mrs. Carson, an elderly lady who lived on the sixth floor of his Chicago housing project, get ripped off and assaulted. The guys who assaulted her were members of the Wolves, a gang whose turf was in the housing project. The cops had questioned Leroy, but he hadn't told them anything. He had kept his mouth shut. He knew if he told the cops, they'd get him. Nevertheless, the cops found out who was involved and arrested Elton, Howard, and BJ. And that meant Leroy was in trouble. BJ wouldn't believe he hadn't told the cops anything. BJ would think Leroy had identified them, and he was just crazy and mean enough to come after Leroy. The cops said they would protect Leroy and his mother or he could move. But if he and his mother moved, they could always find him at work. When Leroy came home from work the next day and found the door to his apartment bashed in, he and his mother moved out. Leroy was sent to his paternal grandfather in Pass Christian, Mississippi; his mother would stay in a hotel for a few days while looking for a new place to live. Leroy's father couldn't help because he had disappeared when Leroy was in the sixth grade. He just hadn't come home from work one night. When his mother had called the place where he worked, they told her that they had let him go. And that was the last they ever saw or heard of him.

Leroy had never met his grandfather and decided soon after meeting him that he was crazy. His grandfather was a shrimp fisherman on the bayou who worked long, hard hours, lived in a shack (the house had been blown away by a hurricane and had never been rebuilt), and carried all of his money in a wad in his pocket. His grandfather was highly respected by those who knew him; he was forthright, clever, stubborn, had all the answers, made Leroy feel stupid, and was unimpressed by the danger Leroy faced at home in Chicago.

He didn't realize that putting Elton, Howard, and BJ in jail wouldn't solve the problem. There would still be other Wolves on the loose to get him. The old man didn't really know what it was like. Everything was black and white to him. The Wolves had assaulted Mrs. Carson, so they should get punished for it. He thought once you did what the cops wanted you to do, that would be the end of it. He just didn't understand what it was like in the project. Doing what the cops wanted you to do was a good way to get yourself killed. He had two sets of people, the cops and the old man on one side, and the Wolves on the other, both telling him to "do right" or face the consequences. And no matter what he did, one group wouldn't like it. He was right in the middle. He didn't know what to do. He could run, disappoint the old man whom he had come to love and respect, or he could testify—and get himself killed.

— *Judy Druse*

LET THE CIRCLE BE UNBROKEN   YA
By MILDRED D. TAYLOR

Cassie Logan and her three brothers—older, serious Stacey, and younger, fun-loving Christopher-John and Little Man—belong to one of the most prosperous black families around Strawberry, Mississippi. The Logans are well-off because they have a five-room house with fireplaces instead of a one-room, tar-papered dirt-floor shack like many of their neighbors. They have several cows and horses, and hired man Mr. Morrison to help work their land. Their land—that's the most important thing, because the Logans own all two hundred acres of it themselves. That means that what small profit they make from selling their cotton crop, they can keep. Their sharecropper neighbors aren't so lucky; their crops go first to the greedy white landowners who skim all the items they bought on credit right off the top, leaving very little behind. We see this world through eleven-year-old Cassie's eyes in 1934, in the middle of the Depression. Cassie has a hard time keeping her mouth shut about things that don't seem right, and there is so much she doesn't understand, such as:

—why the government folks up in Washington make the farmers plow up acres of beautiful blooming cotton to keep cotton prices up, promising to send government checks for the loss, money the farmers never see, since the white plantation owners keep it for themselves.

—why young black neighbor T. J. is hanged for the murder of a white storeowner, after a trial by white folks in which all the evidence points to the white Simms brothers, boys who used to be T. J.'s "friends."

—why pretty black Jacey Peters gets in trouble for talking to a white boy, and why Uncle Hammer throws Cassie's photo of her white friend Jeremy into the fire.

—why Uncle Hammer hates Cousin Bud for marrying a white woman in New York.

—why everybody loves Bud's daughter Suzella when she visits, so pretty and light-skinned she could pass for white.

—why Suzella refuses to call herself black.

—and most of all, why her favorite brother, fourteen-year-old Stacey, doesn't want her to hang around him anymore, and why one morning he leaves a note saying he has run away to make money for the family to pay the new cotton tax.

How can Cassie grow in this hard, confusing, unfair world? Well, there are marble games to play in the red dust, fishing in the pond, chewing sweet gum peeled right off the tree, smelling all the green, growing things around her, munching on warm peanuts. And basking in the understanding love of wise Papa, respected by the whole black community, the warm love of Mama and Big Mama, who would do anything for their children; feeling the unspoken bond with hot-tempered Uncle Hammer, so much like Cassie herself, and the loyalty and companionship of her brothers, who always stick by her.

—*Cathi Edgerton*

LIFE, THE UNIVERSE, AND EVERYTHING   YA/Adult
By DOUGLAS ADAMS

This is the third book in *The Hitchhiker's Guide to the Galaxy* series, and if you liked the first two, you'll really enjoy this one.

These books tell about the best-selling book in the universe—*The Hitchhiker's Guide to the Galaxy*—which is very popular partly because of all the really useful information it contains, but mostly because it has the words DON'T PANIC written in large bright letters on the cover.

This is a handy message to have if you're Arthur Dent, who escaped the planet Earth just before it was destroyed to make way for a hyperspace bypass. Through no fault of his own, mild-mannered Arthur was hurled from one end of the universe and back again, joined by a bizarre assortment of companions, including Zaphod Beeblebrox, the two-headed, three-armed ex-President of the Universe.

Finally Arthur was returned to Earth, but it was an Earth two million years in the past. There, stranded in a prehistoric swamp with no hope of escape, having lived as a hermit for two years (and still wearing the same tattered bathrobe he was wearing the morning Earth was blown up) Arthur found himself visited by a spaceship. Rescue! he was certain.

Thus Arthur Dent, one-time radio copywriter, clambered out of his prehistoric cave to boggle at the alien creature. "It was . . . very alien, [with] a peculiar alien flattened head, peculiar slitty little alien eyes, . . . and pale gray-green alien skin that had that lustrous sheen about it that most gray-green races can acquire only with plenty of exercise and very expensive soap."

The alien gazed levelly at him for a moment, frowned briefly, and consulted a clipboard it was holding in its skinny alien hand.

"Arthur Dent? Arthur *Philip* Dent?"

"Er—yes," Arthur said and waited.

"You're a jerk — a complete kneebiter."

"Er—er . . ."

"Don't give me that!" snapped the alien. And then he walked up the ramp and into the ship, which proceeded to take off, leaving Arthur still stranded.

Arthur Dent would never know that he had met one of the universe's very small number of truly immortal beings—Wowbagger the Infinitely Prolonged, who had decided to relieve the boredom of immortality by taking up a worthwhile project. He had decided to insult everyone in the universe—in alphabetical order. Whenever someone pointed out that his plan was impossible because of all the people being born and dying every minute, Wowbagger would glare haughtily at them and say, "A man can dream, can't he?"

But Arthur Dent would never know all this. Arthur Dent, a very short time later, would be pulled off of prehistoric Earth and into an adventure involving the white killer robots of Krikkit and their plot to destroy the rest of the universe. The adventure would also involve talking elevators, depressed robots, a God of Thunder, and of course that famous book *The Hitchhiker's Guide to the Galaxy.*

And you can read all about it in *Life, the Universe, and Everything*, by Douglas Adams.

—Alan Stewart

LISTEN FOR THE FIG TREE   YA
By SHARON BELL MATHIS

I had been having a hard time, but I felt that with some planning I could handle things. The Holidays were coming, and that would be the hardest time—Christmas, the first Christmas since my father died. Life for Momma and me had become days of screaming or no-talking-at-all and always the smell of whiskey.

If I could get us through Christmas, my mother might allow me to go to the Kwanza celebration.

Ms. Geneva, who lived downstairs, and Mr. Dale, who lived upstairs, would help when Momma got too difficult, but she was often too much for either of them. Momma made Ms. Geneva end up crying by saying, "How can you tell me how to feel about my man, when you never had anyone of your own—you've spent your life taking care of other people's children!"

Mr. Dale couldn't handle Momma when she got to fussing. He sat on the bed and listened until she ordered him off the bed and out of the house.

Mr. Dale was nice. He was designing my dress for Kwanza. He cut it out and I was going to sew it myself. Ernie would take me to the dance—Ernie loves me and someday . . .

I had punched out my grocery list and a list of presents—I punch lists because I'm blind. When Momma asked for some of her medicine, I couldn't give her the pills, because she'd been drinking and couldn't have them. Momma says if she isn't drinking or taking pills she sees Daddy bleeding on Christmas day, dying.

That's when she said I couldn't go anywhere on the Holidays. No dancing. No company. No food. Nothing. And in six days it would be Christmas—Kwanza.

—Akiba Patton-Shabazz

LISTEN TO US!   Grades 6-8
THE CHILDREN'S EXPRESS REPORT
Ed. by DORRIET KAVANAUGH

Listen to Us! The Children's Express Report is about the things we all have to cope with as we grow up—divorce, school, sex, substitute teachers, enemies, trouble, changes. There are lots of books on these subjects, but this is the only one that's written entirely by kids—over a thousand of them across the country, all under sixteen. You'll find people in it who think exactly like you do and others who live and think in totally different ways. Have your parents ever embarrassed you? You'll discover kids who are embarrassed about the way their parents dress, talk to their friends, and treat them like little kids, plus a boy whose mother really embarrasses him every time she takes her sick houseplants to the emergency room of the local hospital, saying they're dying. Then Richard talks about being in a mental institution—he can't even wear tennis shoes because they are afraid you might strangle yourself with your shoelaces. Other children live in prisons, orphanages, foster homes, or nowhere—they're runaways. You'll meet children in trouble—with their parents, or schools, or the law, or their own brothers and sisters. And you'll meet kids who fight back—against parents who abuse them, against drugs, bullies, sex in the wrong situations. Listen to them in *Listen to Us!*

—Elizabeth Overmyer

LIZARD MUSIC   Grades 6-8
By DANIEL MANUS PINKWATER

When Victor's parents go away on vacation, his older sister is supposed to take care of him. But then she decides to take a trip of her own with some friends, and Victor is left alone for two weeks. That's fine with him—at last he can live exactly as he likes. For Victor, that means eating TV dinners, working on his model airplane, and watching the evening news with Walter Cronkite. He especially likes the way Walter signs off at the end of each show, so you can imagine his disappointment when he learns that Walter is on vacation, too. Nevertheless, there's a real good horror movie on the late show, so Victor stays up watching that, and then, just as the station is going off the air, something strange happens: the picture changes, and suddenly he is watching a band of lizard musicians playing weird music on saxophones. Then he meets a strange character on the bus, who keeps changing his name and has a pet chicken under his hat. The Chicken Man seems kind of weird, but he's the only other person who seems to know about the lizards. He believes that there's an invisible community of intelligent lizards living somewhere in the area, and together he and Victor set sail on the lake to search for the island of the lizards. The chicken comes along, too—she's the only one who knows where to find them.

—*Richard Russo*

LIZZIE   YA/Adult
By FRANK SPIERING

Lizzie Borden took an ax
And gave her mother forty whacks.
Then when she saw what she had done,
She gave her father forty-one.

That's how the legend goes. But is it really true? What really happened in the Borden household on that hot, muggy Thursday, August 4, 1892, in Fall River, Massachusetts?

Abby Borden was making the bed in the guest room when someone she never even heard walked up behind her and swung a wickedly sharp ax at the back of her head. She never had a chance to cry out for help. Bridget, the maid, who was upstairs, saw and heard nothing. The ax swung again and again, until the room was filled with a fog of blood, and every surface was covered with it. The ax didn't stop until Abby's head was all but severed from her body. Then the murderer retreated, to wait for the next victim, Andrew Borden, Abby's husband, who was expected home for lunch.

Andrew was sick and came home early. He lay down on the sofa in the sitting room and went to sleep. He woke up just in time to see the contorted face of the murderer who was standing over him, ax raised high. But he, too, had no time to cry out or to defend himself. Once more the weapon rose and fell, and the savage blows didn't stop until Andrew's face was no longer recognizable, and his head was virtually severed from his neck. Once more blood covered every surface of one of the rooms of the Borden household. Then it was quiet. The murderer vanished, as if by magic, and so did the closed carriage that had been waiting just down the street from the Borden house at 92 Second Street. There were only two people left alive on the Borden property—Bridget, the maid, half sick herself and now asleep in her attic room, and Andrew's daughter Lizzie, who was out in the barn looking for something. Emma, her older sister, was away, visiting friends in Fairhaven.

Lizzie found the body of her father and called Bridget to go for help and for the police. Then she retreated outside to sit on the steps by the side door, to wait until someone else arrived before she went back into the blood-splashed house. She was still wearing the blue dress she'd put on before breakfast, and those who saw her testified that there was no blood on it at all. Andrew's blood had not yet clotted when the neighbors and the police arrived. Lizzie had no time to change clothes, no time to wash herself—yet there was no blood.

And was there even a motive? Neither she nor Emma liked their stepmother, but Lizzie had learned to get along with her, while Emma had not. Her father's only piece of jewelry was the ring that Lizzie had given him. But he had just betrayed her and Emma, and stripped them of their inheritance. They were both more angry than they had ever been with him—were these killings some form of revenge? A last attempt to gain control of the Borden estate—worth, in today's terms, twelve million dollars?

Those weren't the only questions. Where did the murder weapon come from, and where did it vanish to? Why was it never found? How did the murderer get into the house with all the doors locked and the front door triple-locked? Why did Lizzie stick to her story about being in the barn long after it had been disproven to the satisfaction of at least two policemen? And if she was innocent, why did she not speak up at the trial? Was she protecting someone? Did Lizzie know who actually committed the murders? And if she was protecting someone, who was it?

The author claims that this book has the answer to these and other questions about the Borden case, and that it includes facts that have never been made public before—including what happened to Lizzie and Emma after the trial. You'll have to decide for yourself whether you agree with his theories or not—whether Lizzie Borden really did swing that ax, or whether it was someone else. . . .

—Joni Bodart

LONG TIME BETWEEN KISSES   YA
By SANDRA SCOPPETTONE

Most of you might think it would be pretty interesting to live in a Greenwich Village loft with your artist mother, especially if your father had his own jazz combo, called Ted James and the Commanders, and spent a lot of time stoned out on dope, which he would offer to you anytime you wanted.

But Billie doesn't even appreciate her situation. For her problem is, With such talented, with-it parents, what can she show for herself? [Read from page 9.]

"You see, I don't have any talent. Don't think I haven't tried to develop one. I've tried writing, painting, acting, singing, playing the guitar, and photography. And guess what? Nada. Zero. Zip. You can't imagine what it's like to want to be creative and there's just nothing there. Well, maybe you can imagine. It's depressing. It makes me feel like a nobody. A nothing. . . . Mother says you're not what you do, but that's easy for her to say. I hate not doing something special. It's boring. I hate to be bored or boring. I especially hate to be boring. There's nothing worse.

"So I thought it would be interesting to cut my hair real short and dye it purple. There's nothing boring about that."

It takes Billie a lot of coping with comments about her hair, a lot of cups of cappuccino with her best friend Elissa, a lot of worry about senile old Captain Natoli, and a lot of heartache over her hopeless love for handsome, older, wheelchair-bound Mitch, before she discovers what her own talent is.

—*Cathi Edgerton*

LONG VOYAGE BACK   YA/Adult
By LUKE RHINEHART

Neil Loken, captain of the trimaran *Vagabond,* is sailing in the Chesapeake Bay, preparing to pick up the owner of the boat and a group of friends for a leisurely cruise. The radio news that day has been filled with reports of increasing hostilities between the United States and Russia, but Neil is unconcerned: U.S.–Soviet relations have always been on a roller-coaster.

Suddenly Neil freezes, standing fascinated as a strange, steadily increasing glow spreads like a cobra's hood, slowly filling the northwestern sky. As he stares, he tries to visualize the map of the Chesapeake. Washington! There are no other cities along the northwest edge of the Chesapeake. As the northwest sky fills with a glow, Neil is filled with horror.

Half of the major American cities—with as many as eighty million killed—explode under nuclear attack, and the *Vagabond* becomes a floating refuge for a small group of survivors. As the group tries to control their panic and face the loss of family and friends, they realize that they must forge ahead to survive. They cannot rescue their families. In the "new world," your family will be whoever you find yourself with. Neil Loken must convince this group of refugees that survival in the new world is most likely out on the open sea. The group must cope with the effects of radiation, starvation, a deadly plague, the attacks of pirates, the refusal of the Caribbean islands or South American countries to accept refugees from the northern hemisphere, and the ongoing but faltering world war. As the journey continues, the group sees first-hand the unspeakable effects of the ultimate inhumanity. There is a rising sense of desperation among the crew of the *Vagabond,* as they face one threat after another. Will it ever end? Are they doomed to sail forever, never reaching the safe harbor they want so much to find?

—Barbara Lynn

THE LONG WALK   YA
By RICHARD BACHMAN

The Long Walk is the ultimate competition in an ultra-conservative America of the not-too-distant future. It is the country's number-one sports contest, a grueling 450-mile marathon walk. The competitors are the cream of the nation's youth, 100 red-blooded American boys. The very finest youngsters from coast to coast join the marathon to keep the spirit of the New American Government alive. The prize is a fortune in money, fame, everything the heart desires for the one and only winner. Sixteen-year-old Ray Garraty joins the marathon against the protests of his mother. Mrs. Garraty blames herself for his decision. She had been too wrapped up in her own sorrows to realize what he was doing, until after he was irrevocably committed to The Marathon. Now there is no way out, and she's afraid for her son. She thinks he doesn't really understand about the race, and she's right. Ray tells himself that a thing like this must have some deeper meaning. A thing like this must provide an answer to every question he has. But there are no answers, only sacrifice and pain. The pain of walking mile after mile with blisters; walking long after his shoes have given out; walking until he just can't take another step. And if he stops, he will get his ticket; then he will make the ultimate sacrifice. Because before the race is over, 99 of the 100 marathoners will make the sacrifice of their lives

—Judy Druse

LORD VALENTINE'S CASTLE   YA/Adult
By ROBERT SILVERBERG

After what seems to have been a long time of wandering, Valentine finds himself on a hill overlooking the provincial capital of Pidruid. It isn't long till a young herdsman comes down the road with a group of fifteen or twenty mounts, headed also for the city to sell his purple-skinned beasts at the market and go to the festival. Valentine trades him some wine for a ride into town. There're all kinds of things going on in Pidruid, because the Coronal has come to make his great processional. He is visiting every part of his realm—which is the whole, huge world of Majipoor. Valentine and the boy Shanamir head into town, and as they talk, Shanamir discovers that though Valentine is a man, there are many simple things he doesn't know. He's either a fool, a simpleton, or the most carefree man in Majipoor. Shanamir doesn't know which, and when he asks Valentine, discovers that Valentine doesn't know either!

They stop at the inn where mount-sellers stay, and the next morning, after Shanamir has gone to sell his mounts, Valentine discovers a troupe of jugglers practicing in the courtyard—six Skandars, huge things with heavy gray pelts and four arms, and two humans, a man with white hair and a lithe dark-haired woman. First they all juggle daggers together, then the Skandars begin to juggle just among themselves, and the woman calls to Valentine to come and join the game. She and the man with her begin to throw daggers at Valentine—and soon, almost before he knows it, he is juggling three of the daggers, throwing them back and forth with the two humans. He's very good, although he's never juggled before, and since the Skandars have need of another human in the troupe, he is asked to join them. He accepts but asks that they take Shanamir along as well, as a groom or valet—the leader agrees. After the festival, where they perform for the Coronal, they begin traveling through the country, juggling wherever they can. Valentine has never been so happy—juggling is fun, Carabella is the love he has always wanted, Sleet, the white haired man, and his other traveling companions are his good friends and comrades. If only he didn't have those dreams—strange, sinister dreams that involve the Coronal (Lord Valentine) and the Isle of Dreams and the Lady of Dreams who lives there. Valentine can't explain them—it is the wizard, Autifon Deliamber, who finally helps him understand. Deliamber is a Vroon—tiny, almost doll-like, with ropey tentacle-like arms and greenish skin. It is his wisdom that helps Valentine realize his true destiny: where he came from, and why they must all make a pilgrimage across the huge planet of Majipoor to the great Castle Mount, where Valentine the juggler must face Lord Valentine, the Coronal of all of Majipoor.

— *Joni Bodart*

THE LOVE BOMBERS   YA
By GLORIA D. MIKLOWITZ

Jenna and her older brother Jeremy were very close. They had uncanny insights about each other; they knew things or felt things they could not have known. It had always been this way between them. So when Jeremy called from college to say he was staying there a couple of weeks to talk to some kids into Eastern-Western philosophy, Jenna was scared. It just didn't sound like Jeremy. He was not into any kind of religion. He had also requested that his parents send his savings account book. Jenna thought at that point that she had heard someone in the background coaching him. In the weeks after the call, Jenna had gone over the conversation a hundred times, and each time her uneasiness had grown. She needed someone to help her understand what was going on and what she could do about it. She decided to talk to Jeremy's best friend, Rick Palmer. But Rick only increased Jenna's anxieties. He said Berkeley was a hotbed of weirdos, especially those new religious cults. Jenna and Rick decided to go to San Francisco to find Jeremy and discover for themselves what he was involved in.

The return address on a letter from Jeremy leads them to the Church of the World. Every time they get close to where Jeremy is, the Church moves him elsewhere. Meanwhile, Jenna and Rick are being "bombed with love"; the Church is trying to recruit them. But Jenna can see beyond the friendliness, the sincerity, and the dedication of the "love bombers." They pass themselves off as one thing when in reality they are something else. They talk about the drug programs and charity they sponsor when the money they raise actually goes into the pockets of their messiah, Ibram ben Adam.

When Jenna and Rick finally confront Jeremy, the war to save him really begins.

—*Judy Druse*

LOVE BY ANY OTHER NAME   YA
By JUNE FOLEY

The summer before she started high school, fifteen-year-old Billie Quinn grew two inches, lost twelve pounds, got a tan—and Bubba Umlauf. Bubba Umlauf was the sports star at Central High, and a big blond hunk. Just about every girl in school drooled over Bubba Umlauf. But that summer, when he was working at her uncle's garage, it was Billie he noticed. Soon, when school starts and kids see her hanging around with all the popular, pretty girls, they ask, "Who is *she*?" "That's Bubba's girl," is the answer. Half of Bubba-and-Billie.

Even though Bubba sometimes seems to think more of himself than of Billie, she enjoys her new-found popularity—she's in because she's Bubba's girl. But along with the popularity comes extra responsibility. Bubba expects Billie to come to all his football practices as well as the games. Bubba's friends have noticed Billie's exceptional sense of humor and have dubbed her the class clown, the Qeeen of Comedy. And Billie is expected to drive the teachers batty.

But one day Billie sees for the first time that being Bubba Umlauf's girl isn't going to solve all her problems.

Problems like how to get herself to do all that English, Spanish, sociology, biology, and drama homework, when she's gone through the last ten years without doing any homework at all.

Like whether or not to torture the drama teacher.

Like how far to go with Bubba.

When it seems as though the problems have built up so much that there's no turning back, Billie meets Cameron, who likes sharing ideas and being together . . . and who just might be more than a friend. But she can't even think about Cameron when being Bubba's girl is the most important thing in her life. Or is it? To find out about the decisions Billie makes, read *Love By Any Other Name*.

—*Diane Tuccillo*

LOVE MATCH   YA
By JANET QUIN-HARKIN

Being the only girl in a family of jocks doesn't bother Joanna. At fifteen she has already decided she wants to be a professional tennis player, and competition with her brothers is good training. And although her girl friends are interested in clothes and boys, Joanna has no time for stuff like that. She's trying out for the tennis team.

When tryouts come, Joanna doesn't make the girls' team—she's too good for them. Instead, the boys' coach sees her play and wants her for *his* team. Joanna knows she'll have to fight hard to be the top player, but when she sees Rick, her main competition, she isn't sure she wants to. Rick is tall, dark, and handsome, and Joanna suddenly realizes there may be more to life than tennis

—*Diana Hirsch*

THE MACHINE GUNNERS
Grades 6–8
By ROBERT WESTALL

Chas McGill was sixteen and lived in Garmouth, England, during World War II. Garmouth was on the coast of England, and suffered nightly from fierce German air raids; during the day all the townspeople could talk about were the rumors that Hitler and his troops would soon be invading. Bodser Brown had the best collection of war souvenirs in all of Garmouth; besides the normal shrapnel and bullets, he had the nose cone of an anti-aircraft shell and the flying helmet he had taken from a dead German pilot. Chas had the second-best collection, and he would have done anything to beat Bodser and have the best—and he knew he could, as soon as he saw the downed German aircraft, a Heinkel 111, with its machine gun still intact.

Although the police soon found the plane and launched a huge search for its missing weapon, Chas organized a gang that hid the gun in a fortress they built in the garden of a bombed-out home. They planned carefully to use the gun to shoot down the German hit-and-run bombers. They didn't plan to let a war orphan live in the fortress, and they never expected to actually capture a German flyer and hold him prisoner, but when these things happened, they just made the group more determined to continue as a military unit. Until the night of the great invasion, when a foreign army advanced upon the fortress—and at last the machine gunners swung into action.

—Elizabeth Overmyer

THE MAN IN THE WOODS
Grades 6–8/YA
By ROSEMARY WELLS

The second day of school, Helen locked all her books and lunch money in her locker before she found out the combination was wrong and she couldn't get them out; met Pinky Levy, a boy she disliked almost instantly; was appointed art assistant on the school paper; and saw the Punk Rock Thrower hit another car.

She and Pinky had just gotten off the schoolbus and were walking down by the highway, several yards apart. About the time Helen started yelling at him for being a chauvinist pig, a gravel truck roared by. There was a crash of breaking glass, and the car just behind the truck went out of control. The windshield had been shattered. It was up to Helen and Pinky to rescue the mother and daughter inside.

Helen saw a man in front of the house on the hill, watching them all, and when he disappeared, she thought he'd gone inside to call the emergency squad. But when she and Pinky helped the victims up to the house, it was empty. Then she glimpsed him in the woods and ran after him. She didn't catch him—she only heard the haunting melody he whistled.

But the Punk Rock Thrower didn't know that Helen couldn't identify him.

Now she's afraid someone's watching her, following her. And she gets a locket and a tape in the mail. *Her* locket, with a picture of her mother inside—the eye sockets have been colored blood-red. The tape is blank, except for five lines from a Christmas song, whistled *very* clearly:

> He sees you when you're sleeping,
> He knows when you're awake,
> He knows if you've been bad or good,
> So be good, for goodness' sake!
> Oh, you better watch out . . .

—Joni Bodart

MANWOLF   YA
By GLORIA SKURZYNSKI

Count Reinmar von Galt, a soldier-knight in medieval Poland, always wore leather headgear that covered most of his face. No one really knew why, but there were rumors that he had been horribly scarred while fighting the Lithuanians. On his way to Vienna on important business for the Teutonic Order, the Count stopped at Pan Lucas' estate for a night's lodging. While he was there, he saw Danusha, a sixteen-year-old serf girl, and asked Pan Lucas if she could go along on the remainder of the journey to serve and cook for him and his knight. Pan Lucas could not afford to offend the Teutonic Order so Danusha was sent with Reinmar. And when Reinmar came to her in the night, she also could do nothing but relent. In the weeks that followed, Danusha fell in love with Reinmar and he with her. But when the pack horse she was riding went lame and she would no longer be able to keep up, Reinmar made arrangements for her to return to Pan Lucas with some monks going in that direction. He had also by this time begun to reconsider the holy vows he had taken; he just couldn't keep Danusha with him.

Less than nine months later, Danusha bore a son she named Adam. As Adam grew, Danusha noticed unnatural traits that marked him. His urine was pink; his first tooth was pink; his teeth turned a deep, dull red as he grew older; his face and hands scarred from exposure to the sun; and then dark facial hair grew over the scars. Danusha kept her son hidden to save him from becoming an object of ridicule. Adam didn't know why he looked so different, but he suspected it had something to do with his father, whose identity Danusha would not reveal.

Adam, upon hearing a monk's tale that the new queen could perform miracles, let himself hope that she could remove his ugliness. But when he emerged from his seclusion to beg Jadwiga's help, his deformities were exposed, and he found himself at the mercy of a fearful mob who thought he was half man, half wolf—a werewolf.

—Judy Druse

THE MARK OF CONTE YA
By SONIA LEVITIN

During Conte's first year at Vista Mar High School, the computer gave him two schedules—one for Conte Mark, his real name, and one for Mark Conte. Two schedules, with two completely different sets of classes. It seemed really crazy, until he realized that if he went to all his courses and passed them all, he could graduate in two years instead of four. Of course, he had to solve a few problems first, with the help of the people who really ran the school—Flint the Fence and Zelinkowitz the Rat. Like, how was he going to get the same algebra teacher not to notice he was in two of her classes, and how would he do homework for twelve classes a semester? Things really got tough when he had to keep running back and forth to classes so fast that the coach spotted him and made him join the track team as well.

How long will he have the energy to keep it all up? And why was a Great Dane a bona-fide member of the graduating class? Find out in *The Mark of Conte*!

—Elizabeth Overmyer

MARKED BY FIRE YA
By JOYCE CAROL THOMAS

If people would ask Abyssinia whose child she was, she would have to answer "the daughter of patience and strength." Indeed, her mother's name was Patience and her father's was Strong. She was born on September 6, 1951, in a cotton field and she was marked by fire. The foreman had built the fire so that the water could be boiled for birthing. Patience spread out on the pallet of cotton sacks and when the baby who would be named Abyssinia emerged, "an ember jumped out of the blaze and branded" her.

"Marked by the fire!"

"Baptized with the fire!"

"Marked at birth!"

The women of Ponca City were present at her birth, and the baby was their special project. Everyone took pride in her and cared for her. The mothers of the church claimed she could recite by heart whole chapters from the Book of Psalms. She would be summoned to read the Black Dispatch to older people like Mother Barker whose eyes had seen too much already. She was her parents' pride and joy. When she visited the Better Way Barbershop which her father owned he would sit her in front of the store and say, "Having my pretty daughter here is better than having a bowl of flowers in the place."

"[One day the entire Crispus Attucks summer school student body assembled to honor its most worthy scholars. After Principal Mosely handed out the award for the most mannerly student, he] looked over to Abby and began to speak. 'A race is judged by its literacy, the ability of its members to read. The young lady I'm about to call up here not only has read just about every book in the library but when school is out she goes around town and reads to the elderly and shut-ins. This habit of reading is most wonderful. Her teacher, Miss Pat, has given me a long list of the books this student has read. . . . Miss Abyssinia.' Abby started to stand, when the school bell began to clang. Mr. Mosely stopped talking, and the students moved restlessly in their seats. 'Tornado,' someone whispered, 'Tornado!'

"Mr. Mosely quickly folded the paper on which he had written the awards and stuck it in his pocket.

"'We will quietly file down to the storm cellar. In order. In order,' he said.

"Both students and staff lined up and filed down to the basement. Whenever the word 'tornado' buzzed through the line, Mr. Mosely admonished, 'There'll be no talking.'

"In the cellar they played spelling-bee games and tic-tac-toe . . . and told ghost stories.

"Three hours later, they emerged from the dark cellar into the open air. The entire student body stood gaping in awe. A giant broom had swept a clean path through the world. There was virgin earth where houses, cars, and cattle had once been. Some structures had been leveled to the bare foundations." One of those structures was the Better Way Barbershop.

For the first time in her life, Abby was truly afraid. And she had good reason to be. Not only did the tornado deprive her of her father, her protector, but it also brought forth an enemy, who targeted Abby for a campaign of terror.

—Linda Lapides

THE MASQUERADE   YA
By SUSAN SHREVE

Rebecca Walker has always been a very cautious young lady. She's spent her high school years doing exactly what is expected of her—by her stylish, aristocratic mother, by her father whom she adores, by her teachers, by her friends. Rebecca doesn't make waves. She suits the elegant house her family lives in. She knows her way will be paid to the college of her choice. She knows that her parents support and love her. Then one day Rebecca Walker's father is arrested. She is in the kitchen making fudge when she sees the two men in dark blue suits come up the driveway. And she watches as they lead her father away in handcuffs. It seems that money is missing from her father's office—a lot of money. Mr. Walker is charged with embezzlement, and suddenly Rebecca's world is turned upside down. Her mother tells her that her father will only be gone for a few days. But days stretch into weeks, then into months. There's no more money. The house must be sold. College plans are canceled. Rebecca can accept all that. She can stand the loss of the house. She can deal with not going to college. Because she knows her father is innocent. He's innocent. He *is* innocent—isn't he?

—Christy Tyson

MAX AND ME AND THE TIME MACHINE   Grades 5-7
By GERY GREER AND BOB RUDDICK

Steve was sure he had found Action, Adventure, and Excitement when he bought, for $2.50, an honest-to-goodness time machine.

Max, Steve's best friend, did not respond with "Bravo" or "Fantastic" or "Way to go" or even "You don't say!" Max just snorted and said, "Who're you trying to kid, Steve? There's no such thing as time travel."

But Steve was not discouraged. The words stamped on the side of the crate clearly said: "Mainly one genuine, completely automated, easily assembled, one-of-a-kind Time Machine! Fully Guaranteed!"

Max still didn't believe it.

One way to convince a nonbeliever is to provide proof, and that is what Steve set out to do.

Putting the time machine together was easy since it came with step-by-step instructions for "assembling Flybender's Fantastic Fully Guaranteed Time Machine." By 1:00 p.m. it was together.

Max and Steve stood back to survey their hard work. As Steve examined the seven-foot-tall contraption he was reminded of a giant jellybean dispenser . . . from outer space. Dials, meters, switches, and colored lights covered a good deal of the thing. A tiny world map and an enormous on/off lever finished it off.

Steve set the controls for Medieval England. He figured he and Max would have plenty of action, adventure, and excitement fighting dragons and rescuing damsels in distress. Max, however, wasn't so sure.

The time had finally come to prove the machine's worth. Before Max could protest, Steve pulled the lever. "The Clubhouse began to vibrate . . . faster . . . Max began to look fuzzy around the edges . . . faster . . . Now he was blue . . . faster. . . . "

The time machine worked, but not the way Steve thought it would in *Max and Me and The Time Machine*, by Gery Greer and Bob Ruddick.

—*Sally Long*

MIND-CALL   YA
By WILANNE SCHNEIDER BELDEN

Tallie knew exactly what was going to happen, right down to the last detail. She'd dreamed all of it—and in her dreams, she'd figured out just what to do. So when she woke up one morning and found her bed and the floor of her room covered with broken glass, she knew what had happened and what she had to do.

There had been an earthquake, and her aunt, uncle, and cousin had all left. She was alone. She would have to be responsible for her own survival. She got out of bed and began to pack. She already knew where things were and what to take—she'd made all those decisions in her dreams. The last things she packed were a cameo locket that belonged to her aunt and her cousin Paul's parka. They were both laid out, waiting for her. But if Paul had had time to leave those things out for her, why hadn't he waked her, so she could go too? Why would her aunt leave her behind? Tallie wasn't the only one who'd been left, she discovered—her aunt's elegant Siamese cat, Pandora, hadn't gone either. Tallie took Pandora, two hugh backpacks, three bags of food, and some odds and ends and left the apartment building. It took several trips to get everything stored on Paul's sailboat, but Tallie finished—only seconds before the second earthquake and tidal wave struck!

Tallie survives—she hasn't yet come to the end of her dreams. That lies ahead—after she rescues Andy, a baby only a few months old, and goes to a strange and sinister house high on a cliff, where she and six others have been called by the menacing man who lives there—"Mad Duke" Logran of the House of Logran—whose powers not even Tallie's dreams have predicted.

To find out who he is, and how and why Logran has gathered these survivors around him, read *Mind-Call.*

—*Joni Bodart*

THE MINDS OF BILLY MILLIGAN   YA/Adult
By DANIEL KEYES

In October 1977, the Columbus, Ohio, police arrested twenty-two-year-old William Stanley Milligan, the Ohio State University "Campus Rapist." The case appeared open and shut—until one day the examining psychologist walked in and greeted Billy. "I'm not Billy," came the reply. "I'm David."

This book is a factual account of the life, up to now, of William Stanley Milligan, the first person in U.S. history to be found not guilty of major crimes, by reason of insanity, because he possessed multiple personalities. Twenty-four different persons live in Billy Milligan's body. Beaten and raped by his stepfather when he was nine years old, Billy's mind, his emotions, his personality, and his soul fragmented into twenty-four parts as he discovered he could not cope with life. He decided he didn't want to be Billy anymore—and so he wasn't—he was twenty-four other people.

And who are the people who live inside? There are ten main ones, known to everyone at his trial.

First, there's "William Stanley Milligan ('Billy'), 26. The original, or core, personality . . . high school dropout. Six feet tall, 190 pounds. Blue eyes, brown hair.

"[Second,] Arthur, 22. The Englishman. Rational, emotionless, he speaks with a British accent. Self-taught in physics and chemistry, he studies medical books. Reads and writes fluent Arabic. . . . He dominates in safe places, wears glasses.

"[Third,] Ragen . . . , 23. The keeper of hate . . . Yugoslavian, he speaks English with a noticeable Slavic accent, and reads, writes, and speaks fluent Serbo-Croatian. A weapons and munitions authority, as well as a karate expert, he displays extraordinary strength, stemming from the ability to control his adrenaline flow. . . . The protector of the family . . . dominates the consciousness in dangerous places. . . . Weighs 210 pounds, has enormous arms, black hair, and a long, drooping mustache. He sketches in black and white because he is color-blind.

"[Fourth,] Allen, 18. The con man . . . he . . . most often deals with outsiders. He plays the drums, paints portraits, and is the only one of the personalities who smokes. . . . Same height as William, though he weighs less . . . He is the only one who is right-handed.

"[Fifth,] Tommy, 16. the escape artist. . . . He is generally belligerent and antisocial. Plays the saxophone and . . . [paints landscapes. Muddy-blond hair and amber-brown eyes.

"[Sixth,] Danny, 14. The frightened one . . . he was forced to dig his own grave and was then buried alive. Thus he paints only still-lifes. Shoulder-length blond hair, blue eyes, short and slender.

"[Seventh,] David, 8. The keeper of pain, or the empath . . . Highly sensitive and perceptive. . . . Dark reddish-brown hair, blue eyes, physically small.

"[Eighth,] Christene, 3. The corner child. She was the one to stand in the corner in school. A bright little English girl, she can read and print, but has dyslexia . . . Blonde shoulder-length hair, blue eyes.

"[Ninth,] Christopher, 13. Christene's brother. . . . Plays the harmonica. Hair brownish-blond like Christene's. . . .

"[Tenth,] Adalana, 19. The lesbian. Shy, lonely and introverted, she writes poetry, cooks and keeps house for the others. . . . Long, stringy black hair and brown eyes . . . "

There are thirteen more personalities that Arthur suppressed because they were undesirable, and that were only recently identified. And finally, the personality who brings them all together—"The Teacher, 26. The sum of all twenty-three alter egos fused into one. Taught the others everything they've learned. Brilliant, sensitive, with a fine sense of humor. He says, 'I am Billy all in one piece,' and refers to the others as 'the androids I made.' The Teacher has almost total recall, and his emergence and cooperation make this book possible."

And is it real? Is Billy a real victim of multiple personality or a brilliant con man? The courts have made their decisions, Daniel Keyes has made his, but *you* have to decide for yourself about *The Minds of Billy Milligan.*

—Joni Bodart

MR. RADAGAST MAKES   Grades 6–8
AN UNEXPECTED JOURNEY
By SHARON NASTICK

Have you ever been so bored in class you wished you could disappear, or better yet make your teacher disappear? That's how boring it was in Mr. Radagast's science class. Students were daydreaming, watching the clock, doodling, and throwing spitballs.

But then Mr. Radagast began to discuss the theory that objects exist only if we believe they exist. This subject really interested the class. It didn't take long for one of the students, Conrad McDermont, to ask, "If you can think something into existence, can you think something *out* of existence?" Mr. Radagast was so pleased to have aroused some interest that he let the class try several experiments. First, they concentrated, to make Mr. Radagast's desk disappear. It didn't work. The desk was still there. Next, they tried to make the science book disappear. It didn't work. The science book was still there. But Conrad McDermont noticed the book got blurry around the edges for a few seconds. Mr. Radagast was so excited he snatched the book, held it close, and told the class to concentrate. Make the book cease to exist!

Thirty bodies leaning forward out of their seats. Sixty eyes staring at the front of the room. Thirty minds thinking the same thought.

But they weren't thinking about the book.

One moment Mr. Radagast was in front of his science class. The next moment he was gone. Where did he go? Could they bring him back? *Do they want to?* To find out, go along when *Mr. Radagast Makes an Unexpected Journey.*

—Vickie Grannan

NOTE: Don't use this in Mr. Radagast's classroom.

MORE MAGIC IN YOUR POCKETS   Grades 6–8
By BILL SEVERN

Make a magic telephone-answering service that records silent messages, or make your own magic ruler. Turn 4 pennies into 28 cents, or make a computer out of an envelope. Make a flying toothbrush, or a pencil that writes by itself. All the secrets are here, and the secret ingredients are ordinary things that you can find around the house. Plus these magic tricks are so easy to do and handy to carry with you that you can pull them out of your purse or pocket wherever you are!

—Elizabeth Overmyer

MOVIE STUNTS, AND THE PEOPLE   Grades 6–8
WHO DO THEM
By GLORIA D. MIKLOWITZ

How many of you have been watching the movies or TV and seen the hero (or the villain) drive off in an ordinary-looking car that suddenly explodes and bursts into flames? Maybe you've even seen the driver get out, all his clothing and body covered with flames. It's hard to believe that anyone could escape from such a situation alive—and even harder to imagine that anyone would want to make a living doing things like that every day. This book, *Movie Stunts and the People Who Do Them*, tells about the people who perform these stunts, from ten-year-old Curtis Epper to Kitty O'Neill, the first woman member of Stunts Unlimited—who has been deaf since the age of four months. You'll find out how these people became stunt performers, how and where they practice, and how the actual stunts—high falls, stair falls, fights, car stunts, explosions—are done.

— Elizabeth Overmyer

MURPHY MUST HAVE BEEN A MOTHER!   Adult
(AND OTHER LAWS I LIVE BY)
By TERESA BLOOMINGDALE

There's only one thing worse than waking up to find out that you have a case of The Bug. That is when you realize that you told your ever-helpful husband that he could take care of the kitchen and the kids while you got some rest. When you dash down to the kitchen your worst fears are realized. While you were upstairs sick and unable to raise a hand to defend your kitchen, your husband has cleaned it all up. Why should that be disturbing? Let me tell you about my experience. When I opened the refrigerator door to survey the cleaning job, I realized that my loving husband had not only thrown out the moldy bacon and curdled cottage cheese, but he had also pitched the roast beef I was sure I could get another meal out of for this family of ten children. His only comment was, "How long has it been since you cleaned this thing? And how about that oven?" Not the oven, I cringed. "If you clean the oven it throw the temperature control all out of whack." To which he replied with a smile, "I fixed it." Swell, just swell. I was used to adjusting the heat control to match the way my oven cooked. Now I'd have to guess whenever I turned on the temperature. I'm not used to cooking in an oven that works the way it's supposed to. My husband went on with the grand tour. "See how neat and tidy the shelves are now. Everything is accessible now." I looked at my six-foot husband and tried to think how to break it to him that a five-foot three-inch woman might have a little trouble reaching *his* accessible shelves. I finally decided just to keep my mouth closed and see what the next project was.

"Look how clean your junk drawer is now," he said.

"I'm afraid to ask this, but where in the world did you put all the things from my thingamajig drawer?"

"I threw them all away," he said with a smile. "It was all no-good junk, like broken crayons, old report cards, bent forks, motels from the Monopoly game, half a deck of playing cards, and at least a dozen things I could not even identify. If you haven't used something in months, for heaven's sake, just throw it away. It isn't needed anymore."

"You don't understand. As long as things are in the thingamajig drawer they *are* unimportant, they may even be just junk. But the minute you throw them away, everyone in the house starts clamoring for the missing dice, the lid to the baby food jar, the rest of the deck of cards to play Crazy Eights—you've just created a disaster that's about to happen. Prepare yourself."

My husband suddenly sat down at the table. "I can't be prepared for anything," he said. "I feel so lousy. I think I must be coming down with something."

Oh, no! A husband with The Bug! And I'm not even over mine completely. With ten children to care for, that's a *real* disaster.

—Pat Powell

MY ROBOT BUDDY   Grades 3–5
By ALFRED SLOTE

Jack Jameson lives so far in the future that people can buy robots that talk, play ball, go to school, and act and think almost exactly like real people. And since Jack lives so far out in the country that he has no friends to play with, he decides that for his tenth birthday he wants a robot. And so he is taken on a tour of the factory and is allowed to pick his own robot friend, Danny One. When they leave the factory, they are given strict warnings about robotnappers, who kidnap robots and hold them for ransom, but nobody believes that robotnappers will bother them in the country—until a mysterious blue solar car begins to follow Jack and Danny wherever they go, and suddenly Jack has to figure out how a ten-year-old boy and a robot can outwit a kidnapping gang!

—Elizabeth Overmyer

A NIGHT WITHOUT STARS   Grades 5-7
By JAMES HOWE

Maria had a lot of worries. She was worried about the pounding in her chest. She was worried about the operation that was supposed to cure the pounding. And she was worried about coming home from the hospital. What if her friends laughed at the long scar that would be left on her chest?

Everyone told Maria that the doctors would "fix her up." They told her not to worry. They told her that she would be just fine.

But Maria worried anyway. Why not? She was going to have open heart surgery to fix a hole in her heart. The doctors were going to cut her chest open and hold her heart in their hands. Who wouldn't worry?

More than anything, Maria wanted to know exactly what her operation would be like. Her parents didn't really know, and the doctors and nurses used words that only they understood. No one seemed to want to talk to her.

Then Maria met the Monster Man. Donald was his real name.

Donald was used to being in the hospital. He had been there many times for operations. As a baby he was in a house fire and was badly burned all over his body and face. The doctors were trying to overcome the damage done to him with surgery. Donald knew all about operations.

The night before Maria's operation she couldn't sleep. She was scared. She had still not been told what the operation would be like. Maria worried about her heart. She worried that she might die.

Wide awake, Maria walked through the quiet halls of the children's section of the hospital. She knew where she was going. She was going to talk to the only person who could help her, the Monster Man, in *A Night Without Stars,* by James Howe.

—Sally Long

NIGHTMARE ISLAND   Grades 3–5
By RON ROY

Scoop and Harley go camping overnight on a tiny island in the bay off the coast of Maine. They promise their mother not to light a fire. When they discover a pack of matches in their sack, though, they cannot resist the temptation to roast their marshmallows.

An oil slick that has silently surrounded the island during the night bursts into flames and sets the entire island ablaze. The boys are trapped, and their lives depend on using their wits and finding barren ground. They wet down their sleeping bags, race through the flames, hide in rock crevices. But little Scoop becomes too exhausted to outrun the flames. How can Harley save his younger brother, and save his own life as well?

Nightmare Island, by Ron Roy. After you read this, you may never let anyone light a match again. And if you like this, try *Fire Storm*, by Robb White.

—Paul H. Rockwell

ONE CHILD   YA/Adult
By TOREY L. HAYDEN

I should have known. I read the article about the six-year-old girl who had abducted a three-year-old neighborhood child and tied him to a tree and burned him.

I should have known no teacher would want a child like that in her classroom—no parents would want her attending school with their children.

I should have known she would end up in my program. I taught what was affectionately known as the "garbage class" in our district—before the effort to mainstream began. I had the eight who were left over—after the retarded, the emotionally disturbed, the physically handicapped, and the learning disabled were put into classes.

Her name was Sheila—a tiny little thing with matted hair, hostile eyes, and a bad smell. Her records showed she lived alone with her father in a one-room shack with no heat, plumbing, or electricity. At four years old, she had been abandoned by her mother and had been found clinging to a chain-link fence between freeway lanes. Old abrasions and healed fractures showed she had been abused.

Her father had spent most of Sheila's early years in prison on assault and battery charges, but she was released to his custody after her mother left.

A memo for the county's consulting attorney stated: Chronic Maladjustment to Childhood. The test battery summary stated she was untestable—she had refused to answer any questions.

I knew she would be a hard child to love because she worked at being unlovable. She would not be an easy child to reach but I hoped she was not unreachable.

One Child, by Torey L. Hayden.

—*Eileen Gieswein*

ONLY LOVE   YA
By SUSAN SALLIS

When sixteen-year-old Fran Adamson arrived at Thornton Hall, she decided immediately to shake things up as much as possible—and she succeeded far beyond her wildest imaginings.

Thornton is a private hospital for the handicapped—very exclusive and very expensive. Fran knows when she ends up there her time has about run out. Abandoned as an infant and a paraplegic since birth, Fran has spent her whole life in state hospitals. And the state wouldn't send her to Thornton Hall if they expected to have to pay the bills for very long. But Fran swears Dr. Beamish—"boss man"—to silence. She has no intention of letting other people feel sorry for her and spoil her fun! She starts off by deciding that Beamish and Nurse Casey, who looks like Marilyn Monroe, should get together. She papers the door to her room with flowers, snitches fresh ones from the garden, goes outside at night without permission, laughs a lot, and teases everyone incessantly so they'll laugh with her. She swipes Mrs. Gorman's false teeth, tries to fix her up with old Mr. Pope, and generally shakes everyone up. Then Lucas Hawkins arrives—who's eighteen, just lost his legs in a motorcycle accident and hates everyone. Now that the Beamish-Casey romance is going well, Fran decides her next project is to get Hawkins out of his room. But she doesn't expect the consequences, as she and Hawkins fall in love and she has to decide whether she can tell him her secret or not. She can't ever leave Thornton Hall, marry him, raise a family, and live happily ever after. Fran Adamson is living on borrowed time, and it may run out any day.

—*Joni Bodart*

OWLS IN THE FAMILY   Grades 4–6
By FARLEY MOWAT

Most families have some interesting characteristics, but owls in the family? That's quite unique. Farley Mowat's family already had about thirty gophers, some rats, a box full of garter snakes, at least ten pigeons, some rabbits, and of course Farley's dog Mutt, when Farley got a yen for an owl—and then, another owl. Weeps, the smaller of the two, had been rescued from the bottom of an old oil barrel where some mean boys were tormenting him with rocks, and he was very timid and never did learn to fly. He did, however, come to feel secure between Mutt the dog's paws and would always head for that protected spot whenever he was let out of his cage. Mutt was pretty good-natured and didn't mind too much, except when Weeps' feathers tickled his nose and made him sneeze.

Mutt's relationship with Wol, the larger, more aggressive owl, was never quite that cozy. Wol definitely had the upper hand and enjoyed teasing Mutt whenever he could. His favorite game with Mutt was The Tail-Squeeze. "Wol would first make sure that Mutt was really fast asleep, then he would begin to stalk the old dog the way a cat will stalk a bird. He always did it on foot. He would sneak across the lawn moving so slowly and carefully he hardly seemed to move at all. If Mutt happened to raise his head he would see Wol standing stock-still on the grass and staring innocently up at the sky, as if he were wondering whether it was going to rain. After a long, suspicious look at Wol, Mutt's eyelids would begin to droop, his head would sag, and soon he would be fast asleep again. He snored, too, and as soon as the snores started, Wol would continue his slow and careful approach. Sometimes it took Wol an hour or more to cross the lawn, but when he had sneaked up close enough, Wol would raise one foot and—very, very gently— lower it over the end of Mutt's long and bushy tail. Then Wol would let out a piercing scream and at the same moment he would give the tail a good hard squeeze. Poor Mutt would leap straight into the air, yelping with surprise and pain, and Wol would fly to the limb of a near-by tree and peer down at Mutt as if to say, 'Good Heavens! What a terrible nightmare you must have been having!' Then he'd close his eyes and pretend to be sound asleep."

Having owls in the family can certainly keep your life interesting, as Farley found out when Wol followed him to school, attracting crows by the dozens, attacked the postman, and chased the minister right out of the house. Find out for yourself what it's like in this true story by Farley Mowat—*Owls in the Family*.

—*Bonnie Janssen*

A PASSING SEASON   Grades 6–8
By RICHARD BLESSING

Craig caught the ball on the snap from center. He took several steps backwards and lifted his passing arm. Then he saw five of the big Steelers heading straight for him with *nothing* to stop them.

Ever since he could remember, Craig had dreamed of playing football for the Oiltown Owls. His father had taken him to every hometown game since he was four, and Craig remembered the excitement when the hometown team made a good play. Someday he would be a part of the game too.

His father had hung an old tire from the tree in the backyard, and Craig had spent numerous hours throwing a football through that tire. He would throw from different angles and from different distances. He would throw when the tire hung steady and when it blew back and fourth in the wind. The old tire was his friend when everyone else was upset with him. There were days when he had thrown more than three hundred passes through the tire and there were days when he threw none.

His father would run with him in the evenings. Together they would race around the block, sprint across the yard, or jog to town. Craig knew that someday he would wear the black and white uniform of the Owls. . . .

Tonight was the first home game of the season. Craig was too excited to eat—the coach had told him to suit up.

He was not only wearing the Owls' jersey, he was on the field and the ball was in his hands. The Steelers were rushing towards him. He panicked. Closing his eyes, he threw the ball blindly.

A Passing Season, by Richard Blessing.

—Cheryl Ress

PASSING THE HAT: YA/Adult
STREET PERFORMANCE IN AMERICA
By PATRICIA J. CAMPBELL

Have you ever passed a street performer—a mime, musician, or juggler—stopped to watch for awhile, entranced by the performance, and then hurriedly walked on when it was over, studiously ignoring the open guitar case or hat lying on the sidewalk, waiting for your contribution?

Maybe you have—I know I have—but I won't again, not after reading this book—*Passing the Hat,* by Patty Campbell. In it you'll meet mimes, musicians, jugglers, magicians, and more—all the pickers and pluckers who ply their trade on the city streets.

Patty is a tall, vivacious redhead with a wicked and wacky sense of humor, whose business card reads, "Patty Campbell—author, columnist, library consultant, belly-dancer." She used to perform on the beach and boardwalk of Venice, California, where she lives. That experience gave her a different point of view, and her empathy with the people she talked to allowed them to open up with her and tell her things perhaps no other interviewer could have learned. You'll meet all kinds of people, and as Patty describes them, you can almost see them sitting cross-legged on the sidewalk between performances, or talking over a glass of wine or a beer afterwards. Sometimes I even knew how their picture would look before I turned to it, or I remembered having seen their performance on the sidewalks of San Francisco.

But my favorite is the Butterfly Man, who performs at Pier 39 in San Francisco. He's the son of a Nobel prize winner and use to be a scientist himself, but now he's a skilled juggler, respected by his colleagues, adored by his fans—and for the first time, a completely whole and satisfied man. He closes his performance—after mad juggling, a wild unicycle ride through his audience, and much laughter—on a serious note.

He goes to the center stage, squeaks at the hecklers, "Shut up, you guys, this is serious," and recites this poem [page 115, "It matters not."] Then he sweeps off his hat to show the butterflies tattooed all over his head, insuring he will never go back to the straight world. Robert Armstrong Nelson III—it's been a long trip, but he's finally made it.

The Butterfly Man is my favorite, Patty has her favorites—but you will have to find your own favorites from all the people you meet passing the hat.

—Joni Bodart

PEPPERMINTS IN THE PARLOR   Grades 4–6
By BARBARA BROOKS WALLACE

Eleven-year-old orphaned Emily Luccock peered into the San Francisco fog looking for tall blond Uncle Twice. Through the fog she heard a thin, scared voice call, "Emily, Emily Luccock." Emily turned around and saw only a shabby, stoop-shouldered woman, but upon looking more closely she recognized her Aunt Twice. Aunt Twice called for her and then hurried her into a cab. Insistently she made Emily promise to do as she was told, ask no questions, and agree with whatever she said.

Out of the fog Sugar Hill Hall rose as elegant and beautiful as Emily remembered. She remembered beautiful bright chandeliers, velvet chairs, and Uncle Twice's laughter. She knew now that this was all just an Uncle Twice joke. As Emily and Aunt Twice hurried up the steps to the front door, Emily could hardly keep from laughing out loud. The door swung open, revealing a dark musty interior. Instead of the laughing Uncle Twice she'd been expecting, Emily saw two women. One of them was as plump as a pudding in a lavender dress, but the other figure turned Emily to stone. A tall woman. Emily's eyes went past a black skirt, past a gold medallion with a ruby eye, past a high black collar coiled around a serpent neck, past a thin pointed chin, past pale lips under a pinched nose, to the most evil eyes Emily had ever seen. The evil eyes caused Emily to shake with terror—Miss Meeching! Miss Meeching sent Aunt Twice and Emily to the kitchen to prepare supper.

On the way to the kitchen Emily discovered moving shadows— shadows that were old people who stared silently through her. And she saw a table with a velvet cloth trimmed in golden braid in the parlor. Even in the dim light the crystal bowl on the table almost twinkled. In the bowl were some of Emily's favorite candies—big, puffy, red-and-white-striped peppermints. As her hand went to the bowl, her knuckles were cruelly struck. Miss Meeching hissed her to the kitchen and glared evilly at Aunt Twice.

Why had Miss Meeching taken over Sugar Hill Hall? Would Emily be able to find the answer in time to save herself and Aunt Twice? *Peppermints in the Parlor.*

—*Karen Cole*

PET SEMATARY* YA/Adult
By STEPHEN KING

It was a huge old farmhouse near Ludlow, Maine, that overlooked a busy two-lane highway. In back of it a huge field sprawled in front of wooded hills. Rachel and Louis Creed and their children fell in love with it immediately. Even their neighbors across the road were perfect—Jud and Norma Crandall soon became friends and substitute grandparents.

It was Jud who showed the family the pet cemetery (the sign, carefully lettered by some long-gone child, says "Pet Sematary"), where generations of pets have been buried in an eerie spiral pattern. The markers are easy to read at first, but as they get closer and closer to the center, the graves are older and the markers almost impossible to read. Between the cemetery and the woods beyond was a huge pile of fallen trees—a blowdown—and as Louis looked at it, just before they turned to go, he thought how deliberately convenient it seemed to be, almost too convenient for nature to have put it there.

It was months before Louis found out just how deliberate everything about the cemetery was—from the pattern of the graves, the perfectly circular clearing, to the jackstraw pile of whitened tree limbs. Rachel and the two kids, Ellie and Gage, had gone to her parents for Thanksgiving. Louis, avoiding conflict, elected to stay behind with Church (Winston Churchill), Ellie's cat. It was Jud who found Church where the speeding car or truck had tossed him in the Crandalls' front yard. Louis was sick—Ellie adored her cat—how would he break the news that Church was dead?

He decided to just bury Church and tell Ellie he ran off. Jud insisted on doing it that night—immediately. Louis felt uneasy about Jud's haste and silence as they walked up the hill and into the clearing. Suddenly, he realized Jud wasn't stopping there—he had crossed the spiral of markers and turned just in front of the blowdown. "Just follow me," Jud said. "Follow me and don't look down. . . . " The path continued. Suddenly Louis was aware of the power of the place—almost an electricity in the air. They went along the edge of a swamp full of noises and eerie lights, and up a long flight of steps into the rock, and onto a flat mesa—an ancient Indian burial ground, a place of enormous and unholy power.

Together they dug a grave, buried the cat, and covered the mound with a cairn of stones. The walk home was almost a dream to Louis, and when he questioned Jud about the whole bizarre experience—"We just buried your daughter's cat, that's all." But was it all?

It was one o'clock the next afternoon when Church came back. Caught on his whiskers were two shreds of green plastic . . . the Hefty Bag they'd buried him in.

—Joni Bodart

------

*Published in part in the *Emporia Gazette,* December 10–11, 1983, in an article entitled "On the Shelf at the Emporia Public Library."

PHILIP HALL LIKES ME,   Grades 4–6
I RECKON, MAYBE
By BETTE GREENE

Have you ever been very sure of something? But not so sure you'd place a bet on it? That's Beth Lambert. Beth is very sure that she likes Philip Hall, the number-one-best arithmetic solver, the number-one-best speller, the number-one-best reader in Miss Johnson's class, and the number-one-best everything in Pocahontas, Arkansas. And she knows that Philip Hall likes her. But she wouldn't make a bet on it.

However, one thing is for certain: Beth's father is losing his turkeys during the long cold December nights. Initially, Mr. Lambert thought chicken hawks were responsible. But even chicken hawks wouldn't mess around with a twenty-pound turkey. "Maybe a fox would," suggests Beth. "That fox would have to crawl under this fence, which is pretty dang smart seeing as there ain't no crawl-through space. And he couldn't have gone over six-foot-high fencing without taking flying lessons." "Besides," Beth says, "a fox couldn't climb back out over the fence with the turkeys anyway, so he'd have to eat the turkeys on the premises." "Right," said Mr. Lambert, "which proves it wasn't no fox 'cause there ain't no blood or bones or turkey remains in this here yard." Next Beth and her Pa search for a passageway that a groundhog might have used but find no such tunnel opening. Suddenly Beth has the answer to this mystery. She explains that perhaps some low-flying airplane in the area is scaring their poultry into taking to the air and roosting in some nearby trees. But unfortunately they find no turkeys in any of the trees.

The following night, another six turkeys disappear. "So how's a man supposed to earn a living? 'Cause the chicken hawk, red fox, groundhog, airplane, or whatever the critter calls himself ain't one to be fooled by me," says Mr. Lambert, disgustedly.

But Beth isn't giving up. So she takes Philip Hall aside at recess and begs him to help her solve the mystery of the missing turkeys. They meet down at the turkey yard to stand guard. In the middle of the night, armed with Philip's flashlight and BB gun, the two settle into the branches of a tree to keep watch. Soon they see the lights of a truck up on the road. The lights are extinguished, but the truck doesn't stop until it reaches the gates of the turkey yard.

While Philip runs to get Beth's Pa and her brother, Luther, Beth holds the thieves at bay with Philip's gun.

This is just one of many adventures that Beth finds herself involved in, and somehow Philip Hall is always a part of them too.

—Shelia Barnett

PORKO VON POPBUTTON Grades 3-5
By WILLIAM PÈNE du BOIS

His real name is Pat O'Sullivan Pinkerton, but I'm sure you understand why he's called Porko, or Fatty Unbuckle, or Oink-Oink, or Sir Cumference Girth, or just Blimpy Splitseam. On Porko's birthday, there are two cakes—one for him and one for the rest of his guests. Just as he finished his birthday cake, the two chairs he has to use suddenly break. Furious, he starts to rush upstairs but forgets that he has to walk sideways through the door, and sticks fast. When he finally gets upstairs, he throws himself onto his bed—and it collapses beneath him. Then the bedroom floor caves in. He crashes right back down to the dining room, onto the top of the table—and the second birthday cake.

Needless to say, this is the last straw for his parents. And Porko ends up at a boarding school where the most important thing in the world is playing hockey. If you'd like to see what Porko looks like in his uniform, I can show you. . . . And if you'd like to know what happens when the school's star player is knocked out in the most important game of the season and Porko is sent in to replace him—on ice that is melting in the first spring thaw—you'll have to read the book!

—Elizabeth Overmyer

POSTCARD POEMS: YA/Adult
A COLLECTION OF POETRY FOR SHARING
Edited by PAUL B. JANECZKO

What can you do with a poem?

—Study it in English class?

—Shake your head in confusion as you try to figure out what it means?

—Look up the words you don't know in the dictionary?

—Swear you hate it and just can't read it?

Or have you ever had a poem capture you because it so perfectly describes a sight or memory or feeling you've had, that it seems to come from inside your own head?

Has a poem ever reminded you of someone?

If so, or if not, here's a new idea about what you can do with a poem. Paul Janeczko, the editor of this collection of poetry called *Postcard Poems,* believes that poems are "gifts from the poet, meant to be shared. Each poem is a sharing of a vision that is unique to each poet."

When you read a poem, you share the poet's vision of his or her experience.

Not every poem will reach you or touch you or mean anything to you at all. But when one special poem *does* get you—and it will—and it makes you smile, or cry, or feel instant recognition, you don't have to leave it there.

You can make a gift of it to someone else. That's what this book, *A Collection of Poetry for Sharing,* intends. Each poem is short enough to jot down on a postcard or notecard or scrap of paper, to share with just the right person you choose.

Take them as a gifts for yourself, or pass them on to someone you are thinking of while I am reading. [Read: Page 1, "Gift"; Page 9, "Man on Wheels"; Page 45, "What Kind of Guy Was he?"; Page 53, "Zimmer's Head Thudding Against the Blackboard"; Page 63, "After the Rain."]

—Cathi Edgerton

THE PRINCESS BRIDE   YA
By WILLIAM GOLDMAN

Ever remember being told fairy tales when you were little? William Goldman remembers one—a story his father told him when he was ten and sick and stuck in bed for three weeks. Every night his father would read him a chapter from S. Morgenstern's *The Princess Bride,* and long after he grew up he'd remember his father and this story and his fear and excitement. Then, when his son turned ten, he gave him a copy. But something went wrong. His son read the first chapter and put the book away, completely bored. And Goldman felt hurt, betrayed, confused by his son's reactions, and went back to read the book himself for the first time since he was ten. He found that his father hadn't been completely honest with him. Oh, he'd told the story that was in Morgenstern's book. But when the going got dull, he skipped ahead to the exciting parts. When Mr. Morgenstern spent 65 pages describing Florinese hat designs, his dad just skipped ahead to the kidnapping. And when Morgenstern used up 32 pages on Florinese history, he got right into the part about the bloodthirsty Prince Humperdink and the Zoo of Death. And William Goldman has done the same for you in his "good parts" version of *The Princess Bride.* No dull history or social comment here. Instead you have 283 pages of "Fencing. Fighting. Torture. Poison. True Love. Hate. Revenge. Giants. Hunters. Bad Men. Good Men. Beautiful Ladies. Snakes. Spiders. Beasts of All

Natures and Descriptions. Pain. Death. Brave Men. Coward Men. Strongest Men. Chases. Escapes. Lies. Truths. Passions. Miracles.*"*

It is the story of Buttercup, the dairyman's daughter, seventeen and already among the Ten Most Beautiful Women in the World, and Westley, the orphaned stable boy who loves her. But Buttercup never notices him until the day the Count and Countess come to visit. The Count has heard of a girl of stunning beauty living in the village—and one glance tells him that the rumors are true. But while the Count only has eyes for Buttercup, the Countess can't take her eyes off Westley. That night, Buttercup can't sleep. Sure, Westley has eyes like the sea before a storm, but who cares about eyes? And his shoulders are broad enough, but the Count's are almost as broad. It must be the teeth. Westley has perfect teeth. That must be it! But still sleep won't come. Before dawn Buttercup is at the door of Westley's house. She tells him of her love for him and Westley closes the door in her face. Without a word! The next day he tells her he is leaving. He'll go to America, he says, and earn enough money to buy a farm and send for her. Finally, the light begins to dawn. Westley loves her. But their love is doomed, for on his way to America, Westley's ship is attacked by The Dread Prince Roberts, the one who *leaves no survivors.* Grief-stricken, Buttercup swears never to love again and locks herself in her room. At the end of two weeks, paler but even more beautiful than before, she emerges. Before, she was just an impossibly lovely girl, but now grief has made her glorious! She immediately leaves the bottom of the list and assumes the number-one spot as The Most Beautiful Woman in the World. So when Prince Humperdink decides to take a wife, there's really only one choice—Buttercup!

The Princess Bride is the answer to the question, "What happens when the most beautiful girl in the world marries the handsomest prince in the world—and he turns out to be a son-of-a . . . " Well, read it youself.

—*Christy Tyson*

NOTE: For a short talk, use the last paragraph only.

THE QUARTZSITE TRIP YA/Adult
By WILLIAM HOGAN

It was the spring of 1962, and at John Muir High School in Los Angeles County, California, PJ Cooper gave out invitations to the Quartzsite Trip. PJ Cooper taught English at John Muir High and was the only person who had been on all of the Quartzsite Trips. He had been born in Quartzsite, Arizona, and had invented the trip on a whim seven years ago.

The Trip was held every year during spring vacation—the week before Easter. Only seniors were invited, and only thirty-six—one school bus-load. PJ Cooper invited them on the Monday two weeks before spring vacation. In 1962, that was April 2nd. No one had ever been on the Trip who had not been in school the day invitations were given out. On April 2, 1962, there were no absences in the senior class at John Muir High School. No one knew how or why PJ Cooper decided whom to invite on the Quartzsite Trip. Some were invited in hallways or during classes. Some found notes in their lockers or at the bottom of the papers PJ handed back to his senior English class—"You are invited to the Quartzsite Trip. PJ" Some of these papers were As, some were Bs. Two boys were even cornered and invited in the boys' restroom. It was the most sought-after invitation at John Muir High School, and it couldn't be obtained by beauty or brains or strength or popularity. No skill, reputation, office, achievement, virtue, or vice could assure it. It *was* the ultimate status, and PJ Cooper bestowed it.

Every spring vacation, a school bus took PJ Cooper, thirty-six incompatible seniors, and four Muir High School graduates who had been on the Trip during their senior years out into the desert, seven miles north of Quartzsite, Arizona. Five days later it returned. In between was the Quartzsite Trip.

In 1962, John Glenn was the first American to orbit earth in a spacecraft. Tricia Nixon celebrated her sixteenth birthday, and Jack Paar left the *Tonight Show*. In 1962, Katherine Anne Porter published *A Ship of Fools, West Side Story* won the Oscar for Best Picture, and *Ben Casey* was the hit of the TV season. In 1962, there was a new singing group called Peter, Paul and Mary, and their biggest hit, and the favorite song sung on the Quartzsite Trip, was "Where Have All the Flowers Gone?"

In 1962, coffee was 59¢ a pound, gasoline 21¢ a gallon, and at Bob's Big Boy in Los Angeles County, California, a cheeseburger with fries was 55¢. 1962 was the Jerk, the Slop, and the Hully Gully. 1962 was the flattop and the flip, pinning, giving BA, makeout parties, and drive-in movies.

And for thirty-six seniors at John Muir High School, 1962 *was* PJ Cooper and the Quartzsite Trip. In 1962, Deeter Moss, Margaret Ball, Ann Hosak, Phil Baker, Stretch Latham, Mary Allbright, and Horace Clay and twenty-nine others were invited on the Quartzsite Trip.

It was the seventh trip. It began on April 16, 1962.

—Joni Bodart

QUEENIE PEAVY
By ROBERT BURCH

Grades 4–6

Queenie Peavy's aim was sure and deadly. The day she was called into district court to see Judge Lewis she took three of her friends along, all boys. They made their way to the vacant front bench just in time to hear the judge charging the jury. Floyd found a plug of Brown Mule chewing tobacco on the end of the bench. He borrowed Queenie's knife to cut off a wad of it and passed it on to the other boys. When it came Queenie's turn she just bit hers off. When it came time to spit, she waited until the judge's attention was on the jury and then she took careful aim and hit the stove, near the bottom where it was extra hot, and it made a crackling, spattering noise. The judge figured it was one of the boys—but after their denials he looked at Queenie and said, "It wouldn't be you, would it?"

"Me, oh no sir, your noble honor."

"I should know that a girl wouldn't do such a thing."

At that she said angrily, "There's nothing I can't do!" and spat the rest of the tobacco at the stove. She was ordered by the judge to leave and come back tomorrow, to which she said, "I might or I might not."

. . .

On the way home she passed little Tilly Evans playing in the yard. Tilly edged closer to her front porch and started chanting, "Queenie's daddy's in the chain gang. Queenie's daddy's in the chain gang." Queenie reached down and picked up two stones and hit the facing of the door just after Tilly rushed inside.

Tilly's mother came out to see what was going on and Queenie explained that Tilly was telling lies about her. Mrs. Evans told her that that wasn't an excuse for throwing stones at a seven-year-old. "I wasn't throwing at her. If I'd been throwing at her I'd have hit her. I've got better aim than anyone." And she proved it as she threw the second stone and killed a squirrel from sixty feet away.

Queenie was always in trouble with the law and at school—because she couldn't take the remarks made about her father being in prison without retaliating. Mr. Hanley, the school principal, tried to make her see that her tormentors were hurting themselves when they teased her and she should ignore these remarks. But Queenie had a long way to go. *Queenie Peavy,* by Robert Burch.

—*Eileen Gieswein*

NOTE: The first half of the talk can be used alone.

THE QUEEN'S GAMBIT   YA/Adult
By WALTER TEVIS

In the Methuen Home in Mt. Sterling, Kentucky, Beth Harmon got two tranquilizers a day. All the children got them—to even their dispositions and make them easier to handle.

The janitor was Mr. Shaibel. He stayed in the basement, and when Beth was sent there to clean erasers she saw him, always sitting behind a checkerboard with strangely-shaped pieces of plastic on it. He moved them from one square to another, one by one. Each one had its own way of moving—some on diagonals, some up and down or back and forth. He said the game was called chess.

Mr. Shaibel wasn't very encouraging at first, but he finally agreed to teach her to play. It only took four moves for him to beat her—but Beth played the game over and over in her mind, and the next week it took him fourteen moves to trap her queen. She won the third game and then sometimes two or three a week. After every game, she lay in bed at night, visualizing the chessboard on the ceiling, replaying the games, and figuring out how she could have won—or won more quickly. Frequently she saved her tranquilizers so she could stay awake longer. She stashed them in her toothbrush holder. Chess was better than pills for relaxing her.

After three months, Mr. Shaibel introduced her to Mr. Ganz, and she played them simultaneously—and won, almost effortlessly. Mr. Ganz was in charge of the chess club at the local high school. Beth played his twelve best players simultaneously, beating all of them in an hour and a half, without one false or wasted move. She wasn't quite nine, and had been playing chess for less than six months.

Then they stopped the tranquilizers—against the law now, they said. Beth couldn't sleep—or survive—without them, so she broke into the infirmary to steal some. She was caught, and part of her punishment was no more chess.

When she was thirteen, the Wheatleys adopted her. It was a strange family—Mr. Wheatley traveled, and was hardly ever home. Mrs. Wheatley was kind, but definitely odd.

Beth had been with them just a few months when she saw an announcement of the Kentucky State Championship Chess Tournament. She entered in open competition although she hadn't played for almost *five years*—and she won. First prize was $100. She was only thirteen, and so she needed Mrs. Wheatley's signature to open a bank account. Mrs. Wheatley was delighted to find that Beth could play chess for money. Mr. Wheatley was "permanently delayed" in the Southwest, and they needed all the money they could get. She faked medical excuses and they traveled all over the United States, and Beth supported them on her winnings. She was still a junior high school student. By the time she was in high school she was a Master chess player, well on her way to becoming a Grandmaster—and U. S. Champion. Too old to be called a prodigy and still addicted to the green pills (Mrs. Wheatley took them too, so Beth could steal her own supply), Beth was gaining an international reputation—at sixteen.

But she'd arranged her life so that there was room for nothing but chess—what if chess turned out to be not nearly enough? What if she discovered she needed friends—or lovers? Was the chance to be the world champion worth the sacrifice? Could she make it alone?

The incredible story of a girl who in ten years goes from having no one and nothing to—how far?

I'll let you find that out for yourself.

—Joni Bodart

RABBIT HILL   Grades 1–6
By ROBERT LAWSON

Pretend you're a small creature: a Southern gentleman rabbit, or a skunk named Phewie. How about Porky, the woodchuck, or Red Buck, a deer? The Hill where you live is all excited. There's a continual chattering and squeaking, whispering and whistling—New Folks Coming.

Who are the New Folks? Will they have guns, dogs, or poison? Will they be planting folks, or shiftless like the last?

The house is made ready, the grounds are worked, and the great day arrives. First the moving van and now the Folks . . . a man, a woman, and a cat named Muldoon, and books! Lots of books.

Some folks on the Hill say reading rots the mind. Discover the truth with the creatures who live on Rabbit Hill.

—Sandy Hudson

RAINBOW JORDAN   YA
By ALICE CHILDRESS

Fourteen-year-old Rainbow says, "I never really had a mama and a daddy. I got a Kathie and a Leroy."

Rainbow's mother, Kathie, says, "If I burn a dress with a hot iron, I can throw it away if it can't be fixed. But you gotta live forever with other mistakes. If I had a dollar for every time I goofed . . . I could buy a Cadillac, cash on the line. One mistake I have to live with each and every day is my daughter, Rainbow; the other I telephone now and then . . . my ex-husband, Leroy. Fifteen was too young for me to have a child. Mother Nature made me able to give birth from the age of twelve . . . but she didn't bother to turn my mind on the same year."

Then there's Miss Josie, who says, "I must be out of my mind. Why do I trap myself? I've had twenty [different foster] children during the last twenty years plus one repeater, Rainbow Jordan, who is fourteen and walks around with her nose slightly in the air . . . as if she is superior and is merely allowing me to handle her situation. She is a definite case of child neglect but puts on like it's all some kind of misunderstanding. Her mother acts like she's been off to Paris and left Rainbow behind in a finishing school."

And then there is Rainbow herself, saying, "Miss Josie, she's okay, but she's fifty . . . and always boastin' about it. No way I can talk my feelings to a 'fifty.' But I do better with her than talkin' with my mother, who is twenty-nine while I am fourteen. I look nearly as old as she does."

Rainbow not only has problems with her mother and Miss Josie, but with her boyfriend, Eljay. Eljay, says Rainbow, is always singing the same song: "Girl, you got hang-ups about sex. Nothing wrong with sex. It's a natural thing. A guy can break his health from holding back his feelings." "But I'm still holding out," says Rainbow. "I don't like bein' asked to make love to save his health. Make me feel like I'm the Red Cross or Cancer Aid."

But Eljay begins hangin' out with a girl named Janine. Trying to make Rainbow jealous so she'll see things his way.

—Linda Lapides

RAMONA AND HER FATHER   Grades 2–4
By BEVERLY CLEARY

When do you start your Christmas list? Well, Ramona was happily dreaming up her Christmas list in September. Today was payday. They would eat supper at Whopperburger.

Beezus knew that something was wrong. She could hear Mom and Dad whispering. When she and Ramona went into the kitchen, Mom told them that Dad had lost his job. Mrs. Quimby looked at the leftovers and began to prepare supper.

There would be no money for Christmas. Ramona began crossing off her Christmas list with a black pen.

Ramona wished she had a million dollars so her father would be fun again. One day she saw a boy her age do a commerical on television. Her father said the boy probably made a million dollars. Ramona begain practicing television commercials at home and at school in order to earn a million dollars. Her favorite commercial was, "Look, Mommy, the elephant's legs are wrinkled, like your pantyhose!" Ramona skipped into the classroom and what did she see but Mrs. Rogers, her second-grade teacher, with wrinkles around her ankles. "Mrs. Rogers, your pantyhose are wrinkled like elephants' legs!" Mrs. Rogers looked kind of surprised. Ramona felt she might have displeased her teacher.

Ramona also felt that her father didn't love her anymore. All he did was sit near the telephone and smoke cigarettes, hoping that someone would call him for a job. Mother and Beezus were awfully busy and grouchy, and Picky-Picky, the family cat, was grumpy and would not eat his cheap cat food.

Did Ramona succeed in making a million dollars so that the family, including Picky-Picky, could be happy again? Read *Ramona and Her Father* and find out.

—Clara Lovely

RAMONA AND HER MOTHER By BEVERLY CLEARY Grades 2–4

Talk 1

Ramona grabbed the toothpaste and squeezed as hard as she could. She squeezed again. Soon the sink was full of a small mountain of quivering toothpaste. Ramona felt great—she had always wanted to do that—until her mother found out what she had done. Ramona does other things, like wear her pajamas to school and dye her feet blue. To find out more about her and her family, read *Ramona and Her Mother,* by Beverly Cleary.

—Billie McKeever

Talk 2

Ramona was a little girl in the second grade who wanted more than anything to have her mother say about her, "Ramona? Why I couldn't make it without her," as she had said about Ramona's older sister, Beezus. But instead, Ramona was always getting herself into a mess.

One night her mother gave her a new pair of flannel pajamas. This was the first time Ramona had had a brand new pair that weren't hand-me-downs from Beezus. They felt so warm and soft and cuddly that Ramona didn't want to pull them off next morning. So, remembering that firemen often pulled on their firemen's suits over their clothes, she quickly pulled on her pants and then her sweater over her pajamas. That way she could enjoy the cuddly softness of her pajamas all day, and no one would know. She raced off to school, making noises like a fire engine. But as she ran down the block, she began to sweat. Sweat ran down her back and down her legs. Her pajamas no long felt soft; they just felt wet. When she arrived and sat down at her seat, the boy in the next desk said, "Boy, Ramona, you look fat." Time dragged. She couldn't sit still, she was so uncomfortable. She'd squirm this way and then that way. Her teacher finally sent her to the office to have her temperature checked because her cheeks were so flushed. The secretary stuck the thermometer into Ramona's mouth and promptly forgot about her. All the time Ramona sat there, she hoped she would have a temperature and they would call her mother to come get her and her mother would tuck her in bed and read stories about rabbits to her and bring her orange juice. But she had *no* temperature. Her bubble burst, and she was faced with a horrible day, sweating and squirming in wet pajamas.

To see how she survived, read *Ramona and Her Mother*.

—Billie Harding

RATHA'S CREATURE   YA
By CLARE BELL

Twenty-five million years in the past, at a time when Earth and its creatures are undergoing profound changes, intelligent wild cats have evolved from the ancient sabertooth. Ratha and her band are the Named. They have developed a society based on herding forest animals, deer and horses mostly, and have laws and leaders. The need for more herders is so great that female cubs are being trained, and cubs like Ratha who have only partially completed their training are taken to guard the herds. She is standing guard on the night a group of predatory cats raid the herd. These predatory cats, the Un-Named, lack the intelligence and social organization of the Named. Ratha, although under strict orders from Thakur not to fight but to climb a tree to safety, fights, nevertheless, to protect the herd-beasts. During the attack, she hears an Un-Named speak—but they are supposed to be stupid! If they can talk, maybe they aren't stupid after all. But Thakur refuses to admit the Un-Named ones can speak, even though he asks Ratha what the Un-Named one said. Ratha begins to question and to doubt. She senses that something is wrong, that there is another fear keeping Thakur silent. Ratha discovers that Thakur's father was Un-Named and that his brother still runs with them.

The Un-Named are pushing the Named close to extinction. This season is the first time that the number of animals killed in raids has exceeded the number of young born. The clan knows the imbalance cannot continue for long. And even their best efforts can only slow the loss of herd-beasts to the enemy. And the fire which blazes across clan ground, destroying the grass for grazing, compounds the problem. However, Ratha tames the power of fire, that no other animal has dared approach. She learns how to put out the Red Tongue by kicking dirt on it; she learns how to feed it dry twigs so it won't die. She takes the Red Tongue to the clan, to show then how they can warm themselves beside it. For her boldness, she is exiled by the clan leader, who feels threatened by her new power. She is stripped of her name, her kin, and all that she knows and values. She is now clanless, outcast and outlaw. Her training as a herder is worthless now, for she has no beasts to keep. There will be no more gatherings, no sharing with the clan. From now on she will have to provide for herself, and that no one has taught her. She has lost her world and everything in it.

"The way of the herder was old, but there was another way, ancient beyond memory. It went back to the time before the beginning. The way of the hunter." Ratha could do nothing to change the fate of her people. She could only look out for herself and try to survive. The clan was no more. She would live each day, trying not to think about the past or the future. A new trail lay before her.

—Judy Druse

RED AS BLOOD YA/Adult
By TANITH LEE

I'm sure you've all heard of—and even read—Grimm's Fairy Tales. But have you ever heard of the Tales of the Sisters Grimmer? Tanith Lee has collected some of them here, in *Red as Blood.*

We all think fairy tales have to end happily ever after—love always wins. But not these tales! For instance:

Maybe waking Sleeping Beauty is a mistake—she has, after all, been asleep for a hundred years. Isn't it possible that it's a gulf too wide to be bridged by a mere kiss?

And as for stepmothers, they're the wicked ones, of course, with beautiful and good stepdaughters. But what if it was reversed—a good stepmother and an unrepentantly evil stepdaughter?

The Rapunzel that we met in the traditional story bears little resemblance to the woman we see here—and her keeper is truly a witch, who means to sacrifice her to the Lords of Darkness.

In the old fairy tales, Beauty always falls in love with her Beast-like captor when he turns into a prince. But what if he doesn't change—and *she* does?

These are only a few of the strange and eerie tales you'll find here— fairy tales for adults, with a new twist added, in *Red as Blood*.

—*Joni Bodart*

THE RIDDLE-MASTER OF HED   YA/Adult
By PATRICIA A. McKILLIP

Morgon woke from a dream to find himself in a real nightmare. When he had gone to bed he was safe, in a protected home with guards in many rooms. Now as he opened his eyes he saw one of the shape changers shimmering in the colors of the sea and playing a deadly harp. At that harpist's song, Morgon could feel the life flowing out of him, and he could feel the horror of knowing that his death alone would not be enough. His own country of Hed, a peaceful quiet island land with no riches to speak of, would also be overwhelmed by the sea by the harpist's playing. No one could help him. Even Lyra, the guard at the door, was standing frozen in time. Morgon croaked out some sound— his voice would not form words—but Lyra could not hear even this noise. He shouted again, a horrible croaking noise, and at last he was able to move, very slowly, fighting for muscle control all the way. The harpist with the shimmering skin the color of pearls in sunlight just laughed and kept on playing as Morgon fought for his life. At last Morgon grasped the shape changer in his hands, only to cry out startled as the merman of the sea changed into many shapes, some too hideous to grasp, others like a beautiful butterfly, so fragile he almost let go for fear of crushing it forever.

At his second cry Lyra came to life and turned, throwing her spear. It seemed to move in slow motion, through some power of the shape changer and it fell short, clattering on the floor. The last shape the shape changer formed was one of a marvelous sword with three glittering stars on the hilt, that matched the stars on Morgon's head. As the shape changer resumed his shimmering man-shape he laughed as Morgon bent and slowly picked up the spear. Morgon, who had never killed any animal or bird, much less a human being, sobbed in agony as he held the spear over his shoulder. "Throw it, Morgon!" screamed Lyra from the doorway. Cursing, Morgon drew back his arm and threw the spear at the chest of the laughing shape changer.

Read *The Riddle-master of Hed,* by Patricia A. McKillip.

—*Pat Powell*

ROADSIDE VALENTINE   YA
By C. S. ADLER

I'm a fool—at least, that's what my father thinks—just because I made a five-foot Valentine's Day heart out of snow by the roadside; it said "Jamie loves Louisa." I put it beside the road so Louisa would see it on her way to school. So what, if everyone else in town could see it too! I don't care who knows I love her. However, Louisa doesn't love me. She loves Vince Brunelli. Being in love with someone who is in love with someone else is painful. But Vince (or Bozo, as I prefer to call him) can't be as unbeatable as he looks. After all, the size of a guy's heart has to matter more in the long run than how big he is physically. A guy as self-involved as Vince will never properly appreciate red-haired, bossy, wonderful Louisa. So what, if my progress so far is zilch. I will just have to win her over with deeds of self-sacrifice or daring. Maybe if I win the vaulting competition at the upcoming gymnastic meet, I'll impress her. I'll learn to fly over that horse like Spiderman or Superman—well, maybe I'll settle for a circus acrobat. I'll make Louisa fall in love with me by the veritable grace of my fantastic vault! And even if she never loves me back, I'll still adore her.

It's too bad I can't win over my father the same way. Deep in my heart I know I'm not the son my father would have chosen. It's never been easy between us since my mother left when I was nine. That's when Louisa and I became friends; she was the only one I told about my mother leaving. Louisa tried in little ways to take over the mothering I was missing. Of course, I resisted her, mostly out of pride, but nevertheless, I liked having somebody there watching out for me. By seventh grade, however, Louisa and I were going in different directions. She was class president, busy, popular, good at everything, including sports. I had already fallen into bad ways. I palled around with kids who excelled in negatives, not caring about grades or adult approval, intent on seeing how much they could get away with. My place among these troublemakers was assured because I always had money for cigarettes and beer or pot, and I was always willing to share. But I cut out my drinking buddies in my junior year after I totaled my car. And I stopped the drugs, too, before I killed myself, when I finally found a purpose in life. I decided to grow up to be a doctor like my father, to be a credit to him. But things didn't work out as I planned. Now I'm a senior in high school, and the arguments have gotten worse. I guess the last straw was my public declaration of love on Valentine's Day, because it started a bitter fight. That was when my father called me a fool and a jackass. So I'm going to move out on my own. I had really hoped my father needed me; but all he needs is disease, death, and disaster. I had really hoped he needed me, because if he doesn't, no one does.

—Judy Druse

ROLL OF THUNDER, HEAR MY CRY   Grades 3–5
By MILDRED D. TAYLOR

Cassie and her family were the only black landowners in Spokane, Mississippi, in 1933. Sometimes it seemed as if their life was just one long fight, whether it was the big struggle against the white plantation owner who had promised to take that land away from you or the little everyday struggles—like Cassie and her brother's fight with the school bus. You see, black children then in Mississippi couldn't ride the several miles to school—they had to walk, while the white children, whose school was much closer to Cassie than the black school, got to ride in a brand new shiny bus. And every day that bus would catch Cassie and her brother on the long, cold, muddy patch through the forest—no matter how early or late they left—and when the driver saw them he always did the same thing—step on the accelerator and roar through the deepest puddle while Cassie and Little Man scrambled up the muddy banks for safety. And every morning they got to school wet and filthy. But Cassie knew how to fight back—she'd fix that school bus some day—and her Papa too would stand up to the nightriders and the burnings and hang on to their land, even if it, and they, were destroyed in the process.

—Elizabeth Overmyer

RUN FOR YOUR LIFE   Grade 6–8
By KIN PLATT

Lee needed this job. Darn, he *had* to keep this job. He'd been lucky to get a job on the delivery truck of the local newspaper. The hours worked great with track and his school schedule. Since his dad died, his mom and he had worked to keep the family on its feet. She worked at the Gomez taco plant, and he worked at a lot of jobs.

They were doing okay, too, until yesterday when he had been on the route. He'd taken out yesterday's papers, put in today's, and then pressed the coin release for his collections. Nothing happened. He hit it with his hand. Nothing happened again. No change. Nothing. Then came the thought. He felt a chill all over. "I've got the key. They'll think I did it."

Run for Your Life, by Kin Platt.

—Dee Scrogin

RUNNING LOOSE   YA
By CHRIS CRUTCHER

The year started out pretty smooth for Louie. He had two good jobs so the money was rolling in; he had even bought a '52 Chevy pickup at the end of the summer. He wasn't doing bad in school either. His grades weren't world-beaters, but two of his senior English compositions were entered in the State Prose and Poetry Fair, and the *Daily Statesman,* the local paper, had even printed one of them. In fact, some guy from the paper called long distance to tell him to keep them in mind if he decided to go to college and major in journalism. He had cheerleader Becky Sanders as a girlfriend. And he finally got a starting spot on the football team. His best friend Carter, also quarterback of the football team, had worked out with him all summer. He got to thinking he was pretty hot stuff. Seemed like all he had to do was shove 'er in neutral and coast in to graduation. Yes, the year started out pretty smooth. Probably would have ended up that way, too, if Becky hadn't been in an automobile accident, or if he hadn't quit the football team and made himself look like the Jerk of the Universe, though quitting was the only thing to do.

Coach Lednecky said the team was on the way to another winning season if they could get past Salmon River and their new black transfer student, named Washington. He was the Salmon River quarterback and had scored as many as six touchdowns in a single game. Coach was worried about Washington so much so that he told his players to hurt him, get him out of the game early. Louie couldn't believe it. Lednecky was telling them to play dirty ball and everyone was eating it up, especially Boomer Cowans. Boomer Cowans was the running back and dumber than a cinderblock. If Coach said to hurt Washington, Boomer would do it. So when it happened, Louie just threw down his helmet and walked off the field. The whole thing ruined his idea of what sports was supposeed to be about. Not only was he off the team, but out of school. He was suspended. The principal said he couldn't have someone with Louie's attitude running loose in school.

Louie couldn't have gotten through the year without his friends, girlfriend, and parents. They were always there when he needed them, and they did surprisingly little judging considering some of the stuff he pulled. Louie learned a lot that year, about friendship and love and how there's no use being honorable with dishonorable men. He learned to accept himself and responsibility for what he did. He learned that losing someone to death is vicious, miserable, and ugly, but that he could get through almost anything if he had people around who cared about him. A few things he didn't learn. He didn't learn to like people who didn't like him and he didn't learn not to push his luck.

—Judy Druse

SADAKO AND THE THOUSAND PAPER CRANES
By ELEANOR B. COERR

Grades 3–5

Sadako learned to run before she walked. Her mother always said she would be a runner, and no one was surprised when she was on the winning relay race team and began to plan for the junior high school track team. Sadako lived in Hiroshima. She had been two years old when her grandmother was killed by the Thunderbolt, the atom bomb that had been dropped at the end of World War II. She was eleven now and spent all her time training so she would be selected for next year's team. But then one day she fainted as she was running, and when she had finished with the tests at the Red Cross Hospital, she was told she had leukemia, the "atom bomb disease." She was sure nothing could help her until her best friend Chuzuko told her she had figured out a way to get well. She quickly folded a piece of gold paper into a paper crane and told her the story—if a sick person folds a thousand paper cranes, the gods will grant her wish and make her healthy again. From then on, whenever Sadako wasn't doing her homework, writing letters to friends and pen pals, or talking to visitors, she would make paper cranes. Three hundred, four hundred, five hundred—until she was more than halfway to a thousand.

This is a true story based on the letters of a very real girl who is always remembered every peace day when children in Japan still make thousands of paper cranes in her honor.

—Elizabeth Overmyer

SAVE QUEEN OF SHEBA   Grades 6–8/YA
By LOUISE MOERI

When King David woke up, the first thing he saw was a huge, greenish-black fly crawling along his hand, just in front of his face. He took a breath, felt pain, sat up and looked around. An overturned wagon and a man underneath, a smashed water keg, and more bodies—horses, women, children, with arrows in them.

King David stood up and felt his head, which hurt—he seemed to be half scalped, but he could walk. The Sioux raiding party was gone, and he was the only person left alive. The only one, that is, until he looked under a feather bed thrown out of the farthest wagon—and found his six-year-old sister, Queen of Sheba.

There were twelve bodies, and two live children—King David was only twelve. But it was up to him to see that he and his little sister caught up with the rest of the wagon train—and their parents. They were on their own—with only a small amount of water, in two canteens, a small pack of cornmeal, one little piece of bacon, some apples, and a gun.

King David was almost delirious from the infection in the wound on his head, Queen of Sheba was a stubborn, spoiled brat who would refuse to help or do anything King David asked her to—and they were alone in the middle of the prairie.

But before they'd gone too far, they found one of the horses from the wagon train caught in some bushes—now at least they had a chance, King David thought—if only he could put up with Queen of Sheba till they found the rest of the wagon train.

—Joni Bodart

THE SCIENCE IN SCIENCE FICTION   YA/Adult
Edited by PETER NICHOLLS

Today, more than ever before, we are aware of the future. Starships, alien life forms, cyborgs, space cities, suspended animation, telekinesis. These are all trappings of science fiction. Are they possible? Are they probable? Are they all fantasy? Or do such things have a grounding in "real" science, pointing the way to what will happen in the future?

Long before atomic weapons, tanks, submarines, artificial satellites, and space travel actually existed, novelists like H. G. Wells and Jules Verne had put them in books. And for nearly a hundred years other writers of science fiction have been stretching their imaginations—and ours—to encompass ever more bizarre possibilities, from alternate universes to invaders from outer space, some plausible, some downright weird. But it is no miracle when science fiction writers make good predictions because they keep abreast of scientific and technological developments. Part of this book is about speculative science, like cloning, the creation of machine intelligences, or ramscoop starships; part deals with imaginary science like time machines, hyperspace traveling, and alternate universes; part deals with controversial science like UFOs, telepathy, and whether or not Uri Geller can really bend spoons; finally, part deals with major errors made by science fiction writers, like invisibility, shrinking people, starbows, meteor storms, and a hollow Earth. Here are the hard facts behind ideas from the novels of Robert Heinlein, Isaac Asimov, Frederick Pohl, Arthur C. Clarke, and dozens of others.

—Judy Druse

SECOND HEAVEN   Adult
By JUDITH GUEST

Michael Atwood is a lawyer, tired of the domestic cases he handles and tired of having to rise to the challenge of yet one more client who does not believe in lawyers. He is trying to survive the trauma of his divorce and the loss of his two children, when they moved with their mother to Washington.

Catherine Holzman is also trying to survive. After her divorce, the world had suddenly been filled with people she couldn't believe in. She couldn't bear asking people for money or time or even opinions. She felt hollow and useless. So she got a job working part-time in an art gallery. And then Gale Murray, a sixteen-year-old runaway, shows up on her doorstep, looking for refuge. He's moved out of his own home and into Catherine's after his father severely burned Gale's hand on an electric stove.

When Gale moves in with Catherine, his parents take him to court. He is charged with chronic truancy, chronic absence from home, lying, stealing, general disobedience, and lack of respect in the home. He is removed from Cat's and taken to the Juvenile Center. At the Center, Gale has no room to move or think or even to breathe unless he has permission. He wants to be free. But he hides his tangled feelings behind a protective wall of silence. He has suffered so severely from child abuse throughout his sixteen years and felt such senseless rage at the unfairness of constant punishment that he can no longer trust anyone.

Gale believes mistakes happen when you start depending on other people, so he will never do that again.

Cat wants Michael to represent Gale and place him in her custody. So Michael tries to get Gale out of the Juvenile Center, working against substantial odds and the disappointment of being separated from his own teenage son, as well as Gale's distrust.

These three vulnerable people, thrown together by past hurts, find the courage to reach out and help one another as they join forces in a custody battle against Gale's brutal, vengeful father, a battle they have a one-in-a-million chance of winning.

—Judy Druse

THE SECRET LIFE OF
THE UNDERWEAR CHAMP
By BETTY MILES

Grades 3–5

The whole thing began for Larry Pryor on a street corner in New York City. He didn't even live in New York—he was there to go to the dentist, and his mouth was still numb with Novocain when a man and woman he'd never seen before started yelling from across the street: "That's him! That's him! The answer to our prayers!" These are the Zigmunds, and Larry soon learns that the Zigmunds run the Zigmund Model Agency—and they happen to need an eleven-year-old red-headed baseball player for a ChampWin Knitting Mills commercial. At first Larry is pretty excited. His only worry seems to be that the TV shootings may conflict with his baseball practice schedule. But when he finds out *what* he will be advertising on the commercials, his real worry turns out to be keeping his TV career a big secret! What will happen when everyone in his class sees him on TV, playing baseball in his underwear?

—Elizabeth Overmyer

THE SECRET OF ANNIE OAKLEY
By MARCY HEIDISH

YA/Adult

In the fall of 1876, two theater managers wired Annie and Frank Butler informing them that they were ready to hire them as an act in Cincinnati, but they wouldn't, if they insisted on being billed as the husband-and-wife team of Butler & Butler.

Annie considered the problem for days. She totally rejected the idea of using her maiden name. Only years later would her husband Frank realize how desperate Annie was to dissociate her current life from her past.

After a week of trying hundreds of names on her writing pad, she still hadn't found the right one. On an autumn afternoon, she and Frank were practicing their act in an open field and they ran out of gunpowder. As they entered a nearby village to get some more, Annie's gaze was transfixed by a small, neatly painted signboard with the name of the village, Oakley.

Annie wrote the name carefully, studying it. She said it aloud, over and over. "Annie Oakley, Annie Oakley."

It was right. Both Frank and Annie knew it. It went on that week's program and every program after that. It went on the trunk, on the gun rack, on everything that she owned. Over the next forty-six years that name would appear on programs and advertisements around the world.

Annie Oakley was a crack shot and a brilliant performer—one of the best of her time. With her husband Frank as manager, she became one of the most sought-after acts in the world, with billings from California to Paris.

In spite of the fame, for all those years Annie continued to hide her past. The Chicago business of 1905–1906 finally brought it to light. Her past had been so carefully concealed that not even her husband knew anything about it. She had even gone to the point of having the last names on her father's and older sister's gravestones changed, and all the church and family records altered.

What was the horror in Annie Oakley's past? What happened in the Darke County Infirmary, and in the home of the wealthy family she called "the wolves"? What happened in those years after her fifth birthday, when first her father died and then, a year later, her beloved older sister Maryjane? What horrors had the child named Phoebe Ann Moses endured? What *was* Annie Oakley's secret?

—*Barbara Lynn*

A SECRET RAGE   Adult
By CHARLAINE HARRIS

Nickie Callahan has always loved making lists. At twenty-seven she is at a turning point in her life, and on a muggy, smoggy New York afternoon, she sits down and lists her blessings, hoping to crystallize a decision.

1. A small-town Southern girl who came to New York and found success.
2. Five years a top model in New York.
3. Nice apartment, good location.
4. Money in the bank, money invested.
5. Two completed novels, but not published.
6. Friends.
7. Beauty—straight nose, high broad cheekbones, blue eyes, beautiful skin; blond hair to frame it all.
8. Furniture and books.
9. Jewelry.
10. Clothes.
11. Brains, but undisciplined ones.
12. Southern background.
13. Fair education, as far as it goes.

On the negative side, Nickie's agent has just told her that he is dropping her. At twenty-seven, Nickie is washed up as a model. Her agent says she is overexposed; the agency is looking for a new face.

When Mimi Houghton calls, her best friend since their days at Miss Beacham's Academy for girls in Memphis, Tennessee, the decision suddenly seems easy. After two failed marriages Mimi is living in her Grandmother Celeste's house in Knolls. This beautiful old home, which Mimi has inherited, has always been one of Nickie's favorite places.

Nickie has been considering going back to college to finish her degree program, which was interrupted by her modeling career. Mimi is encouraging her to come back to Knolls and attend Houghton College.

Everything is easy after that. Nickie is going home. All the continual struggle and fear Nickie has experienced in New York is over. No more clawing to be on top, no more fear, no more memories of a dead woman on the sidewalk in front of her New York apartment.

On Nickie's first night back in Knolls, Mimi suddenly blurts out, "A girl got raped here this summer."

Heidi Edmonds, a beautiful young freshman coed who had everything going for her was attacked in the gardens between the library and the women's dorm at dusk on a warm summer evening.

The reality of this new fear comes home to Nickie that night when for the first time in her memory a house in Knolls is locked. Mimi double-locks her doors.

A week after her arrival, Mimi holds a party in Nickie's honor. By 8:30 p.m. on that Friday evening it seems the entire population of Knolls is crammed into Mimi's house. By midnight, Knolls, Tennessee, has its second rape victim—Barbara Tucker, a young professor at Houghton College.

As the horror of this second crime reaches Nickie, she again thinks of the dead woman on the sidewalk back in New York. She wonders if every place is the same after all. Has she made a mistake coming back to Knolls? How will Nickie and Mimi face this stalking terror? And who will be the next victim?

—Barbara Lynn

A SHADOW LIKE A LEOPARD   YA
By MYRON LEVOY

Ramon Santiago believes that it is necessary to carry a knife at all times. He is a fourteen-year-old Puerto Rican street kid on his own in New York City, with his father in prison and his mother in the hospital. Ramon desperately wants to win a place in Harpo's gang, whose members are reluctant to accept him because he is too good in school and too fond of writing words down in the little notebook he carries in his pocket with his knife. To prove his worth to the gang, Ramon agrees to rip off an old man in a wheelchair who was seen with a lot of money on him.

Yet when Ramon gets the man at knifepoint in his apartment, he is surprised when the man screams at him that all he has are his paintings. As Ramon looks around at the dozens of paintings lining the walls and stacked in the corners, his eyes are assaulted by their rich, bright colors, and he can't help saying what he thinks [read from page 43, or page 32 in the paperback]:

"That one there." Ramon pointed with his knife at a bright yellow-and-red painting. "And over there. That's good stuff. Yeah. You know what that stuff looks like? Like them kites in Central Park. You know? Like you look at the sky and there's something there you don't expect. The sky is all full of surprises. And that's what your paintings are, they're all—"

"Say that again!" Glasser leaned forward in his wheelchair.

"Huh?"

"What you just said."

"I don't know what I said."

"The sky is . . . "

"Oh. You mean, like the sky is full of surprises? Them kites . . . ?"

"Since you're not going to kill me yet," Glasser continued, "I'll tell you something. What you just said is as good as any of those paintings. Better! Do you understand?"

Ramon does not understand what is so great about kites and surprises, but that begins an unlikely friendship between a faded old artist who remembers what it was like to be famous and a street punk who doesn't yet know that he is an artist with words.

—Cathi Edgerton

THE SILENT VOICE   YA
By JULIA CUNNINGHAM

Ice covered the littered streets and sidewalks of Paris in that early winter dawn, and the wind stirred a ragged scrap of material atop a bony mound huddled against the wall. Suddenly a girl rounded the corner and stopped short. "Mon Dieu! There's been a murder!" she screamed. Her fellow street urchins—Jerome, François and Thomas— came quickly, ready to rob the corpse until Astair stopped them—the boy was in fact alive. She insisted that they bring him to that cellar room in an abandoned hovel that Astair called home, although the boys were convinced that the stranger could not live. Even so, they pitied the poor form as they laid him on Astair's ragged mattress, for they too had experienced starvation and misery in times not too long past. They soon left to sing for their supper in front of the factory gate. Astair stayed behind to care for her new charge. As she removed his coat, she discovered a small box of red velvet. Maybe she could sell whatever was inside for enough to buy herself a new pair of shoes to replace the newspaper-stuffed ones that she now wore. Imagine her surprise and joy when she found that the box contained a gold medallion with a sapphire in its center! What a find! How could such a boy possess such a treasure? Maybe the boy could tell her. He stirred at her touch. Astair quickly closed the box as the boy spoke to her with his eyes. She placed the box in his hands and closed his fingers around it. In response to his faint smile, Astair told him how she and her friends had found him nearly frozen to death, and she asked him who he was and where he had gotten the box that had been pinned to his shirt. Only silence met her questions at first. Then the boy moved his hand over his mouth to indicate that he could not talk. Astair gave him a bit of soup warmed over a can of Sterno and explained how she and the three others managed to live by performing on street corners, pilfering from markets, and running errands to keep their stomachs at least half-filled. Finishing the last drop of his soup, the boy pulled an imaginary pen from the air and began to write on paper that wasn't there. Astair laughed at his cleverness and brought him a stub of chalk to write on the floor, explaining that she could read—a little. He spelled out his name in seven round letters: AUGUSTE. Astair told Auguste that he didn't have to tell her where he had gotten the box but that he'd better keep it hidden. She too had to go out and help perform for their supper. As she left the cellar, she gazed back at someone so frail that he was close to being no person at all, and yet she sensed in him a power unlike any she had ever known.

How did Auguste get that medal to which he clung as to life itself? Was he more than he appeared to be? Would that strange power that Astair sensed in him make itself known? Read *The Silent Voice,* by Julia Cunningham.

—*E. Lynn Porter*

SIXTEEN   YA
Ed. by DONALD R. GALLO

Almost every school has a bully who roams the halls searching for smaller, weaker kids to pick on. In this particular school, it was Monk Kluttner, who led Kluttner's Kobras. They ran the school for him: you had to get a pass to do *everything,* even walk down the hall or go to the restroom. The school was Monk's personal Garden of Eden. The only trouble was, he didn't see the serpent till it was too late. Monk's serpent was a girl named Priscilla Roseberry. She wasn't the sort of person who should have that name at all. She was the biggest student in high school. Not fat, mind you, just big, and even beautiful, in a bionic way. She was basically a loner, but her best friend was a guy named Melvin Detweiler, who was close to the smallest guy in school. He was really nice—but *little.* They even had lockers next to each other.

If anyone was unaware of the Kobras, it was Priscilla—they were simply beneath her notice. That is, until one day after school, when she and Melvin were getting their coats out of their lockers. A Kobra slithered up, slammed Melvin against his locker, and demanded his pass. Priscilla turned, put on her coat, and karate-chopped the Kobra with her enormous hand. "Who's your leader, wimp?" "Monk Kluttner." "Never heard of him—send him to me."

Pretty soon Monk slid up. "Who is it around here doesn't know Monk Kluttner?" "Never heard of him." "Kid," Monk replied, reaching for Melvin, "You're gonna have to educate your girlfriend."

His hands never quite made it to Melvin. Priscilla caught him in a gigantic hammerlock, his neck popping, his eyes bulging—and with a single mighty thrust forward, frog-marched Monk into her own locker. It was incredible—his boots clicked once in the air, and he was gone, neatly wedged in—a perfect fit. Priscilla slammed the door, twirled the lock, and she and Melvin strolled out of school.

"Well, this was where fate, an even bigger force than Priscilla, stepped in." It snowed all that night, a blizzard. The whole town iced up. And school closed for a week.

"Priscilla and the Wimps," by Richard Peck, is only one of the hilarious or tragic or surprising or romantic stories you'll find in this book— there are fifteen more of them.

—Joni Bodart

SLAKE'S LIMBO   Grades 6-8
By FELICE HOLMAN

Aremis Slake is the kind of person everyone picks on. He's small, wears glasses, and can't join any gangs because he always gets sick when he tries to smoke. Not belonging to a gang is bad news in the tough section of New York City where Slake lives; it means you're always the one who gets bullied and beaten up. Slake is too small to fight back, so he has to rely on his speed to protect himself. When he's attacked, he runs through alleys and passageways until he can duck into the nearest subway station and hide there. Usually, he ends up spending the rest of the day riding the trains around New York while he waits for things to cool down in his neighborhood.

One day things go particularly badly for Slake. Some bullies take away his brand new sweater, and when he climbs a tree in the park, an old lady spots him and calls the police. Slake dashes for the nearest subway station but doesn't have any money in his pocket, so he sneaks under the turnstile. Now the station attendant is after him, too. There's only one place left to run—down the tracks and into the tunnels where the trains go. He manages to escape from his pursuers, but he can't stay on the track or he'll get run over by a train, so he hunts around until he finds a hole in the wall, sort of like a small cave. He climbs in, and after a while, he realizes that he doesn't want to go back to the jungle that waits for him aboveground—so he doesn't. For the next 121 days,

Slake lives underground in the NYC subway system. *Slake's Limbo* tells how he managed to survive, and what finally brought him out again.

—*Richard Russo*

THE SNARKOUT BOYS AND THE AVOCADO OF DEATH   YA
By DANIEL MANUS PINKWATER

Walter can't believe that Genghis Khan High School is so boring, nauseating, stupid, and generally crummy. Like, he has this English teacher, Mrs. Macmillan, who hates Jews. Years ago she used to make speeches about Jews in her classroom, so this tradition got started: every semester kids who aren't Jewish and kids who are, but don't have them, borrow Jewish stars to wear around their necks in Mrs. Macmillan's class. It's fun to watch her panic when she walks in the first day and realizes she's facing yet another all-Jewish class. She believes they're creeping around plotting the end of civilization, and all those stars make her crazy.

Walter thinks he'll go crazy too at Genghis Khan—until he meets Winston Bongo, the creative, genius inventor of Snarking Out.

Snarking Out involves sneaking out of the house very late at night, getting on the Snark Street bus and going to the Snark Theater. The Snark Theater is open twenty-four hours round the clock, and shows a different double feature every day. It shows bizarre movies in strange combinations, like *Vampires in a Deserted Seaside Hotel at the End of August* (in Yugoslavian with subtitles) along with *Gidget Goes Hawaiian.*

Winston Bongo holds the world's record for the most successful completed Snark Outs—or he thinks he does, until they meet Rat.

Rat is a natural-born Snarker. She's been snarking for years. She invites Walter and Winston to her house for breakfast to meet her Uncle Flipping H. Terwilliger, another Snarker from way back. Uncle Flipping also happens to be a Mad Scientist. Uncle Flipping is in charge of Research and Development for Bullfrog Industries—the company that makes Bullfrog Root Beer. Mad scientists—really mad ones—aren't that easy to come by. Plenty of companies don't have one, so Bullfrog feels lucky. Uncle Flipping right now is working on the development of an avocado that will grow in the coldest climate.

Walter's father loves avocados (really has this *thing* about them!) and Walter mentions this to Uncle Flipping.

"You're Theobald Galt's boy," says Uncle Flipping. "I know your father well. . . . He has very advanced ideas about avocados!"

Then Uncle Flipping remembers that he has a photograph of Walter's father and a prize avocado. "I'll run upstairs and get it," he said. He never comes down again.

That's how Walter gets involved in a weird adventure involving extraterrestrials, the licensed real estate brokers of the world, a performing chicken, avocados, and the most dastardly, most evil master criminal in the world, Wallace Nussbaum, who does things with egg foo young too horrible to tell.

—Martha Pillow

SO YOU WANT TO BE A WIZARD Grades 5-9
By DIANE DUANE

"My problem," Nita thought, running as fast as she could, "is that I can't keep my mouth shut." When Joanne had asked Nita what she thought of her new bike, Nita had told her. Actually, she'd told Joanne what she thought of *her*—and it wasn't flattering! Now she'd been running for several blocks, and Joanne and her gang were going to catch up with her any minute. She'd have another black eye, and another hassle at home. Her family couldn't figure out why she wouldn't fight back.

Suddenly she spotted the library—it was open late on Saturday. Sanctuary! Mrs. Lesser looked up as she came through the door gasping for breath. "Downstairs—I'll get rid of them for you." Nita dashed down to the children's library and then, while she waited for Joanne to leave, began to prowl around among the shelves, looking for old friends she'd read before. As she ran her hand along the spines of the books, she was suddenly caught by one of the titles—*So You Want To Be a Wizard*. "It must be a joke," she thought—but Nita soon discovered that it was quite the opposite, when she tried her first spell. She met Kit, another novice wizard, and an intelligent, telepathic, flickering spark of light that they thought was probably a white hole that had lost its mass. Because, you see, by opening the book and repeating the Oath of Power Nita and Kit had helped let magic loose in the world—and they were part of magic now. Nita, Kit, and their world would never be the same!

So You Want To Be a Wizard. . . . find out what happens when you are!

—Joni Bodart

SOMETHING'S WAITING FOR YOU, BAKER D.
by PATRICIA WINDSOR

Grades 6–8/YA

Is something waiting for Baker Dilloway? He certainly thinks so. He's convinced that the Slynacks are waiting for him, and he's been keeping a log of suspicious activities that he attributes to the Slynacks. He keeps this log locked inside his desk drawer. So far he's figured out this much about the Slynacks: they come from outer space, they like dark narrow spaces where there aren't too many people, and they can change shapes and slip through cracks. He's not sure yet whether they ever appear in human form. Baker feels pretty safe in his room because he has it Slynack-proofed. He has strips of garlic putty in the window cracks and also in the cracks of the desk drawer where the Slynack activity log is kept. He even has an electric alarm rigged up around his bed so that he will have extra protection when he's asleep. Whenever Baker leaves the apartment building, he prefers to climb out the window and go down the fire escape so he can avoid the narrow hallways.

Baker is right about one thing: someone *is* following him. Mary is following him. She's a girl about his age and one of her favorite pastimes is following interesting-looking people in the hopes that she will witness something exciting. She finds Baker particularly interesting because of the way he acts: he avoids doorways, crosses and recrosses the street—he really acts paranoid. Mary follows him around and somehow develops this protective feeling about him, so when she notices that others are following too she tries to warn him about it. This really freaks him out. He doesn't want to hear what she's telling him and moves on toward the school. Mary is quite upset by the encounter, and feels that she really made a mistake talking to him, but she just happens to still be watching him when he reaches the school.

She sees the car pull up, Baker walk over to it and disappear into it. The car takes off fast, running the light at the intersection. How Mary wants to get to the bottom of this. What is this paranoid kid's story? Who was the strange man following him? Did she just see him kidnapped? Go along with Mary and find out if something really is waiting for Baker D.

—*Bonnie Janssen*

SOONER OR LATER   Grades 6–8
By BRUCE and CAROLE HART

Jessie Walters was about to get caught. Or was she? Surely there had to be a way out of this lie. She had first seen him, Michael Skye, last week at the mall playing his guitar with a band. Gosh, she and her best friend Carolyn could have missed him. They'd been at the makeup counter while Jessie got a free lesson. Eyes, blush, lipstick, the works. "You look sixteen," the saleslady had said. She'd stood in front of the band and watched only him for twenty minutes. He was wonderful— tall, blond, a senior at one of the high schools, and seventeen.

Life was funny. Who would have thought when she went for her first guitar lesson that he would be her instructor? He liked her right away. By the second lesson, he asked her to go to the show. Her, Jessie Walters—short, brunette, an eighth-grader at JFK Junior High, and thirteen. But that makeup lesson did make her look sixteen: at least he believed her when she said "sixteen" with a gulp. He was so wonderful. Age doesn't matter in a relationship. Does it?

Sooner or Later, by Bruce and Carole Hart.

—Dee Scrogin

STAIRWAY TO DOOM   Grades 1–2
By ROBERT QUACKENBUSH

Miss Mallard is a world-famous ducktective, who arrives at Duckinbill Castle to hear the will of her great aunt Abby. As she enters the castle, lightning rips across the sky and there are terrible crashes of thunder. Thirteen relatives have come to hear the will, which is very simple. They must all try to stay in the castle for one night—Warning: BEWARE OF COUNT KISSCULA. Aunt Abby's castle had once belonged to Count Kisscula, a terrible kisspire. He hunted for victims when the moon was full—and if there's one thing that ducks absolutely hate, it's to be kissed. As the lawyer leaves, the storm is still raging outside, but when they all go to their rooms, the thunder and lightning stop—and then they notice that Aunt Effie has disappeared! The sky begins to clear and a full moon appears. As the clock strikes midnight, ear-piercing quacks are heard—the Eider sisters have seen the kisspire! Soon there is another disappearance, and a strange discovery in the library. When at last Miss Mallard discovers a hidden staircase, she doesn't know if it's a stairway to doom—or to the terrible Count Kisscula!

—Elizabeth Overmyer

STARVING FOR ATTENTION   YA/Adult
By CHERRY BOONE O'NEILL

"I thought I had to be perfect—and I nearly killed myself trying." For
ten years Cherry struggled with anorexia nervosa, a disease that causes
people to starve themselves to death—and twenty percent of those who
suffer from this disease do indeed die of it. Cherry is one of the lucky
ones, but her story is so bizarre it almost seems like fiction.

It began when she was thirteen, 5´7˝, and weighed 140 pounds. She
couldn't fasten her school uniform and embarked on a diet-and-
exercise program that gradually took control of her whole life. She exer-
cised four hours a day and ate only one small meal at night—the only
one she "couldn't get out of." She weighed only ninety-two pounds
when her parents discovered how thin she was—"I can see your bones
through your clothes, Cherry!" Clothes, at that moment, meant a heavy
sweatshirt and sweatpants. That's how the battle began. For the next
ten years, Cherry lived in a world of threats, spankings, tears, reproach-
es, and guilt from first her parents and then her husband. Her self-
hatred grew as she realized she was no longer in control—her disease
controlled her. She was in the grip of an emotional octopus with tenta-
cles on every part of her life. She couldn't escape even after she had decided she wanted to! By then, she only weighed eighty pounds, and no
one could convince her to gain! But then a new person entered the picture, and it began to look as if there might be hope after all.

A special story of a special woman—*Starving for Attention.*

—Joni Bodart

STEFFIE CAN'T COME OUT TO PLAY   YA
By FRAN ARRICK

Well, I did it. I ran away from home tonight. I know it's the start of
a new life for me. My heart hasn't stopped pounding since the minute
I knew what I had to do. There's so much out there waiting for me! I've
got to grab it while I'm young. I don't want to look like Mama at forty-
two, doing other people's laundry, or Anita, always home now since her
husband ran off. I'm going to have a career. A great career. And I'm
going to be appreciated.

My dreams aren't just dreams. I'm going to be a famous fashion
model. People will pay attention to me. They'll know my name. People
who don't live in a world of washing and cleaning and baby-sitting and
complaining.

I have nine dollars with me. I'm not sure where I'll sleep tonight. Sure, I've got to find a job until I'm discovered. But it shouldn't take long. My cheekbones are my best feature. And when I put my hair up, I don't look fourteen. New York is big, but it's going to be easy and wonderful, just like I planned. Someone will have *big* plans for me, I just know.

And someone did have plans for her, just as soon as she got off the bus. To find out what they were, read *Steffie Can't Come Out to Play,* by Fran Arrick.

—Dee Scrogin

STEPHEN KING: THE ART OF DARKNESS   Adult/YA
By DOUGLAS E. WINTER

Did you ever wonder what he was *really* like? Who he was, the man behind all those hair-raising, bloodcurdling horror stories? The one who created Carrie, the Trashcan Man, Traveling Jack, Christine? Who thought of the Mangler, the Mist, the Shining, the Talisman, and the Pet Sematary?

He's tall, hulking, and seems almost brooding when he's not laughing, something he does a lot. He has broad shoulders, shaggy dark hair that seldom looks combed, dark-rimmed glasses, and during the winter a full black beard. He watches—observes—and he listens—and I mean *really* listens. How do I know? Because the year *Cujo* and *Danse Macabre* came out, I met Stephen King. Or rather, I finally met him in person, and we talked about his passion for beer, my kelly-green–rimmed glasses, and I acquired a copy of *Danse Macabre* signed "Love, Steve King." But I'd really met Stephen King years before, on a chilly, windy fall night in 1973 when I took home a galley copy of *Carrie* to review for the magazine I wrote for. I thought it was going to be just another high school novel, and by the time I realized differently, it was too late. I was hooked. I finished it almost without moving. Then I had to relock all the doors and windows and turn on every single light before I dared to take a shower and wash my hair. It was waist length, and took a lot of water, but I couldn't even bring myself to close the shower doors, so I spent what seemed like hours mopping up afterwards. Then I went to bed—with the closet light on, to make sure no bogey-persons could creep out and pounce on me. I don't sleep with the light on anymore, but I *do* make sure the covers are tucked in and no feet or hands stick out—there may be a clammy-handed *thing* just waiting to grab me!

Obviously, I'm a King fan—and this new analysis of his life and work is fascinating. In addition to Steve King's own account of why and how he wrote his books and short stories, Winter gives details of his life, has the only interview that King will ever do on *Pet Sematary*—why he said he'd never publish it and why he finally did—and gives glimpses of what's next—like *It*—"where I pull out all the stoppers." Meet the man behind the books—loud, intense, beer-drinking; with a custom-made fence of bats, cobwebs, and spiders around his house; who still checks under his own bed before he climbs in at night!

—Joni Bodart

STILLWATCH YA/Adult
By MARY HIGGINS CLARK

"I don't want to punish you. Don't make me do it. Forget your television program on Senator Abigail Jennings. Remember, the Lord said, 'Whoever harms one of these, my little ones, better he be drowned in the sea.'"

The phone connection went dead.

After the shock, Pat decided it was only a crank call. Probably some wacko who thought women belonged in the kitchen, and not in public office.

Pat Traymore, a talented young television journalist, was about to break into the powerful world of Washington, DC, politics with a documentary series called *Women in Government*.

Pat had come home to Washington, back to her house for the first time since that awful night so long ago.

For a long time now, bits and pieces of memory had intruded on her like wreckage from a ship. In the past year, she had had persistent dreams of being a small child again—in this house—awakening in an agony of fear—trying to scream and being unable to utter a sound. Coupled with this fear was a pervading sense of loss.

The truth is in this house, Pat thought. It was here that it had happened.

Lurid headlines flashed through her mind.

"Wisconsin Congressman, Dean Adams, murders beautiful wife and then commits suicide. Their three-year-old daughter, beaten by her father, fights for life." Later headlines told of the death of that daughter after months of lying in a hospital in a coma.

Pat Traymore was that child.

What could she remember? What had she seen?

This call. Was it just a crank call? Or was it something to do with that night?

Perhaps someone was violently angry with Senator Jennings—the lady who was to become the first woman Vice-President of the United States.

What did I see that night? Why can't I remember?

I remember sitting at the top of the stairs. I heard Mommy and Daddy arguing and then there were loud noises. I ran down the stairs and into the living room. I screamed, "Daddy, Daddy!" I tripped over my mother's body . . . there was blood all over the floor . . . I looked up. . . .

Stillwatch, by Mary Higgins Clark.

—*Linda Henderson*

THE STRANGE THING THAT HAPPENED Grades 1-2
TO OLIVER WENDELL ISCOVITCH
By HELEN KRONBERG OLSON

Oliver Wendell Iscovitch had the pinkest, roundest cheeks of anyone, anywhere. He had been told that often enough. By Mama, by Daddy, by Grandma. And even by strangers. He knew it was true, but he didn't know what else it meant until the day he went to the supermarket and saw the box of Goody Woody cereal with a free gift in it. And when his mother wouldn't buy it for him, he began to hold his breath—and he held it, and he held it. Now if anyone else held his breath that long he might burst or collapse or at least get a headache. But because Oliver Wendell Iscovitch had the fattest, roundest cheeks of anyone, anywhere, he didn't burst. He didn't even get a headache. Instead something very strange happened. Suddenly, just like that, his cheeks puffed out like two pink balloons. And then, very slowly, his feet left the floor, and he floated up until he was bumping against the supermarket ceiling like a balloon. As soon as he opened his mouth, all the air whooshed out of him and down he fell—right into the bananas. And that night, Oliver Wendell Iscovitch told Mama and Daddy he was sorry and would never do that again. But then came the emergencies— there was the emergency with the baby birds, and the emergency with the jumping contest in the park. Oliver Wendell flew when he had to, and each time he got a little better, until he was good enough to tackle the biggest emergency of all—the robbers and the raging bull!

—*Elizabeth Overmyer*

STRANGER WITH MY FACE YA
By LOIS DUNCAN

Talk 1

It all started the summer Laurie Stratton turned sixteen. It had been a very good summer for Laurie. She had finally gotten a figure *and* a boyfriend, and was really looking forward to school in the fall. She was also looking forward to the last party of the season, a dinner dance given by her friend Natalie, but at the last minute Laurie came down with a virus and had to stay home. She was fine the next morening, but the kids at school avoided her as if she'd had the plague. When she finally found Natalie, she asked her what was wrong. "If you didn't want to come to my party, Laurie, you could have just said so—you didn't have to sneak around. You weren't sick. I saw you on the beach last night with some guy." Laurie finally convinced Natalie it must have been a case of mistaken identity.

When Laurie got home, she had a funny feeling when she entered her room—she sensed someone had just been in there. (You know the funny feeling you get when someone is sneaking up behind you.) More and more, Laurie felt that someone was watching her; someone who looked just like her; someone who wanted something from her. A sixth sense told her the someone was evil.

Lois Duncan writes books you may not want to read when you're all alone at night. This one may make you hesitate to look into your own mirror.

—*Diana Hirsch*

Talk 2

Laurie didn't know what was happening to her, but she didn't like it, whatever it was. It started when she got the impression that someone was spying on her—even going into her bedroom when she wasn't there. Then her friends said they had seen her places where she hadn't been, doing things she hadn't done. Her boyfriend said he'd seen her with another boy. Laurie came to realize that another Laurie, from another place, was trying to take over her life. The first time she saw this other Laurie, this evil Laurie, was in a mirror. She looked in a mirror one day and saw her reflection. Her reflection began to smile— but Laurie wasn't smiling.

—*Roger Carswell*

SUMMER TO DIE   YA
By LOIS LOWRY

Meg and Molly are sisters. Molly is sixteen, with long blonde hair. She's a cheerleader, popular, and makes friends easily. When the family moves, Molly is immediately accepted as a member of the cheerleading squad, acquires a boyfriend, and quickly becomes part of the school scene.

Meg is fourteen, with brown hair and glasses. She is shy and finds it hard to make friends. Her adjustment to the new school is difficult.

In the new house, they have to share a room, which causes problems because Meg is a slob and Molly is neat. The two girls get along the way many sisters do—they love each other but fight all the time, over the dishes, their room, etc.

Their parents treat them alike and are generally quite fair, but gradually Meg notices that they are taking Molly's side more and more. Molly's personality is also gradually changing—she's grouchy, sleeps a lot more. She has dropped out of extracurricular activities and is missing a lot of school.

At the beginning of the summer, Molly wakes Meg up one night. "Go get Dad, quick." When Meg turns the light on, Molly's face, hair, and bed are covered with blood. Molly is put in the hospital. Now Meg knows something is really wrong.

—Marion Hargrove

SUNFLOWER FOREST   YA
By TOREY L. HAYDEN

Leslie's mother isn't like other mothers. When she is well, she's vibrant, creative, full of stories about her childhood in Wales, and even a little wacky. But more and more, the memories of the dark years of World War II close in around her, every day driving her closer to insanity.

She had been sent to college in Germany just before the war started. Then the Nazi regime took over completely. Because of her intelligence and her Aryan good looks, she was sent to Ravensbrück, a breeding hospital. She was kept locked in one small room and allowed almost nothing to read, write, or do. Every night, she was raped by one or more SS members, over and over and over, until she got pregnant. Then as soon as her child was born, it started again. She bore two sons, both of whom were almost immediately taken from her to be raised by the Nazis.

This is the past Mara can't escape, that haunts her—and now her family. She's always reaching out for happiness and never finding it. She's always searching for her two lost sons, who stay eternally young in her mind.

No matter where the family is, peace of mind is always just over the *next* hill. Nowhere suits Mara for long. She wants to live where it's cooler—or warmer; the country—or in the middle of town. She wants flowers in January, lots of them—a forest of flowers.

Because of Mara, the family live like gypsies. Leslie hates the moves, the discouraging routine of leaving friends and having to make new ones, always knowing she'll have to leave them, too, sooner or later. She wants a normal life, so she can concentrate on her senior year in high school, on getting into college, and on her relationship with Paul. Her biggest fear is that Mara's condition will force the family to move again before she graduates.

But in the end, moving would have been far less agonizing for Leslie *and* Mara than the tragedy of what happened instead.

—*Joni Bodart*
—*Judy Druse*

SWEET BELLS JANGLED OUT OF TUNE   YA
By ROBIN F. BRANCATO

The people of Windsor tolerate Eva Dohrmann because she was once wealthy and respected. But lately, Eva's behavior has grown unbelievably eccentric: she wears gaudy hats and a fur cape straight through the summer; drives battered though once stylish cars stuffed with other people's junk and garbage; hoards these things in her run-down mansion; and strolls through local restaurants sweeping tips right off the tables into her purse. Rumor is that she collects things so she'll be prepared when the end of the world comes. Lots of rumors and stories are circulated about Eva. According to one, she was once the most beautiful woman in Windsor. According to another, she's hiding something terrible in her run-down East Windsor Mansion. Little kids run from her; teenagers joke about her and tell gruesome stories about her mysterious past. But for Ellen Dohrmann, Eva is no laughing matter . . . because Eva is Ellen's grandmother.

But Ellen, who is now fifteen, is not allowed to see Eva anymore. She defies her mother's orders to stay away and takes her best friend, Josie, with her to investigate the truth behind the gossip and perhaps rescue Eva from what sounds like a deteriorating situation. But the terrible reality of what Eva has become is a shock Ellen never expected. Now Ellen is forced to recognize Eva Dohrmann as she is today—no longer the gentle grandmother she once knew so well, but a grave responsibility that no one wants to face. But Eva's bizarre lifestyle cannot continue. She is putting herself in real danger. Sooner or later, someone will have to step in. Can Ellen do it?

—*Judy Druse*

A TASTE OF BLACKBERRIES   Grades 4-6
By DORIS BUCHANAN SMITH

What's it like to be dead?

Jamie is my best friend in the whole world. He can beat me at just about anything, but I don't care—not really. We like to race each other to the creek, climb trees, steal apples from the farmers' orchards, skip rocks, and laugh—but most of all, we like to eat summer blackberries till we're sick.

Once Jamie and I were hiding from our friend, Heather. We ran into a big blackberry patch and it didn't take us long to start stuffing ourselves with the sweet berries. Heather never did find us, but, boy, were we ever sick that night!

I remember all the fun we had, but I remember *that* day, too. Jamie was jumping up and down and waving his arms as the bees swarmed all around him.

"It's your own fault," I told him. "You should've been scraping the Japanese beetles off the grapevines and putting them into the jars like Heather and me, instead of poking that ol' stick down a bee hole."

Jamie kept on screaming and jumping up and down. Then he fell down and started to roll on the ground. At first I laughed at Jamie; then he made me mad. I was sick of all his clowning around. That's when I decided to go home.

Today the only thing I want to do is to sit here in Mrs. Mullins' yard and watch the butterflies. They're alive; the flowers—the trees—the birds—Mrs. Mullins—me. We're all alive.

Jamie's dead. He will never laugh or send Morse code messages or taste summer blackberries again. They say he looks like he's sleeping, but I know better. They can't fool me. Jamie isn't sleeping—he's dead.

What's it like to be dead?

A Taste of Blackberries, by Doris Buchanan Smith.

—*Cheryl Ress*

THEM THAT GLITTER AND THEM THAT DON'T   YA
By BETTE GREENE

Talk 1

"In a land where no one ever goes, where water never flows, there lives a flower, one wild, wild flower. People ask, Can this be so? but only the flower, the wild, wild flower, really knows. Yes, it really knows!"

Carol Ann Delaney wrote this song, and the wild flower she sings of is herself. You see, Carol Ann is the daughter of a thieving gypsy fortuneteller and a drunken father, and like the wild flower in her song, she has had to thrive and blossom on her own strength. And it hasn't been easy.

Although Carol Ann is intelligent, talented, and determined to make something of herself with her music, her mother is equally determined to hold Carol Ann to the gypsy ways. She tries to discourage her daughter's ambitions by predicting failure and death for Carol Ann if she breaks with gypsy tradition. Although Carol Ann's childhood faith in her mother's ability to read the future has diminished over the years, she still finds herself torn between her old belief in gypsy magic and her new belief in herself.

Her struggle and her decision are in *Them That Glitter and Them That Don't,* by Bette Greene.

—*Sherry Cotter*

Talk 2

Carol Ann Delaney is the daughter of the town drunk and the town crazy. Her papa, nicknamed Painter when he worked for the highway department painting the line down the middle of the highway, is a drunk and a weak man dominated by his wife. Mama Delaney is a gypsy fortuneteller and inventor of money-making schemes that invariably fail. Carol Ann no longer believes in her mama's crystal-ball prophecies. Her mama will never forgive Carol Ann for letting go of make-believe, and Carol Ann will never forgive her mama for hanging on to it. She needs Mama to be a mother, a caring, seeing-to-everything, taking-charge mother. But half the time, Mama is just one of the kids herself, and that goes double for Papa.

Carol Ann's natural-born talent for making music may be her only ticket out of her poverty-stricken life in Bainesville, Arkansas, with her irresponsible parents She clings to a secret dream of becoming a famous star of country/western music, using the name Carlotta Dell. Her best friend is her guitar. She writes and sings music to show folks what it feels like to see what she sees and feels. She wants to *be* somebody, but she cannot get her parents to understand that having something is not the same as being something.

The applause Carol Ann hears in her heart is nothing like the sneers of "Little Gyp!" that she hears in the corridors of Bainesville High School. Being a gypsy means belonging to the most put-down, put-upon people on the face of the earth. She always has to be fighting, fighting and tearing other people off her back. She would settle for being treated decently. Then one day, unexpectedly, Carol Ann is asked to sing in front of the whole school, and the roars of approval become real for the first time. And this time the spotlight feels just right.

As graduation approaches, everybody's pulling Carol Ann in different directions. Will Bellows, the handsome and cocky farmer's son, offers to marry Carol Ann so she can "settle down and have a decent life for a change." Mama's crystal ball reveals no stardom in her daughter's future, just a lot of heartache for having such highfalutin' ideas. Only Jean McCaffrey, her music teacher, recognizes Carol Ann's special gift. She says Carol Ann has not only the talent to go far but also the discipline. Mrs. McCaffrey gives Carol Ann the formal training she needs, and the caring she's never known.

Although Carol Ann figures she's got about one chance in a million of making it big in Nashville, the part of her that's Carlotta Dell feels differently, because Carlotta Dell knows beyond any doubt that there's just no end to the songs she can write or the notes she can reach.

—Judy Druse

THERE IS A CARROT IN MY EAR   Grades K–3
AND OTHER NOODLE TALES
By ALVIN SCHWARTZ

A noodle is a very silly person, and this book is about a whole family of noodles and the silly things they say and do. They are Mr. and Mrs. Brown, their children Sam and Jane, and Grandpa. Mr. Brown shouts at his underwear and throws tomatoes at it. Grandpa tries to hatch a baby horse from a pumpkin.And when Sam and Jane go camping, they run into some very strange mosquitoes. Altogether there are six noodle tales about the noodle-head Browns in this book: *There is a Carrot in my Ear and Other Noodle Tales.*

—Zoë Kalkanis

THINGS ARE SELDOM WHAT THEY SEEM   YA
By SANDY ASHER

Debbie Palmero is nervous about starting high school. Grade school wasn't bad, but junior high was the pits. When you aren't an athlete or beautiful, it's hard to make it in junior high. Being smart doesn't count in junior high. To make matters worse, her popular big sister Maggie, who might have helped her get used to high school, has become distant and aloof. This has been going on ever since Maggie became involved with the Drama Club and with its sponsor, Mr. Caraway, her idol.

Things start out even worse than Debbie expects when her best friend Karen also becomes involved in the drama group and starts to imitate Maggie's aloofness. Both of them have a terrific crush on Mr. Caraway. Feeling more alone than ever, Debbie suddenly finds herself becoming friends with another outsider. Murray Gordon turns out to be one of the smartest kids in school, and six inches shorter than Debbie. Before long, they are such good friends that none of that matters anymore.

High school is going fairly well for Debbie, until Karen resigns from one of the lead parts in the school play just two weeks before the scheduled performance. Debbie asks her old friend what happened—and is stunned by Karen's answer. . . .

—Barbara Lynn

THE THIRD EYE   YA
By LOIS DUNCAN

Seven-year-old Bobby Zenner disappeared. Later, under police questioning, Karen Connors, eighteen, pinpointed it sometime between noon and one o'clock. Karen had been baby-sitting the Zenner children since ten that morning. Bobby and two of his friends spent the morning tearing around the house like mad things, engaged in one noisy game after another. Finally, around noon, she had sent them all outside to run off energy and to give her some peace to feed the baby lunch. When she called Bobby for lunch about one, he was nowhere to be found. Karen's immediate reaction to Bobby's disappearance had been more one of exasperation than worry; in spite of his promise not to leave the yard, he had evidently moved on to some other play area with his friends. It wasn't as though there was anything to really worry over; disappearing was a common childhood occurrence. Karen decided that if Bobby was old enough to wander, he was old enough to come home. But when Bobby didn't come home, Karen became concerned. She tracked down his playmates, who told her they had been playing hide-and-seek but they couldn't find Bobby; he had hid too good. He didn't even show up when they called Ally-ally in free. The police feared Bobby had been kidnapped, but Karen had a vision of him caught in a box. How could she feel so certain about this? She couldn't offer any explanation for this vision of Bobby in a confined space with his knees drawn tight against his chest; she saw him with an inner eye. Through the years she had learned to accept without question knowledge that came to her in this abrupt and chilling manner, because experience had taught her that it was always right. And right she was again. Bobby was found, unconscious but alive, trapped in the trunk of a car he had crawled into while playing hide-and-seek. Karen was glad when that day was over.

However, the day's events had repercussions. The newspaper article detailing the incident reported that the child had been found with the help of a psychic. Almost immediately, parents around the country began calling to see if Karen Connors could help them find their missing children. But the vision of Bobby had come to Karen of its own accord, springing effortlessly into her mind. Accepting a spontaneous revelation from her third eye was one thing, but deliberately trying to create one was something else. But Ronald Wilson, a young police officer, convinced Karen to use her powers to locate another missing child. This time her efforts would result in a tragedy that would be a part of her until the end of her life.

—Judy Druse

THIS FAMILY OF WOMEN   Adult
By RICHARD PECK

It was a family of women—women related to each other by blood, by circumstance, by necessity.

Lena was the first. She came from nowhere, adopted as an infant by Frank Wheatley and his wife. A neighboring family had died of diphtheria, leaving only a baby girl as a survivor. They called her Lena, and when she was fourteen, they started out for California. She tells her story first—of hardship, of nights in the wagon, the morning her foster-mother died, and of the day her best friends, Sarah Anne and Beatrice, were kidnapped by Indians. Seven years later, when Lena was married and had a baby girl, Sarah Anne came back, more Indian than white—and also pregnant by her Indian husband. But Sarah Anne didn't seem interested in caring for her child, and early California was no place for a half-breed. Lena named her, and raised Effie as her own daughter.

Effie recalls growing up in a household where she had two mothers and no mothering at all. When, as a teenager, she discovered her birthright, she left.

Her daughter, Constance, picks up the story, as Effie, now Eve Waring, goes on to become one of the world's great exotic beauties and a celebrated actress. Constance tells of her own struggle to become an architect—and the man who helped her realize her dream.

Her friend Rose continues the story of Constance's marriage and of her own, and of the contrasts between them—for Rose is now a member of the family by marriage as well as by friendship.

June, Rose's daughter, tells how she fights World War I in her own way—as a nurse.

But it is her lover, Andy, Constance's son, who finishes the tale, with his story, and that of Claire, his daughter.

The lives of these women sweep around the globe and across the centuries as they fight and love and laugh—and through it all, live to the very utmost.

Their stories, their lives, and their courage make me proud to be, in some sense, one of their descendants—part of my own, and of this, family of women.

—Joni Bodart

THE TIE THAT BINDS   YA/Adult
By KENT HARUF

I'm mad! I'm mad at Bud Sealy, who's turned out to be a real SOB. I'm mad at the laws that keep Edith Goodnough shut up in the hospital, that say she'll have to have handcuffs on her frail eighty-year-old wrists when she finally goes to trial. I'm mad at the empty life she saw no way out of, the life that led her to this mockery of a trial, at a time when she ought to be resting, looking back on all her accomplishments. But there's nothing I can do—not with Sheriff Bud Sealy, and not with Edith. Being mad is all I've got left.

Why am I so mad? What do I care about her? Well, I'm glad you asked that question and I'll tell you, but I warn you, it's a long story. I'm gonna need some more beers before I'm through—OK?

It's a hard land here. You can tell that. Farmers try to grow their crops and run their cattle on the bare, sandy hills—and it wasn't any different in the late 1800s, when Roy Goodnough brought his wife Ada from the east to homestead here. She had two children on the homestead, Edith and Lyman, and she died there. Any softness Roy might have had died with her. Years later, it was on that same farm that Roy got caught in the harvester and lost nine of his fingers. Whey they saw that, Edith and Lyman knew they were trapped—for good.

Lyman was able to get away after Pearl Harbor, but there was no way out for Edith. She never left, not even after Roy died. She never lived anywhere else. And now she's only a week away from being eighty years old. She never in her life hurt a living thing—never said no to anyone but herself, and Bud Sealy wants to put her on trial for murder. Like I said, Bud's turned into a real SOB. Too bad—he used to be a nice guy. Now I'll do anything I can to keep him away from her—to keep her safe.

Who am I? Sorry, I'm so wrapped up in this, I forget the proprieties. I'm Sanders Roscoe—Edith and I were neighbors for years. In fact, if Roy Goodnough hadn't deliberately chopped his tenth finger, Edith might have been my mother.

—Joni Bodart

TIGER EYES   YA
By JUDY BLUME

It all happened so fast, in just a few seconds it was over. Life would never be the same again—not for Davey, or her little brother, or her her mother. All that was left were headlines—"Local Man, Adam Wexler, Murdered in Store Holdup"—and the funeral (Davey couldn't even cry) and fear, fear that kept Davey and her mother from sleeping or even leaving the house. Fear that kept them from beginning again. They needed some time out to recover, and so they went to Los Alamos, New Mexico, to visit Adam's sister and her husband.

But Los Alamos wasn't the safe place they'd expected—partly because all three had brought their sorrow with them, and partly because no one could feel completely safe in a town where most of the people made a living inventing and testing bigger and better atomic weapons.

Their aunt and uncle had every minute planned out, but finally Davey had to be alone and persuaded them to leave her behind. In the desert, she found a beautiful canyon and a dark-haired boy who said his name was Wolf, and finally was able to grieve for her father.

Davey didn't know it then, but that's when she began to recover.

There are many things to be afraid of—of living or dying, staying or going, of being with other people or being alone. As Davey makes friends in Los Alamos, she begins to see that she's not the only one who's running away from something that seems too awful to face. And she also learns that sooner or later, she will have to stop running.

To see how Davey deals with running or staying, dying and living, read *Tiger Eyes*.

—*Joni Bodart*

TO TAKE A DARE YA
By CRESCENT DRAGONWAGON and PAUL ZINDEL

"Luke has been saying that I should write all this down, this whole crazy period from when I was twelve or so until now, which is sixteen. He says I've been feeling guilty about it long enough, and the best way for me to stop is to get it out of my head and down on paper. Luke is big on writing things down.

"It's so complicated. Where do I begin? Do I start in Benton? Or in Excelsior Springs? Who started all those things that snowballed into that sad mixed-up time and the mixed-up kid that Dare was and that I was?

"I don't know, though I do know where it ends—with my starting to be happy for the first time in my life, and in love, and straighter (at sixteen) then I ever, ever dreamed I'd turn out to be. It also ends with Dare, who went the other way. And there was nothing I could do for Dare, nothing but let him go.

"I will always feel sad, though, just sad, sad, sad when I think about crazy Dare with his stringy blond hair and his one wild earring. He had half the girls in Excelsior saving earrings for him. If they lost one of a pair of pierced earrings, they'd know what to do with the other—save it for Dare.

"And when I remember Dare's thirteenth birthday, which was the last time I saw him, I want to cry, still. His thirteenth birthday was even worse than mine, and mine was pretty bad.

"That seems as good a place as any to start."

On my thirteenth birthday, my dog got killed, my father called me a slut once too often, and I lost my virginity, or what was left of it.

It all started when I was twelve—the bad part, that is. Some things had always been weird—but there had been some good things too. My mother was fat—and I mean circus-lady fat—size forty-eight or more. There wasn't much we could talk about. But my father and I could talk—I'd go in the bathroom and watch him shave, or go out and watch him work on the car, and tell him about books I'd read. But then I got this figure that I didn't even know what to do with—and the boys started to notice me. And one day, my father really looked at me and decided I was too old to watch him shave. After that, he hardly spoke to me, except to yell. What with my dad at home and the boys at school, I began to change. I wasn't sweet little Chrissie any longer, in shirtwaist dresses and penny loafers, who never said boo to anyone. I was Chris—tough, cold—with a hard outside that didn't show how scared I was inside. I wore jeans, as tight as I could get into, tight tee shirts or sweaters—sometimes with a string of beads just long enough so that the end dangled off into space. And lots of makeup, especially eye makeup—so much that even my spaced-out mother noticed! That made my father hassle me even more. The only time I could be real was with my dog. He was the only one who loved me.

Then I came home from school on my thirteenth birthday, found out that my dog had been run over by a car—my father called me a slut once more—and I decided, why not?! My reputation says I do it, my father's sure of it, my mother doesn't care—why not?

So that night I lost my virginity. It wasn't at all what I'd expected, but I guess somehow I thought it might change me—keep me from being lonely—and that night I was so *very* lonely and alone.

—*Joni Bodart*

TRINITY'S CHILD   YA/Adult
By WILLIAM PROCHNAU

Suddenly the world is plunged into its worst nightmare: the Third World War . . . nuclear holocaust.

As the book begins, the US is picking up on radar what appears to be Russian missiles headed for the United States. The SAC Command in Omaha, Nebraska, has about thirty minutes before it will be hit and totally destroyed. Other parts of the United States have even less time, especially the East Coast and Washington, DC. The United States deploys a limited number of its missiles, that will cause comparable damage to the Soviet Union. At the same time, our B-52 bombers are alerted and sent airborne, and our nuclear submarine fleet, the heart of our nuclear defense, is put on war alert and deployed toward targets throughout the world. A second command plane is sent aloft from Omaha to join the ever-flying "Looking Glass."

After the first wave of missiles has hit both countries, a courageous American President digs his way out of the rubble. He tries to escape through the air, only to have his helicopter crash from the heat wave of the second round of missiles striking Andrews Air Force Base. As communication with him is lost, the President is considered dead, and the "chain of command" finds that the seventh person in the line of succession is the only one who can be located. He is the Secretary of the Interior, a man brought into the administration for his specific talents as a hatchet man. The fate of the entire world now rests on this man, whose pattern of making decisions does not alter in the face of this grave crisis.

A dozen of the US B-52 bombers did manage to get airborne before the first wave of missiles hit. They are heading toward the arctic, awaiting further orders. They are the US's second line of defense in a nuclear strike. The book closely follows what develops in one of these B-52s as the horror of a nuclear war closes in. In the cockpit are Kazaklis, the smart-talking, womanizing jet jockey, and Moreau, his strong-willed female copilot. Much of the time they are out of radio contact, and they have a crew that is cracking under the strain. Kazaklis and Moreau mistrust each other almost as much as they mistrust themselves in making a decision that could end the world—or save what remains.

In the twenty-one crucial hours following the nuclear exchange between the United States and the Soviet Union, the entire planet teeters on the verge of extinction. The thread of survival is held by an irrational American President giddy with ultimate power; a Russian Premier threatened by mutiny within his own government; a small town civil defense director in rural Maryland overwhelmed with what fate has suddenly thrust into his lap; an uneducated black woman and her two children who are just trying to cope with the initial horror; and the American B-52 crew who are circling the North Pole, awaiting further instructions to continue the slaughter of mankind.

—Barbara Lynn

THE TV KID　　Grades 3–5
By BETSY J. BYARS

Lennie's head is like the inside of a TV set. Commercials and game shows, *Bewitched* and *Star Trek,* run through his head every minute, even when he isn't watching the set. In real life, though, Lennie isn't very happy, living with his mother in a hotel and failing at school. So TV and daydreaming are all he wants, until he is bitten by a rattlesnake and has to survive a real-life disaster.

—Diana McRae

THE TWO-THOUSAND-POUND Grades 6–8/YA
GOLDFISH
By BETSY J. BYARS

How many of you like horror movies—really outrageous ones, like *The Blob* or *Godzilla* or *The Swarm*? Warren spends all the time he can at horror movies. Sometimes he'll stay at the theater all day, until his grandmother has to call the theater manager to send him home. And when he's not watching horror movies, he's writing them. His favorite is the one he calls *The Two-Thousand-Pound Goldfish:*

"What lives in the sewer beneath the city, weighs two thousand pounds, and wants to slurp you to death?"

And his favorite piece of dialogue is this bit from his snail movie:

"SNAILS! Millions of snails, man-eating snails! It's the slime of centuries!"

"I know, don't slip!"

But Warren's real life is not nearly as satisfying as his movies. His mother has disappeared—he hasn't seen her in three years, not since the FBI came looking for her. All his life, she had always been involved in demonstrations of all kinds: against the Vietnam War, against nuclear power plants, against the use of dangerous pesticides. But when Warren was five, she stopped demonstrating peacefully and began throwing bombs instead, and then she disappeared, and the FBI began watching their mail and tapping their phone lines in case she tried to get in touch with them. The night Warren started planning his movie on the two-thousand-pound goldfish was the night that he first suspected that his sister Weezie had been talking to their mother on the telephone. She won't tell him anything, but his Aunt Pepper finally tells him that she has spoken to their mother. Now all his practice making up outrageous plots just may come in handy, as he tries to piece together the clues of his own family's mystery!

—Elizabeth Overmyer

UNICORNS IN THE RAIN YA
By BARBARA COHEN

The weather was horrible. It had been raining for days, and Nikki wished she was anywhere except on a train, on her way to visit a grandmother she didn't want to see, and who didn't want to see her.

But then Sam sat down next to her—he was extraordinarily handsome—and he invited her home for dinner at his family's place. Nikki accepted, but almost immediately began to realize she'd gotten mixed up in something strange.

Sam didn't wear a helmet, and in a world where speed was legal and ninety-nine percent of the population was stoned seventy-five percent of the time, where murderers terrorized every city and town and even old people carried guns to defend themselves, Sam used his gun to defend someone else and didn't believe in drugs. Then Nikki met the rest of his family—all handsome, all different and all with a secret, and an urgency they wouldn't explain. Nikki was ready to go back to the station and to her grandmother's, but Sam's father persuaded her to stay. He promised to explain everything later. At dinner, a very strange thing happened: before they ate, Sam's father asked a blessing—something Nikki had never seen anyone do. She asked about this One God they prayed to, but no one could describe him, show her a picture, or even tell her his name.

The next morning at breakfast she looked at the newspaper headlines ("Thousands Starve as Famine Increases—Bankrupt Nations Lack Funds to Buy Grain Rotting in Silos"; "Sociologists Say New Renaissance Dawns—Five New Novels Published This Year"; "War Continues—203rd Month") and the ads ("a two-and-a-half-inch TV to fix on your bathroom soapdish"—but Nikki wasn't interested, there were only two or three new programs a year). Katherine, the wife of one of Sam's two older brothers, said, "Don't you feel sometimes there should be another way for the world to be, instead of like that?" Then as Nikki began to read the weather forecast ("Rain all day, no clearing trend in sight") Katherine said to Jaspar, her husband, "Nikki has to be told—she has to know! Go get Sam—he's the one to tell her." So then Sam took her outside and showed her all the animals in the corrals surrounding the house; and in the field nearby, a huge boat—an ark. And then he showed her one last pen, far away from the others, with two animals in it. Two beautiful white animals with deep blue eyes—a pair of unicorns.

And then Sam explained what all the urgency was about, why they'd collected all those animals, and why the weather forecast couldn't predict an end to the rain.

—Joni Bodart

VISION QUEST YA
By TERRY DAVIS

Victories came easy for Louden—they always had. But this would be the showdown, the hardest match he'd ever had. He would have to face his toughest opponent ever.

Louden Swain is a senior in high school and a championship wrestler. He has only a few weeks to get ready for his most important meet. His body must be in perfect shape—and that doesn't just mean the pain of practice and workouts, it also means taking several pounds off his already lean frame so he can fight in a lighter class. And even while he's on a rigid diet, he still has to maintain his strength, agility, and energy level. It's not easy or fun, it's difficult and at times it's painful.

If he's going to win, his concentration and preparation must be perfect. He can't afford any distractions, either now or during the match. But there *are* other things on Louden's mind—he's trying to graduate early from high school, and he wants to spend time at the river and work on his beautifully-restored 1951 DeSoto. Finally, there's his biggest distraction—Carla. Where is their relationship going? Will he win his match only to lose his girl?

—Joni Bodart
—Judy Druse

WALLS YA
By JAY DALY

The Shadow is a graffiti artist—a "phantom kamikaze defiler of virgin surfaces" is how he'd put it. He has a way with words, especially words on walls.

The Shadow's real name is Frankie O'Day. He's almost seventeen, looks a little like a taller Mick Jagger, and is a star basketball player on the all-city team.

Frankie is a good enough student at Loyola High, a boys' Catholic high school in San Francisco, and he figures he'll get a basketball scholarship to college. The idea of going to college doesn't thrill him, but it seems to be what's expected. Meanwhile, with a big letter on his sweater, Frankie knows he's acceptable at school. But mostly he just wants to be left alone.

Frankie has no close friends because his father is an alcoholic. He doesn't shout or get violent, just lies around in his bathrobe watching TV, drooling, crying, and falling asleep. When Frankie was about thirteen, he and Bob, a friend, found Frankie's father passed out on the stairway landing of their apartment house. They had to get Frankie's mother and lug him up to his bed. Neither one ever mentioned it again, but Frankie noticed that he saw less and less of Bob after that.

With no close friends to talk to and a mess of feelings inside, Frankie lets it all out by writing on walls. It began one day when he was feeling unusually bored and disgusted with school, and it struck him that the gray concrete walls there looked deadly dull. So Frankie wrote his first "statement," a not-very-original jibe at one of the teachers. He signed it "the Shadow."

The students at Frankie's school were usually a pretty apathetic bunch, but there was a huge uproar when the writing was discovered. More statements followed. Frankie enjoyed hearing everybody speculate about who the Shadow really was. He felt like an agent behind enemy lines. No one suspected him. He was driving the high school administration crazy. When teachers began to patrol all over the school, Frankie decided to cool it there. He took to the walls of the city—and the Shadow's fame spread.

In search of inspiration one day, Frankie noticed, not far from school, the unused back door of a police station (the ultimate thrill!). So he wrote, "Help me, please! I don't want to kill again!—the Shadow." It was supposed to be a joke, but the police connected it with a very real series of murders. Soon police detectives were swarming all over Loyola High. Frankie was interrogated, and it was rough. They let him go, but he knows they're watching him, playing cat-and-mouse. And it's a little late to come on out and announce: "Heh, heh, fooled you, didn't I? Just a joke, guys!"

—Pat Lichter

THE WAR WITH GRANDPA   Grades 4–6
By ROBERT KIMMEL SMITH

This is the true and real story of what happened when Grandpa came to live with us and *took my room!* It began when Jennifer, my little sister, came into my room with that look on her face that usually means she knows something that I don't. That's one of the things Jennifer likes best in life—a secret. Not that she is so good at keeping secrets. She is no good at all in that department. In fact, I can usually get her to tell me anything I want because I'm her big brother and she's only a little kid. This time was no exception.

Grandpa Jack was too lonely down in Florida since Grandma died, so he sold their house, and he was coming to live with us. That was great news! However, that wasn't all. Grandpa had a bad leg and couldn't climb to the top floor of the house, so he was going to be given my room. Let me take a minute here to tell you about my room. I love my room! I have lived in this room all my life. All my favorite things are in this room: bed, bookshelves, desk, toy cabinets with shoeboxes on top full of baseball cards, and a Hank Aaron poster. I can get out of bed in the middle of the night and walk around my room without even looking because I know where every single thing is. And most of all, in the middle of the night there is nothing in my room that is scary.

Well, I suggested that my parents give Grandpa Jennifer's room, but they said they couldn't move her because she was still a baby and needed to be close to them. As you probably know, there's a thing that happens when parents want a kid to do something and the kid doesn't want to.What happens is that the parents usually win. That's one of the big advantages of being a parent. You get to win arguments. So my bed, bookshelves, desk, toy cabinets, baseball cards, and Hank Aaron poster were moved to the third-floor guest room. The last thing that was moved into the guest room was me. It wasn't fair! No one bothered to ask me about giving up my room. We were supposed to treat Grandpa like a member of the family, with respect and courtesy. That was easy; I love Grandpa. He fixed my rocking chair and takes me fishing. But what about showing me respect and courtesy? Why was I the only one in the house who had to give up something for Grandpa? There must be a way I can fight to get back what is really mine. Think about the people who fought in the Revolutionary days. They fought the king, who was kind of a father to them. They stood their ground and fired the shot heard round the world. But I can't shoot at my grandfather. Then I got a funny thought, and the whole idea of what I could do became clear to me—I would declare war on Grandpa.

—Judy Druse

WARDAY: AND THE JOURNEY ONWARD   YA/Adult
By WHITLEY STRIEBER and JAMES KUNETKA

October 28, 1988, is known as Warday. Thirty-six brief minutes. The equivalent of a long coffee break or a short lunch break. At the end of those thirty-six minutes, much of the world lay untouched, but the United States and the Soviet Union were destroyed. Five years after Warday, when two survivors, Whitley Strieber and Jim Kunetka, travel across America, they find a nation still dying from the shortest war in their country's history.

In the space of thirty-six minutes, Washington, DC; San Antonio, Texas; Cheyenne Mountain, Wyoming (NORAD headquarters); and most of the Dakotas were laid to waste. New York City, while suffering immense damage, was spared total annihilation because of a fluke misfire.

Many other population centers (including Omaha, Nebraska, where the SAC was located) were temporarily spared, because the war was so brief. But seven million people in the US died in those thirty-six minutes. Over the next five years, seventy million more died from radiation sickness, cancer, malnutrition, and epidemics of plague proportions.

The President of the US died. The central government ceased to exist. Seventy-five percent of all elctronic communication and transportation was destroyed. Giant commercial airliners literally fell from the sky on Warday when their electronic controls ceased to function. For the survivors of Warday, life would never be the same.

On that clear blue fall afternoon in October, 1988, Whitley Strieber, a writer of horror-occult books, found himself riding the Number 5 bus down Fifth Avenue on his way home when the missiles meant for New York City detonated. They misfired, and instead of exploding at 8,000 feet over metropolitan Manhattan, they detonated at ground level in Queens. A misfire in a nuclear war doesn't really mean much: New York City died anyway. Whitley and his wife and son survived. Whitley suffered a massive dose of radiation and has been "triaged"—since he is undoubtedly going to die from cancer anyway, he is not allowed to have any medical treatment, not even aspirin. Five years after Warday, Whitley and his family have resettled in his home state of Texas—as hydroponic farmers in Dallas.

Jim Kunetka was forty-four years old on Warday. Jim was also a writer, but of scholarly nonfiction. Ironically, his best-known work was about J. Robert Oppenheimer, the scientist who developed the original atomic bomb.

Jim and Whitley had grown up together in San Antonio. On Warday, Jim, who still lived in San Antonio, was in Dallas on business. His wife, whom he would later lose, was with him. Their children and all other family members were in San Antonio.

Like Jim, Whitley lost all his family in San Antonio, except his wife and son who were living with him in New York.

These two Texas authors and longtime friends begin a journey across America five years after that thirty-six-minute war on October 28, 1988. They must face all kinds of dangers as they travel across the fragmented remains of the once proud and powerful United States of

America. This book *Warday* is their account of their eight-week trek across the land that they—as survivors—view after war has unleashed the ultimate horror upon it.

—Barbara Lynn

THE WAVE   YA
By MORTON RHUE

It all began when history teacher Ben Ross showed his senior class a film on the atrocities committed by the Nazis in World War II concentration camps. Afterwards the major question was, "Why didn't someone notice? How do you kill ten million people without someone noticing? Why didn't anyone do anything?" Ben didn't have the answers—but he decided to try an experiment that might provide some of them. And "The Wave" was born. The next day, Ben's class walked in to discover "Strength Through Discipline" in large letters on the blackboard. Class that day was a new experience, one that resulted in an exciting discovery: by acting as a unit, the class gained a new and different kind of power—and a new high as well. The Wave was beginning to work, and work better than anyone had believed it would. The rules: Strength Through Discipline, Strength Through Community, Strength Through Action. And with that strength, that unity, came power! More power than even Ben had ever foreseen! To his horror, Nazi Germany is coming alive again—in his high school classroom.

This is based on an actual event. It took place in Palo Alto, California, in 1969. For three years afterward, no one talked about it. According to the teacher, "It was one of the most frightening events I have ever experienced in the classroom." This book is scary even as a novel—the fact that it is based on truth makes it absolutely chilling. You may not agree with it. You may say, "It could never happen in *my* school." But I warn you—don't try it!

—Joni Bodart

THE WESTING GAME   Grades 6–8
By ELLEN RASKIN

Talk 1

Who killed Samuel W. Westing? That's the question asked of sixteen people who are his heirs and invited to the reading of his will. The right answer could make them millionaires. All sixteen are residents of the

Sunset Towers apartment building, owned by Samuel Westing and visible from his mansion. Who killed Samuel Westing? Was it Tabitha-Ruth-Alice Wexler, otherwise known as TURTLE? She was in the mansion the night of the murder and it was she who found the corpse. Or was it her mother, GRACE W. WEXLER, who fancies herself, an interior decorator, or her father, JAKE WEXLER, a podiatrist with a bookmaking operation on the side? It might even have been Turtle's perfect sister ANGELA, who spends most of her time embroidering, or Angela's fiancé DR. DENTON DEERE, an intern in plastic surgery. Surely no one would suspect HER HONOR JUDGE J.J. FORD of murder! We might be more likely to choose JAMES SHIN HOO, a restaurant owner who once sued Mr. Westing over a patent for disposable diapers, or SANDY, the doorman at the Sunset Towers—he was fired from the Westing Paper Products Plant. Could we suspect Hoo's wife MADAME SUN-LIN HOO, who doesn't speak English, or his son DOUGLAS, a jogger getting ready for his big race? What about THEO THEODARAKIS, the writer and chess player, or his crippled brother CHRIS? Chris spends a lot of his time bird-watching and saw someone limping across the lawn of the mansion the night Mr. Westing was killed. How was Samuel Westing connected to the Towers cleaning woman, BERTHA, or OTIS, the delivery man, or FLORA BAUMBACK, dressmaker, or SYDELLE PULASKI, secretary?

When the will was read, the sixteen were paired off and each pair was given $10,000 and a set of clues—none of them alike. The players were snowbound for several days and spent their time trying to figure out what all the other clues were. The Westing game was tricky and dangerous, but the heirs played on in spite of blizzards, burglaries, and bombs bursting in air.

But who *did* kill Samuel Westing? Only Turtle knows and she isn't telling. You'll have to read *The Westing Game* by Ellen Raskin to find out.

—*Claranell Murray*

Talk 2

Listen, Chris. I'll tell you about that haunted castle on the hill. Somebody is up there, but nobody is there. Just rich Mr. Westing, and he's dead. Dead as a squashed june bug, and rotting away on a moth-eaten oriental rug.

Turtle, brave girl, took a bet. She would stay in the haunted house on Halloween night, and the bet was two dollars for every minute she could stay inside. Dressed in her witch costume, Turtle approached the dark that lay within the French doors. "There is no such thing as a ghost—I'm not scared, I'm not scared. . . . "

At two dollars a minute, she could stay all night—she wasn't scared. Turtle checked her pockets: two sandwiches, a flask filled with orange pop, a flashlight, her mother's silver cross to ward off vampires. The putty wart was soaked in Angela's perfume in the event she was locked up with a stinking corpse.

The boys checked their stopwatch. Nine minutes, ten minutes, eleven minutes. . . .

Suddenly a terrified scream, a young girl's scream, pierced the night.

Turtle had seen the corpse, not rotting on a rug, but tucked in a four-poster bed. The Westing Game had begun.

Sixteen people were called to the reading of rich Mr. Samuel Westing's will.

One of them would inherit his estate of two hundred million dollars. They were mothers, fathers, and children. A dressmaker, a secretary with painted crutches, an inventor, a doctor, and a judge. And oh, yes—one was a bookie, one was a burglar, one was a bomber, and one was a mistake.

"I, Samuel W. Westing, hereby swear that I did not die from natural causes. My life was taken by one of you. Who among you is worthy to be my heir? He who finds the killer shall inherit." And Turtle knew!

Read *The Westing Game,* by Ellen Raskin.

—*Linda Henderson*

WHAT THE WITCH LEFT   Grades 5–8
By RUTH CHEW

A long bathrobe with a big floppy hood colored a wild, bright orange; a pair of tight-fitting, flesh-colored gloves; a pair of rather beat-up red rubber boots; and a dented metal box that had a picture of a fruitcake on the lid. What a pile of junk! But what was it doing in a *locked* dresser drawer in Katy's room?

Katy and her friend Louise were playing in Katy's room one rainy day when Louise asked her what in the world could be in the locked drawer of the dresser. The dresser itself was all scarred and beat up and didn't look very valuable. Maybe there was a secret treasure hidden in that drawer. Katy remembered seeing a key in the nightstand by Mom's bed, and when she and Louise tried it out, it fit just right. They kept digging through the drawer, through old clothes and jumbled objects, but they could not see any hidden treasure or anything that even looked valuable. Katy had tried on the flesh-colored opera-length gloves, and she was surprised when Louise didn't notice she had them on. They had such a smooth, wonderful fit too, as if they had been made just for her.

Just then they heard someone at the door downstairs. They stuffed everything quickly back into the drawer, locked it, and raced to put the key back in Mom's nightstand.

As Katy hurried downstairs to answer the door she realized that she had not taken off the gloves, but they fit so closely she couldn't feel them—she couldn't even see them! No time now to take them off.

When Katy opened the door, there stood her piano teacher. Katy groaned inwardly, for she hadn't practiced in days and Miss Medwick was sure to make her go over those dreary scales again and again. Katy sat down to the piano, and was she ever surprised. She played the first song with no trouble at all. She played all her scales perfectly. Miss Medwick was so surprised she had Katy open the piano book further along and play a brand new song. Katy played every note perfectly. Louise came downstairs and listened. She usually held her ears all through Katy's lesson. Today, though, she sat on the sofa and listened for the whole time. After Miss Medwick left, Louise said, "Katy, I didn't ever hear you play that well before." Katy looked down at her hands and said, "That didn't even feel hard, to play all those long songs." Suddenly she noticed that the flesh-colored gloves were still on her hands. Miss Medwick hadn't even noticed. Louise couldn't even see them until Katy peeled them off. Both girls started wondering if the gloves could be magical. Katy sat down to the piano again and tried to play one song, and all she got was a lot of missed notes.

Could those gloves be magic? If they were, what about the other objects in the drawer—the orange bathrobe, the red rubber boots, and the dented metal box with a fruitcake painted on the lid? Katy and Louise were about to embark on a series of magic adventures they would never forget.

—*Pat Powell*

WHEN THE WIND BLOWS YA/Adult
By RAYMOND BRIGGS

James Bloggs and his wife Hilda are an elderly British couple living on a small farm outside of London. The radio warns them to prepare for an imminent nuclear attack. So, being conscientious citizens, James and Hilda begin to do just that, following the confusing directions for safety measures in the official literature James picked up at the library. They fuss about the inconvenience, and think back to the Blitz in World War II. However, science has leaped forward with giant strides since then. The "powers that be" are making much better wars now.

Nevertheless, James and Hilda proceed to follow the instructions, assured that the civil defense plan will provide them maximum protection. They emerge from their ineffectual shelter after the initial attack before they are supposed to, and find that the utilities don't work and the garden is scorched. They begin to show symptoms of radiation sickness, but don't realize what's the matter. They are not concerned, because they're alive, and now the government will make everything right again.

Does the government *really* know how you can protect yourself in a nuclear war?

—*Judy Druse*

WHERE THE BUFFALOES BEGIN Grades 1-2
By OLAF BAKER

Little Wolf was only ten years old, but he could run faster than any of his friends. And the wildest pony was not too wild for him to catch and ride. But the great thing about him was that he had no fear. He knew that if an angry bull bison or a pack of prairie wolves ran him down, there would be nothing left of him but his bones. And he was well aware that if he fell into the hands of his people's enemies, the Assiniboins, he would be killed and scalped as neatly as could be.

But of all the thoughts that ran this way and that in his quick brain, the one that galloped the hardest was the thought of the great lake to the south where the buffaloes began. According to Indian legend, if you arrived at the right time, on the right night, you would see the buffaloes rise out of the middle of the lake and come crowding to the shore; for there, it was, said was the sacred spot where the buffaloes began.

The thought of the lake grew bigger and bigger in Little Wolf's mind. At last it was so very big that Little Wolf could not bear it any longer, and so one morning, very early, before the village was awake, he crept out of the tepee and stole along below the junipers and tall firs till he came to the spot where the ponies were hobbled. Little Wolf unhobbled a pony, slipped on the bridle he had brought with him, and leaped lightly upon its back. A few minutes afterward, horse and rider had left the camp behind them and were out on the prairie, going due south.

Did he find the lake he was searching for? Read *Where the Buffaloes Begin* and find out.

—*Judy Druse*

WHERE THE SIDEWALK ENDS   Grades 4-8
By SHEL SILVERSTEIN

[Read "Who," from page 63, hardcover edition.]

Anything can happen, anything can be. Come in . . . for where the sidewalk ends, Shel Silverstein's world begins. An acrobat and a bottomless boat; a flying shoe and Captain Hook; a hug o' war, and a double-tailed dog, and Sarah Cynthia Sylvia Stout, who would not take the garbage out.

It is a place where you can auction off your sister, find a recipe for a hippopotamus sandwich, a place where a Yipiyuk can bite your toe.

Where else would you find my minnow, Minnie, swimming in your Ovaltine, or pity poor Benjamin Bunn, who buttons will not come undone. It all comes down to your point of view. [Read "Point of View," page 98, and "Invitation" at the beginning of the book—"If you are a dreamer, come in. . . . "]

To the place *Where the Sidewalk Ends,* by Shel Silverstein.

—*Linda Henderson*

WHITE COAT, WHITE CANE   YA/Adult
By DAVID HARTMAN and BERNARD ASBELL

Do any of you know a blind person? I'd like to introduce you to David Hartman, totally blind since the age of eight. When David first learned of his blindness, his instant reaction was one of glee—he would not have to wear glasses any longer. But his second reaction was of dismay—he would not be able to ride the new bike his father had just given him. He was overcome by a peculiar thrill despite the heavy news that had been dropped on him. "Everybody's going to feel sorry for me now. I'll be everybody's little angel, and they'll all pay attention. I'll get a lot of presents." But David was not allowed to get away with a thing.

Until the seventh grade he attended a school for the blind with 350 students; then he went to a public school of 1,800. "The experience was not only new for me but for everyone else, and it made me suddenly aware, as I never was before, of my blindness.

"At Overbrook, the school for the blind, I had been wrestling since third grade. It was more or less required in gym because wrestling is one of the few sports blind kids can engage in without greatly modifying the rules. The upshot was that now, entering public school, I had experience in wrestling, I knew the tricks of the mat better than these sighted guys. I had another slight advantage over sighted kids in wrestling. They weren't sure how to deal with me. My opponent and I would go out to the middle of the mat, face each other off, the whistle would blow, and I could just hear his hesitation: Gosh, if it's not fair to hit a kid with glasses, what do you do with a guy who can't see at all? In that split second, he was all mine. Wham! I'd lunge at him and take him down. He'd be shocked, then embarrassed that the coach and all his teammates and maybe some girls watching from the walls of the gym were all seeing this blind kid beat the hell out of him, and finally he'd get mad. By that time I was on top, working him over. When you're that close, it's all feel. Seeing doesn't help.

"I remember my first match against Upper Darby, our big rival high school. I pinned my opponent in forty-five seconds. That's very fast—a match usually lasts six minutes. To pin a guy in the last two-minute period match is like being God. Power. Control. You're not only on top of your opponent, you're on top of the world. And, Upper Darby being our rival, the whole gym was packed. All those people watching, admiring. Look at that blind guy! He crippled that brute from Upper Darby. It still stands as the biggest thrill of my life."

David Hartman is a determined individual. He was not only determined to win at wrestling, but even though he was blind he was determined to become a doctor. *White Coat, White Cane.*

—*Linda Lapides*

NOTE Linda also uses David's conversation with his physics teacher, who doesn't realize he can't see the blackboard, in her presentation.

THE WHITE MOUNTAINS   Grades 3–5
By JOHN CHRISTOPHER

In the year 2000, villagers churn butter by hand, drink camomile tea, and walk on cobbled roads. There are no machines and no cities. At the age of thirteen, every child is made to go through a capping ceremony. He is lifted into the body of one of the great metallic tripods that have descended from another planet to control Earth. And when he is returned several hours later, his head is shaved and a metallic cap has been implanted, which insures that from now on all his thoughts and actions will be controlled by the terrible tripods.

Three boys refuse to be capped. Will, Henry, and Beanpole escape the tripods before the capping and start towards the White Mountains, where a small band of men have gathered together to overthrow the tripods. Will, Henry, and Beanpole have to travel at night, always hiding from the tripods—until Will is finally captured.

This is the first of three books about the struggle to free the earth from the tripods. In this book, the goal is to join the other outlaws in the White Mountains. There are two other books—*The City of Gold and Lead* and *The Pool of Fire*—that continue the story.

— *Elizabeth Overmyer*

WILD FOODS   Grades 3–5
By LAURENCE PRINGLE

If regular food sounds a little too tame for you, why not try some wild foods? How about some cattail muffins, sheep sorrel pie, or daylily tubers with dip? Wash that down with some sumacade (Indian lemonade) and top it off with maple sugar! Recipes for these and other delicacies are in Laurence Pringle's *Wild Foods*; they're all made from common weeds that grow wild across the country, and if you're lucky, you can find all these gourmet treats, for free, in a twenty-four-hour convenience location near you: your own backyard, or maybe that vacant lot down the street, or a nearby park. Along with the recipes, you'll find a guide telling you how to pick out the edible, nonpoisonous parts of wild plants, how to handle and clean them, and (if you're squeamish about accidentally eating insects, spiders, or slugs) a surefire way to make sure they're gone before you dig in.

— *Elizabeth Overmyer*

THE WILD INSIDE: THE SIERRA   Grades 3–5
CLUB'S GUIDE TO THE GREAT INDOORS
By LINDA ALLISON

You've heard of explorers going out into the Wild, imagined the adventures you'd have out in the Wild . . . but have you ever considered the Wild *inside,* the wilderness and adventures you can find if you only go exploring indoors, in your very own house—under the living room rug, behind the kitchen sink, even under your dog's fur? We expect dogs to have fur, but have you ever heard of a fur-lined teakettle? Did you know there's a river that runs through your house, or how come there's a whirlpool when you let the water out of the bathtub? Or why that snake was curled up in the lady's dishwasher? Did you know that the reason many people sing in the shower may have something to do with the air and the falling water? Or that a murder may be happening every day among your houseplants?

And what was going on when the lady said she had birds in her toilet? She called the plumber and said, "Birds, they are the problem. These birds, they fly out of my toilet. They're wet and scared and make a horrible mess, flapping around the bathroom." John, the plumber, thought maybe this lady had some other kind of problem, one that a plumber couldn't fix. But conquering his reservations, he went off to see what he could do. It turned out to be true. Sure enough, this lady did have birds flying out of her toilet, grackles to be exact.

But how did they get there? In *The Wild Inside, The Sierra Club's Guide to the Great Indoors,* you can find the answers to all these questions and more, as well as stuff to send away for (free), and things to make—like soap boats, wind darts, clouds in your kitchen, crystals you can eat, and monster markers.

So the next time you're stuck indoors or just want an unusual adventure, take this new explorer's guide to the Wild inside.

— Joan Ariel

WILEY AND THE HAIRY MAN   Grades 1–2
Adapted by MOLLY G. BANG

Wiley's mother told him he'd have to watch out for the Hairy Man in the swamp. And when Wiley met him, he found out why. He was sure ugly, he was hairy all over, his eyes burned like coals, his teeth were big and sharp and white, and he was swinging a sack. Wiley was so scared, he quickly climbed a tree. "What's in your big old sack?" he asked the Hairy Man. "Nothing, yet," the Hairy Man replied, and he sat down at the foot of the tree. He knew Wiley'd have to come down sometime, and he knew that he could turn himself into any animal he wanted and make things appear and disappear too—and he knew Wiley couldn't escape!

—Elizabeth Overmyer

WINGMAN   Grades 1–2
By DANIEL MANUS PINKWATER

Donald Chen was called Donald at school, but at home he was Chen Chi-Wing or Ah-Wing. The most important thing to him was comic books—he collected them and he had over two hundred! The least important thing to him was school, and after Thanksgiving, he just stopped going. Instead he would climb the George Washington

Bridge—right up the steel girders to the top—and sit up there and read comic books. That was how he met Wingman. Before he met him, Donald never knew there were Chinese superheroes. And then one day Wingman carried him off the bridge and right back to China!

—Elizabeth Overmyer

THE WITCHES
By ROALD DAHL
Grades 1-3

My life was drastically changed by two separate encounters with witches, even before I celebrated my eighth birthday. The first time I escaped unharmed, but on the second occasion I was not so lucky.

There I was at the Hotel Magnificent with Grandma. While exploring the hotel, I came to the ballroom. On the noticeboard was a sign saying:

RSPCC Meeting
—Strictly Private—
This room is reserved for
the Annual Meeting of the
Royal Society for the
Prevention of Cruelty to Children

I crept inside and hid behind a large screen.

Almost immediately I heard a voice saying, "Well, ladies, I am sure you will be quite comfortable in here." Then a man ushered in a great flock of ladies, all dressed in pretty dresses, all wearing hats.

The back row filled up first. I noticed one woman in that row scratching her head. Perhaps she had lice. All of a sudden I noticed the lady next to her scratching her head. They were all scratching their heads. One lady was scratching so hard her fingers went up underneath her hair, lifting up all the hair—in one piece!

She was wearing a wig! She was also wearing gloves. Every one of them was wearing gloves.

My blood turned to ice, and I began to shake all over. I looked for a way out—there was none!

I was shaking because I realized that these ladies were wearing disguises. They were wearing disguises because they were witches! Witches wear gloves to hide their claws. They wear wigs because they are bald. They have large noseholes for smelling out children, which to them smell like dog's droppings! They also have no toes on their feet, and their spit is blue.

This is what their disguise looks like, but this is what a witch is really like! [Show illustrations.]

The Grand High Witch then gave her talk, centering on a special formula called Formula 86 Delayed-Action Mouse-Maker.

To discover the powers of this formula and what happened to me next, read *The Witches,* by Roald Dahl.

—Mary K. Hobson

THE YOUNG LANDLORDS YA
By WALTER DEAN MYERS

It was summer; Paul Williams and his friends were out of school. Gloria felt they should stop just talking about how bad things were and get involved. So the Action Group began, with Gloria, Dean, Bubba, Omar, Jeannie, and Paul as members. Gloria made a list of things that they should deal with. First, the problem of the Stratford Arms—the building at 356—The Joint. The Joint had its share of garbage, graffiti, and grit. It was time to do something about it. The first thing was to contact the owner. Get him to solve the problem. So the committee met face to face with owner Joseph Harley. Mr. Harley had forty-eight hours to do something about the problem at The Joint. However, Mr. Harley sold his problem to Paul for the sum of one dollar. Paul decided that since it was the group's idea in the first place, the group would become owners of The Joint.

It seemed great at first, but then there were gas bills, heat bills, taxes, and building maintenance costs to be paid. The landlords went into the red—fast. How could they pay all those bills, and make the necessary repairs and improvements without any money?

Then there was the problem of Chris, the nice kid on the block. Chris had been arrested for stealing some hi-fi systems from the store where he worked part-time. Gloria decided it was time to get involved with Chris's case. The group had to find the person who was responsible.

—Dwight Malone

YOUR BABY, YOUR BODY Adult
By CAROL STAHMANN DILFER

No, you don't have to get fat during pregnancy, or afterwards either. Not even if your mother did, and your grandmother, and all your sisters and three of your first cousins. It doesn't have to happen to *you.* Your body is *your* body—not your mother's or your grandmother's. And by working with your body, you can avoid becoming a dumpy mother.

How? Watch what you eat and exercise! Now, I'm not saying that it's *easy* to exercise. It isn't always. But you have to live with that body of yours for the rest of your life.

But is it safe to exercise during pregnancy? Yes! Exercise won't solve all your problems of weight control, but it will make your body firm and limber and relieve some of the aches and pains that many pregnant women experience. It will also help you look even better after you deliver than before you became pregnant. Doesn't that sound great?

Are you sitting there smugly thinking, I'm not pregnant—so forget it!? The program in this book is also terrific for those of us with good intentions who never seem to get around to carrying them out. This program will also help saggy bottoms, pouchy tummies, and flabby arms. It's not a miracle, but it is the least time-consuming or boring routine I've seen. Learn how to look better and feel better, whether you're pregnant, a new mother, or just out of shape.

Your Baby, Your Body, by Carol Stahmann Dilfer.

—Becky Blick

Appendix A:
Bibliography by Age Level

Young Children

Baker, Olaf. *Where the Buffaloes Begin.* Warne 1981.

Bang, Molly G., ad. *Wiley and the Hairy Man.* Macmillan 1976.

Berends, Polly Berrien. *The Case of the Elevator Duck.* Random 1973.

Brown, Jeff. *Flat Stanley.* Harper 1964.

Corbett, Scott. *The Great Custard Pie Panic.* Little 1974.

Dahl, Roald. *The Witches.* Farrar 1983.

Fritz, Jean. *And Then What Happened, Paul Revere?* Coward 1973 (op, but widely held).

Goble, Paul. *The Girl Who Loved Wild Horses.* Bradbury 1978.

Lawson, Robert. *Rabbit Hill.* Viking 1944, Penguin 1977.

Olson, Helen Kronberg. *The Strange Thing That Happened to Oliver Wendell Iscovitch.* Dodd 1983.

Pinkwater, Daniel Manus. *Wingman.* Dodd 1975 (op).

Pomerantz, Charlotte. *Detective Poufy's First Case.* Bantam c1976.

Quackenbush, Robert. *Stairway to Doom: A Miss Mallard Mystery.* Prentice 1983.

Schwartz, Alvin. *There Is a Carrot in My Ear, and Other Noodle Tales.* Harper 1982.

Shannon, George. *The Gang and Mrs. Higgins.* Greenwillow 1981.

Shub, Elizabeth, ad. *Clever Kate.* Macmillan 1973.

Williams, Jay. *Everyone Knows What a Dragon Looks Like.* Scholastic 1976.

Middle Grades

Allison, Linda. *The Wild Inside: The Sierra Club's Guide to the Great Indoors.* Sierra Club 1979 (op, but widely held).

Banks, Lynne Reid. *The Indian in the Cupboard.* Doubleday 1981, Avon 1982.

Bellairs, John. *House With a Clock in Its Walls.* Dell 1974, Dial 1983.

Brittain, Bill. *The Devil's Donkey.* Harper 1981, 1982.

Middle Grades (cont.)

Burch, Robert. *Queenie Peavey.* Viking 1966.

Byars, Betsy C. *The Eighteenth Emergency.* Viking 1973, Penguin 1981.

————. *The TV Kid.* Viking 1976.

Christopher, John. *The White Mountains.* Macmillan 1967, 1970.

Cleary, Beverly. *Ramona and Her Father.* Morrow 1977, Dell.

————. *Ramona and Her Mother.* Morrow 1979, Dell 1980.

Clifford, Eth. *Harvey's Horrible Snake Disaster.* Houghton 1984.

Coerr, Eleanor B. *Sadako and the Thousand Paper Cranes.* Putnam 1977, Dell.

Conford, Ellen. *Felicia the Critic.* Little 1973, Archway 1978.

Corbett, Scott. *Here Lies the Body.* Little 1974.

Cunningham, Julia. *Dorp Dead.* Pantheon 1965, Avon 1974.

Dahl, Roald. *Fantastic Mr. Fox.* Knopf 1970, Bantam 1978.

Drury, Roger. *The Champion of Merrimack County.* Little 1976.

Du Bois, William Pène. *Porko Von Popbutton.* Harper 1963.

Fleischman, Paul. *The Half-a-Moon Inn.* Harper 1980.

Fleischman, Sid. *Humbug Mountain.* Little 1978.

George, Jean C. *Julie of the Wolves.* Harper 1972.

Greene, Bette. *Philip Hall Likes Me, I Reckon, Maybe.* Dial 1974, Dell 1975.

Heide, Florence Parry. *Banana Twist.* Holiday 1978, Bantam 1982.

Howe, Deborah and James. *Bunnicula: A Rabbit-Tale of Mystery.* Atheneum 1979, Avon 1984.

————. *Howliday Inn.* Atheneum 1982, Avon 1983.

Howe, James. *The Celery Stalks at Midnight.* Atheneum 1983, Avon 1984.

Hurmence, Belinda. *A Girl Called Boy.* Houghton 1982.

Konigsburg, Elaine L. *Jennifer, Hecate, Macbeth, William McKinley, and Me, Elizabeth.* Atheneum 1967.

Langton, Jane. *The Diamond in the Window.* Harper 1962, 1973.

Levy, Elizabeth. *Frankenstein Moved in on the Fourth Floor.* Harper 1979, 1981.

Lowry, Lois. *Anastasia Again!* Houghton 1981, Dell 1982.

————. *Anastasia Krupnik.* Houghton 1979, Bantam 1981.

Miles, Betty. *The Secret Life of the Underwear Champ.* Knopf 1981.

Morey, Walt. *Kavik, the Wolf Dog.* Dutton 1968.

Mowat, Farley. *Owls in the Family.* Little 1961, Bantam 1981.

Naylor, Phyllis. *How Lazy Can You Get?* Atheneum 1979.

Pinkwater, Daniel Manus. *Fat Men From Space*. Dodd 1977, Dell 1980.

Pringle, Laurence. *Wild Foods*. Scholastic 1978.

Robinson, Barbara. *The Best Christmas Pageant Ever*. Harper 1972, Avon 1983.

Rockwell, Thomas. *How to Eat Fried Worms*. Watts 1973, Dell 1975.

Rodgers, Mary. *A Billion for Boris*. Harper 1974, 1976.

————. *Freaky Friday*. Harper 1972, 1973, 1977.

Roy, Ron. *Nightmare Island*. Dutton 1981.

Silverstein, Shel. *Where the Sidewalk Ends*. Harper 1974.

Sleator, William. *Among the Dolls*. Dutton 1975.

Slote, Alfred. *Jake*. Harper.

————. *My Robot Buddy*. Harper 1975, Avon 1978.

Smith, Doris Buchanan. *A Taste of Blackberries*. Harper 1973, Scholastic 1976.

Smith, Robert Kimmel. *The War With Grandpa*. Delacorte 1984.

Snyder, Zilpha K. *Black and Blue Magic*. Atheneum 1966, 1972.

Taylor, Mildred D. *Roll of Thunder, Hear My Cry*. Dial 1976, Bantam 1978.

Viorst, Judith. *If I Were in Charge of the World, and Other Worries*. Atheneum 1981.

Wallace, Barbara Brooks. *Peppermints in the Parlor*. Atheneum 1980.

Older Children

Adler, C. S. *Footsteps on the Stairs*. Delacorte 1982, Dell 1984.

Ames, Mildred. *Anna to the Infinite Power*. Scribner 1981, Scholastic 1983.

Blessing, Richard. *A Passing Season*. Little 1982.

Byars, Betsy C. *The Animal, the Vegetable, and John D. Jones*. Delacorte 1982, Dell 1983.

————. *The Two-Thousand-Pound Goldfish*. Harper 1982.

Chew, Ruth. *What the Witch Left*. Hastings 1973.

Cohen, Daniel. *The Headless Roommate and Other Tales of Terror*. Evans 1980.

Conford, Ellen. *And This Is Laura*. Little 1977, Archway 1978.

DeWeese, Gene. *The Adventures of a Two-Minute Werewolf*. Doubleday 1983, Putnam 1984.

Duane, Diane. *So You Want to Be a Wizard*. Delacorte 1983.

Froelich, Margaret W. *Hide Crawford Quick*. Houghton 1983.

Gallo, Donald, ed. *Sixteen*. Delacorte 1984.

Greer, Gary. *Max and Me and the Time Machine*. Harcourt 1983.

Older Children (cont.)

Hart, Bruce and Carole. *Sooner or Later.* Avon 1981.

Holman, Felice. *Slake's Limbo.* Scribner 1974, Dell 1977.

Howe, Deborah and James. *Bunnicula: A Rabbit-Tale of Mystery.* Atheneum 1979, Avon 1984.

Howe, James. *A Night Without Stars.* Atheneum 1983.

Jones, Diana Wynne. *Dogsbody.* Dell 1979.

Karl, Jean E. *Beloved Benjamin Is Waiting.* Dutton 1978.

Kavanaugh, Dorriet, ed. *Listen to Us: The Children's Express Report.* Workman 1978.

Kullman, Harry. *The Battle Horse.* Bradbury 1977, 1981.

Levitin, Sonia. *The Mark of Conte.* Atheneum 1976, 1979.

Levoy, Myron. *Alan and Naomi.* Harper 1977.

Lowry, Lois. *Anastasia Again!* Houghton 1981, Dell 1982.

McKinley, Robin. *Beauty.* Harper 1978.

Maruki, Toshi. *Hiroshima No Pika.* Lothrop 1980, 1982.

Marzollo, Jean. *Halfway Down Paddy Lane.* Dial 1981, Scholastic 1984.

Miklowitz, Gloria D. *Movie Stunts and the People Who Do Them.* Harcourt 1980.

Moeri, Louise. *Save Queen of Sheba.* Dutton 1981, Avon 1982.

Nastick, Sharon. *Mr. Radagast Makes an Unexpected Journey.* Harper 1981, Dell 1982.

O'Dell, Scott. *Island of the Blue Dolphins.* Houghton 1960, Dell 1978.

Oppenheimer, Joan. *Gardine vs. Hanover.* Harper 1982.

Paterson, Katherine. *The Great Gilly Hopkins.* Harper 1978, Avon 1979.

Pinkwater, Daniel Manus. *Lizard Music.* Dodd 1976.

Platt, Kin. *Run for Your Life.* Dell 1979.

Prince, Marjorie M. *The Cheese Stands Alone.* Archway 1975.

Raskin, Ellen. *The Westing Game.* Dutton 1978, Avon 1980.

Severn, Bill. *More Magic in Your Pockets.* McKay 1980.

Silverstein, Shel. *Where the Sidewalk Ends.* Harper 1974.

Sleator, William. *Into the Dream.* Dutton 1979, Scholastic 1984.

Tolan, Stephanie S. *Grandpa—and Me.* Scribner 1978.

Viorst, Judith. *If I Were In Charge of the World, and Other Worries.* Atheneum 1981, 1984.

Voigt, Cynthia. *Homecoming.* Atheneum 1981, Fawcett 1982.

Wells, Rosemary. *The Man in the Woods.* Dial 1984.

Westall, Robert. *The Machine Gunners.* Greenwillow 1976.

Windsor, Patricia. *Something's Waiting for You, Baker D.* Harper 1974
Wiseman, David. *Jeremy Visick.* Houghton 1981.

Young Adults

Adler, C. S. *Roadside Valentine.* Macmillan 1983, Putnam 1984.
Adams, Douglas. *The Hitchhiker's Guide to the Galaxy.* Harmony
1979, Crown 1980, 1981.
————. *Life, the Universe, and Everything.* Crown 1982, PB 1983.
Ames, Mildred. *Anna to the Infinite Power.* Scribner 1981, Scholastic
1983.
Arrick, Fran. *God's Radar.* Bradbury 1983.
————. *Steffie Can't Come Out to Play.* Bradbury 1978, Dell.
Asher, Sandy. *Things Are Seldom What They Seem.* Delacorte 1984.
Auel, Jean M. *Clan of the Cave Bear.* Crown 1980, Bantam 1981.
Bachman, Richard. *The Long Walk.* NAL 1979.
Belden, Wilanne S. *Mind-Call.* Atheneum 1981.
Bell, Clare. *Ratha's Creature.* Atheneum 1983.
Bennett, Jay. *The Executioner.* Avon 1982.
Blume, Judy. *Tiger Eyes.* Bradbury 1981, Dell 1982.
Brancato, Robin F. *Sweet Bells Jangled Out of Tune.* Knopf 1982.
Briggs, Raymond. *When the Wind Blows.* Schocken 1982.
Bunting, Eve. *Ghosts of Departure Point.* Harper 1982, Scholastic 1984.
————. *If I Asked You, Would You Stay?* Harper 1984.
Butterworth, W. E. *Leroy and the Old Man.* Scholastic 1980.
Byars, Betsy C. *Glory Girl.* Viking 1983.
————. *The Two-Thousand-Pound Goldfish.* Harper 1982.
Calvert, Patricia. *Hour of the Wolf.* Scribner 1983.
Campbell, Patricia J. *Passing the Hat: Street Performance in America.*
Delacorte 1981.
Chambers, Aidan. *Dance on My Grave.* Harper 1983.
Childress, Alice. *Rainbow Jordan.* Putnam 1981, Avon 1982.
Clark, Mary Higgins. *Stillwatch.* S&S 1984.
Cohen, Barbara. *Unicorns in the Rain.* Atheneum 1980.
Cohen, Daniel. *The Headless Roommate and Other Tales of Terror.* Evans 1980.
Conford, Ellen. *And This Is Laura.* Little 1977, Archway 1978.
Cormier, Robert. *After the First Death.* Pantheon 1979, Avon 1983.
————. *The Bumblebee Flies Anyway.* Knopf 1983, Dell 1984.
————. *I Am the Cheese.* Pantheon 1977, Dell 1978.
Crook, Beverly C. *Fair Annie of Old Mule Hollow.* McGraw 1978, Avon
1980.

Young Adults (cont.)

Crutcher, Chris. *Running Loose.* Greenwillow 1983.

Culin, Charlotte. *Cages of Glass, Flowers of Time.* Bradbury 1979, Dell 1982.

Cunningham, Julia. *The Silent Voice.* Dutton 1981, Dell 1983.

Daly, Jay. *Walls.* Harper 1980.

Danziger, Paula. *Can You Sue Your Parents for Malpractice?* Delacorte 1979, Dell 1980.

―――. *The Divorce Express.* Delacorte 1982, Dell 1983.

Davis, Terry. *Vision Quest.* Viking 1979.

Dear, William. *Dungeon Master: The Disappearance of James Dallas Egbert III.* Houghton 1984.

DeVeaux, Alexis. *Don't Explain (A Song of Billie Holiday).* Harper 1980.

Dragonwagon, Crescent and Zindel, Paul. *To Take a Dare.* Harper 1982, Bantam 1984.

Due, Linnea A. *High and Outside.* Harper 1980, Bantam.

Duncan, Lois. *Daughters of Eve.* Little 1979, Dell 1980.

―――. *Stranger With My Face.* Little 1981, Dell 1982.

―――. *The Third Eye.* Little 1984.

Durrell, Gerald. *Ark on the Move.* Putnam 1983.

Foley, June. *Love by Any Other Name.* Delacorte 1983, Dell 1983.

Gallo, Donald, ed. *Sixteen.* Delacorte 1984.

Garden, Nancy. *Annie on My Mind.* Farrar 1982.

Green, Bette. *Them That Glitter and Them That Don't.* Knopf 1983.

Goldman, William. *The Princess Bride.* Ballantine 1977.

Greenberg, Joanne. *The Far Side of Victory.* Holt 1983.

Greenwald, Sheila. *Blissful Joy and the SATs: A Multiple-Choice Romance.* Little 1982, Dell 1983.

Guy, Rosa. *The Disappearance.* Delacorte 1979, Dell.

Hartman, David and Asbell, Bernard. *White Coat, White Cane.* Playboy, dist. by S&S 1978.

Haruf, Kent. *The Tie That Binds.* Holt 1984.

Hayden, Torey L. *One Child.* Avon 1982.

―――. *Sunflower Forest.* Putnam 1984.

Heidish, Marcy. *The Secret of Annie Oakley.* NAL 1983.

Hogan, William. *The Quartzsite Trip.* Atheneum 1980, Avon 1981.

Hughes, Monica. *Hunter in the Dark.* Atheneum 1983, Avon 1984.

―――. *Keeper of the Isis Light.* Atheneum 1981, Bantam 1984.

Jackson, Shirley. *The Haunting of Hill House.* Penguin 1984.

Janeczko, Paul, ed. *Postcard Poems: A Collection of Poetry for Sharing.* Bradbury 1979.

Keyes, Daniel. *The Fifth Sally.* Houghton 1980.

―――. *The Minds of Billy Milligan.* Random 1981, Bantam 1982.

King, Stephen. *Christine.* NAL 1983, Viking 1983.

―――. *Cujo.* Viking 1981, NAL 1982.

―――. *Different Seasons.* Viking 1982, NAL 1983.

―――. *Firestarter.* Viking 1980, NAL 1981.

―――. *Pet Sematary.* Doubleday 1983, NAL, Hall 1984.

Knudson, R. R. *Just Another Love Story.* Farrar 1983, Avon 1984.

Kullman, Harry. *The Battle Horse.* Bradbury 1977, 1981.

Kurtis, Bill. *Bill Kurtis on Assignment.* Rand 1983.

Lee, Tanith. *Red as Blood.* DAW 1983.

LeGuin, Ursula. *The Beginning Place.* Harper 1980, Bantam 1981.

Leitner, Isabella. *Fragments of Isabella.* Crowell 1978, Dell 1983.

Levenkron, Steven. *The Best Little Girl in the World.* Contemporary 1978, Warner 1979.

Levitin, Sonia. *The Mark of Conte.* Atheneum 1976, 1979.

Levoy, Myron. *Shadow Like a Leopard.* Harper 1981, NAL 1982.

Lowry, Lois. *Summer to Die.* Houghton 1977, Bantam 1979.

McCaffrey, Anne. *Crystal Singer.* Ballantine 1982.

―――. *Dragondrums.* Atheneum 1979, Bantam 1980.

MacCracken, Mary. *City Kid.* NAL 1982.

McKillip, Patricia A. *The Riddle-Master of Hed.* Atheneum 1976, Ballantine 1978.

McKinley, Robin. *Beauty.* Harper 1978.

Magorian, Michelle. *Good Night, Mr. Tom.* Harper 1982.

Marshall, Catherine. *Julie.* McGraw 1984.

Marzollo, Jean. *Halfway Down Paddy Lane.* Dial 1981, Scholastic 1984.

Mathis, Sharon Bell. *Listen for the Fig Tree.* Viking 1974.

Mazer, Harry. *The Last Mission.* Dell 1981.

Michaels, Barbara. *Here I Stay.* Congdon 1983, Hall 1984.

Miklowitz, Gloria D. *The Day the Senior Class Got Married.* Delacorte 1983.

―――. *The Love Bombers.* Delacorte 1980, Dell 1982.

Milton, Hilary. *Blind Flight.* Watts 1980, Scholastic 1982.

Moeri, Louise. *First the Egg.* Dutton 1982, Archway 1984.

―――. *The Girl Who Lived on the Ferris Wheel.* Dutton 1979, Avon 1980.

Young Adults (cont.)

————(Moeri). *Save Queen of Sheba*. Dutton 1981, Avon 1982.

Myers, Walter Dean. *Hoops*. Delacorte 1981, Dell 1983.

————. *It Ain't All for Nothin'*. Avon 1979.

————. *The Young Landlords*. Viking 1979, Avon 1980.

Newton, Suzanne. *I Will Call It Georgie's Blues*. Viking 1983.

Nicholls, Peter. *The Science in Science Fiction*. Knopf 1983.

Nixon, Joan Lowery. *A Deadly Game of Magic*. Harcourt 1983.

Oneal, Zibby. *A Formal Feeling*. Viking 1982, Fawcett 1983.

————. *The Language of Goldfish*. Viking 1980, Fawcett 1981.

O'Neill, Cherry Boone. *Starving for Attention*. Continuum 1982, Dell 1983.

Oppenheimer, Joan. *Gardine vs. Hanover*. Harper 1982.

Patterson, Francine and Linden, Eugene. *The Education of Koko*. Holt 1981.

Paulsen, Gary. *Dancing Carl*. Bradbury 1983.

Peck, Richard. *Amanda/Miranda*. Avon 1981.

————. *Close Enough to Touch*. Delacorte 1981, Dell 1982.

Petersen, P. J. *The Boll Weevil Express*. Delacorte 1983, Dell 1984.

Pfeffer, Susan Beth. *About David*. Delacorte 1980, Dell 1982.

Pierce, Meredith. *Darkangel*. Little 1982, Tor 1984.

Pinkwater, Daniel Manus. *The Snarkout Boys and the Avocado of Death*. Lothrop 1982, NAL (Bantam?) 1983.

Prochnau, William. *Trinity's Child*. Putnam 1983.

Quin-Harkin, Janet. *Love Match*. Bantam 1982.

Rhinehart, Luke. *Long Voyage Back*. Delacorte 1983, Dell 1984.

Rhue, Morton. *The Wave*. Delacorte 1981, Dell 1981.

Sallis, Susan. *Only Love*. Harper 1980.

Santiago, Danny. *Famous All Over Town*. S&S 1983, NAL 1984.

Sargent, Pamela. *Earthseed*. Harper 1983.

Scoppettone, Sandra. *Long Time Between Kisses*. Harper 1982.

Shaw, Richard. *The Hard Way Home*. Dell 1983.

Shreve, Susan. *The Masquerade*. Knopf 1980, Dell 1981.

Silsbee, Peter. *The Big Way Out*. Bradbury 1984.

Silverberg, Robert. *Lord Valentine's Castle*. Harper 1980, Bantam 1981.

Singer, Marilyn. *The Course of True Love Never Did Run Smooth*. Harper 1983.

Skurzynski, Gloria. *Manwolf*. Houghton 1981.

Sleator, William. *Into the Dream*. Dutton 1979, Scholastic 1984.

Spiering, Frank. *Lizzie.* Random 1984.

Strasser, Todd. *Friends Till the End.* Delacorte 1981, Dell 1982.

Strieber, Whitley and Kunetka, James. *Warday: And the Journey Onward.* Holt 1984.

Sweeney, Joyce. *Center Line.* Delacorte 1984.

Tamar, Erika. *Blues for Silk Garcia.* Crown 1982.

Taylor, Mildred D. *Let the Circle Be Unbroken.* Dial 1981, Bantam 1983.

Terry, Douglas. *The Last Texas Hero.* Doubleday 1982.

Tevis, Walter. *The Queen's Gambit.* Random 1983, Dell 1984.

Thomas, Joyce Carol. *Marked by Fire.* Avon 1982.

Thompson, Joyce. *Conscience Place.* Doubleday 1984.

Thompson, Julian. *The Grounding of Group 6.* Avon 1983.

Uris, Leon. *The Haj.* Doubleday 1984.

Voigt, Cynthia. *Homecoming.* Atheneum 1981, Fawcett 1982.

Wells, Rosemary. *The Man in the Woods.* Dial 1984.

Wersba, Barbara. *The Carnival in My Mind.* Harper 1982.

Willey, Margaret. *The Bigger Book of Lydia.* Harper 1983.

Windsor, Patricia. *Something's Waiting for You, Baker D.* Harper 1974.

Winter, Douglas E. *Stephen King: The Art of Darkness.* NAL 1984.

Wiseman, David. *Jeremy Visick.* Houghton 1981.

Wortman, Elmo. *Almost Too Late.* Random 1981, Berkley 1983.

Yolen, Jane. *Dragon's Blood.* Delacorte 1982, Dell 1984.

Adults

Adams, Douglas. *The Hitchhiker's Guide to the Galaxy.* Harmony 1979, Crown 1980, 1981.

———. *Life, the Universe, and Everything.* Crown 1982, PB 1983.

Auel, Jean M. *Clan of the Cave Bear.* Crown 1980, Bantam 1981.

Bloomingdale, Teresa. *Murphy Must Have Been a Mother! and Other Laws I Live By.* Doubleday 1982, Bantam 1983, Hall 1983.

Briggs, Raymond. *When the Wind Blows.* Schocken 1982.

Campbell, Patricia J. *Passing the Hat: Street Performance in America.* Delacorte 1981.

Clark, Mary Higgins. *A Cry in the Night.* Dell 1983, Hall 1983.

———. *Stillwatch.* S&S 1984.

Cormier, Robert. *The Bumblebee Flies Anyway.* Knopf 1983, Dell 1984.

Dear, William. *Dungeon Master: The Disappearance of James Dallas Egbert III.* Houghton 1984.

Adults (cont.)

DeVeaux, Alexis. *Don't Explain (A Song of Billie Holiday).* Harper 1980.

Dilfer, Carol Stahmann. *Your Baby, Your Body.* Crown 1977.

Due, Linnea A. *High and Outside.* Harper 1980, Bantam.

Durrell, Gerald. *Ark on the Move.* Putnam 1983.

Goldman, Peter and Fuller, Tony. *Charlie Company: What Vietnam Did to Us.* Morrow 1983, Ballantine 1984.

Greenberg, Joanne. *The Far Side of Victory.* Holt 1983.

Harris, Charlaine. *A Secret Rage.* Houghton 1984.

Hartman, David and Asbell, Bernard. *White Coat, White Cane.* Playboy, dist. by S&S 1978.

Haruf, Kent. *The Tie That Binds.* Holt 1984.

Hayden, Torey L. *One Child.* Avon 1982.

Heidish, Marcy. *The Secret of Annie Oakley.* NAL 1983.

Hogan, William. *The Quartzsite Trip.* Atheneum 1980, Avon 1981.

Jackson, Shirley. *The Haunting of Hill House.* Penguin 1984.

Janeczko, Paul, ed. *Postcard Poems: A Collection of Poetry for Sharing.* Bradbury 1979.

Keyes, Daniel. *The Fifth Sally.* Houghton 1980.

———. *The Minds of Billy Milligan.* Random 1981, Bantam 1982.

King, Stephen. *Christine.* NAL 1983, Viking 1983.

———. *Cujo.* Viking 1981, NAL 1982.

———. *Different Seasons.* Viking 1982, NAL 1983.

———. *Firestarter.* Viking 1980, NAL 1981.

———. *Pet Sematary.* Doubleday 1983, NAL, Hall 1984.

Kurtis, Bill. *Bill Kurtis on Assignment.* Rand 1983.

Least Heat Moon, William. *Blue Highways.* Hall 1983, Little 1983, Fawcett 1984.

Lee, Tanith. *Red as Blood.* DAW 1983.

LeGuin, Ursula. *The Beginning Place.* Harper 1980, Bantam 1981.

MacCracken, Mary. *City Kid.* NAL 1982.

McKillip, Patricia A. *The Riddle-Master of Hed.* Atheneum 1976, Ballantine 1978.

Magorian, Michelle. *Good Night, Mr. Tom.* Harper 1982.

Marshall, Catherine. *Julie.* McGraw 1984.

Mazer, Harry. *The Last Mission.* Dell 1981.

Michaels, Barbara. *Here I Stay.* Congdon 1983, Hall 1984.

Nicholls, Peter. *The Science in Science Fiction.* Knopf 1983.

O'Neill, Cherry Boone. *Starving for Attention.* Continuum 1982, Dell 1983.

Patterson, Francine and Linden, Eugene. *The Education of Koko.* Holt 1981.

Paulsen, Gary. *Dancing Carl.* Bradbury 1983.

Peck, Richard. *Amanda/Miranda.* Avon 1983.

————. *This Family of Women.* Delacorte 1983, Dell 1984, Hall 1984.

Prochnau, William. *Trinity's Child.* Putnam 1983.

Rhinehart, Luke. *Long Voyage Back.* Delacorte 1983, Dell 1984.

Santiago, Danny. *Famous All Over Town.* S&S 1983, NAL 1984.

Scott, Sir Walter. *Ivanhoe.* many editions.

Silverberg, Robert. *Lord Valentine's Castle.* Harper 1980, Bantam 1981.

Smith, Robert Kimmel. *Jane's House.* Morrow 1982, Hall 1983, PB 1984.

Strieber, Whitley and Kunetka, James. *Warday: And the Journey Onward.* Holt 1984.

Terry, Douglas. *The Last Texas Hero.* Doubleday 1982.

Tevis, Walter. *The Queen's Gambit.* Random 1983, Dell 1984.

Uris, Leon. *The Haj.* Doubleday 1984.

Van Devanter, Lynda and Morgan, Christopher. *Home before Morning.* Beaufort 1983, Warner 1984.

Spiering, Frank. *Lizzie.* Random 1984.

Winter, Douglas E. *Stephen King: The Art of Darkness.* NAL 1984.

Wortman, Elmo. *Almost Too Late.* Random 1981, Berkley 1983.

Appendix B:

Bibliography by Theme and Genre

Adventure/Suspense

After the First Death (Cormier) YA
Almost Too Late (Wortman) YA/Adult
Amanda/Miranda (Peck) YA
Battle Horse (Kullman) 6-8
The Big Way Out (Silsbee) YA
Blind Flight (Milton) YA
Center Line (Sweeney) YA
Dorp Dead (Cunningham) 3-5
Fantastic Mr. Fox (Dahl) 2-4
The Gang and Mrs. Higgins (Shannon)
    1-2
The Great Custard Pie Panic (Corbett)
    1-2
Half-a-Moon Inn (Fleischman) 3-5
Homecoming (Voigt) 6-8/YA
Hour of the Wolf (Calvert) YA
I Am the Cheese (Cormier) YA
Ivanhoe (Scott) Adult
Julie (Marshall) YA/Adult
Julie of the Wolves (George) 2-5
Last Mission (Mazer) YA/Adult
Long Voyage Back (Rhinehart) YA/
    Adult
The Long Walk (Bachman) YA
The Machine Gunners (Westall) 6-8
Marked by Fire (Thomas) YA
Nightmare Island (Roy) 3-5
Peppermints in the Parlor (Wallace) 4-6
The Princess Bride (Goldman) YA
Run for Your Life (Platt) 6-8
Save Queen of Sheba (Moeri) 6-8/YA
Slake's Limbo (Holman) 6-8
Trinity's Child (Prochnau) YA/Adult
TV Kid (Byars) 3-5
Warday (Strieber and Kunetka) YA/
    Adult
The White Mountains (Christopher) 3-5
Wiley and the Hairy Man (Bang) 1-2
Witches (Dahl) 1-3

Biography

Bill Kurtis on Assignment (Kurtis) YA/
    Adult

Don't Explain (DeVeaux) YA/Adult
Home Before Morning (Van Devanter
    and Morgan) Adult
Passing the Hat (Campbell) YA/Adult
Starving for Attention (O'Neill) YA/Adult
Stephen King: The Art of Darkness (Win-
    ter) YA/Adult
White Coat, White Cane (Hartman and
    Asbell) YA/Adult

General

Anastasia Again! (Lowry) 4-6
Anastasia Krupnik (Lowry) 3-5
A Billion for Boris (Rodgers) 3-5
Boll Weevil Express (Petersen) YA
The Champion of Merrimack County
    (Drury) 3-5
The Eighteenth Emergency (Byars) 4-6
*Jennifer, Hecate, Macbeth, William Mc-
    Kinley, and Me, Elizabeth* (Konigs-
    burg) 3-5
Listen to Us! (Kavanaugh) 6-8
More Magic in Your Pockets (Severn) 6-8
*Movie Stunts and the People Who Do
    Them* (Miklowitz) 6-8
Murphy Must Have Been a Mother
    (Bloomingdale) Adult
Passing the Hat (Campbell) YA/Adult
Postcard Poems (Janeczko) YA/Adult
Queenie Peavey (Burch) 4-6
Rabbit Hill (Lawson) 1-6
Ramona and Her Father (Cleary) 2-4
Ramona and Her Mother (Cleary) 2-4
Sadako and the Thousand Paper Cranes
    (Coerr) 3-5
The Tie That Binds (Haruf) YA/Adult
When the Wind Blows (Briggs) YA/Adult
Where the Sidewalk Ends (Silverstein)
    4-8
The Young Landlords (Myers) YA

History/Geography

And Then What Happened, Paul Revere?
    (Fritz) 1-2

Bill Kurtis on Assignment (Kurtis) YA/
Adult
Charlie Company (Goldman and Fuller)
Adult
Clan of the Cave Bear (Auel) YA/Adult
Fragments of Isabella (Leitner) YA
A Girl Called Boy (Hurmence) 3-6
The Haj (Uris) YA/Adult
Halfway Down Paddy Lane (Marzollo)
6-8/YA
Hiroshima No Pika (Maruki) 4-8
Home Before Morning (Van Devanter
and Morgan) Adult
Ivanhoe (Scott) Adult
Jeremy Visick (Wiseman) 6-8/YA
The Last Mission (Mazer) YA/Adult
Lizzie (Spiering) YA/Adult
Manwolf (Skurzynski) YA
Save Queen of Sheba (Moeri) 6-8/YA
The Secret of Annie Oakley (Heidish)
YA/Adult
The Silent Voice (Cunningham) YA
This Family of Women (Peck) Adult

Horror/Occult

Among the Dolls (Sleator) 3-5
And This Is Laura (Conford) 5-8/YA
Beloved Benjamin Is Waiting (Karl) 6-8
Bunnicula (Howe and Howe) 3-5
The Celery Stalks at Midnight (Howe)
3-5
Christine (King) YA/Adult
Cujo (King) YA/Adult
A Deadly Game of Magic (Nixon) YA
The Devil's Donkey (Brittain) 4-6
Ghosts of Departure Point (Bunting) YA
The Haunting of Hill House (Jackson)
YA/Adult
The Headless Roommate (Cohen) 6-8
Here I Stay (Michaels) YA/Adult
Into the Dream (Sleator) 6-8/YA
Firestarter (King) YA/Adult
Jeremy Visick (Wiseman) 6-8/YA
Mind-Call (Belden) YA
Pet Sematary (King) YA/Adult
So You Want to Be a Wizard (Duane)
5-9
Stranger With My Face (Duncan) YA
The Third Eye (Duncan) YA

Humor

Ace Hits the Big Time (Murphy and
Wolkoff) YA
Banana Twist (Heide) 4-6
The Best Christmas Pageant Ever (Rob-
inson) 4-6
Bunnicula (Howe and Howe) 3-5

The Celery Stalks at Midnight (Howe) 3-5
Clever Kate (Shub) 1-2
Flat Stanley (Brown) 1-2
Felicia the Critic (Conford) 3-5
Harvey's Horrible Snake Disaster (Clif-
ford) 3-6
How Lazy Can You Get? (Naylor) 3-5
How to Eat Fried Worms (Rockwell) 3-5
Howliday Inn (Howe and Howe) 3-5
The Hitchhiker's Guide to the Galaxy
(Adams) YA/Adult
*If I Were in Charge of the World and
Other Worries* (Viorst) 4-8
Life, the Universe, and Everything (Ad-
ams) YA/Adult
The Mark of Conte (Levitin) YA
*Mr. Radagast Makes an Unexpected
Journey* (Nastick) 6-8
Murphy Must Have Been a Mother
(Bloomingdale) Adult
Porko Von Popbutton (du Bois) 3-5
The Secret Life of the Underwear Champ
(Miles) 3-5
*The Snarkout Boys and the Avocado of
Death* (Pinkwater) 3-5
Something's Waiting for You, Baker D.
(Windsor) 6-8/YA
There Is a Carrot in My Ear (Schwartz)
k-3
Stairway to Doom (Quackenbush) 1-2
The Two-Thousand Pound Goldfish
(Byars) 6-8/YA
Where the Sidewalk Ends (Silverstein) 4-8

Minorities:
Black

The Disappearance (Guy) YA
A Girl Called Boy (Hurmence) 3-6
Hoops (Myers) YA
It Ain't All for Nothin' (Myers) YA
Let the Circle Be Unbroken (Taylor) YA
Leroy and the Old Man (Butterworth)
YA
Listen for the Fig Tree (Mathis) YA
Marked by Fire (Thomas) YA
Philip Hall Likes Me, I Reckon, Maybe
(Greene) 4-6
Rainbow Jordan (Childress) YA
Roll of Thunder, Hear My Cry (Taylor)
3-5
The Young Landlords (Myers) YA

Hispanic

Famous All Over Town (Santiago) YA/
Adult
Shadow Like a Leopard (Levoy) YA

Jewish

Fragments of Isabella (Leitner) YA

Native American

Blue Highways (Least Heat Moon) Adult
The Girl Who Loved Wild Horses (Goble) k-3
Island of the Blue Dolphins (O'Dell) 6-8
Julie of the Wolves (George) 2-5
Where the Buffaloes Begin (Baker) 1-2

Oriental

Wingman (Pinkwater) 1-2

Mystery

Case of the Elevator Duck (Berends) 1-2
A Cry in the Night (Clark) Adult
Daughters of Eve (Duncan) YA
Detective Poufy's First Case (Pomerantz) 1-2
Different Seasons (King) YA/Adult
Dungeon Master (Dear) YA/Adult
The Executioner (Bennett) YA
Footsteps on the Stairs (Adler) 6-8
Frankenstein Moved in on the Fourth Floor (Levy) 3-5
The Grounding of Group 6 (Thompson) YA
Here Lies the Body (Corbett) 3-5
The House With a Clock in Its Walls (Bellairs) 3-5
Howliday Inn (Howe and Howe) 3-5
Humbug Mountain (Fleischman) 4-6
Lizzie (Spiering) YA/Adult
A Secret Rage (Harris) Adult
Something's Waiting for You, Baker D. (Windsor) 6-8/YA
Stairway to Doom (Quackenbush) 1-2
Stillwatch (Clark) YA/Adult
The Westing Game (Raskin) 6-8

Nonfiction (see also Biography; Poetry)

Almost Too Late (Wortman) YA/Adult
And Then What Happened, Paul Revere? (Fritz) 1-2
Ark on the Move (Durrell) YA/Adult
Blue Highways (Least Heat Moon) YA/Adult
City Kid (MacCracken) YA/Adult
Dungeon Master (Dear) YA/Adult
Fragments of Isabella (Leitner) YA
Listen to Us! (Kavanaugh) 6-8

Lizzie (Spiering) YA/Adult
More Magic in Your Pockets (Severn) 6-8
The Minds of Billy Milligan (Keyes) YA/Adult
Movie Stunts and the People Who Do Them (Miklowitz) 6-8
One Child (Hayden) YA/Adult
Owls in the Family (Mowat) 4-6
Passing the Hat (Campbell) YA/Adult
The Science in Science Fiction (Nicholls) YA/Adult
Wild Foods (Pringle) 3-5
The Wild Inside (Allison) 3-5
Your Baby, Your Baby (Dilfer) Adult

Poetry

Don't Explain (DeVeaux) YA/Adult
If I Were in Charge of the World (Viorst) 4-8
Postcard Poems (Janeczko) YA/Adult
Where the Sidewalk Ends (Silverstein) 4-8

"Problem" books: Aging

Good Night, Mr. Tom (Magorian) YA/Adult
Grandpa—and Me (Tolan) 5-7
The Great Gilly Hopkins (Paterson) 6-8
Leroy and the Old Man (Butterworth) YA
Shadow Like a Leopard (Levoy) YA
Sweet Bells Jangled Out of Tune (Brancato) YA
The War With Grandpa (Smith) 4-6

Anorexia nervosa

Best Little Girl in the World (Levenkron) YA
Bigger Book of Lydia (Willey) YA
Starving for Attention (O'Neill) YA/Adult

Child Abuse

Cages of Glass, Flowers of Time (Culin) YA
Center Line (Sweeney) YA
The Girl Who Lived on the Ferris Wheel (Moeri) YA
Good Night, Mr. Tom (Magorian) YA/Adult
Second Heaven (Guest) Adult
Things Are Seldom What They Seem (Asher) YA

Death/Mourning

About David (Pfeffer) YA
Close Enough to Touch (Peck) YA
A Formal Feeling (Oneal) YA
Friends Till the End (Strasser) YA
Hunter in the Dark (Hughes) YA
Jane's House (Smith) Adult
A Summer to Die (Lowry) YA
A Taste of Blackberries (Smith) 4–6
Tiger Eyes (Blume) YA

Delinquency/Crime

City Kid (MacCracken) YA/Adult
The Disappearance (Guy) YA
It Ain't All for Nothin' (Myers) YA
Masquerade (Shreve) YA
One Child (Hayden) YA/Adult
Shadow Like a Leopard (Levoy) YA
Steffie Can't Come Out to Play (Arrick)
    YA
Walls (Daly) YA

Family Problems

*The Animal, the Vegetable, and John D.
    Jones* (Byars) 6–8
The Big Way Out (Silsbee) YA
Blissful Joy and the SATs (Greenwald)
    YA
Blues for Silk Garcia (Tamar) YA
Carnival in My Mind (Wersba) YA
The Disappearance (Guy) YA
Divorce Express (Danziger) YA
Gardine vs. Hanover (Oppenheimer)
    5–7/YA
Hide Crawford Quick (Froelich) 6–8
It Ain't All for Nothin' (Myers) YA
Leroy and the Old Man (Butterworth)
    YA
Masquerade (Shreve) YA
Roadside Valentine (Adler) YA
Running Loose (Crutcher) YA
Them That Glitter and Them That Don't
    (Greene) YA
The Two-Thousand-Pound Goldfish
    (Byars) 6–8/YA
The TV Kid (Byars) 3–5

Handicapped

Blind Flight (Milton) YA
Hide Crawford Quick (Froelich) 6–8
Listen for the Fig Tree (Mathis) YA
Manwolf (Skurzynski) YA
A Night Without Stars (Howe) 5–7
White Coat, White Cane (Hartman and
    Asbell) YA/Adult

Mental Illness

Alan and Naomi (Levoy) 6–8/YA
The Big Way Out (Silsbee) YA
I Will Call It Georgie's Blues (Newton)
    YA
The Language of Goldfish (Oneal) YA
Sunflower Forest (Hayden) YA

Runaways

Boll Weevil Express (Petersen) YA
Carnival in My Mind (Wersba) YA
Center Line (Sweeney) YA
The Hard Way Home (Shaw) YA
Steffie Can't Come Out to Play (Arrick)
    YA
To Take a Dare (Dragonwagon and Zin-
    del) YA

Sex and Sexuality—Gay

Annie on My Mind (Garden) YA
Dance on My Grave (Chambers) YA

Sex and Sexuality—Straight

Carnival in My Mind (Wersba) YA
The Day the Senior Class Got Married
    (Miklowitz) YA
First the Egg (Moeri) YA
Just Another Love Story (Knudson) YA
A Long Time Between Kisses (Scoppet-
    tone) YA
Love by Any Other Name (Foley) YA
The Quartzsite Trip (Hogan) YA
Rainbow Jordan (Childress) YA
Roadside Valentine (Adler) YA
Sooner or Later (Hart) 6–8
Steffie Can't Come Out to Play (Arrick)
    YA
Things Are Seldom What They Seem
    (Asher) YA
To Take a Dare (Dragonwagon and Zin-
    del) YA

Substance Abuse

High and Outside (Due) YA/Adult
Walls (Daly) YA

Psychology/Sociology

About David (Pfeffer) YA
Alan and Naomi (Levoy) 6–8/YA
The Best Little Girl in the World
    (Levenkron) YA
The Bigger Book of Lydia (Willey) YA
The Bumblebee Flies Anyway (Cormier)
    YA

Cages of Glass, Flowers of Time (Culin) YA
The Cheese Stands Alone (Prince) 6–8
City Kid (MacCracken) YA/Adult
Dancing Carl (Paulsen) YA/Adult
The Fifth Sally (Keyes) YA/Adult
A Formal Feeling (Oneal) YA
The Girl Who Lived on the Ferris Wheel (Moeri) YA
God's Radar (Arrick) YA
Goodnight, Mr. Tom (Magorian) YA/Adult
High and Outside (Due) YA/Adult
I Will Call It Georgie's Blues (Newton) YA
The Language of Goldfish (Oneal) YA
Listen to Us! (Kavanaugh) 6–8
The Love Bombers (Miklowitz) YA
The Minds of Billy Milligan (Keyes) YA/Adult
One Child (Hayden) YA/Adult
The Queen's Gambit (Tevis) YA/Adult
Starving for Attention (O'Neill) YA/Adult
Sunflower Forest (Hayden) YA
Sweet Bells Jangled Out of Tune (Brancato) YA
The Wave (Rhue) YA

Religion/Philosophy

The Best Christmas Pageant Ever (Robinson) 4–6
The Bumblebee Flies Anyway (Cormier) YA
Fragments of Isabella (Leitner) YA
Glory Girl (Byars) YA
God's Radar (Arrick) YA
Leroy and the Old Man (Butterworth) YA
The Love Bombers (Arrick) YA
Unicorns in the Rain (Cohen) YA

Romance

Amanda/Miranda (Peck) YA
Beauty (McKinley) 6–8/YA
The Carnival in My Mind (Wersba) YA
Close Enough to Touch (Peck) YA
The Day the Senior Class Got Married (Miklowitz) YA
Fair Annie of Old Mule Hollow (Crook) YA
The Far Side of Victory (Greenberg) YA/Adult
If I Asked You, Would You Stay? (Bunting) YA
Keeper of the Isis Light (Hughes) YA

Love by Any Other Name (Foley) YA
Only Love (Sallis) YA
Philip Hall Likes Me, I Reckon, Maybe (Greene) 4–6
The Princess Bride (Goldman) YA
Roadside Valentine (Adler) YA
Second Heaven (Guest) Adult
Sooner or Later (Hart) 6–8

Science/Nature

Ark on the Move (Durrell) YA/Adult
The Education of Koko (Patterson and Linden) YA/Adult
Kavik the Wolf Dog (Morey) 3–5
Julie of the Wolves (George) 2–5
Owls in the Family (Mowat) 4–6
The Science in Science Fiction (Nicholls) YA/Adult
Wild Foods (Pringle) 3–5
The Wild Inside (Allison) 3–5

Science Fiction/Fantasy

Adventures of a Two-Minute Werewolf (DeWeese) 5–8
Beauty (McKinley) 6–8/YA
The Beginning Place (LeGuin) YA/Adult
Anna to the Infinite Power (Ames) 6–8/YA
Conscience Place (Thompson) YA
Crystal Singer (McCaffrey) YA
Darkangel (Pierce) YA
Diamond in the Window (Langton) 3–5
Dogsbody (Jones) 6–8
Dragondrums (McCaffrey) YA
Dragon's Blood (Yolen) YA
Earthseed (Sargent) YA
Everyone Knows What a Dragon Looks Like (Williams) k–3
Fat Men From Space (Pinkwater) 3–5
Flat Stanley (Brown) 1–2
Freaky Friday (Rodgers) 3–5
The Hitchhiker's Guide to the Galaxy (Adams) YA/Adult
The Indian in the Cupboard (Banks) 3–5
Keeper of the Isis Light (Hughes) YA
Life, the Universe, and Everything (Adams) YA/Adult
Lizard Music (Pinkwater) 6–8
The Long Walk (Bachman) YA
Lord Valentine's Castle (Silverberg) YA/Adult
Max and Me and the Time Machine (Greer and Ruddick) 5–7
Mr. Radagast Makes an Unexpected Journey (Nastick) 6–8

My Robot Buddy (Slote) 3-5
Ratha's Creature (Bell) YA
Red as Blood (Lee) YA/Adult
The Riddle-Master of Hed (McKillip)
 YA/Adult
*The Snarkout Boys and the Avocado of
 Death* (Pinkwater) 3-5
*The Strange Thing That Happened to Ol-
 iver Wendell Iscovitch* (Olson) 1-2
The White Mountains (Christopher) 3-5

Short Stories

Different Seasons (King) YA/Adult
The Headless Roommate (Cohen)
 6-8/YA
Red as Blood (Lee) Adult
Sixteen (Gallo) YA

Sports/Games

Dungeon Master (Dear) YA/Adult
Hoops (Myers) YA
Hour of the Wolf (Calvert) YA

Jake (Slote) 3-5
The Last Texas Hero (Terry) YA/Adult
The Long Walk (Bachman) YA
Love Match (Quin-Harkin) YA
Passing Season (Blessing) 6-8
The Queen's Gambit (Tevis) YA/Adult
Running Loose (Crutcher) YA
Vision Quest (Davis) YA

Women's Studies

Daughters of Eve (Duncan) YA
The Day the Senior Class Got Married
 (Miklowitz) YA
First the Egg (Moeri) YA
Love by Any Other Name (Foley) YA
Love Match (Quin-Harkin) YA
The Secret of Annie Oakley (Heidish)
 YA/Adult
Sunflower Forest (Hayden) YA
This Family of Woman (Peck) Adult
Your Baby, Your Body (Dilfer) Adult

Appendix C:

List of Publishers

ALA. American Library Association, 50 E. Huron St., Chicago, IL 60611

Archway (PB). Archway Paperbacks, c/o Pocket Books, 1230 Avenue of the Americas, New York, NY 10020

Atheneum. Atheneum Publishers, 597 Fifth Ave., New York, NY 10017

Avon. Avon Books, 1790 Broadway, New York, NY 10019

Ballantine. Ballantine/Del Rey/Fawcett, 201 East 50th St., New York, NY 10022

Bantam. Bantam Books, Inc., 666 Fifth Ave., New York, NY 10103

Beaufort. Beaufort Books, Inc., 9 E. 40th St., St., New York, NY 10016

Berkley. Berkley Publishing Group, 200 Madison Ave., New York, NY 10016

Bowker. R.R. Bowker Co., 205 E. 42 St., New York, NY 10017

Bradbury. Bradbury Press, 2 Overhill Rd., Scarsdale, NY 10583

Congdon. Congdon & Weed, Inc., 298 Fifth Ave., New York, NY 10001

Contemporary. Contemporary Books, Inc., 180 N. Michigan Ave., Chicago, IL 60601

Continuum. The Continuum Publishing Corp. 370 Lexington Ave., New York, NY 10017

Coward. Coward, McCann & Geoghegan, Inc., 200 Madison Ave., New York, NY 10016

Crowell. Thomas Y. Crowell Co., c/o Harper & Row, 10 East 53rd St., New York, NY 10022

Crown. Crown Publishers, Inc., One Park Ave., New York, NY 10016

DAW. DAW Books, New American Library, 1633 Broadway, New York, NY 10019

Delacorte. Delacorte Press, c/o Dell Publishing Co., One Dag Hammarskjold Plaza, 245 East 47th St., New York, NY 10017

Dell. Dell Publishing Co., Inc., One Dag Hammarskjold Plaza, 245 East 47th St., New York, NY 10017

Dial. Dial Press, c/o Doubleday & Co., Inc., 245 Park Ave., New York, NY 10167

Dodd. Dodd, Mead & Co., 79 Madison Ave., New York, NY 10016

Doubleday. Doubleday & Co., Inc., 245 Park Ave., New York, NY 10167

Dutton. E. P. Dutton, 2 Park Ave., New York, NY 10016

Evans. M. Evans & Co., Inc., 216 East 49th St., New York, NY 10017

Farrar. Farrar, Straus, & Giroux, Inc., 19 Union Square West, New York, NY 10003

Fawcett. Ballantine/Del Rey/Fawcett, 201 East 50th St., New York, NY 10017

Greenwillow. Greenwillow Books, 105 Madison Ave., New York, N Y 10016

Hall. G. K. Hall, Inc., 70 Lincoln St., Boston, MA 02111

Harcourt. Harcourt Brace Jovanovich, Inc., 1250 Sixth Ave., San Diego, CA 92101

Harmony. Harmony Books, One Park Ave., New York, NY 10016

Harper. Harper & Row Publishers, Inc., 10 East 53rd St., New York, NY 10022

Hastings. Hastings House, Publishers, Inc., 10 E. 40th St., New York, NY 10016

Holiday. Holiday House, Inc., 18 East 53rd St., New York, NY 10022

Holt. Holt, Rinehart, and Winston General Book, 521 Fifth Ave., New York, NY 10175

Houghton. Houghton Mifflin Co., One Beacon St., Boston, MA 02108

Knopf. Alfred A. Knopf, Inc., 201 East 50th St., New York, NY 10022

Little. Little, Brown & Co., 34 Beacon St., Boston, MA 02106

Lothrop. Lothrop, Lee & Shepard Books, 105 Madison Ave., New York, NY 10016; orders to William Morrow & Co., Inc., Wilmor Warehouse, 6 Henderson Dr., West Caldwell, NJ 07006

McGraw. McGraw-Hill, Inc., 1221 Avenue of the Americas, New York, NY 10020

McKay. David McKay Co., Inc, 2 Park Ave., New York N Y 10016

Macmillan. Macmillan Publishing Co., Inc., 866 Third Ave., New York, NY 10022

Merrill. Charles E. Merrill Publishing Co., 936 Eastwind Dr., Westerville, OH 43081

Morrow. William Morrow & Co., Inc., 105 Madison Ave., New York, NY 10016

NAL. New American Library, Inc., 1633 Broadway, New York, NY 10019

Pantheon. Pantheon Books, 201 East 50th St., New York, NY 10022

PB. Pocket Books, Inc., 1230 Avenue of the Americas, New York, NY 10020

Penguin. Penguin Books, Inc., 40 West 23rd St., New York, NY 10010

Playboy. Playboy Press, 747 Third Ave., New York, NY 10017; distributed by Harper & Row Pubs., Inc., Keystone Industrial Park, Scranton, PA 18512

Prentice. Prentice-Hall, Inc., Englewood Cliffs, NJ 07632

Putnam. The Putnam Publishing Group, Inc., 200 Madison Ave., New York, NY 10016; orders to 390 Murray Hill Pkwy., East Rutherford, NJ 07073

Rand. Rand McNally & Co., P.O. Box 7600, Chicago, IL 60680

Random. Random House, Inc., 201 East 50th St., New York, NY 10022

S&S. Simon & Schuster, Inc., 1230 Avenue of the Americas, New York, NY 10020

Schocken. Schocken Books, Inc., 200 Madison Ave., New York, NY 10016

Scholastic. Scholastic, Inc., 730 Broadway, New York, NY 10003

Scott. Scott, Foresman & Co., 1900 East Lake Ave., Glenview, IL 60025

Scribner. Charles Scribner's Sons, 115 Fifth Ave., New York, NY 10003

Sierra Club. Sierra Club Books, 2034 Fillmore St., San Francisco, CA 94115

Tor. Tor Books, 8 W. 36 St., New York, NY 10018

Viking. Viking, Penguin, Inc., 40 West 23rd St., New York, NY 10010

Warne. Frederick Warne & Co., Inc., 40 West 23rd St., New York, NY 10010

Warner. Warner Books, Inc., 666 Fifth Ave., New York, NY 10103

Watts. Franklin Watts, Inc., 387 Park Ave. S., New York, NY 10016

Wilson. The H.W. Wilson Co., 950 University Ave., Bronx, NY 10452

Workman. Workman Co., Inc., One W. 39th St., New York, NY 10018

Appendix D:

Short Films Suitable for Use in Programs for All Ages*

Ballet Robotique. Pyramid Films, 1982. 8 min.

The Bead Game. National Film Board of Canada, 1978. 6 min.

A Boy, a Dog, and a Frog. Phoenix Films, 1981. 9 min.

Closed Mondays. Pyramid Films, 1974. 8 min.

The Fly. Perspective Films, 1980. 3 min.

Hardware Wars. Pyramid Films, 1978. 13 min.

The Hat. Weston Woods, 1982. 6 min.

The History of the World in Three Minutes Flat. M. Mills Prod., 1980.
4 min.

Hug Me. Churchill Films, 1981. 7 min.

Kick Me. Little Red Filmhouse, 1977. 8 min.

Legacy. Billy Budd Films, 1979. 5 min.

Neighbors. The National Film Board of Canada. 9 min.

A Scrap of Paper and a Piece of String. Comtemporary Films, 1965. 6
min.

Self-Service. Connecticut Films, 1975. 11 min.

Skipping. Churchill Films, 1979. 9 min.

The Wizard of Speed and Time. Pyramid Films, 1980. 3 min.

*Compiled with the help of Penny Northern, Head of the Film Department, Kansas City
Public Library.

Appendix E:

Handouts on Booktalking and School Visiting

1. Tips on Booktalking*

1. Expect the unexpected.

2. Keep the group small if possible. It is better to do two separate sessions than to try to keep the attention of a large group.

3. As far as possible, know the group you are addressing. How many; what age, sex, class (in school), any distinguishing marks (such as hostility to all librarians, bringers of books, females, etc.).

4. Give yourself enough lead time to prepare booktalks. Refuse to accept last-minute engagements unless you always have some talks ready to give and copies of those titles available in your library.

5. *Know your book.* Don't try to fake knowledge of materials. There is bound to be some smart kid who has read the book. Once you lose credibility, it's difficult to recoup.

6. Do not talk down to the kids or call them "boys and girls"; they are young men and women and respond to that title.

7. Talk slowly, clearly, and loudly enough to be heard by all.

8. Maintain eye contact in order to detect restlessness, boredom, etc. Think about whether you are more at ease sitting or standing and try to arrange the physical setting accordingly.

9. Insist that the teacher or adult responsible for the group remain in the room so that you don't have to worry about discipline.

10. Don't talk more than a half-hour to a teenage group; restless groups get up to twenty minutes and the rest of the social studies period to harass the teacher, not you. This is a flexible time limit dependent on *your* style.

11. When possible, compliment the group on something—size of class, school appearance, something. You can always fall back on the oldie that it is nice to be invited to share your enthusiasm for books.

---

*Prepared by Jan Freeman, King County Library Stystem; Susan Tait, Seattle Public Library (YA Work); and Susan B. Madden, KCLS Coordinator of YA Services.

12. When possible, tie one or two titles in with something that has happened of note, either on a local, national, or international level, i.e., politics, civil rights, sports, etc.

13. Keep some talks short, let others run longer. Vary the pace as much as possible. When doing two or three classes in a row, it helps to have one or two alternative books to present to each class in order to keep your approach fresh; or at least vary the order in which you present the titles.

14. For your own self-preservation, learn to tune out extraneous noises while booktalking. In schools you will often be subjected to bells, phones, loudspeaker announcements, etc., in the classroom. Rise above these, if possible; if not, treat with humor.

15. Unless requested to talk around a particular theme, bring a variety of material to assure that you will have something of interest to almost everyone. Figure about ten–fifteen titles. One from each of the following areas should meet most adolescent interests: Horror; Animal; Hi-Lo (call "Quick-read"); Romance; Movie/TV tie-in; Oldie but goodie; Popular nonfiction; Science fiction; Young woman protagonist; Young man protagonist; War; Car/motorcycle; Pop scene or local esoteric; "Problem" novel.

You'll get an automatic reading level spread with this approach, so you can use basically the same books for junior high and high school (let your pre-info aid your selection).

16. Do not use titles on the reserve list. This is frustrating to the students who try to get the books after your talk. It will help your own library staff if you can give them a list of the books you will be doing, so they can have copies readily available. A special "Booktalk" shelf near front desk is often a workable ploy and good PR.

17. The school librarian can arrange your booktalk visits. If teachers contact you directly for booktalks, make sure the school librarian knows why and when you are coming. In a territorial hassle, only the teenagers will be the losers.

18. If you will be doing booktalks again with the same class or audience, find out their particular reading interests for the next time.

19. Science fiction is difficult to present unless you genuinely enjoy it, or have read (not skimmed) the book. Sci-fi enthusiasts are a strange breed who can sense uncertainty.

20. Make a list of the titles you will be using and distribute it to the teacher and students as well as to your staff.

21. Announce upcoming library programs and have a variety of booklists (if available) to hand out to interested students.

22. Book talks are fun. The kids will enjoy them; and you can have fun, too.

2. Guidelines for School Visiting*

School visiting is one of the most effective ways of reaching the majority of teenagers in the city. It is a unique opportunity to publicize the library, its materials, and services. School visiting can take many different forms. It can mean anything from a brief visit to one class, a talk at a faculty meeting or an assembly, to a full day of booktalks in the school library. No one will be expected to begin school visiting without training and assistance. Here are some practical pointers which may contribute to the success of your visit:

1. Librarians should identify the public and non-public junior and senior high schools in their service areas.

2. [Librarians should confer with branch, regional, and YA offices when planning school visits. Once the plans are definite, inform the relevant library office as to dates and times.]

3. Make contact with the school librarians—either visit them in person, or by phone, write a note, or invite them to your branch. Sometimes a school librarian or teacher will contact you first. Let them know that you wish to cooperate and what services you and your library can provide.

4. Preparation is necessary for a successful visit, whether you are presenting a slide or slide-tape show, or talking about books and services. Know your materials.

5. Many practical arrangements and details must be settled before a school visit.

    a. Availability of audio-visual equipment. Does the school have what you need or will you have to provide it? [Booking library AV presentations.]

    b. The number in the audience (if lists or other materials are needed).

    c. Books and lists will need to be selected and sent out in advance. Allow enough time and be aware of school holidays that could delay the arrival of your materials.

    d. The scheduling of classes (if more than one is involved).

    e. Seating arrangements—it may be necessary to have furniture rearranged in advance.

---

*Young Adult Services Office, Enoch Pratt Free Library. Bracketed material has been substituted for instructions specific to Enoch Pratt.

6. Although there may be times when you will be going out with another librarian, chances are your school visits will be solo. How you manage to cover the schools in your community—whether by several short visits over the duration of the school year or one or two full days—depends on you, your branch, and its schedule.

7. In addition to the group services statistics, it is necessary to know the number of books circulated, as the total is added to the branch daily circulation figures (if two librarians go, divide the statistics).

8. Procedures for the circulation of books [need to be decided on].

9. If you do circulate books you might want to consider some kind of follow-up announcement about returning books.

10. If there is an emergency and you cannot follow through on a commitment, [be sure to notify the library and the schools, and reschedule as soon as you can].

11. Try to evaluate your performance and the session.

a. Was your training adequate?

b. Were you organized?

c. Would you use the same techniques next time?

d. Do you have any ideas or suggestons for different presentations that you would share?

e. What would you do the next time that you did not do this time?

INDEX

Numbers in **boldface** type refer to pages where booktalks appear. Books are listed by author in Appendix A.